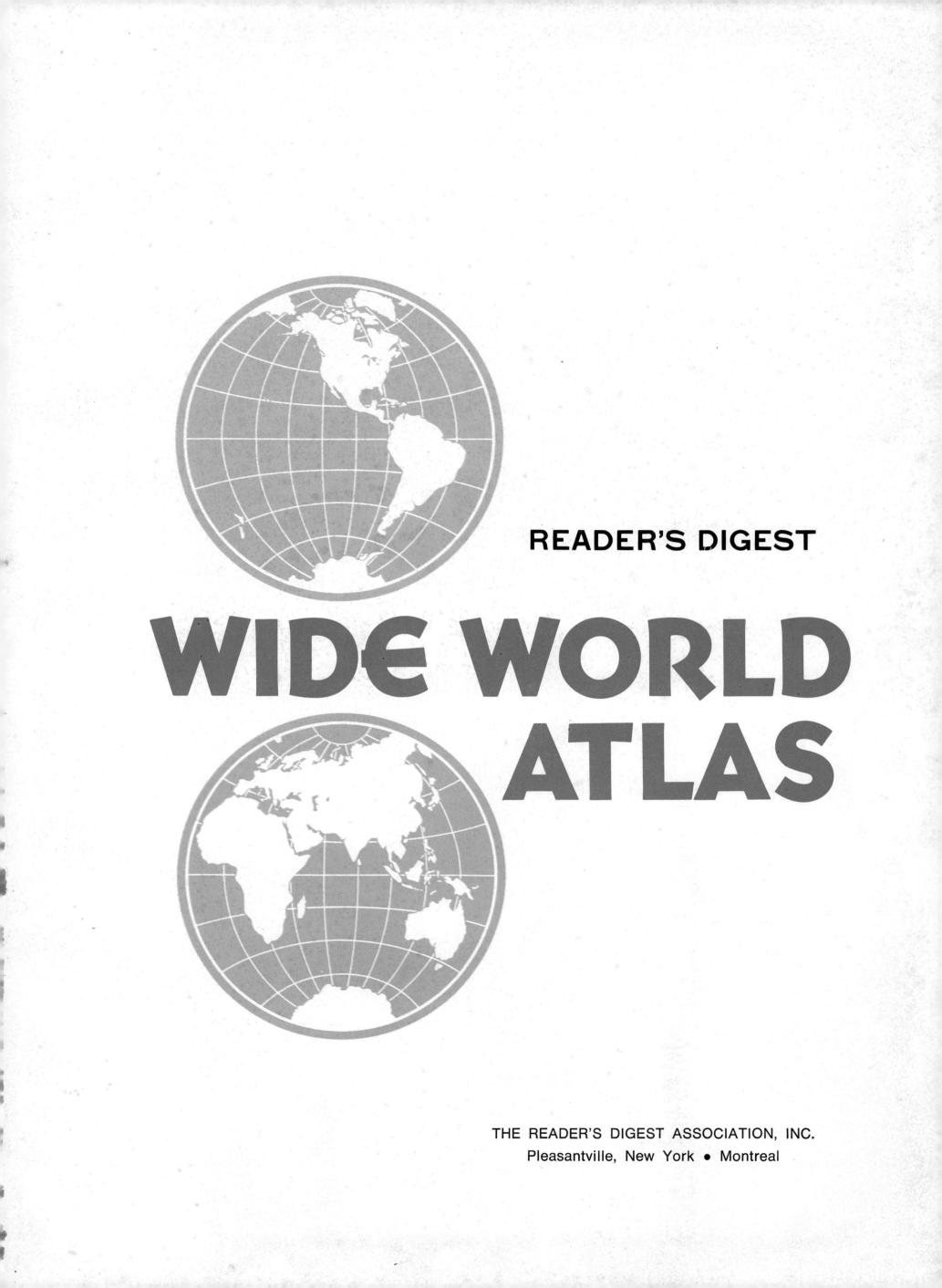

READER'S DIGEST

WIDE WORLD ATLAS

THE READER'S DIGEST ASSOCIATION, INC.
Pleasantville, New York • Montreal

INTRODUCTION

The world in which we live is shrinking. In 1842 it took Charles Dickens 18 days, chugging across the Atlantic in a side-wheel steam packet, to travel from Liverpool to Boston. Less than a century later, in 1927, Charles Lindbergh flew from New York to Paris in 33 hours and 30 minutes. The Boeing 707 jet, introduced in 1959, reduced the New York—London journey to 6 hours 40 minutes. Today the Concorde makes the flight in 3 hours 20 minutes—scarcely time enough for a meal and a catnap.

At the same time, our world has been changing. In 1945 there were 51 founding members of the United Nations; at the end of the 1970's the world body had 150 member states, with nations being added each year. New names keep appearing on the globe. Ceylon is now Sri Lanka; British Honduras is Belize; Cambodia has been renamed Kampuchea; South-West Africa is Namibia; the Congo is now called Zaire. To understand a world drawing ever closer to our doorstep, to keep abreast of the headlines, every home needs a world atlas. To fill this need, Reader's Digest has created *Wide World Atlas*.

Library of Congress Catalog Card Number 78-65321

ISBN 0-89577-062-8

Printed for The Reader's Digest Association, Inc., in the United States of America

Before compiling this work, we looked at the maps and atlases of many publishers—to ensure that we would be offering our readers the best selection available. As a result of this search, Reader's Digest joined Rand McNally, long regarded as America's foremost mapmaker and atlas publisher, to produce this concise yet comprehensive edition of *The International Atlas,* called "the best atlas ever to be produced in the United States."

Wide World Atlas contains the best maps, charts, and tables from Rand McNally's original unabridged work. Then, to make our new volume even more useful and attractive, we added from other sources some special features never before available in a single atlas. Finally, we asked Rand McNally's staff of professionals to review every page for clarity, currency, and accuracy. The result: an up-to-date, reliable atlas as your one-volume guide to the world today.

Maps are the heart of any atlas—and in Reader's Digest *Wide World Atlas* you will find some of the best ever published: *Physical* maps (pages 6—17) of an almost three-dimensional quality present the world and the continents in vivid color. *Political* maps (pages 20—123) show current names and borders for all the countries of the world, half at a generous scale of 1:3,000,000 (see the notes on scale at the bottom of page 5). *Metropolitan* maps (pages 124—144) emphasize, in precise detail, the major features of the largest cities in America and abroad. (For quick access to and easy use of both *Political* and *Metropolitan* maps, consult first the *Locator Maps and Legend* on pages 18—19.)

Most conventional atlases stop with the maps listed above. *Wide World Atlas* in addition contains a unique combination of special features, virtually a second volume, beginning on page 145: *The World in Theme Maps.* Here you will find *The Earth and Space* (pages 146-151), a review of the universe beyond our earth so rapidly being revealed and opened to us. A portfolio of *Environmental* maps (pages 152—167) offers a panorama of our planet's varied terrain and land usage as if seen from a vantage point in outer space. Vivid, easy-to-understand charts and diagrams (*World View,* pages 168—189) contain a wealth of information about the globe's population, religions, languages, wealth and trade, natural resources, energy production and consumption, climate, geology, time zones, and more. *Ocean Floor* maps (pages 190—195) show the world as it would look if drained of all its water. World political information is summed up beginning on page 196. A chart of the largest metropolitan areas appears on page 201. And finally, the 39-page index beginning on page 202 is your key to the 35,000 place-names listed on the *Political* maps that form the core of this volume.

Wide World Atlas is intended to be an indispensable reference work—its pages to be consulted again and again to answer questions, supply interesting facts, find useful information. It is our hope that it will also prove entertaining for the browser, a book to be savored and treasured for its beauty as well as for its utility.

—The Editors

CONTENTS

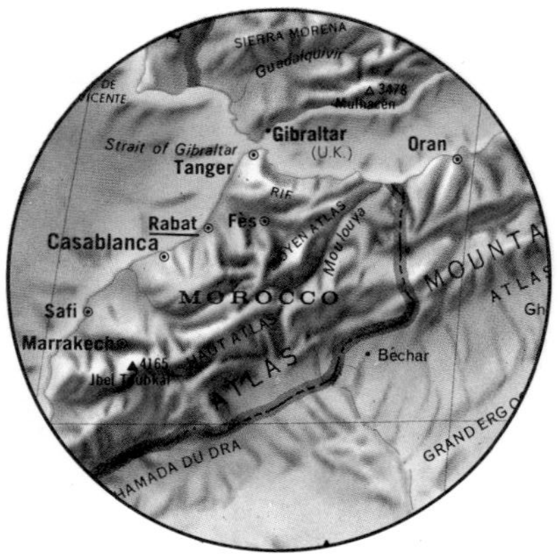

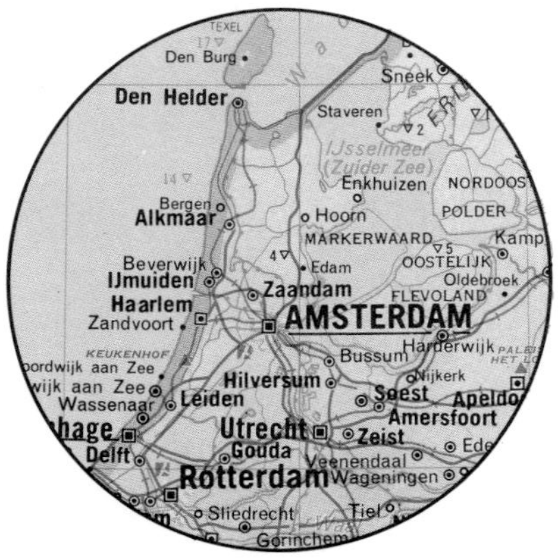

Maps

Physical Maps

Page		Scale*
6–7	World (including Legend)	1:75
8–9	North America	1:24
10–11	South America	1:24
12–13	Europe and Africa	1:24
14–15	Asia	1:24
16–17	Australia and Oceania	1:24

18–19 Locator Maps and Legend for Political and Metropolitan Maps

Political Maps

ANGLO-AMERICA

Page		Scale*
20–21	United States (excluding Alaska and Hawaii)	1:12
22–23	Canada	1:12
24–25	Alaska and Yukon	1:6
26–27	Southwestern Canada	1:3
28–29	South-Central Canada	1:3
30–31	Southeastern Canada	1:3
32–33	Northeastern United States	1:3
34–35	Great Lakes Region	1:3
36–37	Southeastern United States	1:3
38–39	Mississippi Valley	1:3
40–41	Southern Great Plains	1:3
42–43	Northern Great Plains	1:3
44–45	Southern Rocky Mountains	1:3
46–47	Northwestern United States	1:3
48–49	California and Nevada, Hawaii inset	1:3

LATIN AMERICA

Page		Scale*
50–51	Middle America	1:12
52–53	Mexico	1:6
54–55	Islands of the West Indies	1:1, 1:3
56–57	Northern South America	1:12
58–59	Southern South America	1:12
60–61	Colombia, Ecuador, Venezuela, and Guyana	1:6
62–63	Central Argentina and Chile	1:6

EUROPE AND THE SOVIET UNION

64–65	Europe	1:12
66–67	Northern Europe, Iceland inset	1:6
68–69	Southern Scandinavia	1:3
70–71	British Isles	1:3
72–73	Central Europe	1:3
74–75	France and the Alps	1:3
76–77	Spain and Portugal	1:3
78–79	Italy	1:3
80–81	Southeastern Europe	1:3
82–83	Western and Central Soviet Union	1:12
84–85	Eastern and Central Soviet Union	1:12
86–87	Baltic and Moscow Regions	1:3

ASIA

88–89	China, Japan, and Korea	1:12
90–91	Japan	1:3
92–93	Southeast Asia	1:12
94–95	Burma, Thailand, and Indochina	1:6
96–97	Malaysia and Western Indonesia	1:6
98–99	Philippines	1:3
100–101	India, Pakistan, and Southwest Asia	1:12
102–103	Northern India and Pakistan	1:6
104–105	The Middle East	1:6

AFRICA

106–107	Western North Africa	1:12
108–109	Eastern North Africa	1:12
110–111	Southern Africa	1:12
112–113	Egypt and Sudan	1:6
114–115	West Africa	1:6
116–117	Southern Africa and Madagascar	1:6

AUSTRALIA AND NEW ZEALAND

118–119	Australia	1:12
120–121	New Zealand	1:3
122–123	Islands of the Pacific	1:1, 1:3, 1:6

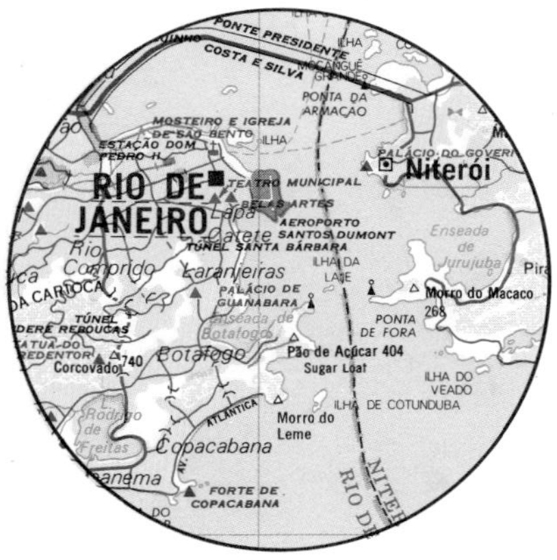

Metropolitan Maps**

Page

124 Montreal • Toronto
125 Boston
126–127 New York
128 Philadelphia
129 Buffalo—Niagara Falls • Baltimore • Washington
130 Cleveland • Pittsburgh
131 San Francisco—Oakland—San Jose
132 Detroit—Windsor
133 Chicago
134 Los Angeles
135 Sydney • Melbourne
136 Mexico City • Havana • Caracas • Lima • Santiago
137 Rio de Janeiro • São Paulo
138 London
139 Paris
140 Berlin • Vienna • Budapest
141 Leningrad • Moscow
142 Rome • Athens • Istanbul • Tehran
143 Peking • Seoul • Singapore • Hong Kong
144 Tokyo—Yokohama

* 1:75 or 1:75,000,000, meaning 1 centimeter on the map represents 750 kilometers on the ground (1 inch represents approximately 1,185 miles)

1:24 or 1:24,000,000, meaning 1 centimeter on the map represents 240 kilometers on the ground (1 inch represents approximately 380 miles)

1:12 or 1:12,000,000, meaning 1 centimeter on the map represents 120 kilometers on the ground (1 inch represents approximately 190 miles)

1:6 or 1:6,000,000, meaning 1 centimeter on the map represents 60 kilometers on the ground (1 inch represents approximately 95 miles)

1:3 or 1:3,000,000, meaning 1 centimeter on the map represents 30 kilometers on the ground (1 inch represents approximately 47 miles)

1:1 or 1:1,000,000, meaning 1 centimeter on the map represents 10 kilometers on the ground (1 inch represents approximately 16 miles)

** All Metropolitan Maps are at a scale of 1:300,000, meaning 1 centimeter on the map represents 3 kilometers on the ground (1 inch represents approximately 4.7 miles)

The World in Theme Maps

Page

145 Introduction

The Earth and Space

146–147 The Planet Earth in Space
148–149 Our Solar System
150–151 The Moon

Environmental Maps

152–153 North America
154–155 United States and Canada
156–157 South America
158–159 Europe
160–161 Northern Asia
162–163 Southern Asia
164–165 Africa
166–167 Australia and New Zealand

World View

Page

168–169 The World, 1979
170–171 Population
172–173 Religions/Languages
174–175 Agricultural Regions/Forests and Fisheries
176–177 Minerals
178–179 Energy Production and Consumption
180–181 Gross National Product/International Trade
182–183 Climate Graphs/Climate Regions/Mean Annual Temperature/Mean Annual Precipitation
184–185 Surface Configuration/Earth Structure and Tectonics
186–187 Natural Vegetation/Soils
188–189 Time Zones/Drainage Regions and Ocean Currents

Ocean Floor Maps

190–191 Atlantic Ocean
192–193 Pacific Ocean
194 Indian Ocean
195 Arctic Ocean/South Polar Ocean

Tables and Index

196–200 World Political Information Table
201 Largest Metropolitan Areas of the World, 1979
202–240 Abbreviations, Introduction to Index, and Index

World: Physical

Kilometers 0 1000 2000 3000 Km.
Statute Miles 0 1000 2000 3000 Mi.

One centimeter represents 750 kilometers.
One inch represents approximately 1200 miles.
Robinson Projection
Scale 1:75,000,000

Land Features

Ice and Snow | High Barren Area | Tundra and Alpine | Needleleaf Trees | Broadleaf Trees | Tropical Rainforest

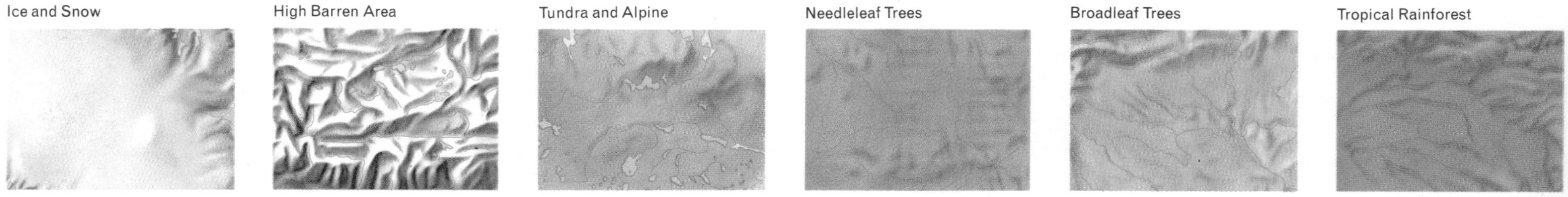

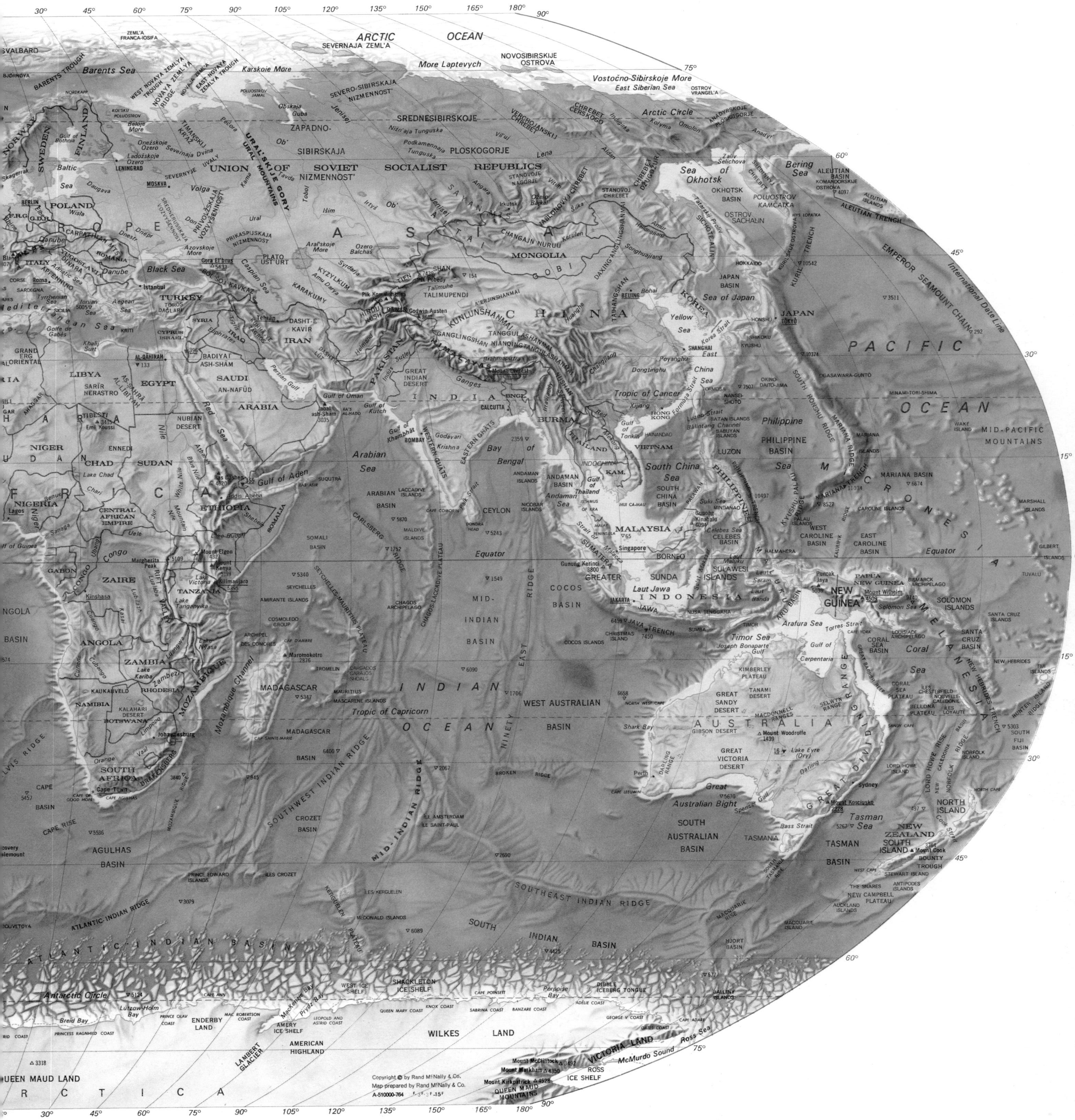

Submarine Features

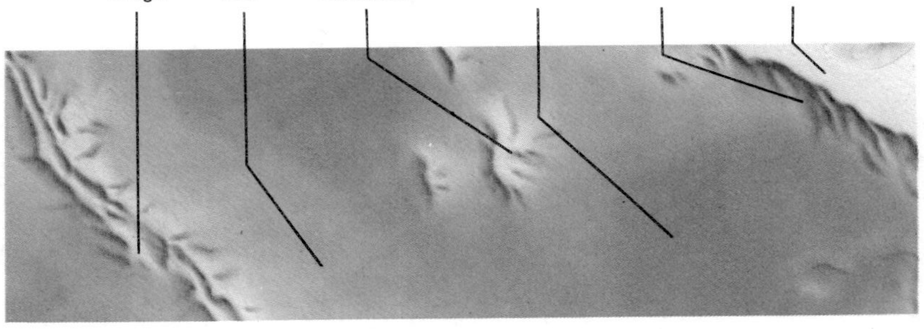

Grassland

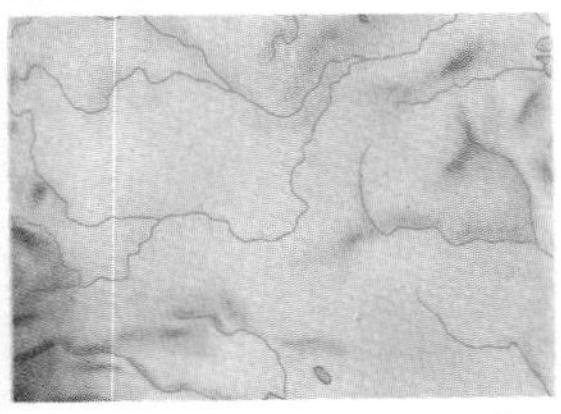

Dry Scrub

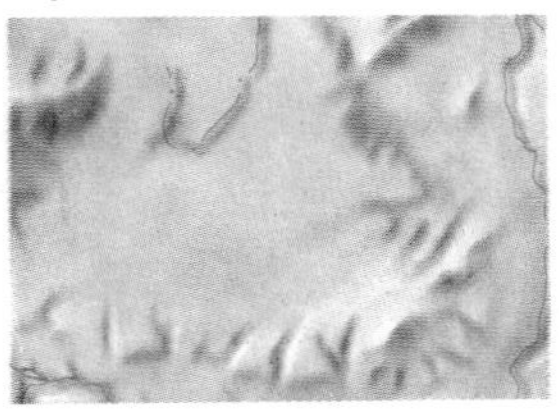

Desert

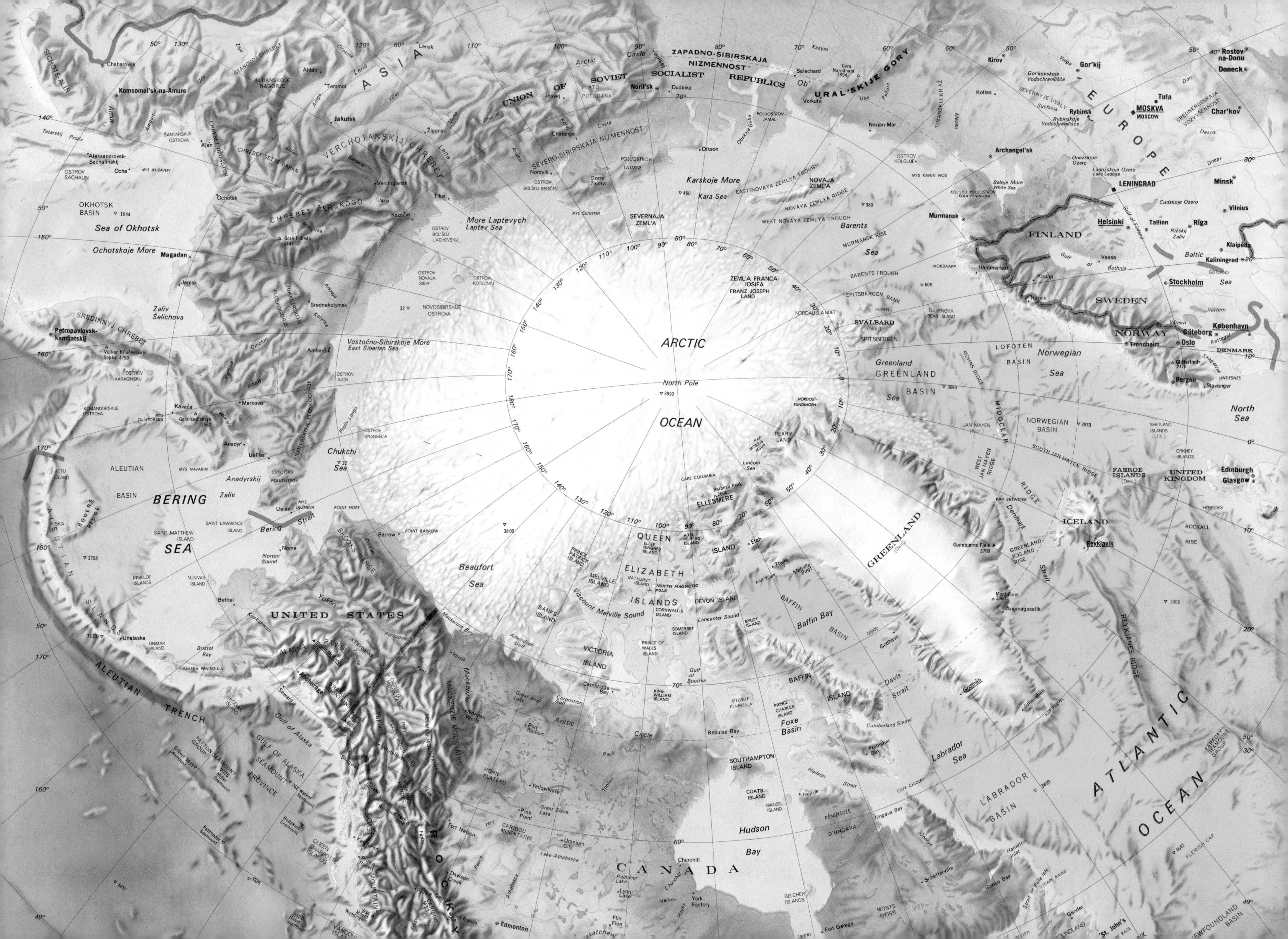

ARCTIC
OCEAN
North Pole
ASIA
EUROPE
UNION OF SOVIET SOCIALIST REPUBLICS
UNITED STATES
CANADA
ATLANTIC OCEAN
GREENLAND
ICELAND
FINLAND
SWEDEN
NORWAY
DENMARK
UNITED KINGDOM
FAEROE ISLANDS
SVALBARD
SPITSBERGEN
ZEML'A FRANCA-IOSIFA
FRANZ JOSEPH LAND
NOVAJA ZEML'A
SEVERNAJA ZEML'A
ELLESMERE ISLAND
QUEEN ELIZABETH ISLANDS
BAFFIN ISLAND
VICTORIA ISLAND
BANKS ISLAND
SOUTHAMPTON ISLAND
Karskoje More
Kara Sea
Barents Sea
Norwegian Sea
Greenland Sea
North Sea
More Laptevych
Laptev Sea
Vostočno-Sibirskoje More
East Siberian Sea
Chukchi Sea
Beaufort Sea
BERING SEA
Bering Strait
Sea of Okhotsk
Ochotskoje More
Baffin Bay
Davis Strait
Labrador Sea
Hudson Bay
Foxe Basin
Gulf of Alaska
ALEUTIAN TRENCH
ALEUTIAN ISLANDS
URAL'SKIJE GORY
ZAPADNO-SIBIRSKAJA NIZMENNOST'
SEVERO-SIBIRSKAJA NIZMENNOST
VERCHOJANSKIJ CHREBET
CHREBET ČERSKOGO
BROOKS RANGE
MACKENZIE MOUNTAINS
ROCKY
REYKJANES RIDGE
LABRADOR BASIN
NORWEGIAN BASIN
GREENLAND BASIN
LOFOTEN BASIN
MIDOCEAN
ALEUTIAN BASIN
OKHOTSK BASIN
Arctic Circle
MOSKVA
MOSCOW
LENINGRAD
Helsinki
Stockholm
Oslo
København
Reykjavik
Murmansk
Archangel'sk
Anchorage
Edmonton
Churchill
Jakutsk
Magadan
Noril'sk

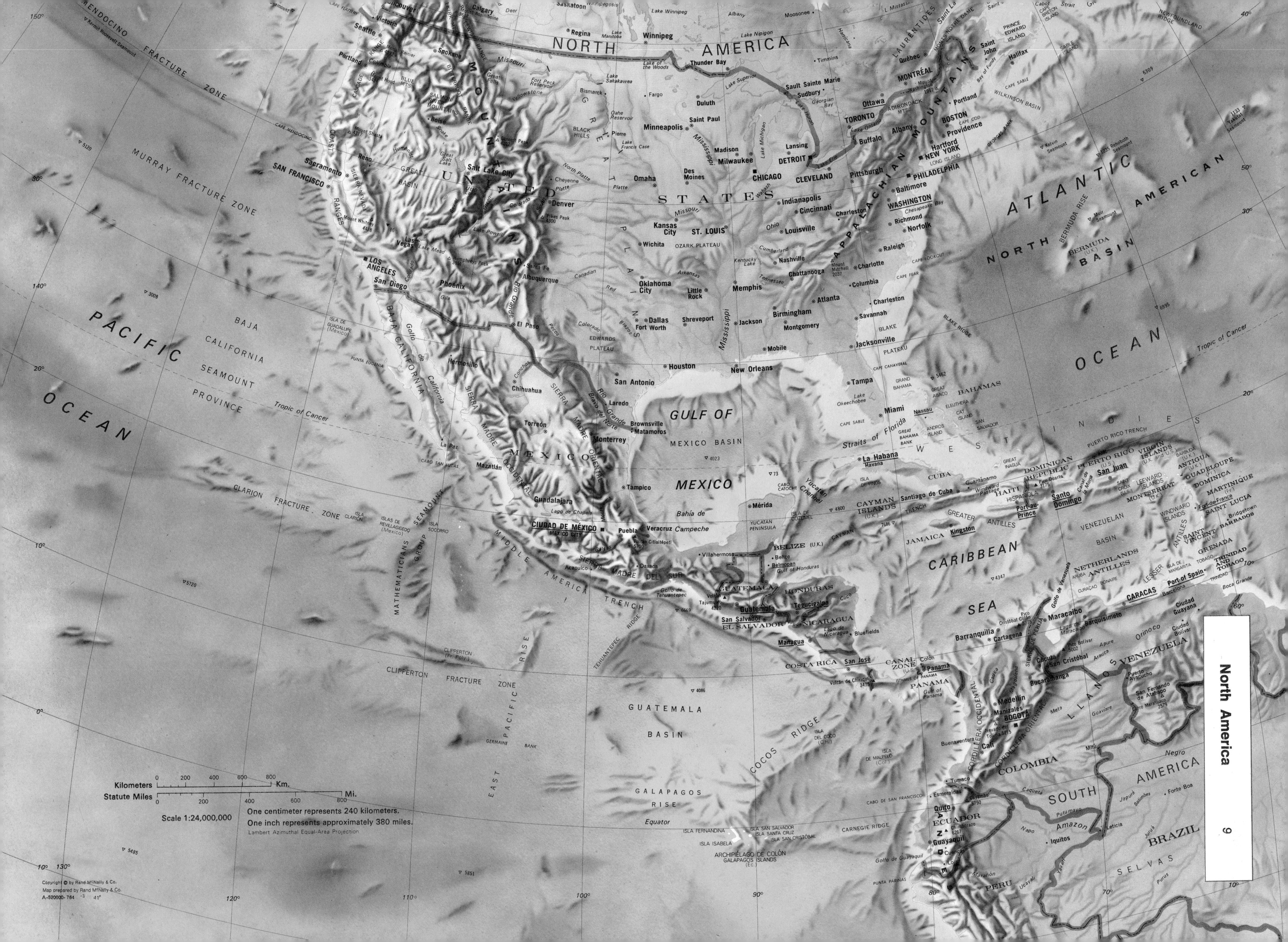
NORTH AMERICA
UNITED STATES
GREAT PLAINS
ROCKY MOUNTAINS
APPALACHIAN MOUNTAINS
LAURENTIDES
ATLANTIC
NORTH AMERICAN BASIN
OCEAN
PACIFIC
OCEAN
MENDOCINO FRACTURE ZONE
MURRAY FRACTURE ZONE
BAJA CALIFORNIA SEAMOUNT PROVINCE
CLARION FRACTURE ZONE
CLIPPERTON FRACTURE ZONE
MATHEMATICIANS SEAMOUNT GROUP
MIDDLE AMERICA TRENCH
EAST PACIFIC RISE
GUATEMALA BASIN
COCOS RIDGE
GALAPAGOS RISE
CARNEGIE RIDGE
GULF OF MEXICO
MEXICO BASIN
CARIBBEAN SEA
VENEZUELAN BASIN
GREATER ANTILLES
NETHERLANDS ANTILLES
WEST INDIES
BAHAMAS
PUERTO RICO TRENCH
BERMUDA (U.K.)
BLAKE PLATEAU
Tropic of Cancer
Straits of Florida
MÉXICO
SIERRA MADRE OCCIDENTAL
SIERRA MADRE ORIENTAL
SIERRA MADRE DEL SUR
CIUDAD DE MÉXICO
MEXICO CITY
GUATEMALA
HONDURAS
EL SALVADOR
NICARAGUA
COSTA RICA
PANAMA
CANAL ZONE
CUBA
HAITI
DOMINICAN REPUBLIC
JAMAICA
CAYMAN ISLANDS
BELIZE (U.K.)
COLOMBIA
VENEZUELA
ECUADOR
PERU
BRAZIL
SOUTH AMERICA
LLANOS
SELVAS
Amazon
Orinoco
WASHINGTON
NEW YORK
PHILADELPHIA
BOSTON
CHICAGO
DETROIT
CLEVELAND
ST. LOUIS
LOS ANGELES
SAN FRANCISCO
TORONTO
MONTRÉAL
Ottawa
La Habana
Havana
Kingston
Port-au-Prince
Santo Domingo
San Juan
CARACAS
Port-of-Spain
BOGOTÁ
Quito
Panamá
San José
Managua
Tegucigalpa
San Salvador
Guatemala
Kilometers 0 200 400 600 800 Km.
Statute Miles 0 200 400 600 800 Mi.
Scale 1:24,000,000
One centimeter represents 240 kilometers.
One inch represents approximately 380 miles.
Lambert Azimuthal Equal-Area Projection
Copyright © by Rand McNally & Co.
Map prepared by Rand McNally & Co.

NORTH AMERICA
UNITED STATES
ROCKY MOUNTAINS
GREAT PLAINS
APPALACHIAN MOUNTAINS
Chicago
New York
Philadelphia
Washington
Cleveland
Pittsburgh
Baltimore
Cincinnati
St. Louis
Kansas City
Omaha
Des Moines
Denver
Wichita
Oklahoma City
Louisville
Nashville
Memphis
Birmingham
Atlanta
Richmond
Norfolk
Raleigh
Charleston
Savannah
Montgomery
Jackson
Jacksonville
Mobile
New Orleans
Houston
Dallas
Fort Worth
Little Rock
Albuquerque
San Antonio
Laredo
Brownsville
Tampa
Miami
Mississippi
Missouri
Ohio
Rio Grande
Colorado
Pecos
EDWARDS PLATEAU
OZARK PLATEAU
GULF OF MEXICO
MEXICO BASIN
MEXICO
SIERRA MADRE ORIENTAL
SIERRA MADRE DEL SUR
Monterrey
Matamoros
Torreón
Tampico
Guadalajara
Puebla
Veracruz
CIUDAD DE MEXICO
Mérida
YUCATAN PENINSULA
Yucatan Channel
Bahía de Campeche
BELIZE
GUATEMALA
HONDURAS
EL SALVADOR
NICARAGUA
COSTA RICA
PANAMA
CANAL ZONE
Managua
San José
Gulf of Honduras
CARIBBEAN SEA
CUBA
La Habana
Havana
Straits of Florida
BAHAMAS
JAMAICA
Kingston
HAITI
Port-au-Prince
DOMINICAN REPUBLIC
Santo Domingo
HISPANIOLA
PUERTO RICO
San Juan
PUERTO RICO TRENCH
CAYMAN ISLANDS
VIRGIN ISLANDS
ANTIGUA
GUADELOUPE
DOMINICA
MARTINIQUE
SAINT LUCIA
BARBADOS
GRENADA
TRINIDAD AND TOBAGO
NETHERLANDS ANTILLES
LESSER ANTILLES
VENEZUELAN BASIN
WEST INDIES
NORTH AMERICAN BASIN
BERMUDA
ATLANTIC OCEAN
MID-ATLANTIC RIDGE
AZORES RIDGE
CAPE VERDE BASIN
GUIANA BASIN
Tropic of Cancer
Equator
MIDDLE AMERICA TRENCH
TEHUANTEPEC RIDGE
GUATEMALA BASIN
COCOS RIDGE
GALAPAGOS RISE
CARNEGIE RIDGE
ARCHIPIÉLAGO DE COLÓN
SOUTH AMERICA
VENEZUELA
Caracas
Maracaibo
Barquisimeto
COLOMBIA
Bogotá
Medellín
Cali
Barranquilla
Cartagena
LLANOS
GUYANA
Georgetown
SURINAME
Paramaribo
FRENCH GUIANA
Cayenne
ECUADOR
Quito
Guayaquil
PERU
Lima
BRAZIL
SELVAS
Manaus
Belém
São Luís
Fortaleza
Natal
Recife
Salvador
Amazon
Negro
Orinoco
ANDES

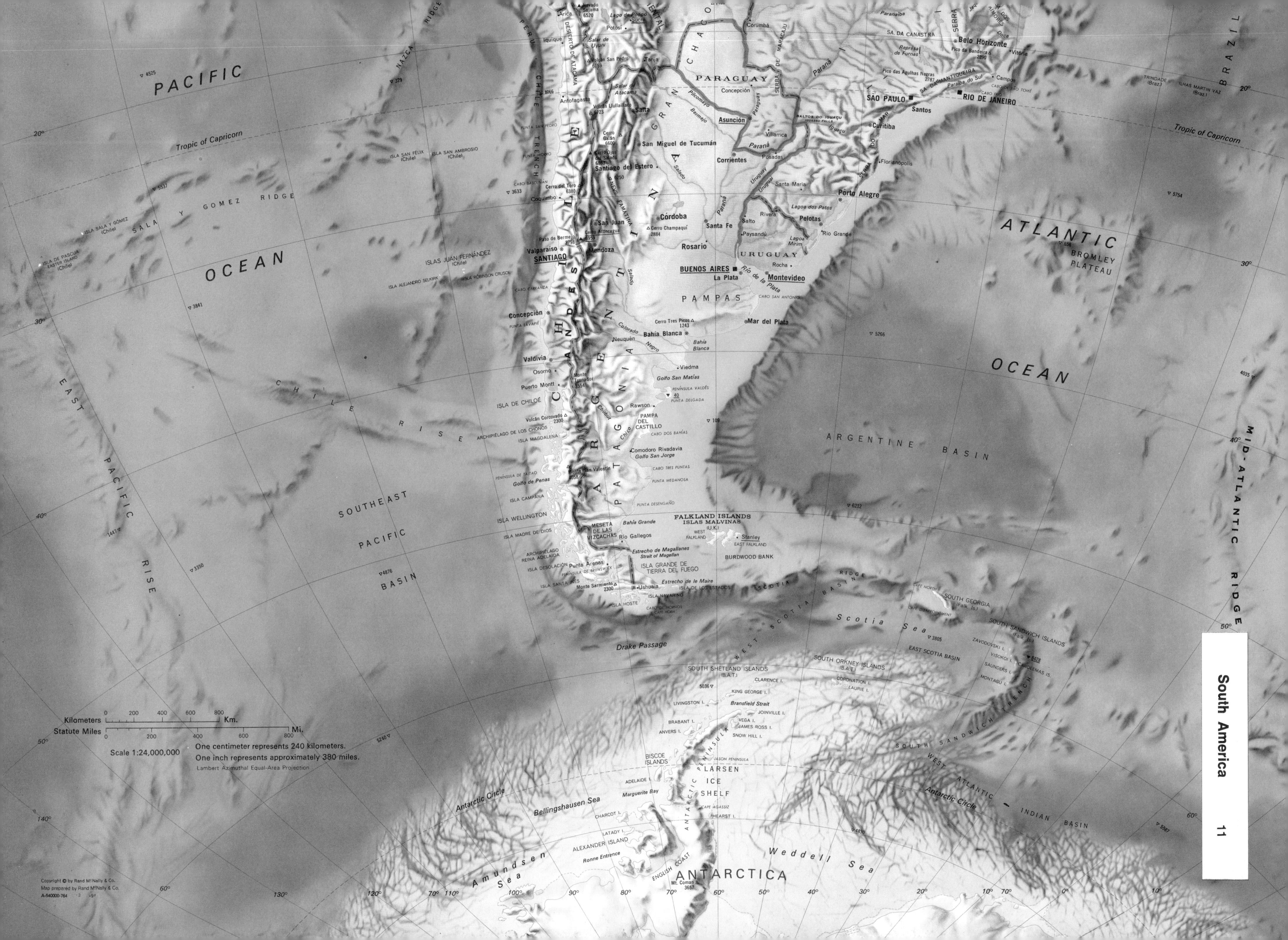
PACIFIC
OCEAN
SOUTHEAST
PACIFIC
BASIN
EAST
PACIFIC
RISE
CHILE RISE
SALA Y GOMEZ RIDGE
NAZCA RIDGE
PERU-CHILE TRENCH
Tropic of Capricorn
ISLA SAN FÉLIX (Chile)
ISLA SAN AMBROSIO (Chile)
ISLA SALA Y GÓMEZ (Chile)
ISLA DE PASCUA EASTER ISLAND (Chile)
ISLAS JUAN FERNÁNDEZ (Chile)
ISLA ALEJANDRO SELKIRK
ISLA ROBINSON CRUSOE
PARAGUAY
Concepción
Asunción
Corrientes
Posadas
Villarrica
San Miguel de Tucumán
Santiago del Estero
Salta
Antofagasta
Iquique
Arica
Potosí
Sucre
Corumbá
GRAN CHACO
ANDES
ARGENTINA
PATAGONIA
PAMPAS
Córdoba
Santa Fe
Rosario
BUENOS AIRES
La Plata
Río de la Plata
Montevideo
URUGUAY
Salto
Paysandú
Rivera
Rocha
Mar del Plata
Bahía Blanca
Cerro Tres Picos 1243
Neuquén
Viedma
Golfo San Matías
PENÍNSULA VALDÉS
Rawson
PAMPA DEL CASTILLO
Comodoro Rivadavia
Golfo San Jorge
Bahía Grande
MESETA DE LAS VIZCACHAS
Río Gallegos
Estrecho de Magallanes Strait of Magellan
ISLA GRANDE DE TIERRA DEL FUEGO
Punta Arenas
Ushuaia
Estrecho de le Maire
ISLA DE LOS ESTADOS
Monte Sarmiento 2300
ISLA NAVARINO
ISLA HOSTE
Mendoza
San Juan
Cerro Aconcagua
Valparaíso
SANTIAGO
Coquimbo
Concepción
Valdivia
Osorno
Puerto Montt
ISLA DE CHILOÉ
Volcán Corcovado 2300
ARCHIPIÉLAGO DE LOS CHONOS
ISLA MAGDALENA
PENÍNSULA DE TAITAO
Golfo de Penas
ISLA CAMPANA
ISLA WELLINGTON
ISLA MADRE DE DIOS
ARCHIPIÉLAGO REINA ADELAIDA
ISLA DESOLACIÓN
ISLA SANTA INÉS
SÃO PAULO
RIO DE JANEIRO
Santos
Curitiba
Florianópolis
Porto Alegre
Lagoa dos Patos
Pelotas
Rio Grande
Lagoa Mirim
Santa Maria
Belo Horizonte
Vitória
Campos
SA. DA CANASTRA
SA. DA MANTIQUEIRA
BRAZIL
TRINDADE (Braz.)
ILHAS MARTIN VAZ (Braz.)
ATLANTIC
OCEAN
BROMLEY PLATEAU
ARGENTINE BASIN
MID-ATLANTIC RIDGE
FALKLAND ISLANDS
ISLAS MALVINAS
(U.K.)
WEST FALKLAND
EAST FALKLAND
Stanley
BURDWOOD BANK
SCOTIA RIDGE
SOUTH GEORGIA (Falk. Is.)
SOUTH SANDWICH ISLANDS (Falk. Is.)
Scotia Sea
SCOTIA BASIN
EAST SCOTIA BASIN
SOUTH SANDWICH TRENCH
Drake Passage
SOUTH SHETLAND ISLANDS (B.A.T.)
SOUTH ORKNEY ISLANDS (B.A.T.)
CORONATION I.
LAURIE I.
CLARENCE I.
KING GEORGE I.
LIVINGSTON I.
Bransfield Strait
JOINVILLE I.
BRABANT I.
ANVERS I.
VEGA I.
JAMES ROSS I.
SNOW HILL I.
BISCOE ISLANDS
ADELAIDE I.
Marguerite Bay
LARSEN ICE SHELF
ANTARCTIC PENINSULA
Bellingshausen Sea
CHARCOT I.
LATADY I.
ALEXANDER ISLAND
Ronne Entrance
ENGLISH COAST
Mt. Coman 3657
Amundsen Sea
Weddell Sea
ANTARCTICA
Antarctic Circle
WEST ATLANTIC-INDIAN BASIN
Kilometers 0 200 400 600 800 Km.
Statute Miles 0 200 400 600 800 Mi.
Scale 1:24,000,000
One centimeter represents 240 kilometers.
One inch represents approximately 380 miles.
Lambert Azimuthal Equal-Area Projection
Copyright © by Rand McNally & Co.
Map prepared by Rand McNally & Co.

ATLANTIC OCEAN
EUROPE
ASIA
ASIA MINOR
UNION OF SOVIET SOCIALIST REPUBLICS
GREENLAND (Den.)
CANADA
ICELAND
Reykjavík
NORWEGIAN BASIN
Norwegian Sea
Greenland Sea
GREENLAND BASIN
LOFOTEN BASIN
MOHNS RIDGE
WEST JAN MAYEN RIDGE
MIDOCEAN RIDGE
GREENLAND-ICELAND RISE
Denmark Strait
Davis Strait
Labrador Sea
LABRADOR BASIN
REYKJANES RIDGE
ROCKALL RISE
WEST EUROPEAN BASIN
MID-ATLANTIC RIDGE
AZORES-GIBRALTAR RIDGE
CANARY BASIN
CAPE VERDE TERRACE
BARENTS TROUGH
MURMANSK RISE
Barents Sea
Kara Sea
SVALBARD (Nor.)
Arctic Circle
Tropic of Cancer
North Sea
Baltic Sea
Gulf of Bothnia
Gulf of Finland
White Sea
English Channel
Bay of Biscay
Mediterranean Sea
Tyrrhenian Sea
Adriatic Sea
Ionian Sea
Aegean Sea
Black Sea
Caspian Sea
Aral'skoje More
Persian Gulf
Red Sea
UNITED KINGDOM
IRELAND
FRANCE
SPAIN
PORTUGAL
ITALY
DENMARK
NORWAY
SWEDEN
FINLAND
POLAND
FED. REP. OF GER.
GER. DEM. REP.
CZECHOSLOVAKIA
AUSTRIA
HUNGARY
ROMANIA
YUGOSLAVIA
BULGARIA
ALBANIA
GREECE
TURKEY
CYPRUS
SYRIA
LEBANON
ISRAEL
JORDAN
IRAQ
IRAN
KUWAIT
SAUDI ARABIA
QATAR
BAHRAIN
UNITED ARAB EMIRATES
OMAN
EGYPT
LIBYA
TUNISIA
ALGERIA
MOROCCO
WESTERN SAHARA
MAURITANIA
MALI
NIGER
SAHARA
LONDON
PARIS
MADRID
ROMA
BERLIN
WIEN
Praha
BUDAPEST
Warszawa
MOSKVA
LENINGRAD
Stockholm
Oslo
Helsinki
København
Bucureşti
Sofija
Beograd
Athínai
İstanbul
Ankara
Tehrān
Baghdād
Dimashq
Bayrūt
AL-QĀHIRAH
Tarābulus
Tūnis
Alger
Rabat
Lisboa
Dublin
Amsterdam
Bruxelles
SVERDLOVSK
VOLGOGRAD
URAL'SKIJE GORY URAL MOUNTAINS
ATLAS MOUNTAINS
ZAPADNO-SIBIRSKAJA NIZMENNOST'
SREDNESIBIRSKOJE PLOSKOGORJE
PRIKASPIJSKAJA NIZMENNOST'

GAMBIA
Banjul
Bamako
UPPER
VOLTA
Ouagadougou
Niamey
Zinder
Lake Chad
Abéché
El Fasher
Al-Ubayyid
White Nile
Blue Nile
Aden
Gulf of Aden
DJIBOUTI
Djibouti
GUINEA
BISSAU
Bissau
GUINEA
BENIN
Kano
Maiduguri
Ndjamena
Kaduna
A F R I C A
Conakry
Freetown
SIERRA
LEONE
IVORY
COAST
GHANA
Lake Volta
TOGO
NIGERIA
Niger
Ibadan
Lagos
Enugu
Kumasi
Accra
Lomé
Porto-Novo
LIBERIA
Monrovia
Abidjan
Sekondi-Takoradi
Bight of Benin
Aba
Port Harcourt
CAMEROON
Douala
Yaoundé
Bight of Biafra
Gulf of Guinea
CENTRAL
AFRICAN
EMPIRE
Bangui
Addis
Abeba
ETHIOPIA
Berbera
Hargeysa
SOMALIA
Mogadisho
Juba
SIERRA LEONE
RISE
SIERRA LEONE
BASIN
UGANDA
Lake Albert
Lake Kyoga
Kampala
KENYA
Lake Rudolf
Nairobi
Lake Victoria
EQUAT.
GUI.
SAO TOME
AND PRINCIPE
Libreville
GABON
CONGO
Congo
Ubangi
Kisangani
ZAIRE
CONGO
BASIN
RWANDA
Kigali
BURUNDI
Bujumbura
Lake Kivu
SERENGETI
PLAIN
Lake Eyasi
GUINEA
BASIN
Equator
ROMANCHE GAP
PAGALU
(Equat. Gui.)
GUINEA RISE
Brazzaville
Kinshasa
Matadi
Pointe-Noire
CABINDA
(Angola)
Kananga
Mombasa
Lake
Tanganyika
TANZANIA
Dar-es-Salaam
INDIAN
OCEAN
SEYCHELLES
SOMALI BASIN
Equator
ASCENSION
(St. Helena)
Luanda
Lake Mweru
KATANGA PLATEAU
Lubumbashi
Lake Bangweulu
Lake Rukwa
RIFT VALLEY
Mtwara
ALDABRA ISLANDS
(Sey.)
COMOROS
Lobito
Huambo
ANGOLA
Ndola
ZAMBIA
Lusaka
Lake
Nyasa
Lilongwe
MOZAMBIQUE
Moçambique
Moçamedes
Blantyre
Diego-Suarez
MASCARENE
ATLANTIC
SAINT HELENA
(U.K.)
Lake Kariba
Livingstone
VICTORIA
FALLS
Salisbury
RHODESIA
Zambezi
Okavango
Tsumeb
KAUKAUVELD
Bulawayo
Beira
Antananarivo
Mozambique
Channel
MADAGASCAR
BASIN
Windhoek
NAMIBIA
(S. Afr. Admin.)
Walvis Bay
(S. Afr.)
BOTSWANA
KALAHARI
DESERT
Limpopo
Gaborone
Pretoria
JOHANNESBURG
SWAZILAND
Maputo
MAURITIUS
REUNION
(Fr.)
MASCARENE ISLANDS
Tropic of Capricorn
Tropic of Capricorn
Lüderitz
NAMIB DESERT
GREAT NAMALAND
Orange
SOUTH AFRICA
Bloemfontein
Maseru
LESOTHO
Durban
DRAKENSBERG
NATAL
BASIN
MADAGASCAR
BASIN
Fort-Dauphin
GREAT KARROO
East London
Port Elizabeth
Cape Town
CAPE OF
GOOD HOPE
CAPE AGULHAS
O C E A N
MID-ATLANTIC RIDGE
BRAZIL BASIN
ANGOLA BASIN
WALVIS RIDGE
CAPE
BASIN
CAPE RISE
AGULHAS
PLATEAU
MOZAMBIQUE RIDGE
MADAGASCAR RIDGE
SOUTHWEST INDIAN RIDGE
TRISTAN DA CUNHA GROUP
(St. Helena)
GOUGH ISLAND
Kilometers 0 200 400 600 800 Km.
Statute Miles 0 200 400 600 800 Mi.
Scale 1:24,000,000
One centimeter represents 240 kilometers.
One inch represents approximately 380 miles.
Lambert Azimuthal Equal-Area Projection
Copyright © by Rand McNally & Co.
Map prepared by Rand McNally & Co.
A-519394-764

ARCTIC
OCEAN
North Pole
ATLANTIC
OCEAN
GREENLAND
(Den.)
ELLESMERE ISLAND
(Can.)
Lincoln Sea
Greenland Sea
Denmark Strait
ICELAND
Reykjavík
JAN MAYEN
(Nor.)
ROCKALL RISE
GREENLAND BASIN
NORWEGIAN BASIN
Norwegian Sea
FAEROE ISLANDS
(Den.)
SVALBARD
(Nor.)
Arctic Circle
Barents Sea
BARENTS TROUGH
ZEML'A FRANCA-IOSIFA
FRANZ JOSEPH LAND
SEVERNAJA ZEML'A
NOVAJA ZEML'A
Karskoje More
Kara Sea
More Laptevych
Laptev Sea
NOVOSIBIRSKIJE OSTROVA
Vostočno-Sibirskoje More
East Siberian Sea
OSTROV VRANGEL'A
Chukchi Sea
Bering Strait
UNITED STATES
Bering Sea
ALEUTIAN BASIN
ALEUTIAN ISLANDS
IRELAND
Dublin
UNITED KINGDOM
LONDON
North Sea
NORWAY
Oslo
SWEDEN
Stockholm
FINLAND
Helsinki
DENMARK
København
Gulf of Bothnia
Baltic Sea
BELGIUM
NETHERLANDS
Amsterdam
BERLIN
POLAND
Warszawa
CZECHOSLOVAKIA
Praha
WIEN
BUDAPEST
HUNGARY
ROMANIA
Bucureşti
BULGARIA
Sofija
E U R O P E
UNION OF SOVIET SOCIALIST REPUBLICS
LENINGRAD
MOSKVA
Archangel'sk
Murmansk
Kijev
ODESSA
VOLGOGRAD
SVERDLOVSK
URAL'SKIJE GORY
URAL MOUNTAINS
ZAPADNO-SIBIRSKAJA NIZMENNOST'
SREDNESIBIRSKOJE PLOSKOGORJE
CHREBET ČERSKOGO
Sea of Okhotsk
OSTROV SACHALIN
KURIL'SKIJE OSTROVA
KURIL ISLANDS
Novosibirsk
Omsk
Krasnojarsk
Irkutsk
Jakutsk
Magadan
Chabarovsk
Vladivostok
Caspian Sea
Black Sea
ISTANBUL
ASIA MINOR
TURKEY
SYRIA
IRAQ
IRAN
TEHRĀN
AFGHANISTAN
Kābul
SAUDI ARABIA
Baghdād
Aral'skoje More
PLATO UST'URT
Ozero Balchaš
TIEN SHAN
PAMIR
HINDU KUSH
TALIMUPENDI
TAKLA MAKAN
KUNLUNSHANMAI
MONGOLIA
Ulaanbaatar
GOBI
CHINA
BEIJING
SHANGHAI
WUHAN
Yellow Sea
EAST CHINA SEA
NORTH KOREA
SOUTH KOREA
SOUL
P'yongyang
Sea of Japan
JAPAN BASIN
HONSHU
ŌSAKA
HOKKAIDO
Sapporo

ARABIAN SEA
Bay of Bengal
INDIAN OCEAN
ARABIAN PENINSULA
AR-RAB' AL-KHĀLĪ
INDIA
DECCAN
PAKISTAN
BANGLADESH
BURMA
THAILAND
LAOS
VIETNAM
KAMPUCHEA
INDOCHINA
MALAYSIA
INDONESIA
PHILIPPINES
SRI LANKA
MALDIVES
SEYCHELLES
MADAGASCAR
MAURITIUS
SOMALIA
ETHIOPIA
DJIBOUTI
YEMEN
P.D.R. OF YEMEN
OMAN
UNITED ARAB EMIRATES
QATAR
HONG KONG
TAIWAN
BRUNEI
BORNEO
SUMATERA
SULAWESI
AUSTRALIA
DELHI
New Delhi
BOMBAY
CALCUTTA
MADRAS
Hyderābād
Bangalore
Colombo
Dacca
Rangoon
KRUNG THEP
Phnum Pénh
Thanh-pho Ho Chi Minh
Ha-noi
MANILA
Kuala Lumpur
SINGAPORE
JAKARTA
VICTORIA
GUANGZHOU
Karāchi
Perth
Antananarivo
Mogadisho
Gulf of Aden
Gulf of Oman
Gulf of Thailand
Andaman Sea
Laccadive Sea
South China Sea
Celebes Sea
Sulu Sea
Java Sea
Philippine Sea
Tropic of Cancer
Equator
Tropic of Capricorn
ARABIAN BASIN
CARLSBERG RIDGE
SOMALI BASIN
MASCARENE BASIN
MASCARENE PLATEAU
MID-INDIAN BASIN
MID-INDIAN RIDGE
CHAGOS-LACCADIVE PLATEAU
NINETY EAST RIDGE
COCOS BASIN
WEST AUSTRALIAN BASIN
MADAGASCAR BASIN
SOUTHWEST INDIAN RIDGE
BROKEN RIDGE
JAVA TRENCH
Kilometers
Statute Miles
Scale 1:24,000,000
One centimeter represents 240 kilometers.
One inch represents approximately 380 miles.
Lambert Azimuthal Equal-Area Projection
Copyright © by Rand McNally & Co.
Map prepared by Rand McNally & Co.

World Index Map

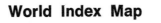

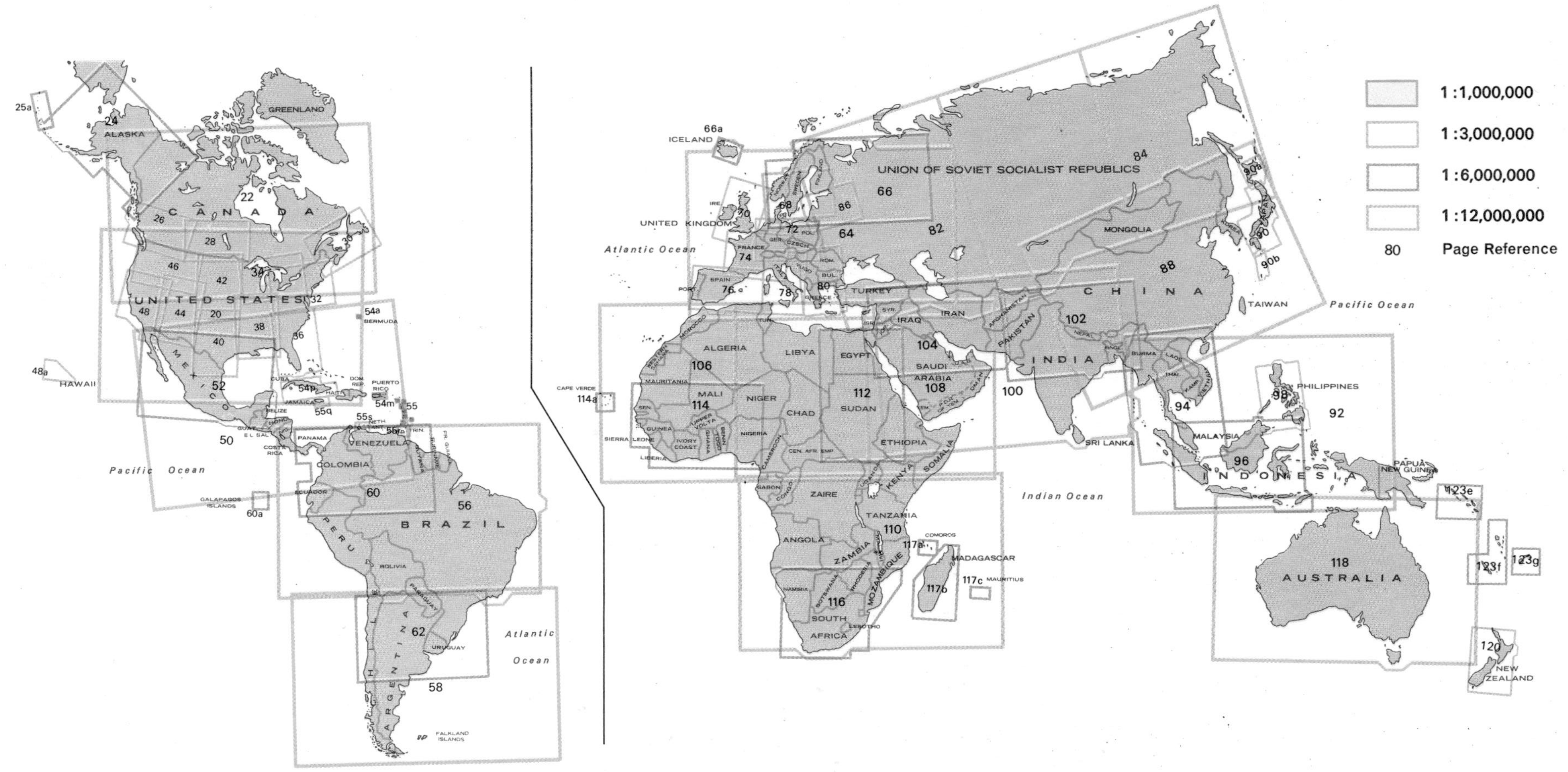

Legend to Maps

Inhabited Localities

The symbol represents the number of inhabitants within the locality

1:300,000 1:1,000,000 1:3,000,000 1:6,000,000	• 0—10,000 ○ 10,000—25,000 ⊙ 25,000—100,000 ▣ 100,000—250,000 ▣ 250,000—1,000,000 ■ >1,000,000	1:12,000,000	• 0—50,000 ⊙ 50,000—100,000 ▣ 100,000—250,000 ▣ 250,000—1,000,000 ■ >1,000,000

Urban Area (area of continuous industrial, commercial, and residential development)

Northland Center ■ Major Shopping Center

Major Industrial Area

Wooded Area

Local Park or Recreational Area

The size of type indicates the relative economic and political importance of the locality

Écommoy	Lisieux	Rouen
Trouville	Orléans	PARIS

Hollywood ▫ *Westminster* — Section of a City, Neighborhood

Bi'r Safājah ° — Inhabited Oasis

Kumdah ° — Uninhabited Oasis

Capitals of Political Units

BUDAPEST Independent Nation

Cayenne Dependency (Colony, protectorate, etc.)

GALAPAGOS (Ecuador) Administering Country

Villarica State, Province, etc.

White Plains County, Oblast, etc.

Iserlohn Okrug, Kreis, etc.

Alternate Names

Basel **Bâle** — **MOSKVA** **MOSCOW** — English or second official language names are shown in reduced size lettering

Ventura **(San Buenaventura)** — **Volgograd** **(Stalingrad)** — Historical or other alternates in the local language are shown in parentheses

Political Boundaries

International (First-order political unit)

1:300,000 — 1:1,000,000, 1:3,000,000, 1:6,000,000, 1:12,000,000

Demarcated, Undemarcated, and Administrative

Disputed de jure

Indefinite or Undefined

Demarcation Line

Internal

Okrug, Kreis, etc. (Fourth-order political unit)

City or Municipality (may appear in combination with another boundary symbol)

GUAIRA — State, Province, etc. (Second-order political unit)

WESTCHESTER — County, Oblast, etc. (Third-order political unit)

ANDALUCIA — Historical Region (No boundaries indicated)

Miscellaneous Cultural Features

PARQUE NACIONAL CANAIMA ▲ — National or State Park or Monument

FORT CLATSOP NAT. MEM. ▲ — National or State Historic(al) Site, Memorial

BLACKFOOT IND. RES. — Indian Reservation

FORT DIX ■ — Military Installation

▲ TANGLEWOOD — Point of Interest (Battlefield, cave, historical site, etc.)

<> — Lock

STEINHAUSEN — Church, Monastery

UXMAL — Ruins

WINDSOR CASTLE — Castle

AMISTAD DAM — Dam

Quarry or Surface Mine

Subsurface Mine

GREENWOOD CEMETERY — Cemetery

Lighthouse

Crib — Water Intake Crib

Regional Index Maps

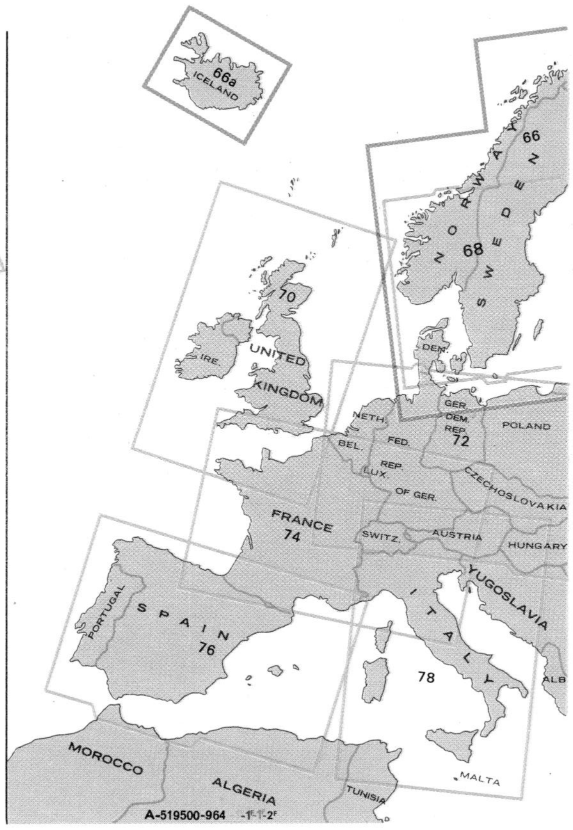

Transportation

1:12,000,000	1:3,000,000 1:6,000,000	1:300,000 1:1,000,000	
		PENNSYLVANIA TURNPIKE	Primary Road
			Secondary Road
			Tertiary Road
			Minor Road, Trail
		CANADIAN NATIONAL	Primary Railway
			Secondary Railway
		DULLES INTERNATIONAL AIRPORT	Airport
		LONDON (HEATHROW) AIRPORT	Airport
		SÜD-BAHNHOF	Rail or Air Terminal

MACKINAC BRIDGE — Bridge

Shipping Channel

GREAT ST. BERNARD TUNNEL — Tunnel

Canal du Midi — Navigable Canal

TO CALAIS — Ferry

Intracoastal Waterway

Metric-English Equivalents

Areas represented by one square centimeter at various map scales

1:300,000
9 km²
3.48 square miles

1:6,000,000
3,600 km²
1,390 square miles

1:1,000,000
100 km²
39 square miles

1:12,000,000
14,400 km²
5,558 square miles

1:3,000,000
900 km²
348 square miles

Meter=3.28 feet
Kilometer=0.62 mile

Meter² (m²)=10.76 square feet
Kilometer² (km²)=0.39 square mile

Hydrographic Features

Shoreline

The Everglades — Swamp

Undefined or Fluctuating Shoreline

SEWARD GLACIER — Glacier

Amur — River, Stream

L. Victoria — Lake, Reservoir

Intermittent Stream

Tuz Gölü — Salt Lake

Rapids, Falls

Intermittent Lake, Reservoir

Irrigation or Drainage Canal

Dry Lake Bed

Reef

(395) — Lake Surface Elevation

764 — Depth of Water

Pier, Breakwater

Los Angeles Aqueduct — Aqueduct

Topographic Features

Mt. Kenya △ 5199 — Elevation Above Sea Level

Lava

76 ▽ — Elevation Below Sea Level

Sand Area

Mount Cook ▲ 3764 — Highest Elevation in Country

Salt Flat

Khyber Pass 1067 — Mountain Pass

A N D E S KUNLUNSHANMAI — Mountain Range, Plateau, Valley, etc.

133 ▼ — Lowest Elevation in Country

(106) — Elevation of City

BAFFIN ISLAND NUNIVAK ISLAND — Island

* — Rock

Elevations and depths are given in meters

Highest Elevation and Lowest Elevation of a continent are underlined

POLUOSTROV KAMČATKA CABO DE HORNOS — Peninsula, Cape, Point, etc.

United States (excluding Alaska and Hawaii)

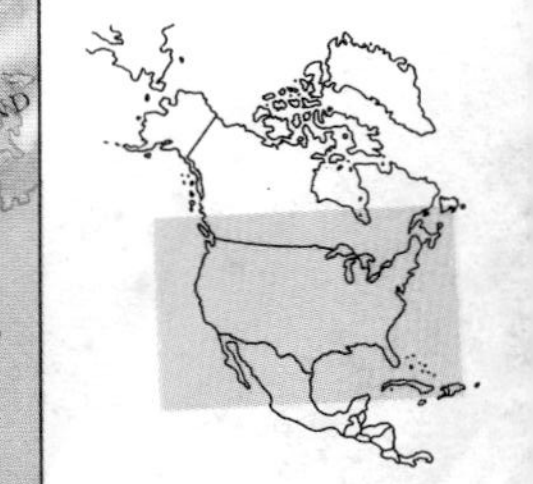

Kilometers 0 200 400 600 Km.

Statute Miles 0 200 400 600 Mi.

Scale 1:12,000,000

One centimeter represents 120 kilometers.
One inch represents approximately 190 miles.

Albers Conical Equal-Area Projection

ROCKY MOUNTAINS
COAST MOUNTAINS
MACKENZIE MTS
SELWYN MOUNTAINS
PELLY MOUNTAINS
CASCADE RANGE
SIERRA NEVADA
BROOKS RANGE
ALASKA RANGE
PACIFIC OCEAN
Gulf of Alaska
Beaufort Sea
UNITED STATES
CANADA
NORTHWEST TERRITORIES
ALASKA
ALBERTA
SASKATCHEWAN
MANITOBA
MONTANA
NORTH DAKOTA
SOUTH DAKOTA
MINNESOTA
WYOMING
OREGON
WASHINGTON
NEBRASKA
COLORADO
UTAH
VICTORIA ISLAND
BANKS ISLAND
Anchorage
Fairbanks
Vancouver
Victoria
Seattle
Tacoma
Portland
Salem
Eugene
Spokane
Calgary
Edmonton
Saskatoon
Regina
Winnipeg
Lethbridge
Great Falls
Missoula
Butte
Billings
Boise
Bismarck
Fargo
Grand Forks
Minneapolis
Salt Lake City
Ogden
Provo
Reno
Sacramento
SAN FRANCISCO
Oakland
San Jose
Stockton
Modesto
Fresno
Prince Rupert
Prince George
Yellowknife
Whitehorse
Dawson
Fort Smith
Fort McMurray
Fort St. John
Fort Nelson
Fort Liard
Fort Simpson
Fort Norman
Inuvik
Aklavik
Tuktoyaktuk
Coppermine
Cambridge Bay
Baker Lake
Rankin
Churchill
The Pas
Flin Flon
Thompson
Brandon
Moose Jaw
Medicine Hat
Red Deer
Lloydminster
North Battleford
Prince Albert
Uranium City
Stony Rapids
Sachs Harbour
Holman Island
All Offshore Islands are within the District of Franklin

Kilometers 0 200 400 600 Km.
Statute Miles 0 200 400 600 Mi.

Scale 1:12,000,000
One centimeter represents 120 kilometers.
One inch represents approximately 190 miles.
Lambert Conformal Conic Projection

Alaska and Yukon

Kilometers 0 100 200 300 Km.

Statute Miles 0 100 200 300 Mi.

Scale 1:6,000,000

One centimeter represents 60 kilometers.

One inch represents approximately 95 miles.

Lambert Conformal Conic Projection

Southwestern Canada

Kilometers 0 50 100 150 Km.
Statute Miles 0 50 100 150 Mi.
Scale 1:3,000,000
One centimeter represents 30 kilometers.
One inch represents approximately 47 miles.
Lambert Conformal Conic Projection

South-Central Canada

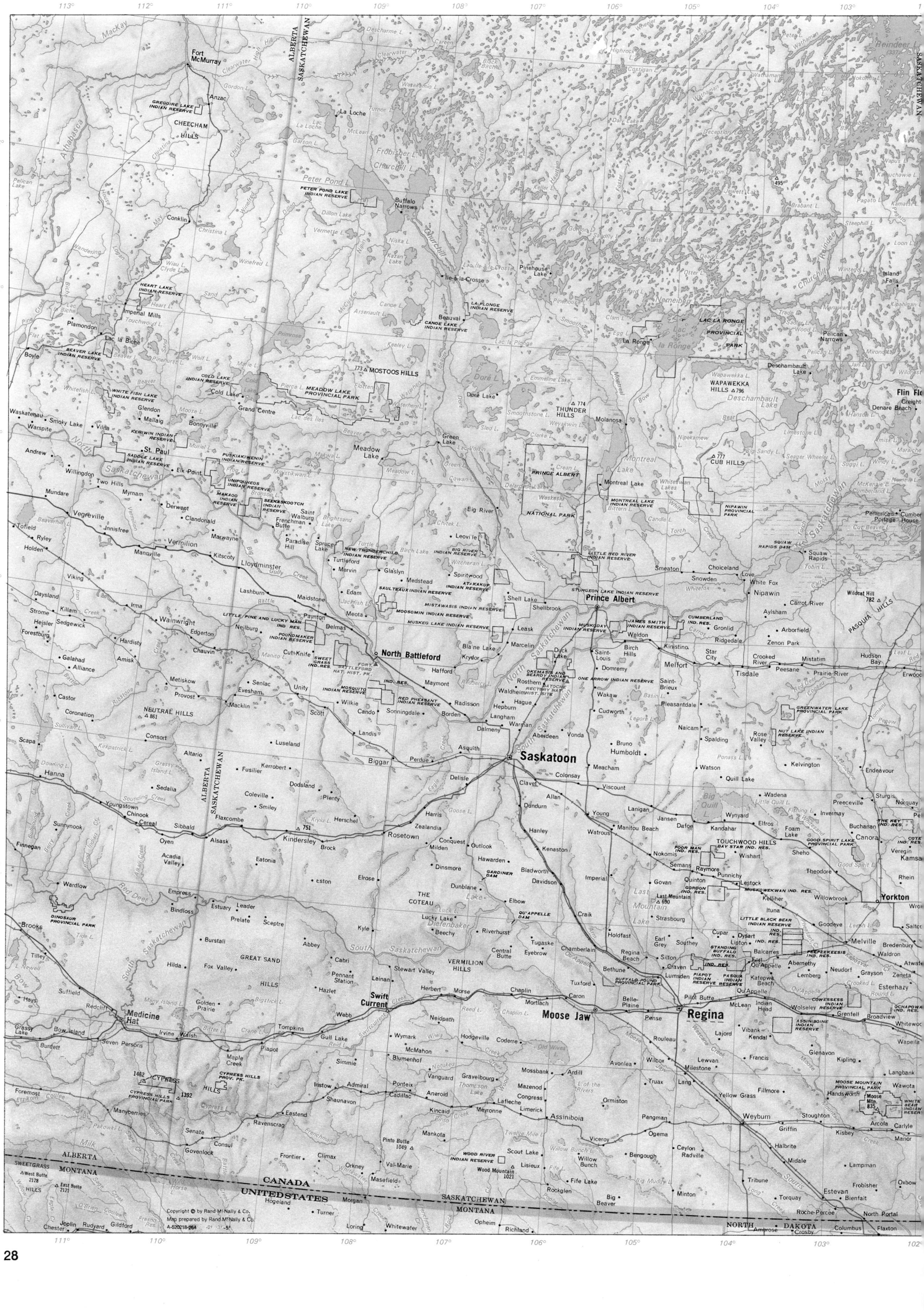

Kilometers 0 50 100 150 Km.

Statute Miles 0 50 100 150 Mi.

Scale 1:3,000,000

One centimeter represents 30 kilometers.

One inch represents approximately 47 miles.

Lambert Conformal Conic Projection

Southeastern Canada

Kilometers 0 50 100 150 Km.
Statute Miles 0 50 100 150 Mi.

Scale 1:3,000,000
One centimeter represents 30 kilometers.
One inch represents approximately 47 miles.
Lambert Conformal Conic Projection

Northeastern United States

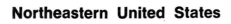

Kilometers 0 50 100 150 Km.

Statute Miles 0 50 100 150 Mi.

Scale 1:3,000,000

One centimeter represents 30 kilometers.
One inch represents approximately 47 miles.
Albers Conical Equal-Area Projection

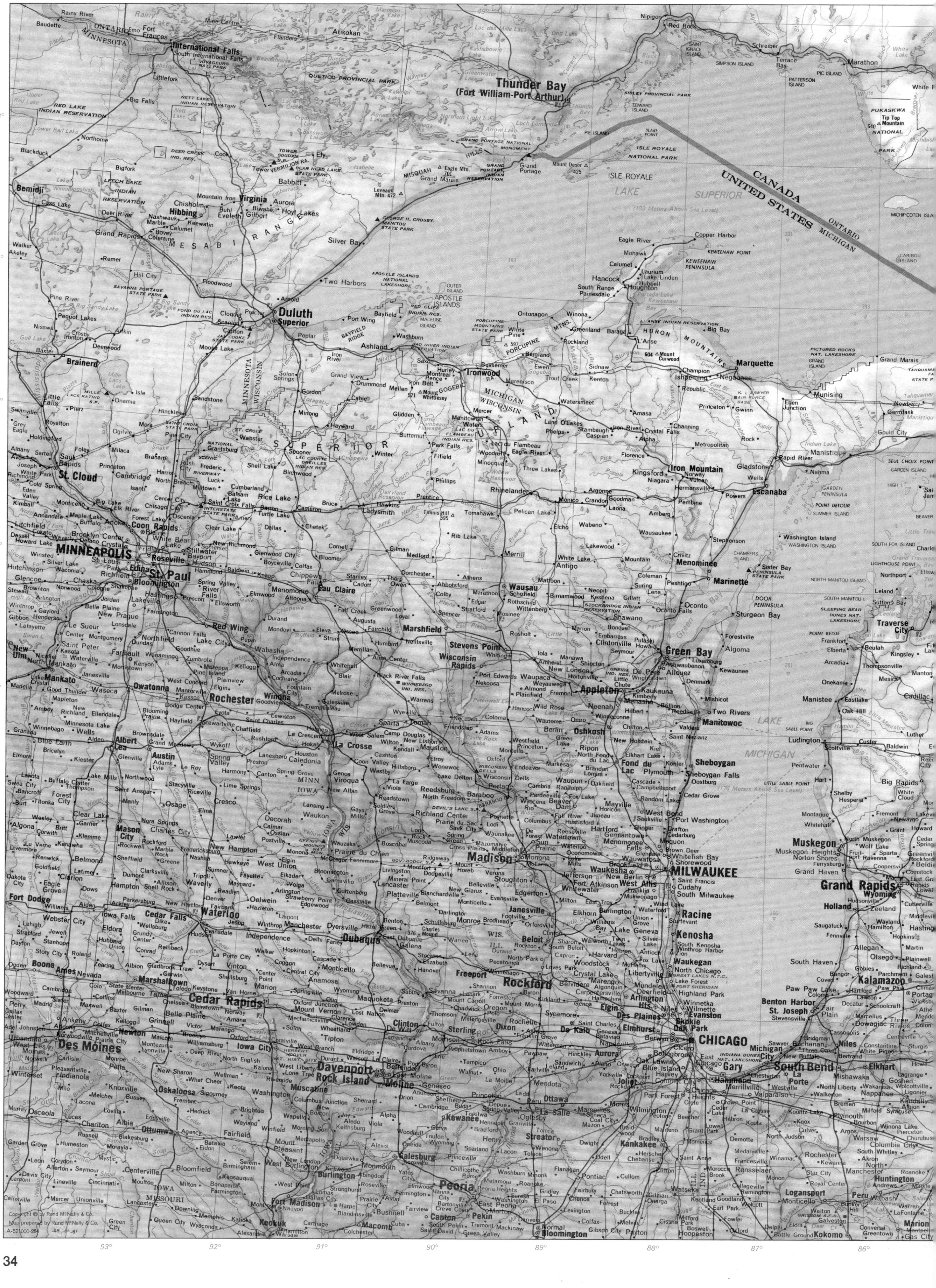
CANADA
UNITED STATES
ONTARIO
MINNESOTA
MICHIGAN
WISCONSIN
IOWA
MISSOURI
LAKE SUPERIOR
(183 Meters Above Sea Level)
LAKE MICHIGAN
(176 Meters Above Sea Level)
Thunder Bay
(Fort William-Port Arthur)
ISLE ROYALE
QUETICO PROVINCIAL PARK
MESABI RANGE
SUPERIOR UPLAND
HURON MOUNTAINS
KEWEENAW PENINSULA
APOSTLE ISLANDS
DOOR PENINSULA
International Falls
Duluth
Superior
Marquette
Escanaba
Iron Mountain
St. Cloud
MINNEAPOLIS
St. Paul
Rochester
Eau Claire
La Crosse
Wausau
Green Bay
Appleton
Oshkosh
Madison
MILWAUKEE
Racine
Kenosha
Rockford
CHICAGO
Gary
South Bend
Grand Rapids
Muskegon
Kalamazoo
Waterloo
Cedar Rapids
Dubuque
Davenport
Rock Island
Des Moines
Peoria
Bloomington
Copyright © by Rand McNally & Co.
Map prepared by Rand McNally & Co.

Kilometers 0 50 100 150 Km.
Statute Miles 0 50 100 150 Mi.

Scale 1:3,000,000
One centimeter represents 30 kilometers.
One inch represents approximately 47 miles.
Albers Conical Equal-Area Projection

Kilometers 0 50 100 150 Km.
Statute Miles 0 50 100 150 Mi.

Scale 1:3,000,000

One centimeter represents 30 kilometers.
One inch represents approximately 47 miles.
Albers Conical Equal-Area Projection

Southeastern United States

ATLANTIC
OCEAN
GULF OF
MEXICO
Straits of Florida
FLORIDA KEYS
UNITED STATES
BAHAMAS
GEORGIA
FLORIDA
Dothan
Headland
Blakely
Columbia
Ashford
Damascus
Bainbridge
Thomasville
Moultrie
Valdosta
Waycross
Brunswick
Saint Simons Island
Okefenokee Swamp
Fernandina Beach
Jacksonville
Atlantic Beach
Neptune Beach
Jacksonville Beach
Ponte Verda Beach
Tallahassee
Marianna
Chattahoochee
Quincy
Panacea
Carrabelle
Port Saint Joe
Apalachicola
Perry
Live Oak
Lake City
Olustee
Starke
Gainesville
Palatka
St. Augustine
Flagler Beach
Ormond Beach
Daytona Beach
New Smyrna Beach
Ocala
Cedar Key
Crystal River
Leesburg
Sanford
Orlando
Winter Park
Titusville
Cape Canaveral
Merritt Island
Cocoa
Cocoa Beach
Melbourne
Kissimmee
Lakeland
Winter Haven
Tampa
Clearwater
St. Petersburg
Bradenton
Sarasota
Venice
Port Charlotte
Punta Gorda
Fort Myers
Cape Coral
Naples
Vero Beach
Fort Pierce
Stuart
Jupiter
Okeechobee
Lake Okeechobee
West Palm Beach
Boynton Beach
Delray Beach
Boca Raton
Pompano Beach
Fort Lauderdale
Hollywood
North Miami
Hialeah
MIAMI
Miami Beach
Coral Gables
Homestead
Florida City
Key Largo
Key West
DRY TORTUGAS
FORT JEFFERSON NAT. MON.
MARQUESAS KEYS
KEY WEST N.A.S.
Everglades
Big Cypress Swamp
EVERGLADES NATIONAL PARK
Florida Bay
JOHN F. KENNEDY SPACE CENTER
CANAVERAL NATIONAL SEASHORE
West End
Freeport
GRAND BAHAMA
LITTLE ABACO ISLAND
GREAT ABACO
Marsh Harbour
Northwest Providence Channel
Northeast Providence Channel
BERRY ISLANDS
ANDROS ISLAND
Nassau
NEW PROVIDENCE
ELEUTHERA
Governors Harbour
Alice Town
BIMINI ISLANDS
31°
30°
29°
28°
27°
26°
25°
85°
84°
83°
80°
79°
78°
77°
76°
Copyright © by Rand McNally & Co.
Map prepared by Rand McNally & Co.
A-521100-264

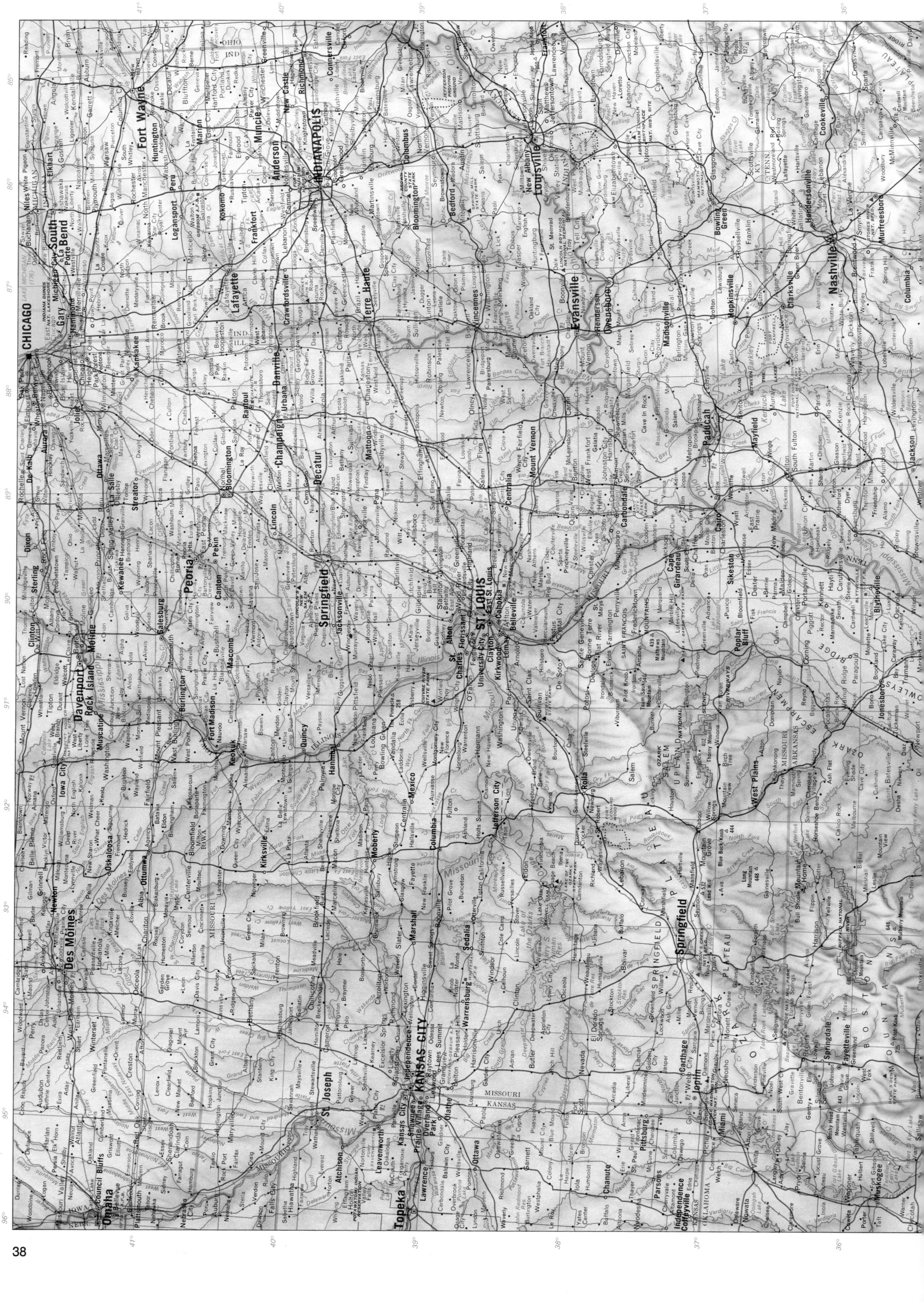
CHICAGO
South Bend
Fort Wayne
Gary
Kankakee
Joliet
Aurora
De Kalb
Dixon
Sterling
Clinton
Davenport
Rock Island
Moline
Iowa City
Muscatine
Des Moines
Omaha
Council Bluffs
Newton
Ottumwa
Oskaloosa
Burlington
Keokuk
Fort Madison
Galesburg
Peoria
Pekin
Canton
Macomb
Quincy
Hannibal
Kewanee
La Salle
Ottawa
Streator
Bloomington
Normal
Champaign
Urbana
Danville
Decatur
Springfield
Jacksonville
Lincoln
Mattoon
Kokomo
Lafayette
Crawfordsville
Terre Haute
Logansport
Peru
Marion
Muncie
Anderson
New Castle
Richmond
Connersville
Frankfort
INDIANAPOLIS
Columbus
Bloomington
Bedford
Vincennes
Evansville
Owensboro
Henderson
Madisonville
Louisville
New Albany
Paducah
Mayfield
Hopkinsville
Bowling Green
Clarksville
Nashville
Murfreesboro
Columbia
Jackson
Cairo
Cape Girardeau
Carbondale
Mount Vernon
Centralia
Belleville
ST. LOUIS
East St. Louis
St. Charles
Alton
Kirkwood
Clayton
University City
Sikeston
Poplar Bluff
Blytheville
Jonesboro
Rolla
Jefferson City
Columbia
Mexico
Moberly
Kirksville
Sedalia
Springfield
Joplin
Marshall
Warrensburg
KANSAS CITY
Independence
St. Joseph
Atchison
Leavenworth
Lawrence
Topeka
Olathe
Ottawa
Chanute
Parsons
Pittsburg
Independence
Coffeyville
Miami
Muskogee
Fayetteville
Springdale
West Plains
Ottumwa
MISSOURI
KANSAS
IOWA
OKLAHOMA
ARKANSAS
BOSTON MOUNTAINS
OZARK PLATEAU
SPRINGFIELD PLATEAU
SALEM UPLAND
85°
86°
87°
88°
89°
90°
91°
92°
93°
94°
95°
96°
41°
40°
39°
38°
37°
36°

Kilometers 0 50 100 150 Km.

Statute Miles 0 50 100 150 Mi.

Scale 1:3,000,000

One centimeter represents 30 kilometers.

One inch represents approximately 47 miles.

Albers Conical Equal-Area Projection

Southern Great Plains

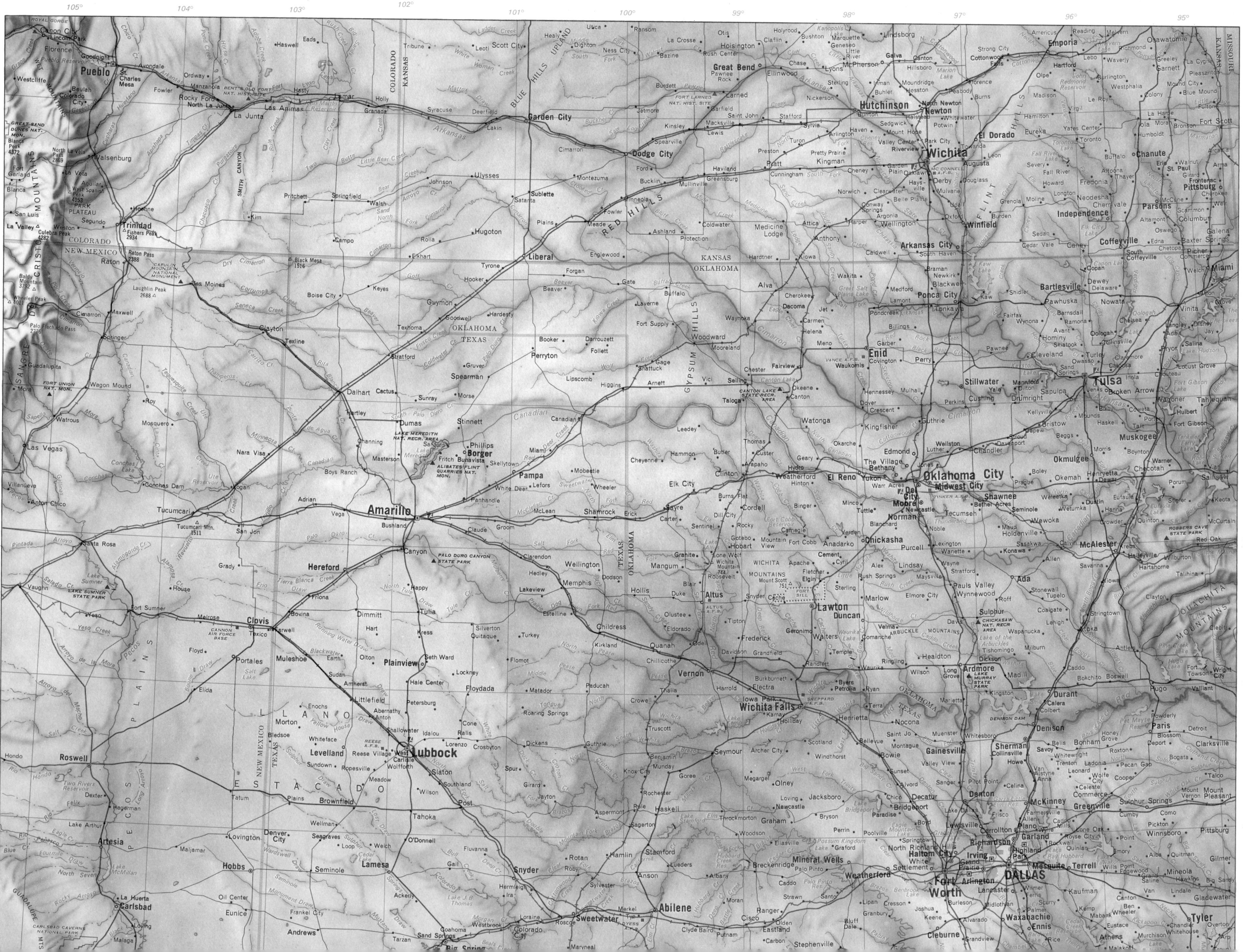

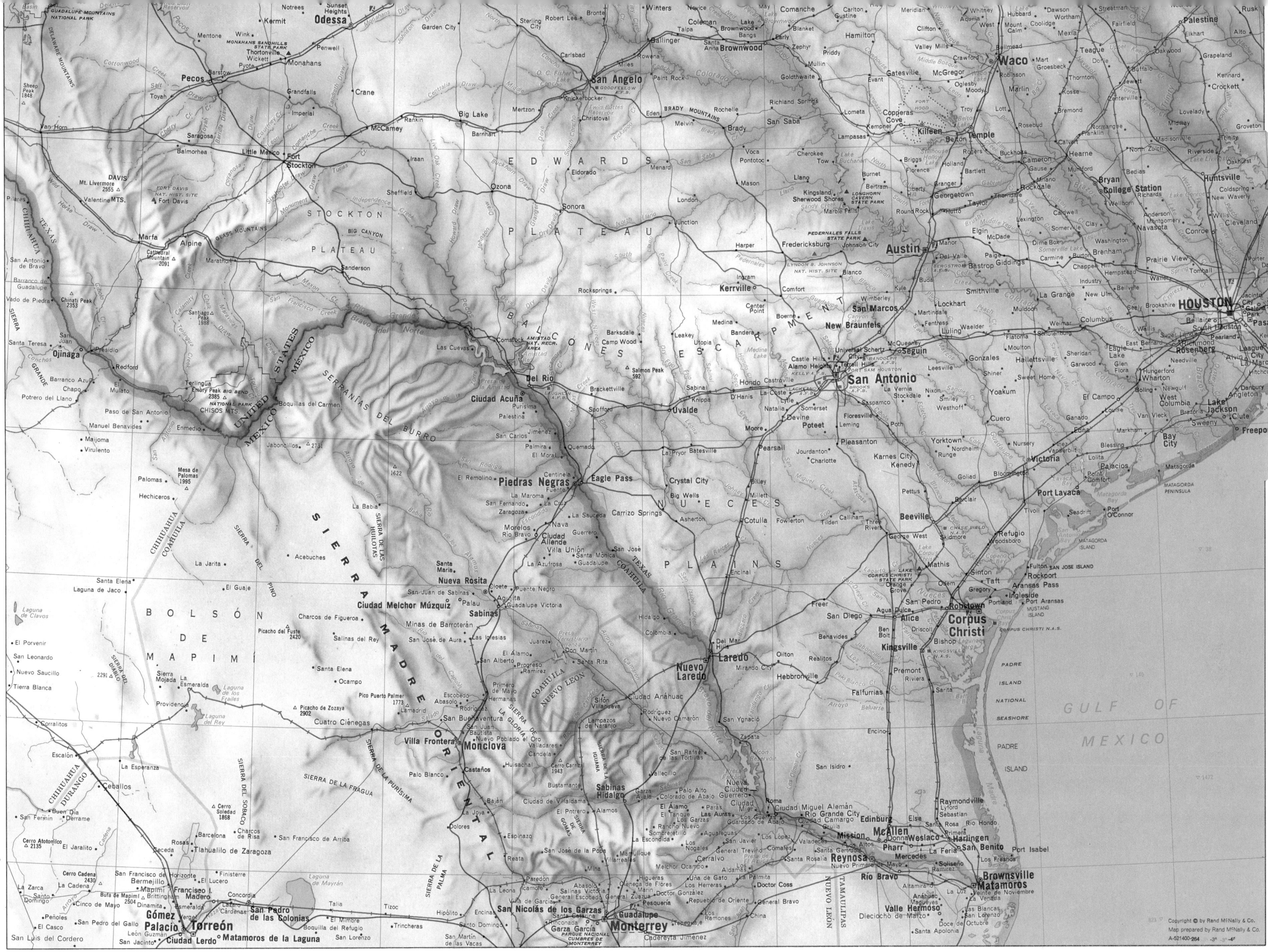

Kilometers 0 50 100 150 Km.

Statute Miles 0 50 100 150 Mi.

Scale 1:3,000,000

One centimeter represents 30 kilometers.

One inch represents approximately 47 miles.

Albers Conical Equal-Area Projection

Northern Great Plains

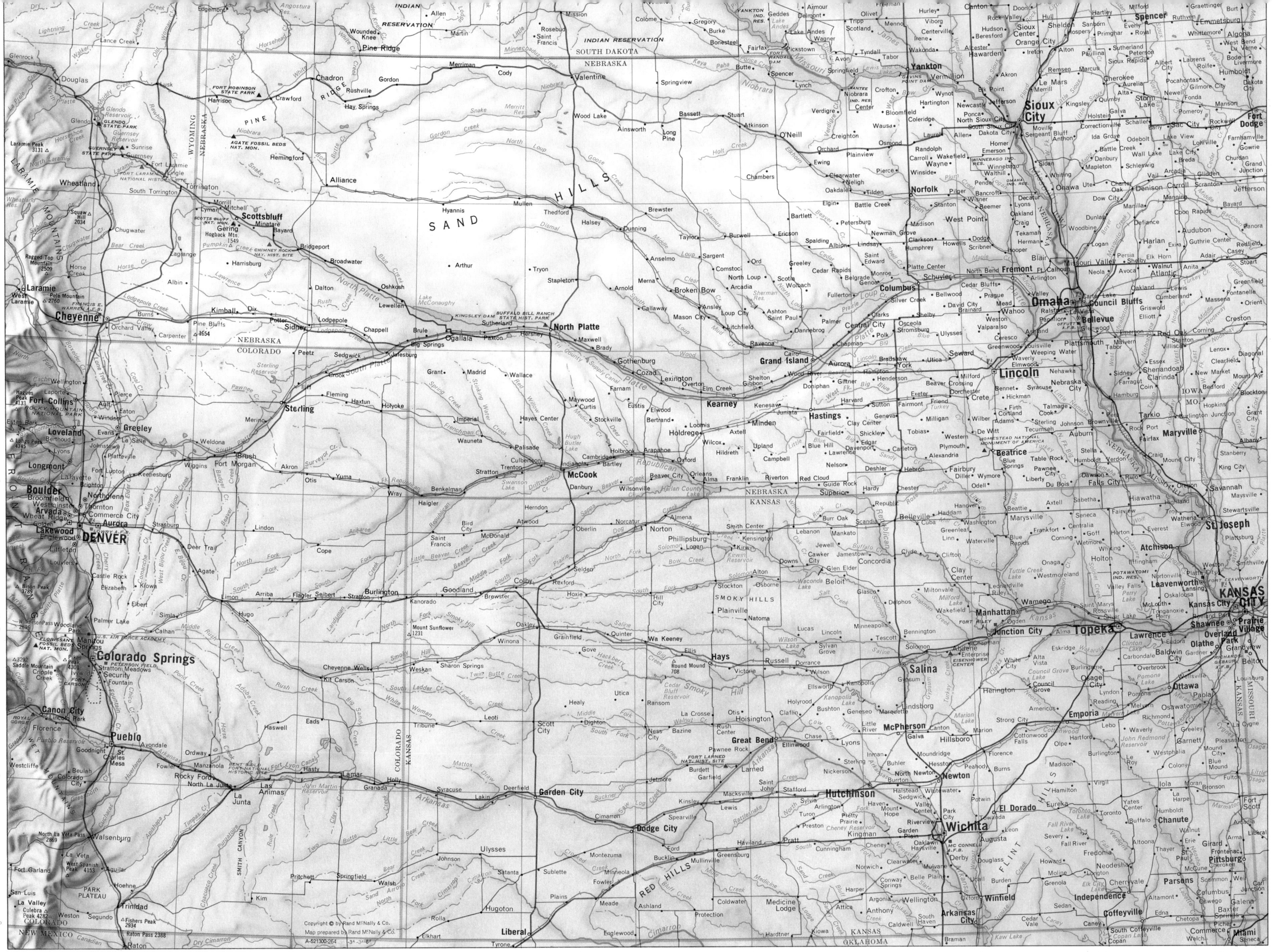

Kilometers 0 50 100 150 Km.

Statute Miles 0 50 100 150 Mi.

Scale 1:3,000,000

One centimeter represents 30 kilometers.

One inch represents approximately 47 miles.

Albers Conical Equal-Area Projection

DENVER
Colorado Springs
Pueblo
Canon City
Lakewood
Boulder
Longmont
Fort Collins
Greeley
Cheyenne
Laramie
Casper
Rock Springs
Grand Junction
Salt Lake City
Ogden
Provo
Orem
Logan
Brigham City
Pocatello
Idaho Falls
Twin Falls
Tooele
ROCKY MOUNTAINS
COLORADO PLATEAU
GREAT DIVIDE BASIN
GREAT SALT LAKE DESERT
SNAKE RIVER PLAIN
WASATCH RANGE
UINTA MOUNTAINS
WYOMING RANGE
FRONT RANGE
PARK RANGE
SAWATCH RANGE
SAN JUAN MOUNTAINS
SANGRE DE CRISTO
LARAMIE MOUNTAINS
WIND RIVER RANGE
BOOK CLIFFS
ROAN PLATEAU
DANFORTH HILLS
GRANITE MTS
BIG HORN MTS.
OWL CREEK MOUNTAINS
105°
106°
107°
108°
109°
110°
111°
112°
113°
114°
115°
116°
38°
39°
40°
41°
42°
43°

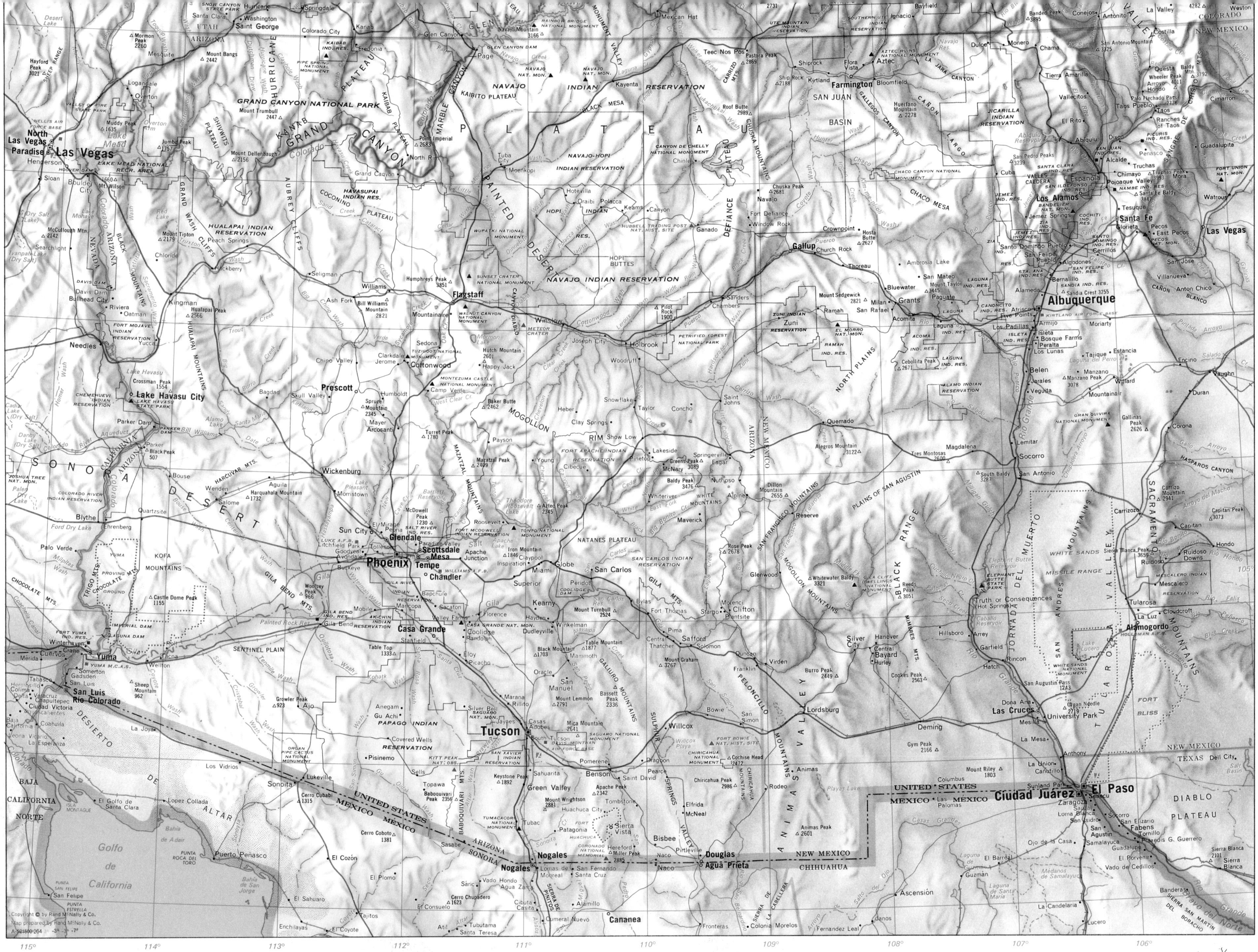

Kilometers 0 50 100 150 Km.

Statute Miles 0 50 100 150 Mi.

Scale 1:3,000,000

One centimeter represents 30 kilometers.
One inch represents approximately 47 miles.
Albers Conical Equal-Area Projection

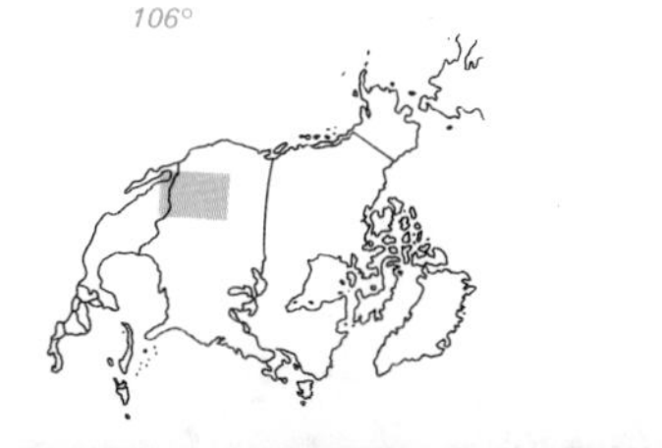

Northwestern United States

Kilometers 0 50 100 150 Km.

Statute Miles 0 50 100 150 Mi.

Scale 1:3,000,000

One centimeter represents 30 kilometers.

One inch represents approximately 47 miles.

Albers Conical Equal-Area Projection

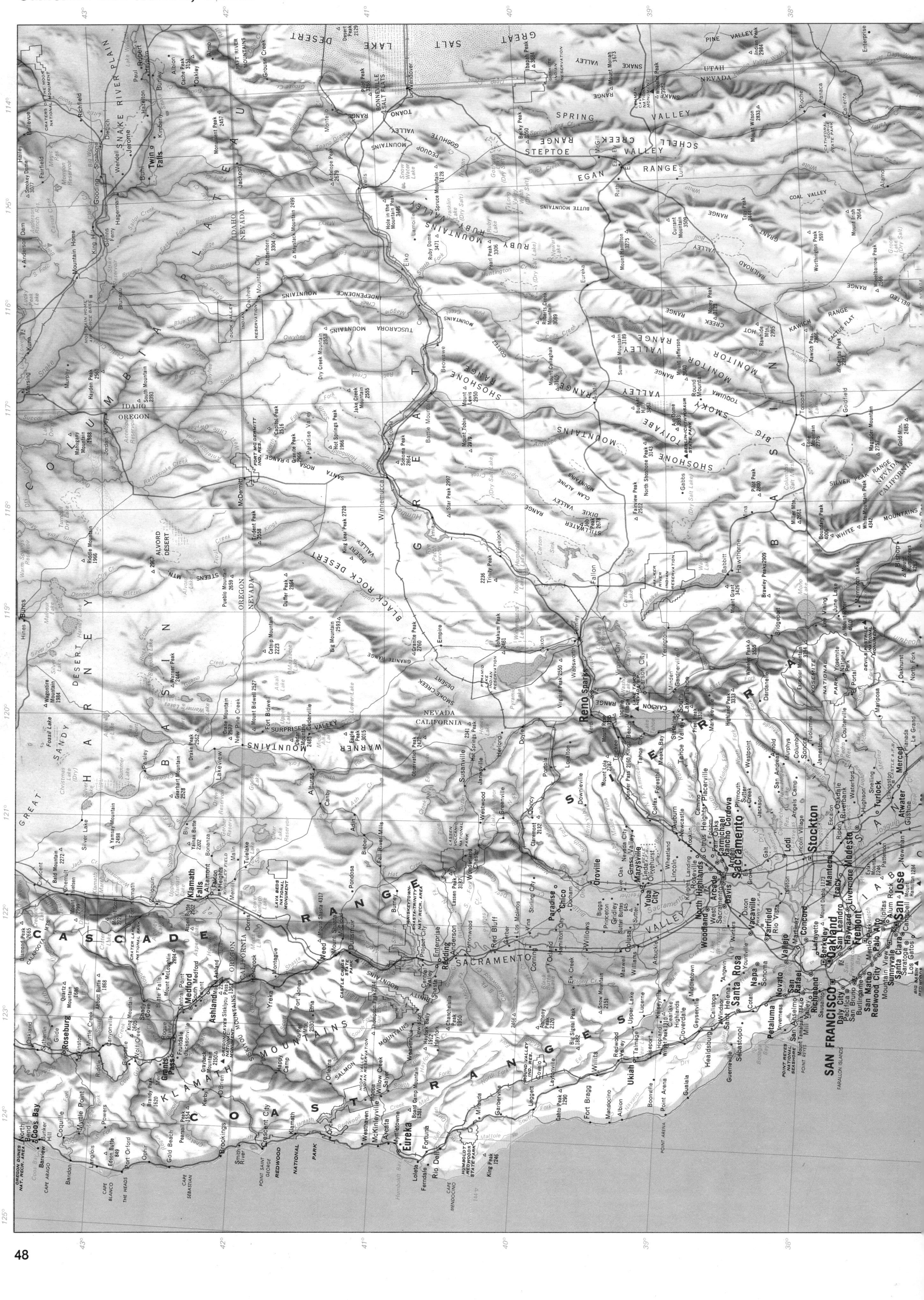
SAN FRANCISCO
Oakland
San Jose
Stockton
Sacramento
Reno
Eureka
Redding
Medford
Klamath Falls
Winnemucca
Elko
Twin Falls
COAST RANGES
CASCADE RANGE
SIERRA NEVADA
SACRAMENTO VALLEY
KLAMATH MOUNTAINS
GREAT BASIN
COLUMBIA PLATEAU
SNAKE RIVER PLAIN
BLACK ROCK DESERT
GREAT SALT LAKE DESERT
HARNEY BASIN
GREAT SANDY DESERT
RUBY MOUNTAINS
TOIYABE RANGE
SHOSHONE MOUNTAINS
MONITOR RANGE
EGAN RANGE
SCHELL CREEK RANGE
WARNER MOUNTAINS
CALIFORNIA
NEVADA
OREGON
IDAHO
UTAH

Kilometers 0 50 100 150 Km.
Statute Miles 0 50 100 150 Mi.

Scale 1:3,000,000
One centimeter represents 30 kilometers.
One inch represents approximately 47 miles.
Albers Conical Equal-Area Projection

Middle America

Kilometers 0 200 400 600 Km.
Statute Miles 0 200 400 600 Mi.

Scale 1:12,000,000
One centimeter represents 120 kilometers.
One inch represents approximately 190 miles.
Oblique Conic Conformal Projection

Kilometers 0 100 200 300 Km.
Statute Miles 0 100 200 300 Mi.

Scale 1:6,000,000
One centimeter represents 60 kilometers.
One inch represents approximately 95 miles.
Lambert Conformal Conic Projection

GULF
OF
MEXICO
Bahía de Campeche
Golfo de Tehuantepec
Tropic of Cancer
Gulf of Honduras
TEXAS
LOUISIANA
MISSISSIPPI
ALABAMA
TAMAULIPAS
NUEVO LEON
HIDALGO
VERACRUZ
TABASCO
CHIAPAS
YUCATÁN
PENINSULA
QUINTANA ROO
GUATEMALA
HONDURAS
BELIZE (U.K.)
SIERRA MADRE ORIENTAL
SIERRA MADRE DEL SUR
Fort Worth
Dallas
Abilene
San Angelo
Waco
Austin
San Antonio
Houston
Galveston
Beaumont
Corpus Christi
Laredo
Brownsville
Shreveport
Jackson
Baton Rouge
New Orleans
Mobile
Monterrey
Saltillo
Matamoros
Ciudad Victoria
Tampico
San Luis Potosí
CIUDAD DE MÉXICO
MEXICO CITY
Puebla
Veracruz
Oaxaca
Acapulco
Coatzacoalcos
Villahermosa
Campeche
Mérida
Belize
Belmopan
Guatemala
Tapachula
San Pedro Sula

Islands of the West Indies

a

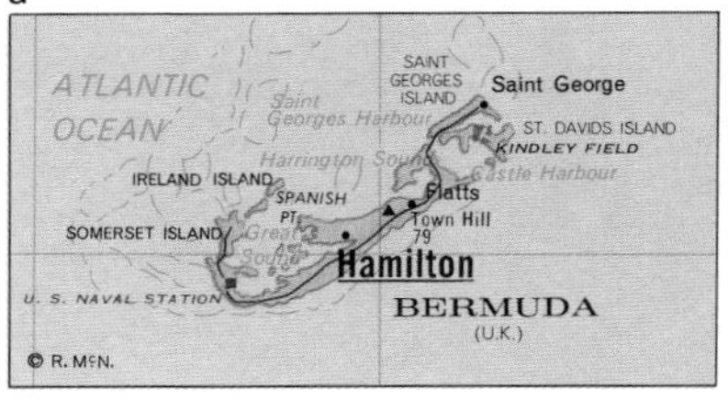

b

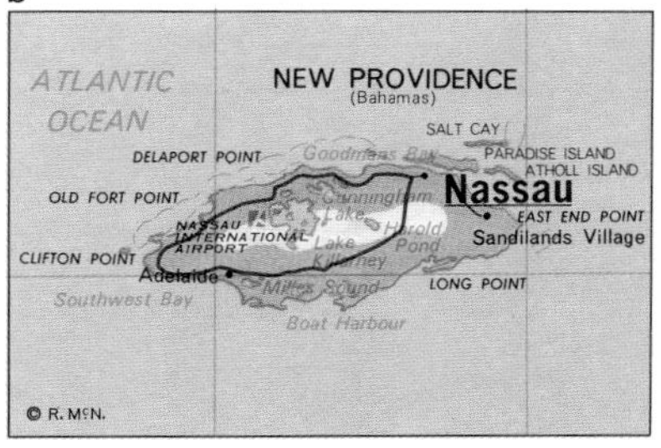

c

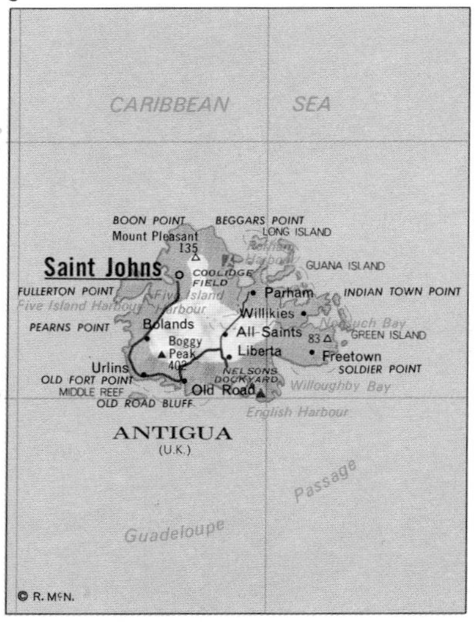

d

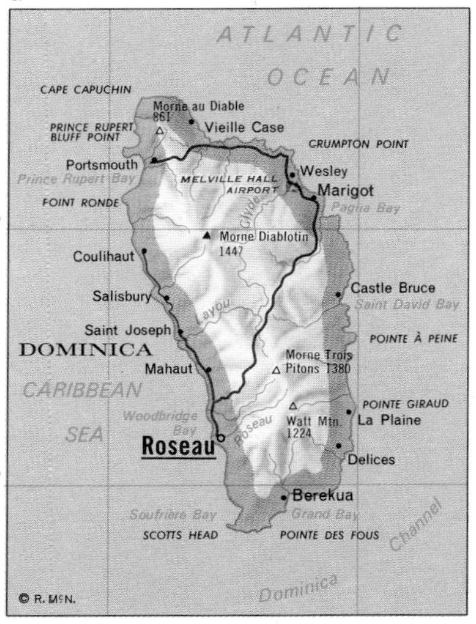

e

m

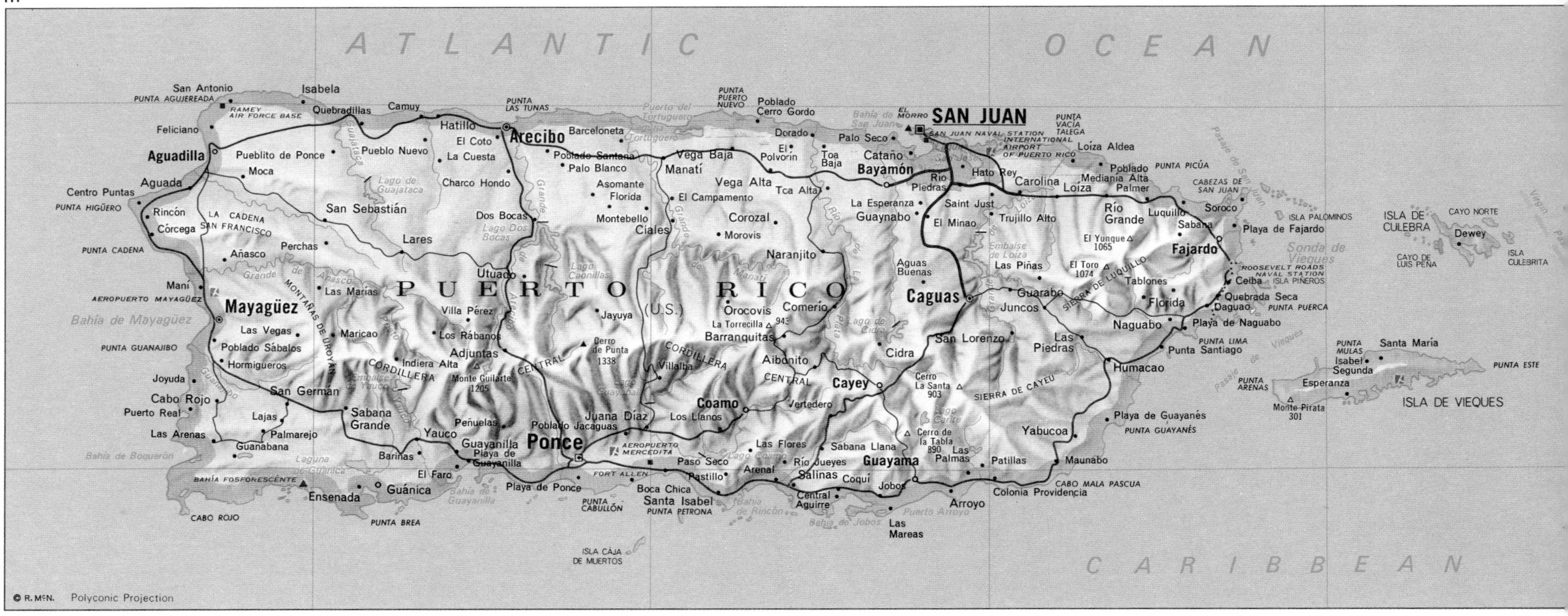

p

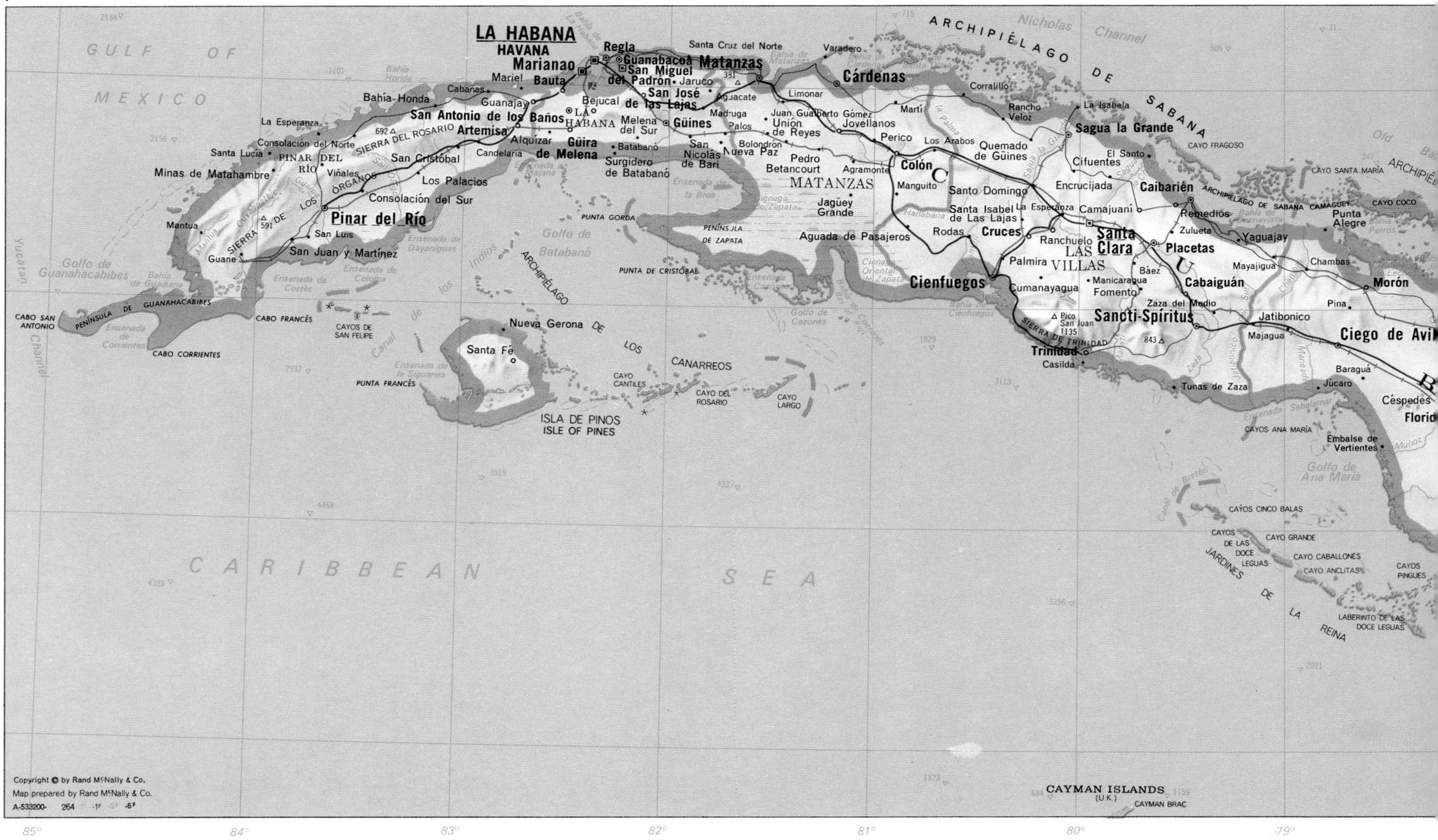

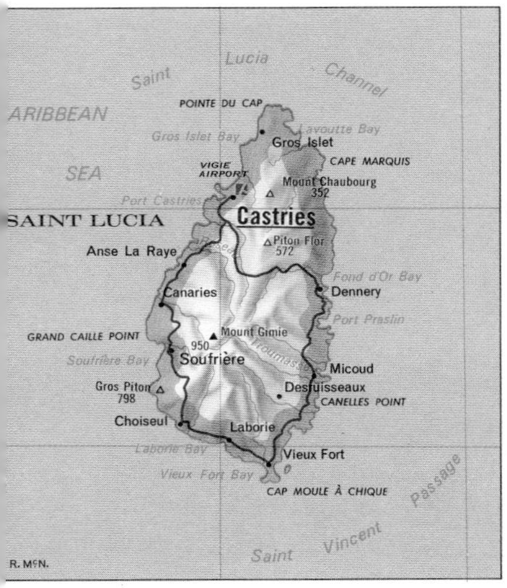

g

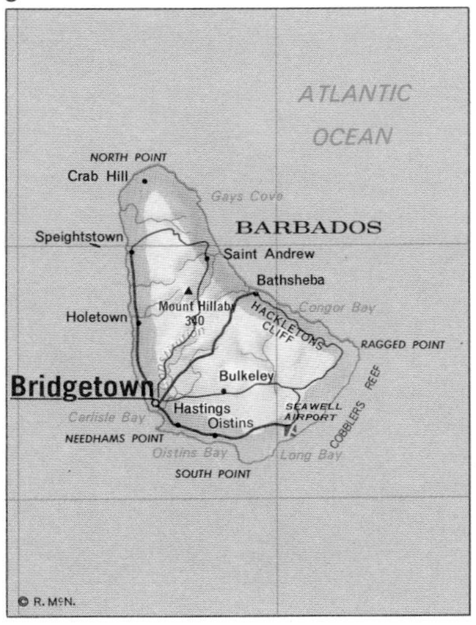

h

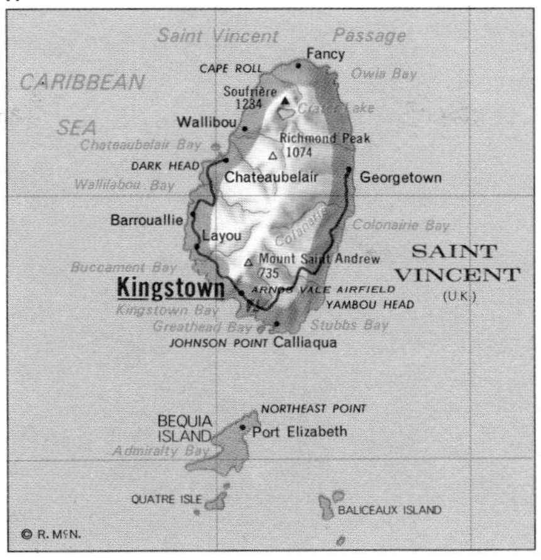

k

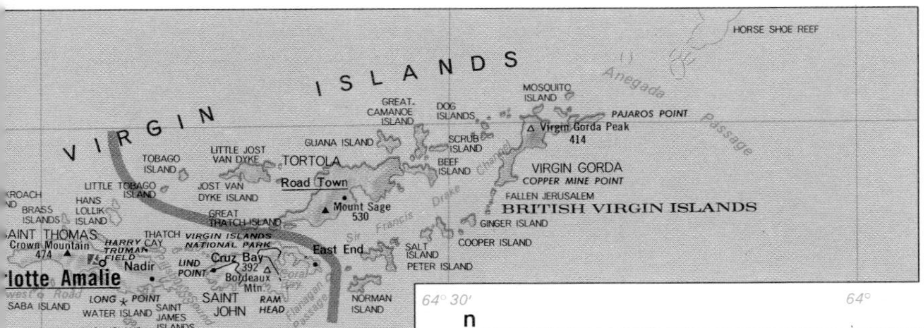

n

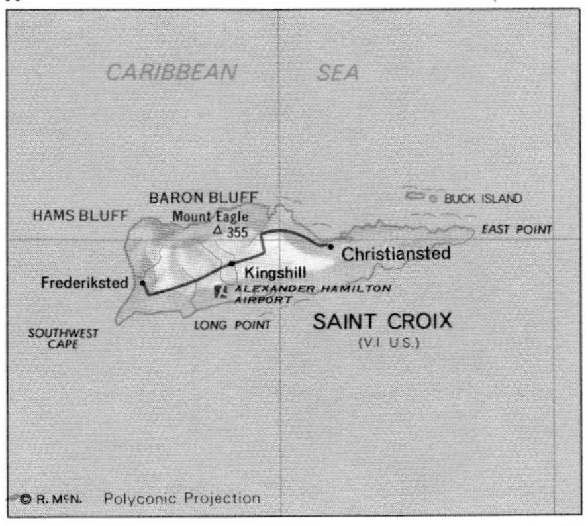

o

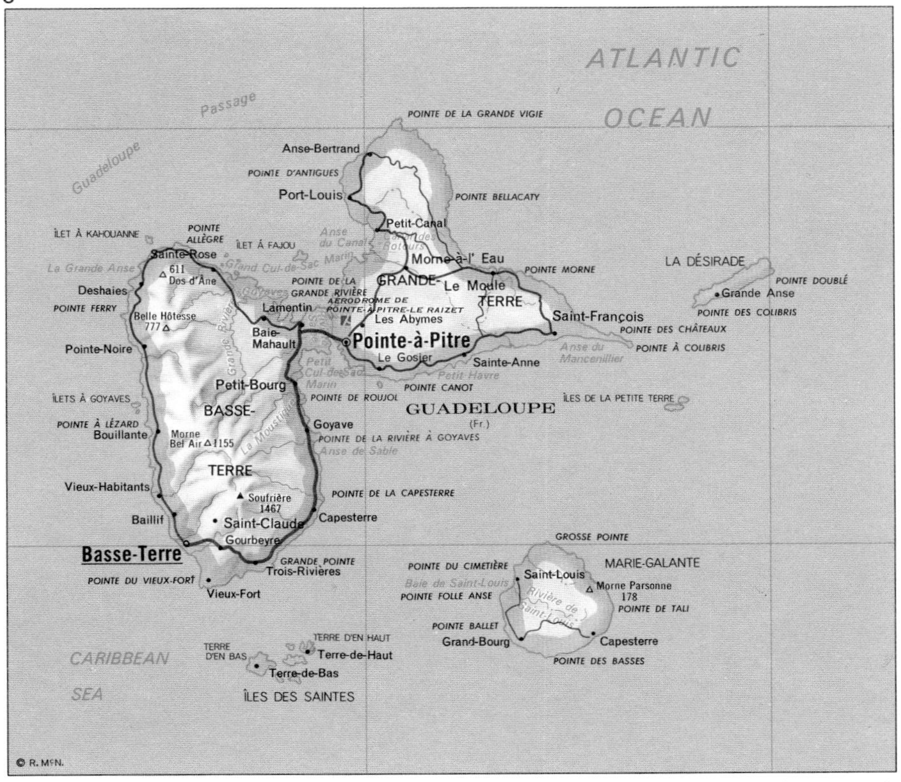

Kilometers 0 10 20 30 40 50 Km.
Statute Miles 0 10 20 30 40 50 Mi.

Scale 1:1,000,000
One centimeter represents 10 kilometers.
One inch represents approximately 16 miles.
Transverse Mercator Projection (except as noted)

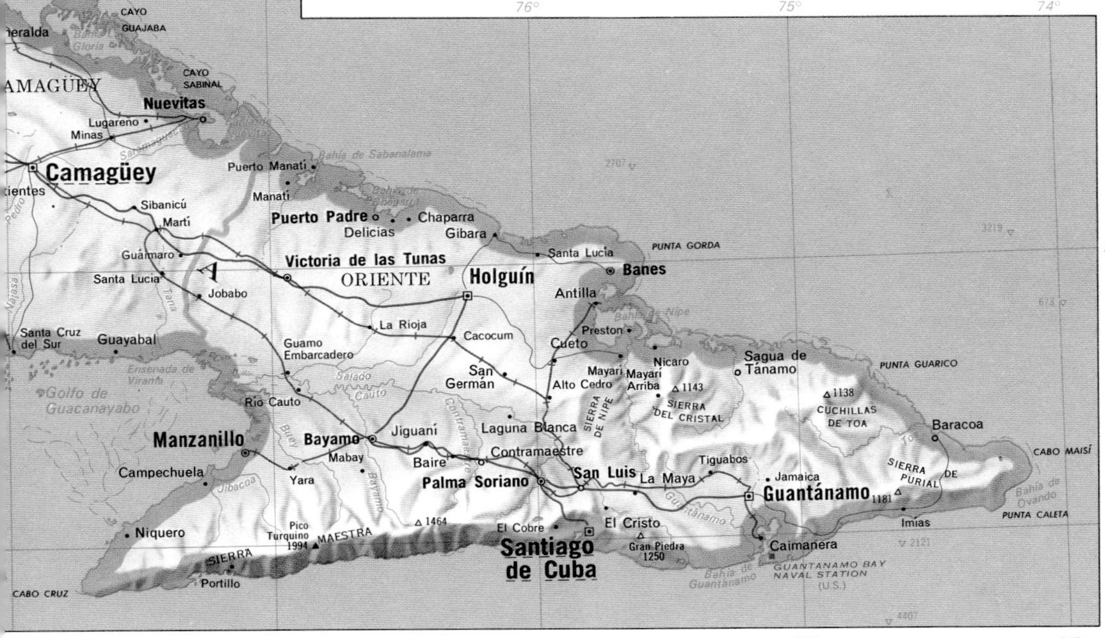

q

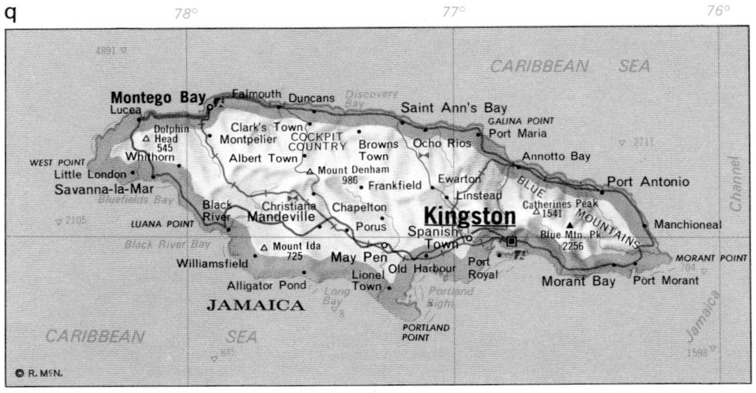

r

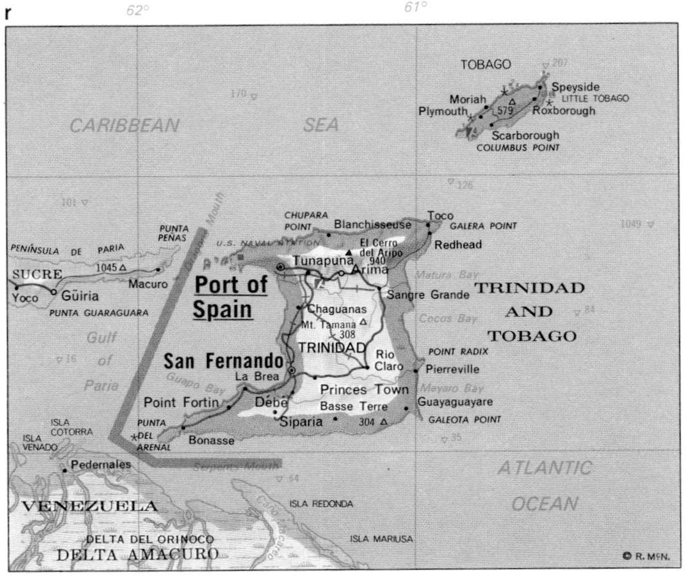

s

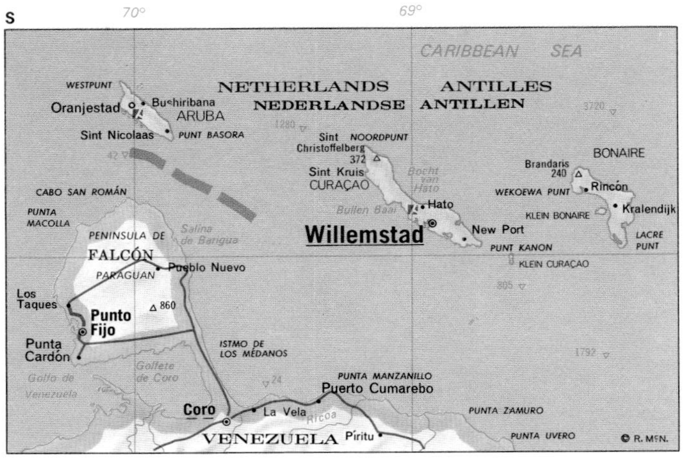

Kilometers 0 50 100 150 Km.
Statute Miles 0 50 100 150 Mi.

Scale 1:3,000,000
One centimeter represents 30 kilometers.
One inch represents approximately 47 miles.
Lambert Conformal Conic Projection

Northern South America

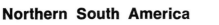

Kilometers 0 200 400 600 Km.

Statute Miles 0 200 400 600 Mi.

Scale 1:12,000,000

One centimeter represents 120 kilometers.
One inch represents approximately 190 miles.
Oblique Conic Conformal Projection

ATLANTIC OCEAN
BRAZIL
SURINAME
FRENCH GUIANA
Georgetown
Paramaribo
Cayenne
TUMUC-HUMAC MOUNTAINS
ILHA DE MARAJÓ
Belém
São Luís
Fortaleza
Natal
João Pessoa
Recife
Maceió
Aracaju
Salvador
Teresina
Brasília
Goiânia
Belo Horizonte
RIO DE JANEIRO
SÃO PAULO
Santos
Vitória
Campo Grande
Cuiabá
Santarém
Macapá
PLANALTO DO MATO GROSSO
PLANALTO CENTRAL
SERRA DO CACHIMBO
SERRA DO RONCADOR
SERRA DOS CARAJÁS
Equator
Tropic of Capricorn

Map prepared by Esselte Map Service AB, Stockholm.
A-549200-264

Kilometers 0 200 400 600 Km.

Statute Miles 0 200 400 600 Mi.

Scale 1:12,000,000

One centimeter represents 120 kilometers.

One inch represents approximately 190 miles.

Oblique Conic Conformal Projection

Colombia, Ecuador, Venezuela, and Guyana

Kilometers 0 100 200 300 Km.
Statute Miles 0 100 200 300 Mi.

Scale 1:6,000,000

One centimeter represents 60 kilometers.
One inch represents approximately 95 miles.
Oblique Conic Conformal Projection

Central Argentina and Chile

Kilometers 0 100 200 300 Km.

Statute Miles 0 100 200 300 Mi.

Scale 1:6,000,000

One centimeter represents 60 kilometers.
One inch represents approximately 95 miles.
Oblique Conic Conformal Projection

Western and Central Soviet Union

Kilometers 0 200 400 600 Km.
Statute Miles 0 200 400 600 Mi.

Scale 1:12,000,000

One centimeter represents 120 kilometers.
One inch represents approximately 190 miles.
Lambert Conformal Conic Projection

Eastern and Central Soviet Union

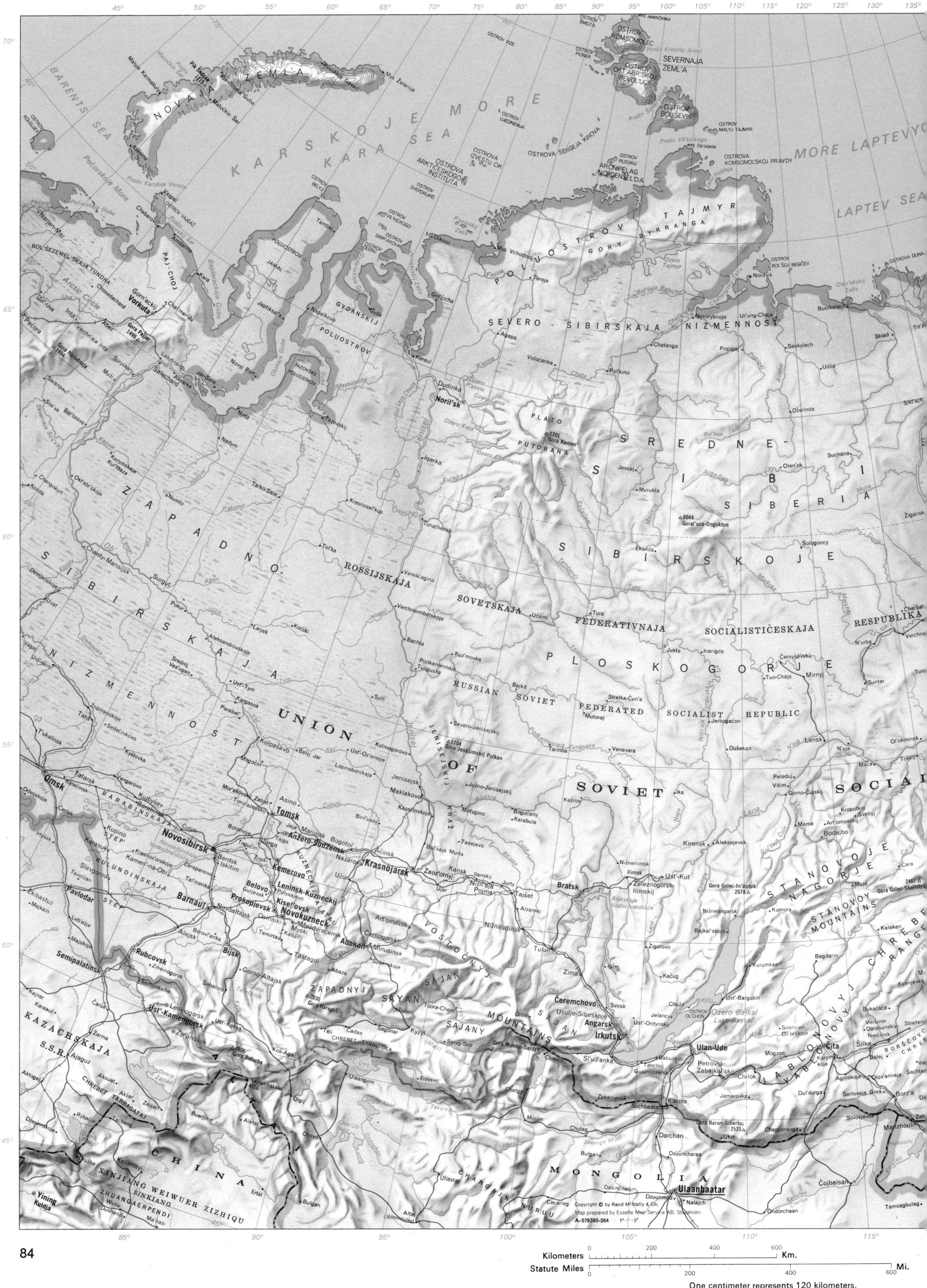

Kilometers 0 200 400 600 Km.
Statute Miles 0 200 400 600 Mi.

Scale 1:12,000,000
One centimeter represents 120 kilometers.
One inch represents approximately 190 miles.
Lambert Conformal Conic Projection

DAXINGANLINGSHANMAI
NEIMENGGU ZIZHIQU
MANCHURIA
CHINA
HEILONGJIANG
Haerbin
Qiqihaer Tsitsihar
Vladivostok
Ussurijsk
Chabarovsk
Komsomol'sk-na-Amure
Blagoveščensk
Jakutsk
Magadan
S T A N O V O J C H R E B E T
A L D A N S K O J E N A G O R J E
REPUBLICS
CHREBET DŽUGDŽUR
BUREINSKIJ CHREBET
S I C H O T E - A L I N '
CHREBET SUNTAR-CHAJATA
CHREBET ČERSKOGO
MOMSKIJ CHREBET
VERCHOJANSKIJ CHREBET
SETTE-DABAN
KOLYMSKAJA NIZMENNOST'
JUKAGIRSKOJE PLOSKOGORJE
ANADYRSKOJE PLOSKOGORJE
ANJUJSKIJ CHREBET
PENŽINSKIJ CHREBET
K O R J A K S K O J E N A G O R J E
SREDINNYJ CHREBET
ČUKOTSKIJ POLUOSTROV
EKIATAPSKIJ CHREBET
NOVOSIBIRSKIJE OSTROVA
OSTROVA ANŽU
OSTROVA DE LONGA
OSTROV NOVAJA SIBIR'
OSTROV KOTEL'NYJ
OSTROV BOL'ŠOJ L'ACHOVSKIJ
VOSTOČNO-SIBIRSKOJE MORE
EAST SIBERIAN SEA
OSTROV VRANGEL'A
Chukchi Sea
Arctic Circle
SHANTARSKIJE OSTROVA
OSTROV SACHALIN
SAKHALIN
Južno-Sachalinsk
SEA OF OKHOTSK
OCHOTSKOJE MORE
SEA OF JAPAN
Tatarskij Proliv
Sapporo
HOKKAIDO
HONSHU
JAPAN
Asahikawa
Hakodate
Aomori
Kushiro
KURIL'SKIJE OSTROVA
KURIL ISLANDS
PACIFIC OCEAN
Habomai, Shikotan, Kunashiri, and Etorofu, occupied by the U.S.S.R. since 1945, are claimed by Japan pending a final peace treaty.
POLUOSTROV KAMČATKA
Petropavlovsk-Kamčatskij
KOMANDORSKIJE OSTROVA
Bering Sea
Anadyrskij Zaliv
Anadyr'
SAINT LAWRENCE ISLAND
SAINT MATTHEW ISLAND
NUNIVAK ISLAND
ALASKA
UNITED STATES

Baltic and Moscow Regions

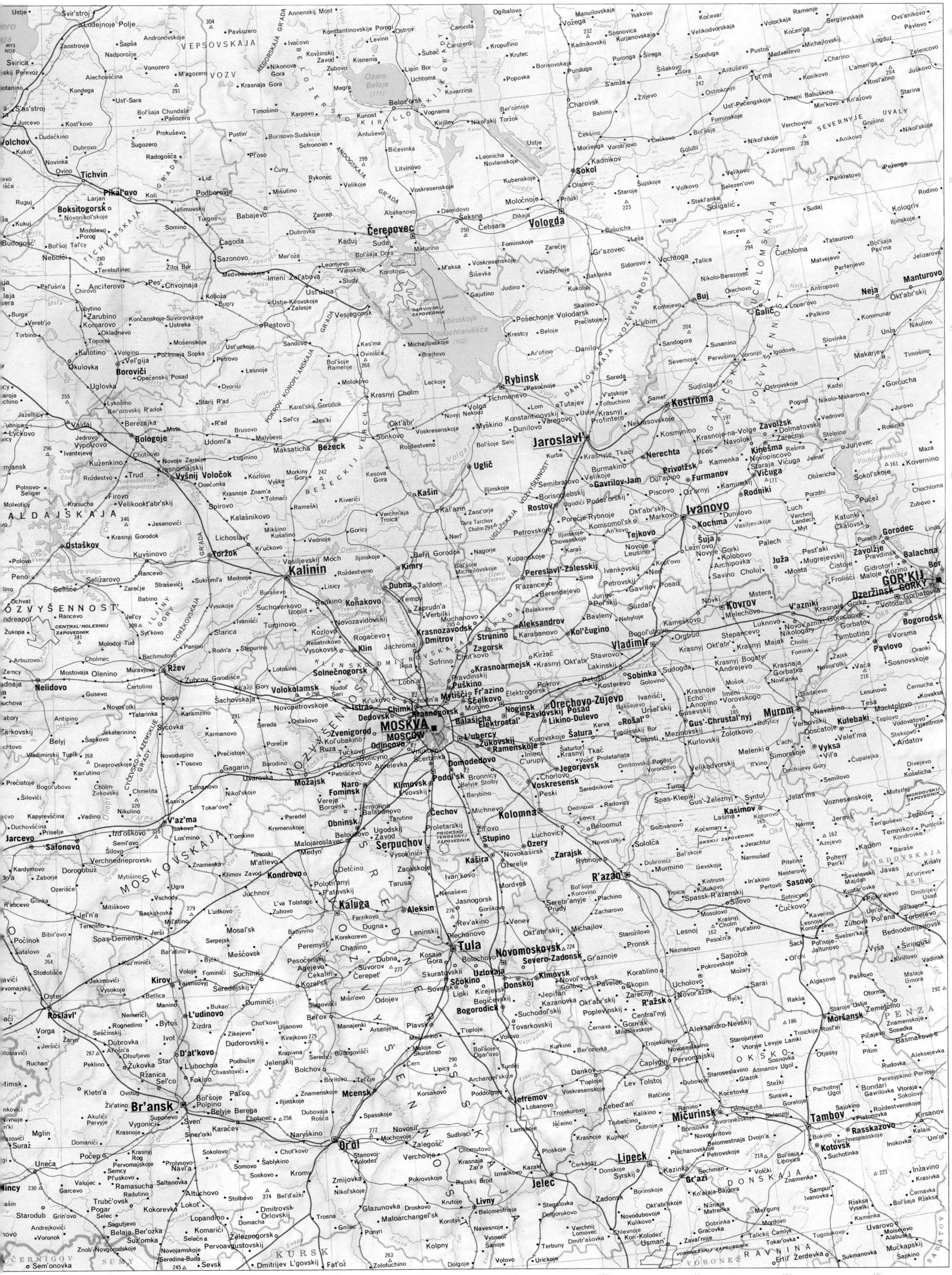

Kilometers 0 50 100 150 Km.

Statute Miles 0 50 100 150 Mi.

Scale 1:3,000,000

One centimeter represents 30 kilometers.

One inch represents approximately 47 miles.

Lambert Conformal Conic Projection

UNION OF SOVIET SOCIALIST REPUBLICS
KAZACHSKIJ MELKOSOPOCNIK
KAZACHSKAJA S.S.R.
BETPAK-DALA
ROSSIJSKAJA S.F.S.R.
CHREBET TANNU-OLA
VOSTOČNYJ SAJAN
Irkutsk
Angarsk
Ulan-Ude
Ust'-Kamenogorsk
Alma-Ata
Frunze
Džambul
Andižan
KIRGIZSKAJA S.S.R.
CHREBET TARBAGATAJ
DZUNGARSKIJ ALATAU
MONGOL ALTAJN NURUU
CHANGAJN NURUU
MONGOL
EDRENGIJN NURUU
GURVAN SAJCHAN UUL
GOBI
Ulaanbaatar
Darchan
Mandalgov'
Dalandzadgad
TIEN SHAN
ZHUANGAERPENDI
Wulumuqi
Urumchi
BOGEDUOSHANMAI
Yining
Kuldja
Hami
XINJIANG WEIWUER ZIZHIQU
SINKIANG
TALIMUPENDI
TAKLA MAKAN
Kashi
Kashgar
Suoche
Yarkand
Akesu
Kuche
BEISHANMAI
AERJINSHANMAI
KUNLUNSHANMAI
KEKEXILISHANMAI
CHAIDAMUPENDI
QILIANSHANMAI
NANSHAN
Yumen
Yinchuan
Lanzhou
Xining
QINGHAI
XIZANG ZIZHIQU
TIBET
TANGGULASHANMAI
GANGLINGSHAN
GANGDISISHANMAI
NYANQINGTANGGULASHANMAI
BAYANKALASHANMAI
ANIMAQINGSHANMAI
MINSHAN
DAXUESHAN
Lasa
Lhasa
HIMALAYAS
KARAKORAM RANGE
ZASKAR MOUNTAINS
NEPAL
Katmandu
BHUTAN
SICHUAN
Chengdu
CHONGQING
Zigong
Yibin
Luzhou
GUIZHOU
Guiyang
YUNNAN
Kunming
Gejiu
Kokiu
WULIANGSHAN
AILAOSHAN
NUSHAN
INDIA
Delhi
Dehra Dūn
Sahāranpur
Meerut
Morādābād
Bareilly
Aligarh
Lucknow
Kānpur
Allahābād
Vārānasi
Benares
Patna
Gaya
Bhāgalpur
Jabalpur
Raipur
Asansol
Jamshedpur
Howrah
CALCUTTA
Kharagpur
SUNDARBANS
Cuttack
Berhampur
Vishākhapatnam
Rajahmundry
Kākināda
EASTERN GHATS
VINDHYA RANGE
BANGLADESH
Dacca
Khulna
Nārāyanganj
Chittagong
Mymensingh
Shillong
Gauhati
Imphāl
Silchar
PATKAI RANGE
CHIN HILLS
ARAKAN YOMA
PEGU YOMA
BURMA
Mandalay
Sittwe
Akyab
Henzada
Pegu
BAY OF BENGAL
LAOS
Louangphrabang
Viangchan
(Vientiane)
THAILAND
Chiang Mai
VIETNAM
Ha-noi
Hai-phong
Nam-dinh
Vinh
Mount Victoria
RAMREE ISLAND
CHEDUBA ISLAND
70°
75°
80°
85°
90°
95°
100°
105°
45°
40°
35°
30°
25°
20°
15°

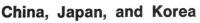

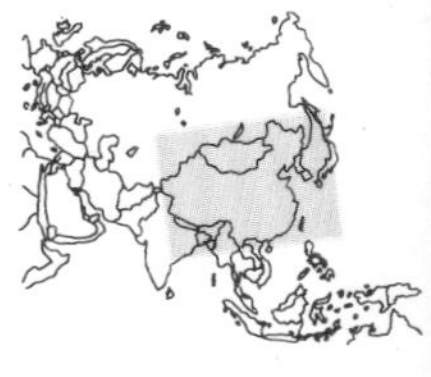

Kilometers 0 200 400 600 Km.

Statute Miles 0 200 400 600 Mi.

Scale 1:12,000,000

One centimeter represents 120 kilometers.

One inch represents approximately 190 miles.

Lambert Conformal Conic Projection

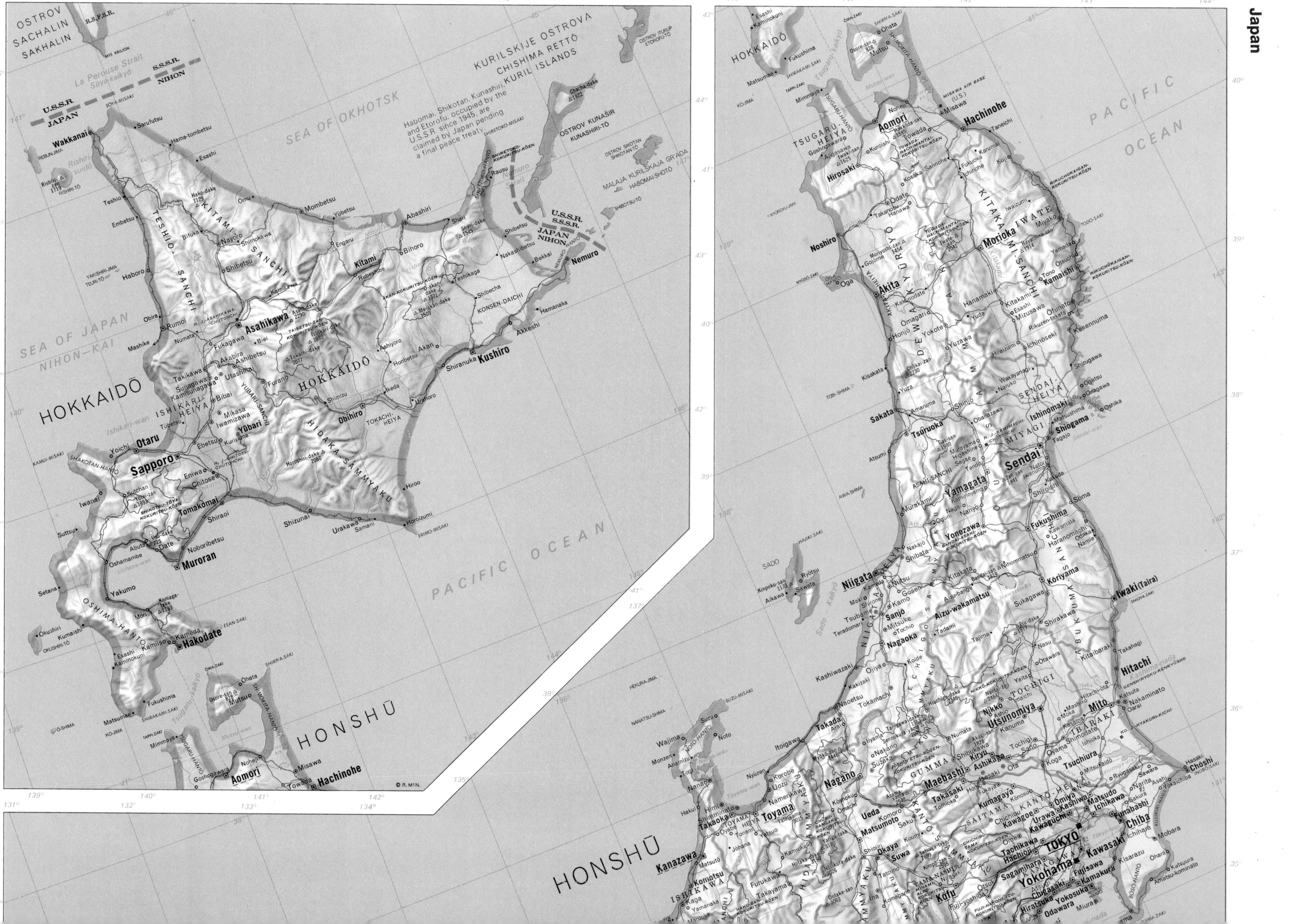
OSTROV SACHALIN SAKHALIN
R.S.F.S.R.
La Perouse Strait
Sōya-kaikyō
U.S.S.R.
JAPAN
S.S.S.R.
NIHON
SEA OF OKHOTSK
KURILSKIJE OSTROVA
CHISHIMA RETTŌ
KURIL ISLANDS
Habomai, Shikotan, Kunashiri, and Etorofu, occupied by the U.S.S.R. since 1945, are claimed by Japan pending a final peace treaty.
OSTROV KUNAŠIR
KUNASHIRI-TŌ
HOKKAIDŌ
SEA OF JAPAN
NIHON-KAI
PACIFIC OCEAN
HONSHŪ
Wakkanai
Asahikawa
Sapporo
Otaru
Kushiro
Obihiro
Kitami
Abashiri
Nemuro
Tomakomai
Muroran
Hakodate
Aomori
Hachinohe
Akita
Morioka
Sendai
Yamagata
Fukushima
Niigata
Toyama
Nagano
Maebashi
Utsunomiya
Mito
TOKYO
Yokohama
Kawasaki
Chiba
Japan

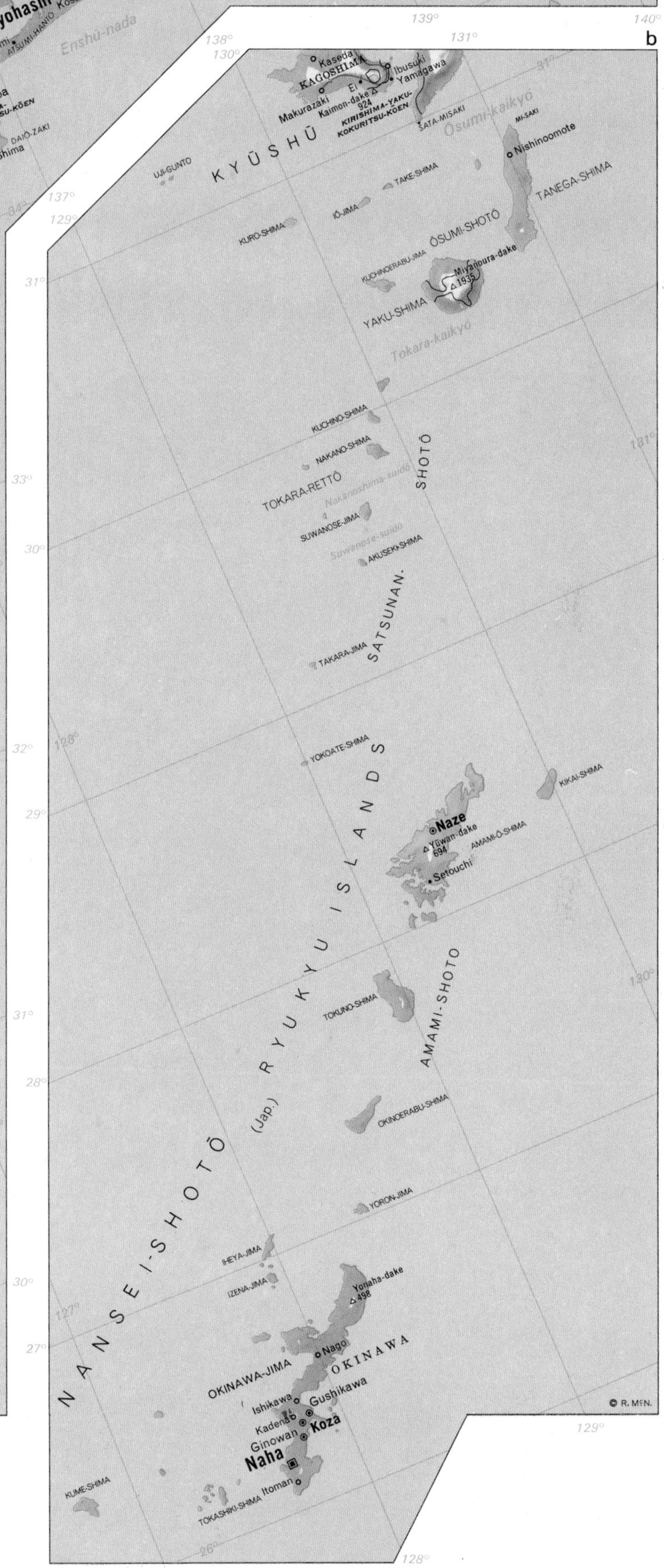

Kilometers 0 50 100 150 Km.
Statute Miles 0 50 100 150 Mi.
Scale 1:3,000,000
One centimeter represents 30 kilometers.
One inch represents approximately 47 miles.
Lambert Conformal Conic Projection

Southeast Asia

Kilometers 0 200 400 600 Km.

Statute Miles 0 200 400 600 Mi.

Scale 1:12,000,000

One centimeter represents 120 kilometers.
One inch represents approximately 190 miles.
Lambert Conformal Conic Projection

Burma, Thailand, and Indochina

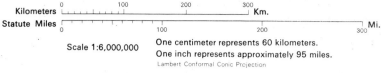

Kilometers 0 100 200 300 Km.

Statute Miles 0 100 200 300 Mi.

Scale 1:6,000,000

One centimeter represents 60 kilometers.
One inch represents approximately 95 miles.
Lambert Conformal Conic Projection

ANDAMAN SEA
MIDDLE ANDAMAN
ANDAMAN ISLANDS
SOUTH ANDAMAN
Port Blair
LITTLE ANDAMAN
ANDAMAN AND NICOBAR ISLANDS
Ten Degree Channel
Duncan Passage
MERGUI ARCHIPELAGO
NICOBAR ISLANDS
CAR NICOBAR
LITTLE NICOBAR
GREAT NICOBAR
Sombrero Channel
Great Channel
INDIA
INDONESIA
BURMA
THAILAND
Mergui
Phet Buri
Hua Hin
Prachuap Khiri Khan
Ban Huai Yang
Bang Saphan
Chumphon
ISTHMUS OF KRA
Ranong
Surat Thani
Nakhon Si Thammarat
Phuket
Songkhla
Hat Yai
Pattani
Narathiwat
GULF OF THAILAND
KO SAMUI
KO PHANGAN
Phnum Pénh
Bătdâmbâng
Kâmpóng Chhnăng
Kâmpóng Cham
Krâchéh
Kâmpôt
THANH-PHO HO CHI MINH (SAI-GON)
Vung-tau (Cap-Saint-Jacques)
Bien-hoa
Gia-dinh
My-tho
Long-xuyen
Rach-gia
Can-tho
Khanh-hung
Bac-lieu (Vinh-loi)
Da-lat
Nha-trang
Cam-ranh
Phan-rang
Phan-thiet
CON SON
SOUTH CHINA SEA
Alor Setar
Kota Baharu
Kuala Terengganu
Pinang (George Town)
Butterworth
Taiping
Ipoh
Telok Anson
Kuantan
Kuala Lumpur
Kelang
Seremban
Melaka
Muar (Bandar Maharani)
Batu Pahat
Johor Baharu
SINGAPORE
KEDAH
PERLIS
PERAK
KELANTAN
TERENGGANU
PAHANG
SELANGOR
NEGERI SEMBILAN
MELAKA
JOHOR
MALAYA
THAILAND MALAYSIA
MALAYSIA INDONESIA
KEPULAUAN BUNGURAN UTARA
NATUNA BESAR
KEPULAUAN BUNGURAN SELATAN
KEPULAUAN ANAMBAS
KEPULAUAN TAMBELAN
KEPULAUAN RIAU
LINGGA
Tanjungpinang
Kuching
SARAWAK
KALIMANTAN BARAT
BORNEO KALIMANTAN
Singkawang
Pontianak
Banda Aceh
Sabang
Lhokseumawe
Langsa
ACEH
Medan
Binjai
Tebingtinggi
Pematangsiantar
Tanjungbalai
Sibolga
Padangsidimpuan
Rantauprapat
SUMATERA UTARA
SUMATERA SUMATRA
RIAU
Pakanbaru
Dumai
Bengkalis
Bukittinggi
Payakumbuh
Padangpanjang
Pariaman
Padang
Solok
SUMATERA BARAT
JAMBI
PULAU SIMEULUE
PULAU NIAS
KEPULAUAN BANYAK
KEPULAUAN BATU
PULAU SIBERUT
Strait of Malacca
INDIAN OCEAN
Equator

Malaysia and Western Indonesia

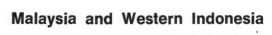

Copyright © by Rand McNally & Co.
Map compiled by Cartographia, Budapest.
Map produced by Rand McNally GmbH, Stuttgart.
A-565500-264

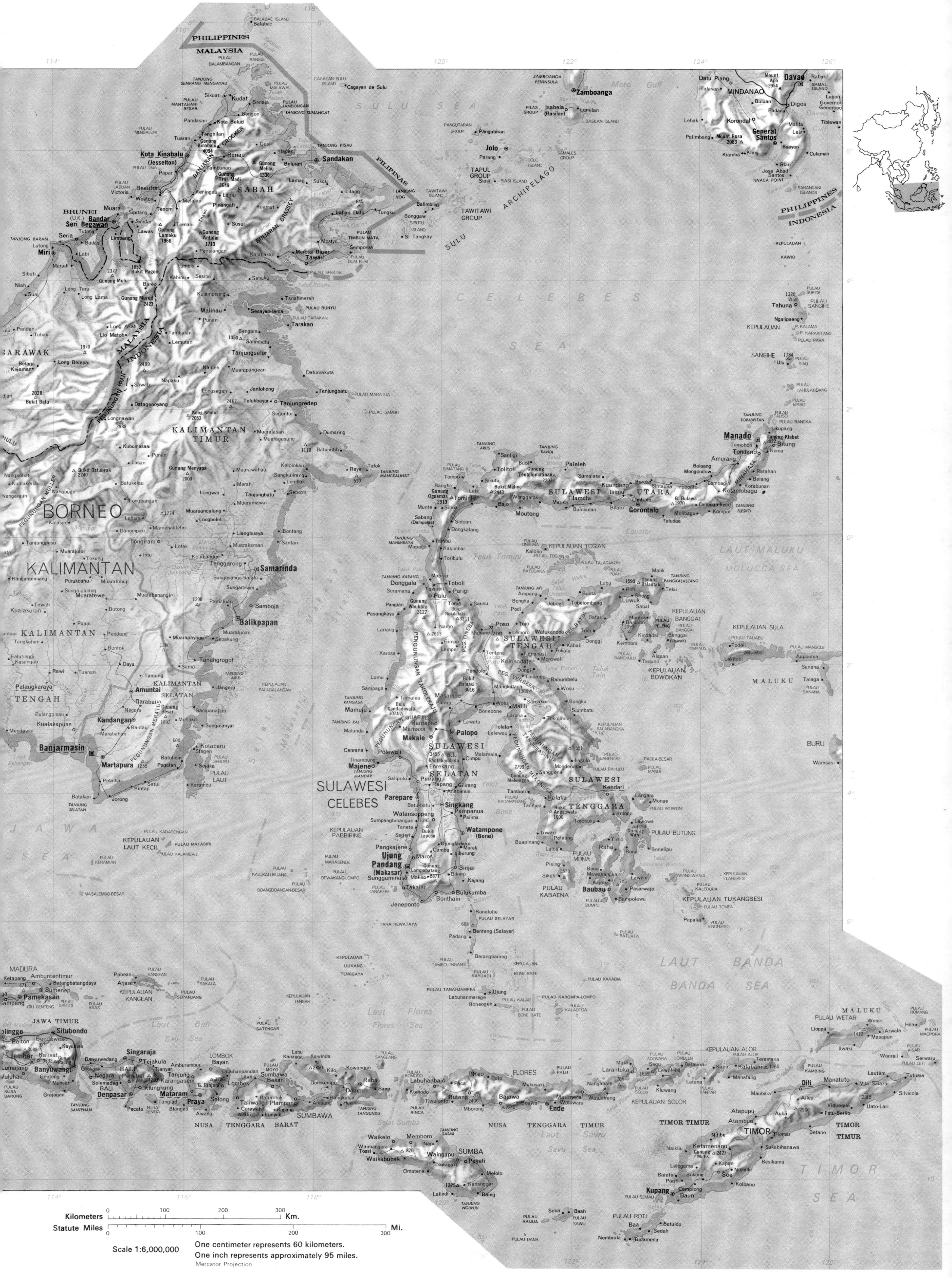

Scale 1:6,000,000

One centimeter represents 60 kilometers.

One inch represents approximately 95 miles.

Mercator Projection

Philippines

SULU SEA
CELEBES SEA
MINDANAO
NEGROS
PANAY
BOHOL
CEBU
LEYTE
SAMAR
PALAWAN
BORNEO
KALIMANTAN
Mindanao Sea
Moro Gulf
Davao Gulf
Panay Gulf
Iligan Bay
Illana Bay
Visayan Sea
Camotes Sea
Leyte Gulf
PHILIPPINES PILIPINAS
MALAYSIA
SABAH NORTH BORNEO
SULU ARCHIPELAGO
CUYO ISLANDS
CAGAYAN ISLANDS
PANGUTARAN GROUP
SAMALES GROUP
JOLO GROUP
TAPUL GROUP
TAWITAWI GROUP
TAPIANTANA GROUP
SARANGANI ISLANDS
QUINILUBAN GROUP
TUBBATAHA REEFS
VICTORIA RANGE
MANTALINGAJAN RANGE
TABLAS PLATEAU
ZAMBOANGA PENINSULA
ZAMBOANGA DEL NORTE
ZAMBOANGA DEL SUR
MISAMIS OCCIDENTAL
MISAMIS ORIENTAL
LANAO DEL NORTE
LANAO DEL SUR
BUKIDNON
COTABATO
DAVAO DEL NORTE
DAVAO DEL SUR
DAVAO ORIENTAL
SURIGAO DEL NORTE
AGUSAN
NEGROS OCCIDENTAL
NEGROS ORIENTAL
SOUTHERN LEYTE
Iloilo
Bacolod
Roxas
Cebu
Tacloban
Catbalogan
Ormoc
Baybay
Maasin
Surigao
Butuan
Cagayan de Oro
Iligan
Marawi
Dipolog
Dapitan
Ozamiz
Pagadian
Zamboanga
Isabela (Basilan)
Jolo
Cotabato
Davao
Digos
General Santos (Dadiangas)
Mati
Malaybalay
Dumaguete
Tagbilaran
Puerto Princesa
San Jose
Victorias
Silay
Talisay
Cadiz
San Carlos
La Carlota
La Castellana
Hinigaran
Binalbagan
Himamaylan
Kabankalan
Bais
Tanjay
Siaton
Kalibo
Sandakan
Cagayan de Sulu
Taytay
Roxas
Brooke's Point
Rio Tuba
Balabac
Tawitawi
Copyright © by Rand McNally & Co.
Map prepared by Rand McNally & Co.

India, Pakistan, and Southwest Asia

Kilometers 0 200 400 600 Km.
Statute Miles 0 200 400 600 Mi.

Scale 1:12,000,000
One centimeter represents 120 kilometers.
One inch represents approximately 190 miles.
Lambert Conformal Conic Projection

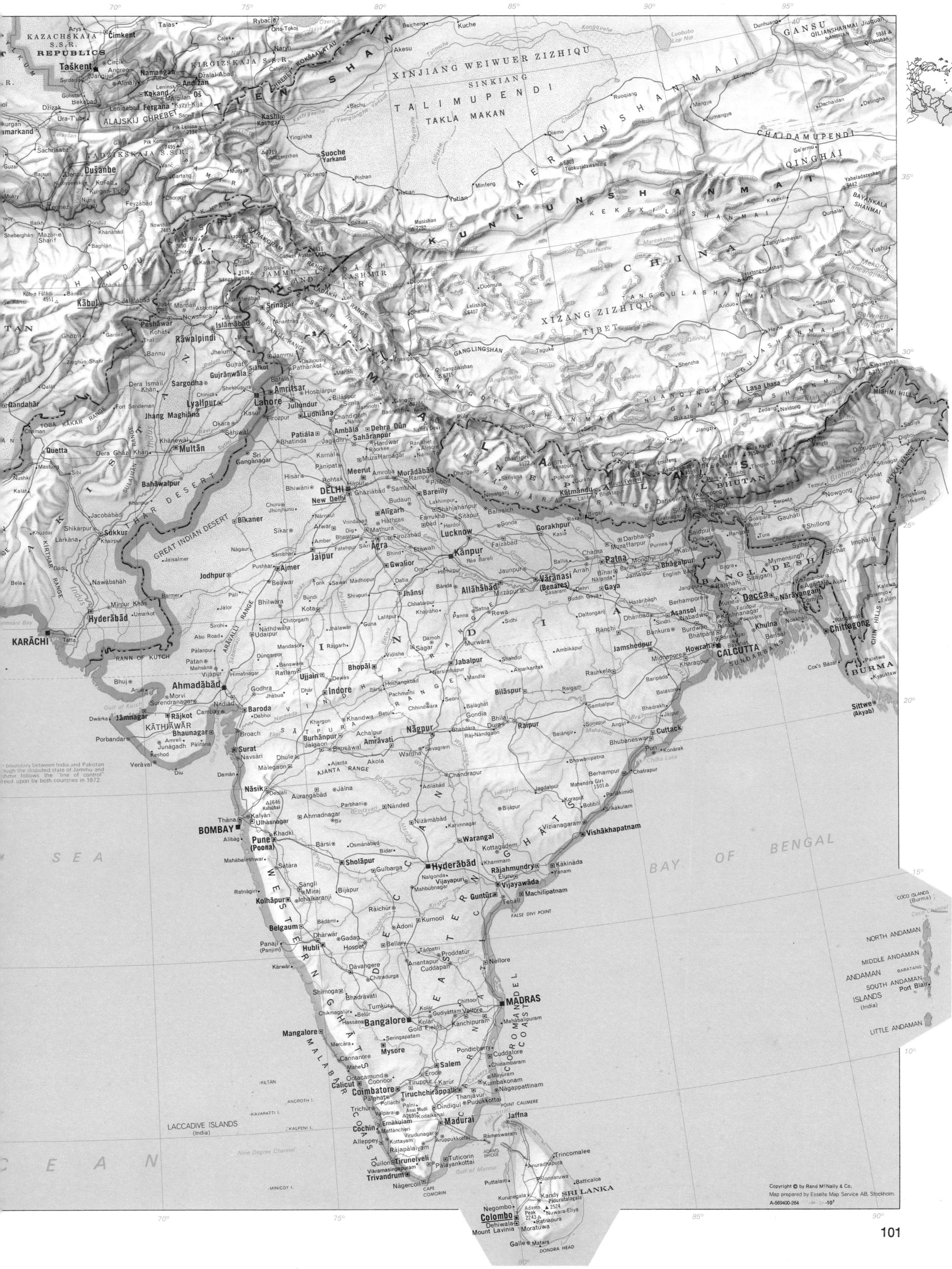
KAZACHSKAJA S.S.R.
REPUBLICS
KIRGIZSKAJA S.S.R.
TADŽIKSKAJA S.S.R.
XINJIANG WEIWUER ZIZHIQU
SINKIANG
TALIMUPENDI
TAKLA MAKAN
TIEN SHAN
KUNLUN SHAN
ALTUN SHAN
CHINA
XIZANG ZIZHIQU
TIBET
TANGGULA SHAN
QINGHAI
CHAIDAMUPENDI
GANSU
HINDU KUSH
KARAKORAM RANGE
JAMMU AND KASHMIR
HIMALAYA
NEPAL
BHUTAN
BANGLADESH
BURMA
GREAT INDIAN DESERT
THAR DESERT
RANN OF KUTCH
KATHIAWAR
ARAVALLI RANGE
VINDHYA RANGE
SATPURA RANGE
AJANTA RANGE
DECCAN
WESTERN GHATS
EASTERN GHATS
MALABAR COAST
COROMANDEL COAST
INDIA
LACCADIVE ISLANDS (India)
SEA
BAY OF BENGAL
ANDAMAN ISLANDS (India)
NORTH ANDAMAN
MIDDLE ANDAMAN
SOUTH ANDAMAN
LITTLE ANDAMAN
Port Blair
COCO ISLANDS (Burma)
SRI LANKA
Colombo
Kandy
Jaffna
Trincomalee
KARĀCHI
Hyderābād
Quetta
Kābul
Taškent
Dušanbe
Lahore
Amritsar
Islāmābād
Rawalpindi
Srinagar
DELHI
New Delhi
Jaipur
Āgra
Kānpur
Lucknow
Allāhābād
Vārānasi (Benares)
Patna
Kātmāndu
Dacca
Chittagong
CALCUTTA
Ahmadābād
Surat
BOMBAY
Pune (Poona)
Hyderābād
Nāgpur
Bhopāl
Indore
Jabalpur
Cuttack
Vishākhapatnam
Vijayawāda
Bangalore
MADRAS
Mysore
Coimbatore
Madurai
Trivandrum
Lasa Lhasa
Sittwe (Akyab)
Copyright © by Rand McNally & Co.
Map prepared by Esselte Map Service AB, Stockholm.
A-569400-264
The boundary between India and Pakistan through the disputed state of Jammu and Kashmir follows the "line of control" agreed upon by both countries in 1972.

Northern India and Pakistan

Kilometers 0 100 200 300 Km.

Statute Miles 0 100 200 300 Mi.

Scale 1:6,000,000

One centimeter represents 60 kilometers.

One inch represents approximately 95 miles.

Lambert Conformal Conic Projection

The Middle East

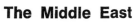

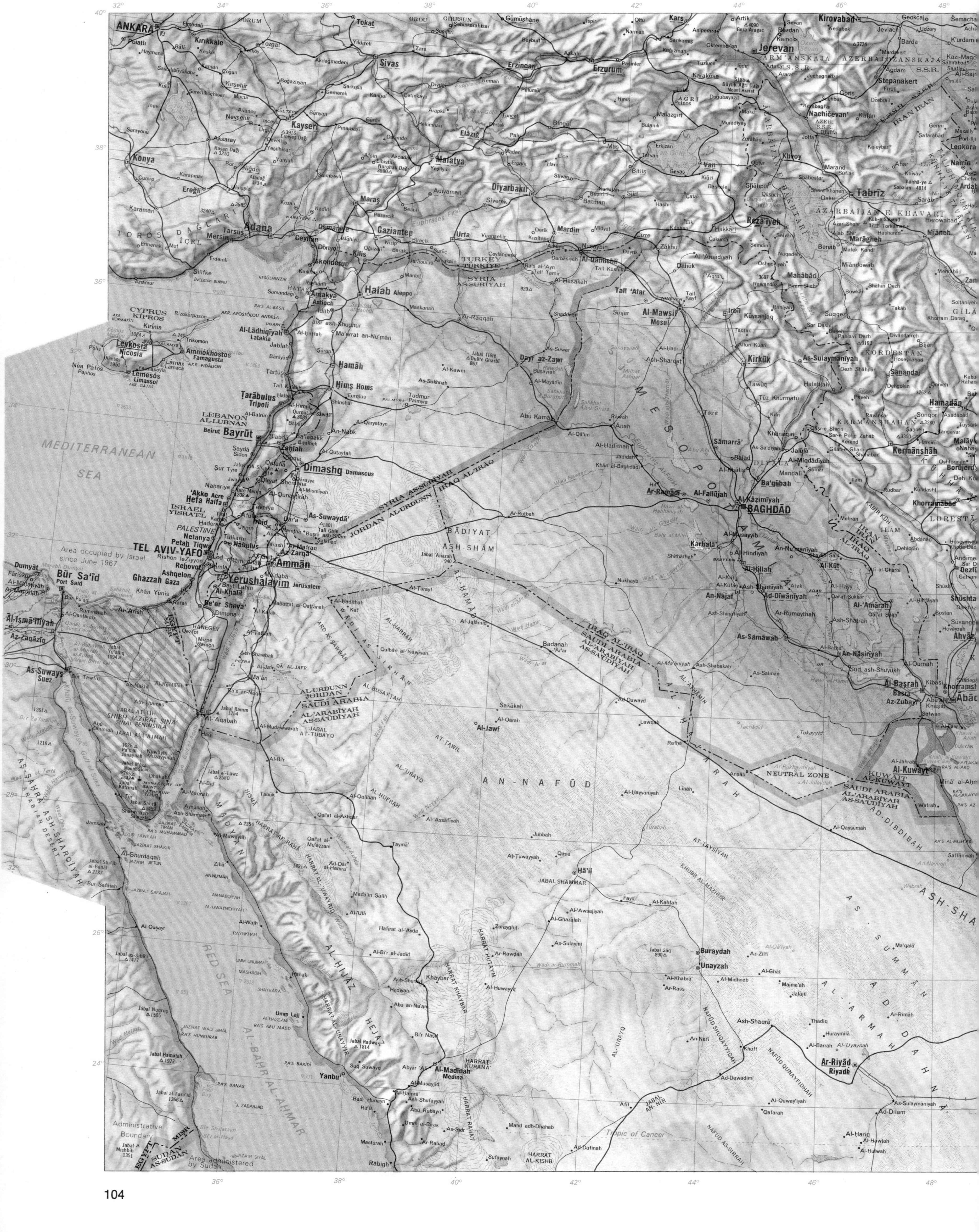

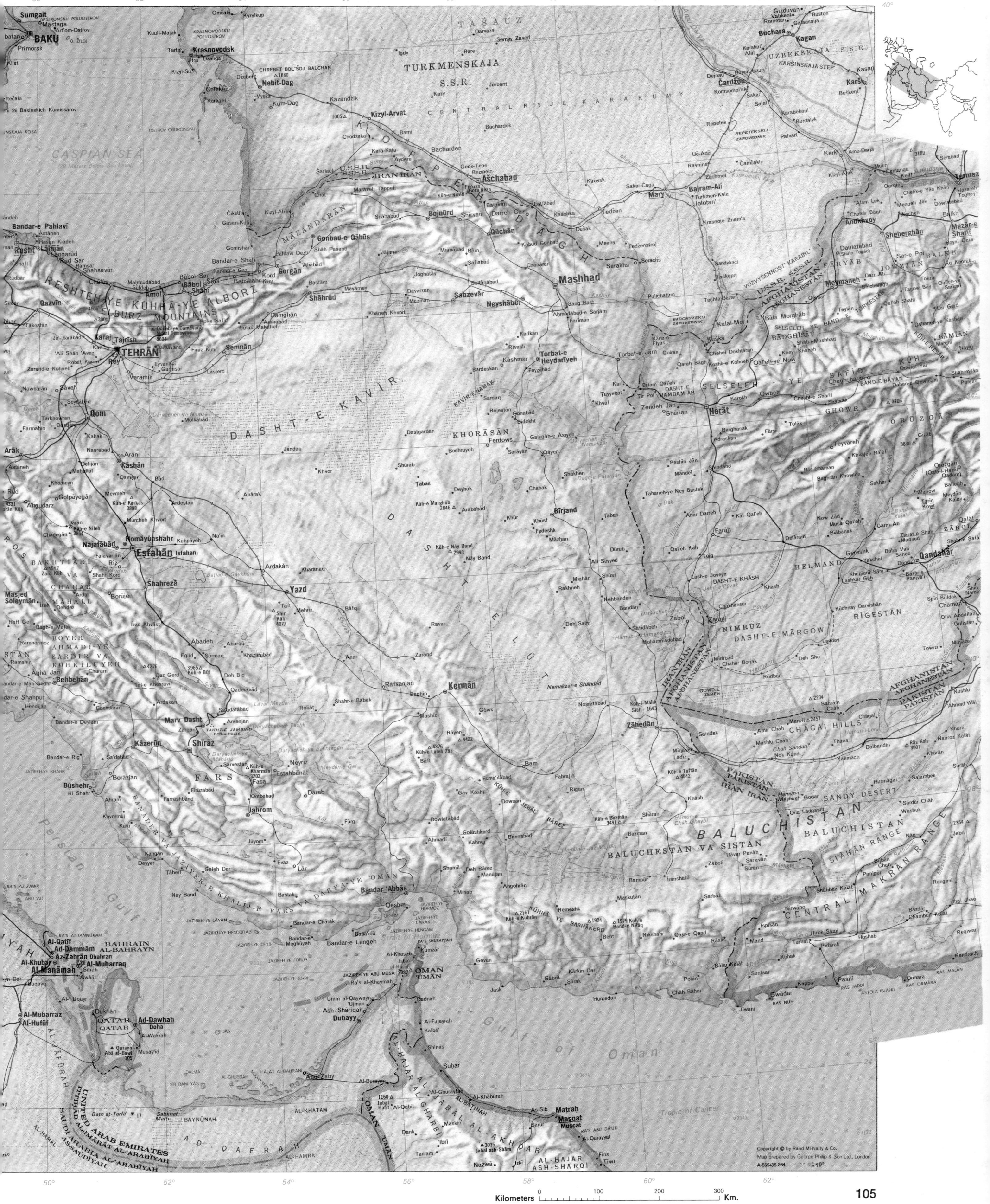

Kilometers 0 100 200 300 Km.

Statute Miles 0 100 200 300 Mi.

Scale 1:6,000,000

One centimeter represents 60 kilometers.
One inch represents approximately 95 miles.
Lambert Conformal Conic Projection

Western North Africa

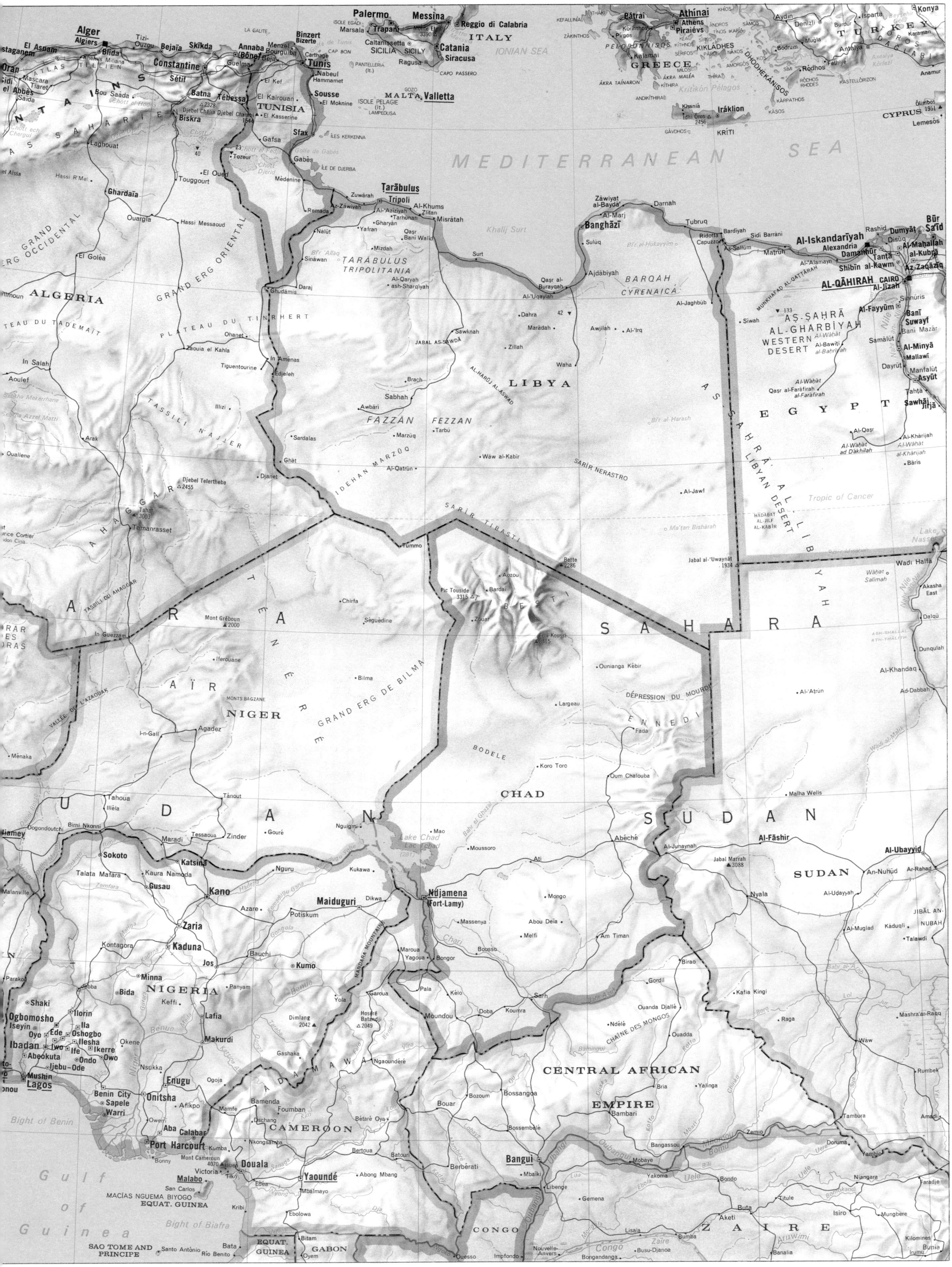

Kilometers 0 200 400 600 Km.

Statute Miles 0 200 400 600 Mi.

Scale 1:12,000,000

One centimeter represents 120 kilometers.
One inch represents approximately 190 miles.
Miller Oblated Stereographic Projection

Eastern North Africa

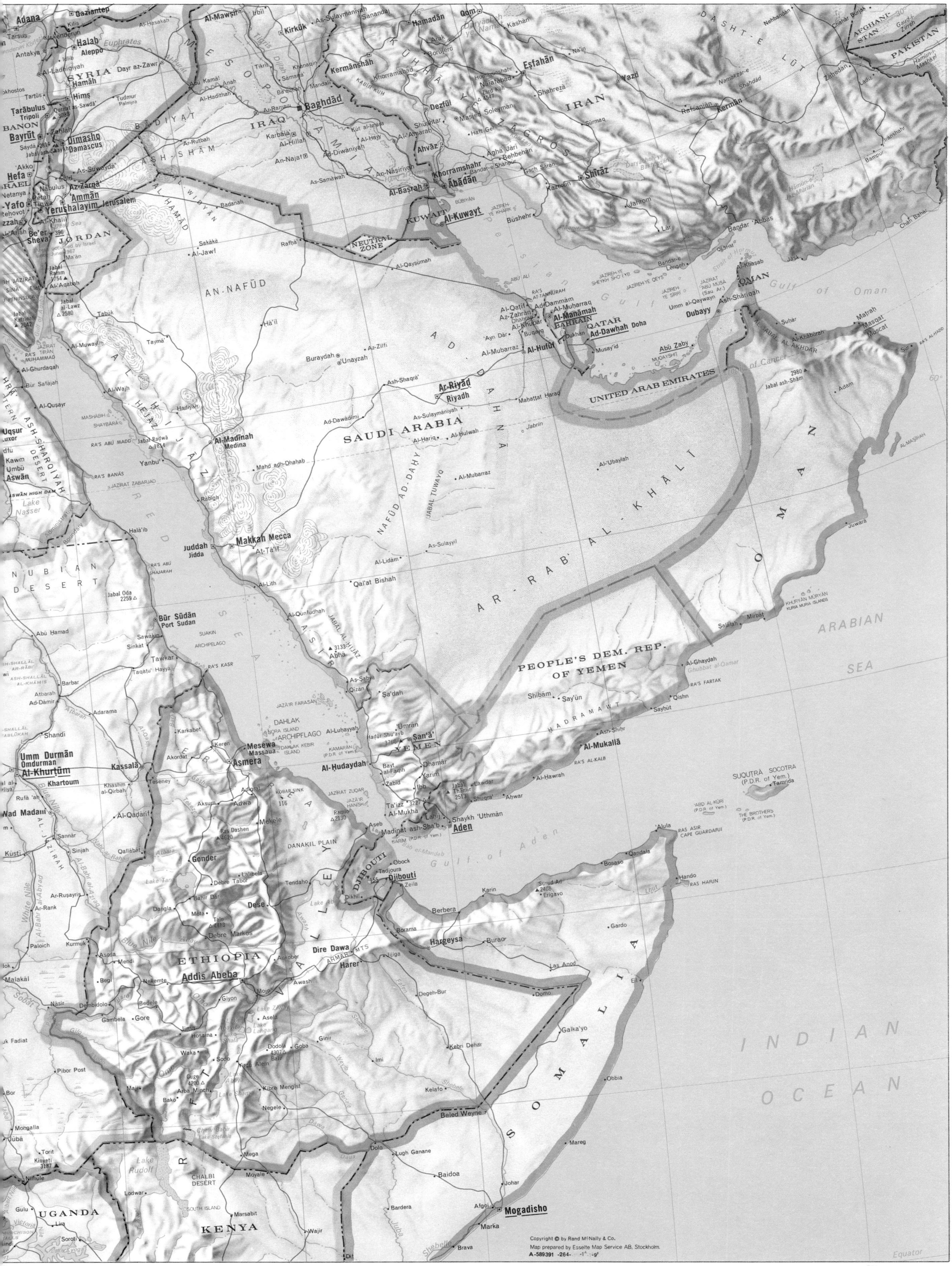

Kilometers 0 200 400 600 Km.
Statute Miles 0 200 400 600 Mi.

Scale 1:12,000,000
One centimeter represents 120 kilometers.
One inch represents approximately 190 miles.
Miller Oblated Stereographic Projection.

ATLANTIC
OCEAN
SAO TOME AND PRINCIPE
EQUATORIAL GUINEA
GABON
CONGO
CABINDA (Angola)
ZAIRE
ANGOLA
ZAMBIA
RHODESIA
NAMIBIA
(S. Afr. Admin.)
BOTSWANA
KALAHARI DESERT
SOUTH AFRICA
LESOTHO
SWAZILAND
RWANDA
BURUNDI
CAMEROON
KATANGA PLATEAU
BAROTSELAND
OVAMBOLAND
DAMARALAND
GREAT NAMALAND
KAOKOVELD
NAMIB DESERT
BUSHMAN LAND
GREAT KARROO
LITTLE KARROO
TRANSKEI
Tropic of Capricorn
Libreville
Port-Gentil
Pointe-Noire
Brazzaville
Kinshasa (Léopoldville)
Matadi
Boma
Luanda
Lobito
Benguela
Huambo (Nova Lisboa)
Moçâmedes
Kisangani (Stanleyville)
Bukavu
Kigali
Bujumbura
Kananga (Luluabourg)
Mbuji-Mayi (Bakwanga)
Kikwit
Mbandaka (Coquilhatville)
Kamina
Kolwezi
Likasi (Jadotville)
Lubumbashi (Elisabethville)
Kalemi (Albertville)
Chingola
Mufulira
Kitwe
Ndola
Luanshya
Kabwe (Broken Hill)
Lusaka
Livingstone
Salisbury
Gwelo
Bulawayo
Windhoek
Swakopmund
Walvisbaai (Walvis Bay) (S. Afr.)
Lüderitz
Tsumeb
Otjiwarongo
Serowe
Francistown
Gaborone
Pretoria
JOHANNESBURG
Kimberley
Bloemfontein
Pietermaritzburg
Durban
East London (Oos-Londen)
Port Elizabeth
Cape Town (Kaapstad)
CAPE OF GOOD HOPE
CAPE AGULHAS
The United Nations declared an end to the mandate of South Africa over Namibia in October, 1966. Administration of the territory by South Africa is not recognized by the United Nations.

Kilometers 0 200 400 600 Km.

Statute Miles 0 200 400 600 Mi.

Scale 1:12,000,000

One centimeter represents 120 kilometers.

One inch represents approximately 190 miles.

Miller Oblated Stereographic Projection

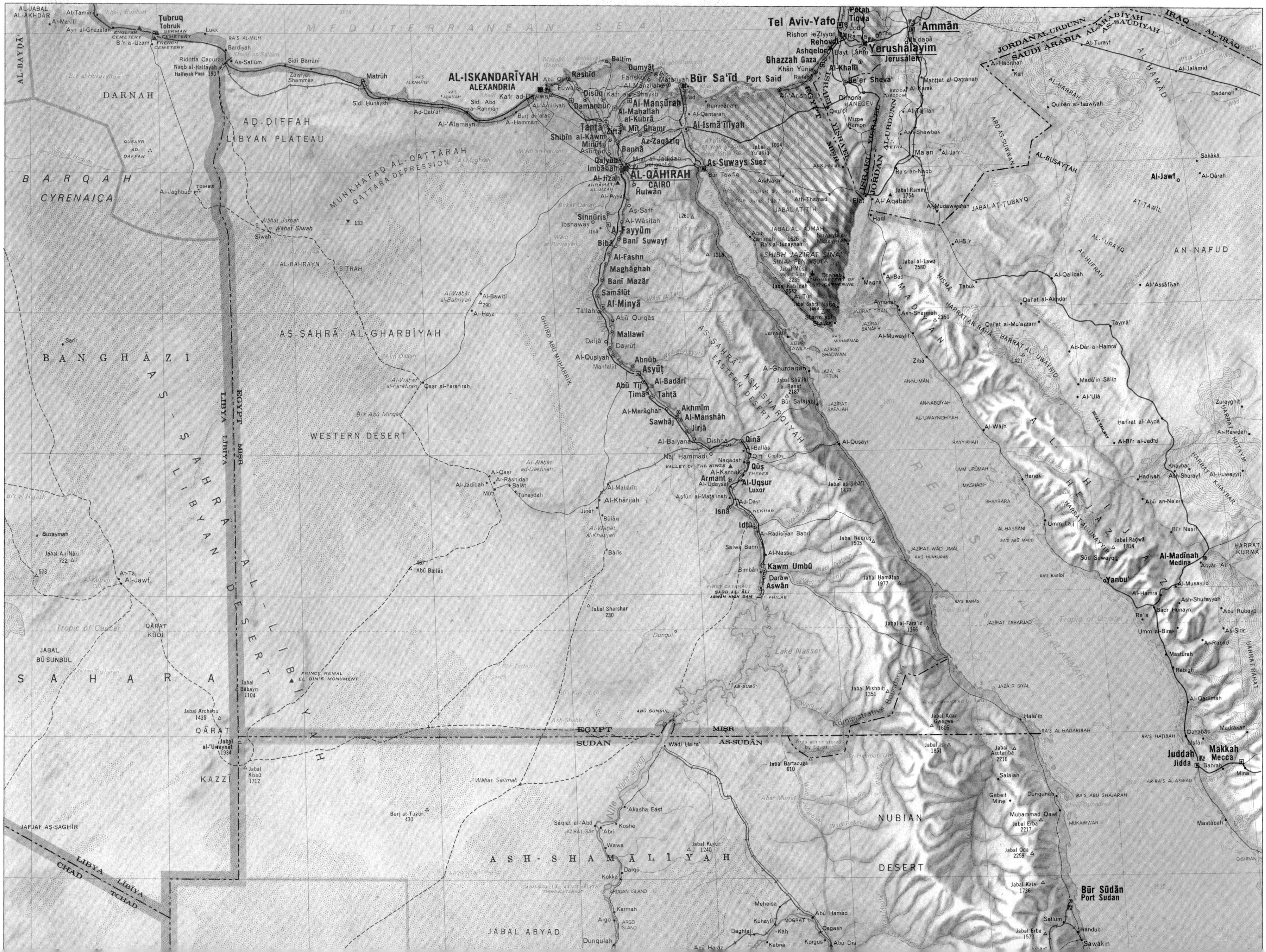
MEDITERRANEAN SEA
AL-ISKANDARĪYAH
ALEXANDRIA
Būr Sa'īd
Port Said
Tel Aviv-Yafo
Yerushalayim
Jerusalem
'Ammān
AL-QĀHIRAH
CAIRO
As-Suways Suez
Al-Ismā'īlīyah
Az-Zaqāzīq
Ṭanṭā
Al-Manṣūrah
Dumyāṭ
Rashīd
Marsā Maṭrūḥ
Tubruq
Tobruk
DARNAH
AD-DIFFAH
LIBYAN PLATEAU
MUNKHAFAḌ AL-QAṬṬĀRAH
QATTARA DEPRESSION
BARQAH
CYRENAICA
BANGHĀZĪ
AṢ-ṢAḤRĀ' AL-GHARBĪYAH
WESTERN DESERT
AṢ-ṢAḤRĀ' AL-LĪBĪYAH
LIBYAN DESERT
SAHARA
EGYPT
MIṢR
LIBYA
LĪBIYĀ
SUDAN
AS-SŪDĀN
CHAD
TCHAD
Al-Fayyūm
Banī Suwayf
Al-Minyā
Asyūṭ
Sawhāj
Qinā
Al-Uqṣur
Luxor
Aswān
Lake Nasser
Wādī Ḥalfā'
Al-Khārijah
Siwah
AṢ-ṢAḤRĀ' ASH-SHARQĪYAH
EASTERN DESERT
SHIBH JAZĪRAT SĪNĀ'
SINAI PENINSULA
RED SEA
AL-BAḤR AL-AḤMAR
Tropic of Cancer
NUBIAN DESERT
ASH-SHAMĀLĪYAH
JABAL ABYAD
Būr Sūdān
Port Sudan
Sawākin
AL-ḤIJĀZ
AN-NAFŪD
Al-Madīnah
Medina
Makkah
Mecca
Juddah
Jidda
Yanbu'
Tabūk
SAUDI ARABIA
AL-'ARABIYAH AS-SA'ŪDIYAH
JORDAN
AL-URDUNN
ISRAEL
YISRA'EL
IRAQ
AL-'IRĀQ

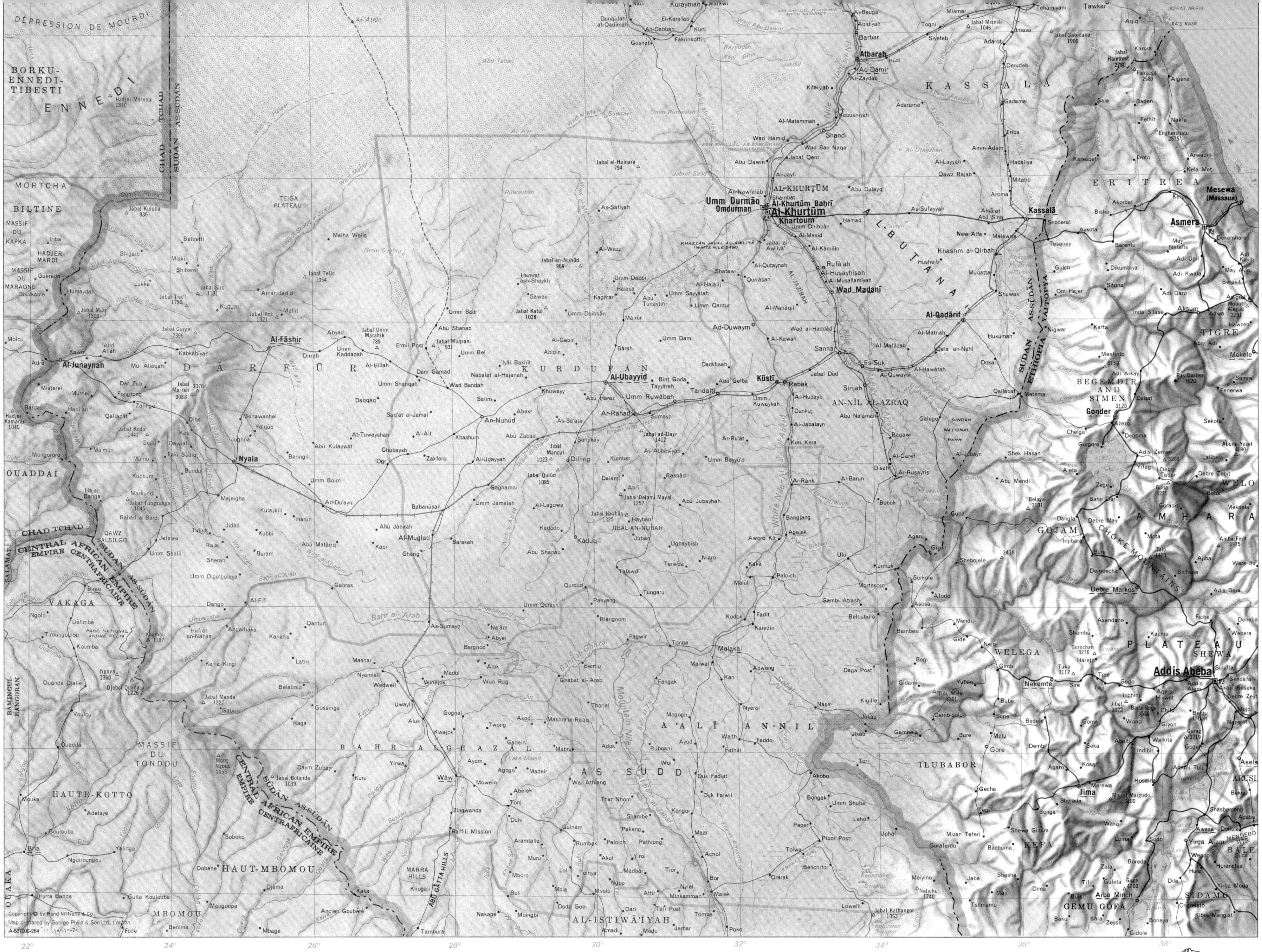

Kilometers 0 100 200 300 Km.

Statute Miles 0 100 200 300 Mi.

Scale 1:6,000,000

One centimeter represents 60 kilometers.
One inch represents approximately 95 miles.
Lambert Azimuthal Equal-Area Projection

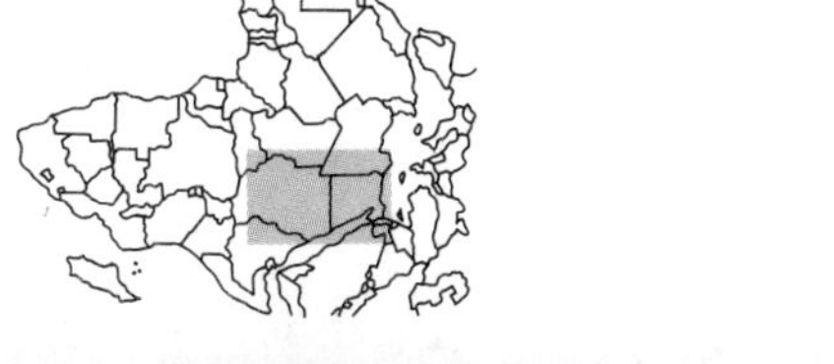

West Africa

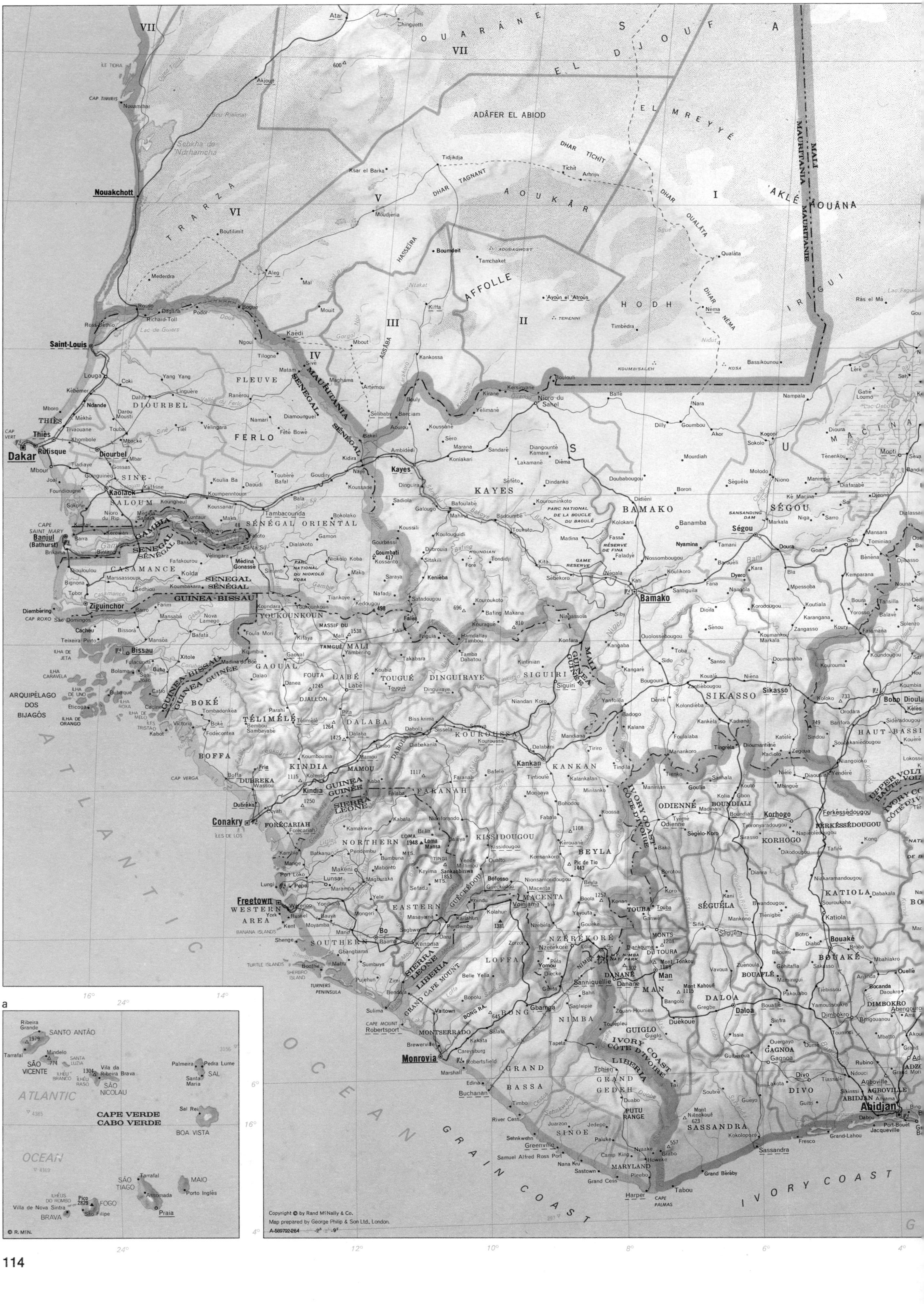

MAURITANIA
MAURITANIE
MALI
SENEGAL
SÉNÉGAL
GAMBIA
GUINEA-BISSAU
GUINEA
GUINÉE
SIERRA LEONE
LIBERIA
IVORY COAST
CÔTE D'IVOIRE
UPPER VOLTA
HAUTE-VOLTA
Nouakchott
Saint-Louis
Dakar
Thiès
Rufisque
Kaolack
Banjul
(Bathurst)
Ziguinchor
Bissau
Conakry
Freetown
Monrovia
Bamako
Ségou
Kayes
Sikasso
Abidjan
Bouaké
Kankan
ATLANTIC OCEAN
GRAIN COAST
IVORY COAST
ARQUIPÉLAGO DOS BIJAGÓS
CAPE VERDE
CABO VERDE
SANTO ANTÃO
SÃO VICENTE
SÃO NICOLAU
SAL
BOA VISTA
MAIO
SÃO TIAGO
FOGO
BRAVA
Praia
Copyright © by Rand McNally & Co.
Map prepared by George Philip & Son Ltd. London.
A-589792-264

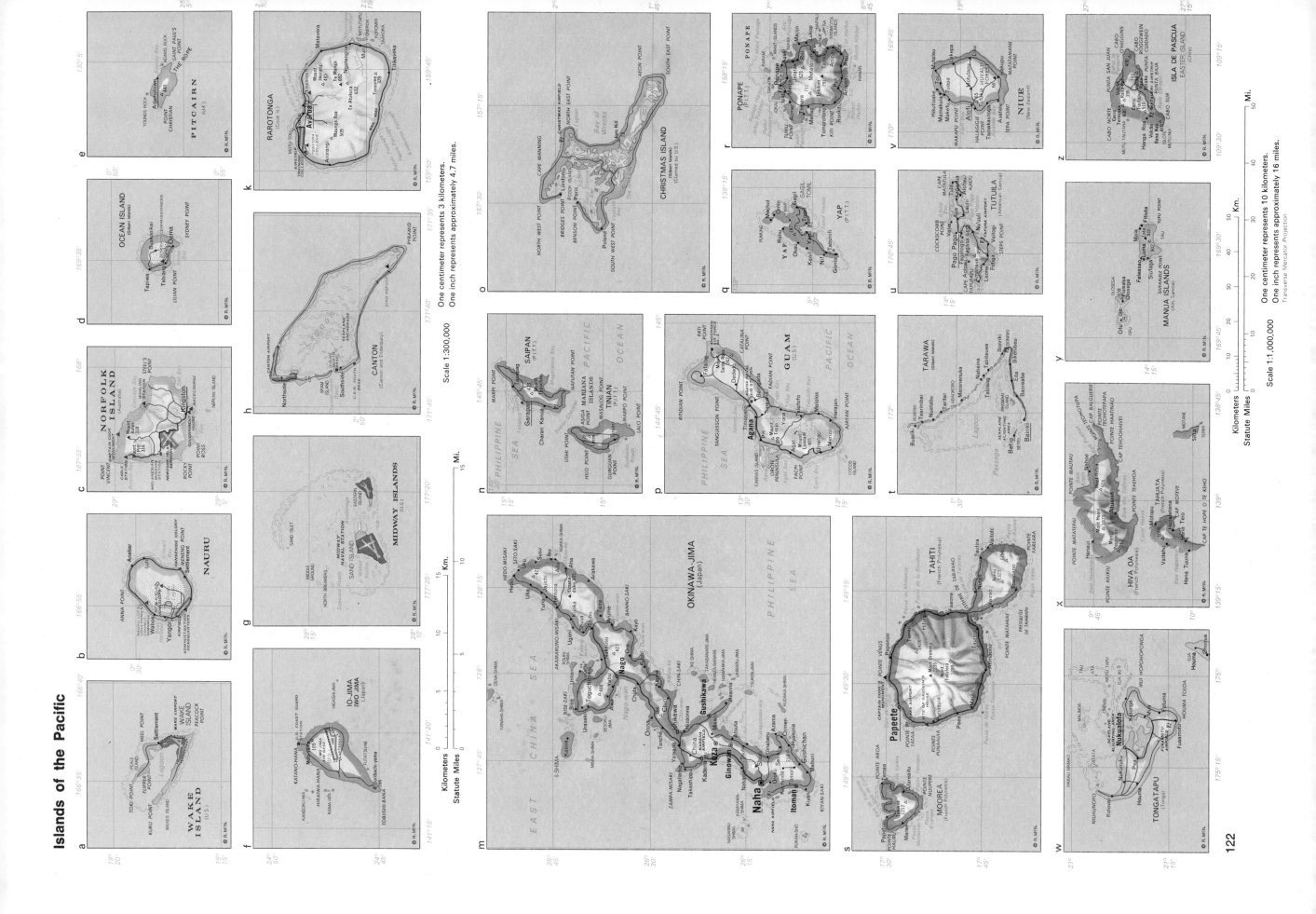

Kilometers 0 100 200 300 Km.
Statute Miles 0 100 200 300 Mi.

Scale 1:6,000,000
One centimeter represents 60 kilometers.
One inch represents approximately 95 miles.
Lambert Azimuthal Equal-Area Projection

Southern Africa and Madagascar

The United Nations declared an end to the mandate of South Africa over Namibia in October, 1966. Administration of the territory by South Africa is not recognized by the United Nations.

Kilometers 0 100 200 300 Km.
Statute Miles 0 100 200 300 Mi.

Scale 1:6,000,000

One centimeter represents 60 kilometers.
One inch represents approximately 95 miles.
Lambert Azimuthal Equal-Area Projection

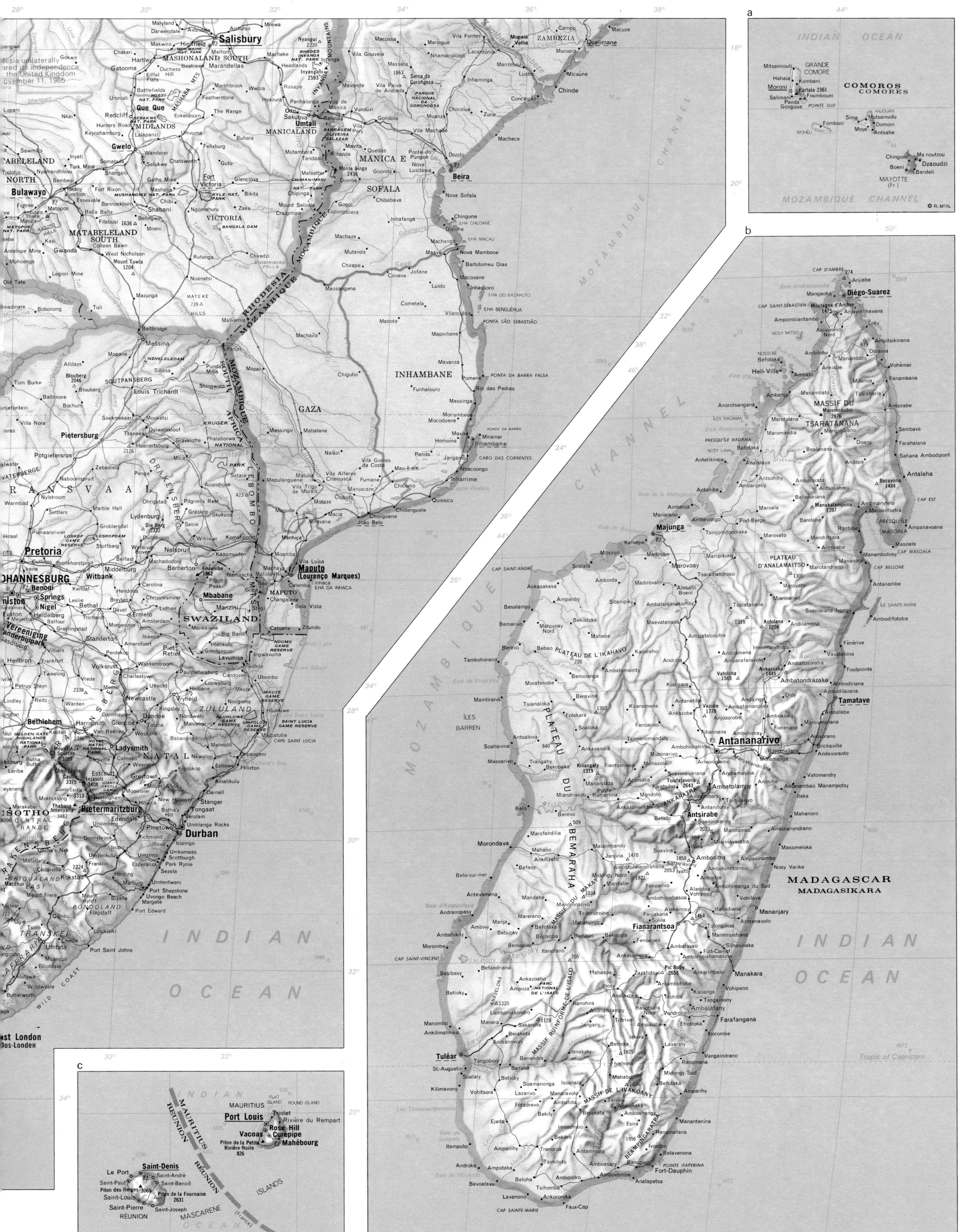

Salisbury
MASHONALAND SOUTH
MIDLANDS
MANICALAND
MATABELELAND SOUTH
Bulawayo
Gwelo
Que Que
Umtali
Fort Victoria
VICTORIA
RHODESIA
MOZAMBIQUE
MANICA E SOFALA
Beira
ZAMBEZIA
Quelimane
Chinde
INHAMBANE
GAZA
Maputo
(Lourenço Marques)
SWAZILAND
Mbabane
TRANSVAAL
Pretoria
JOHANNESBURG
Pietersburg
NATAL
ZULULAND
Durban
Pietermaritzburg
Ladysmith
LESOTHO
TRANSKEI
East London
INDIAN OCEAN
MOZAMBIQUE CHANNEL
COMOROS
COMORES
Moroni
GRANDE COMORE
MAYOTTE
(Fr.)
Dzaoudzi
MADAGASCAR
MADAGASIKARA
Antananarivo
Majunga
Diégo-Suarez
Tamatave
Fianarantsoa
Antsirabe
Tuléar
Fort-Dauphin
Manakara
MASSIF DU TSARATANANA
PLATEAU DU BEMARAHA
MASSIF DE L'IVAKOANY
Tropic of Capricorn
MAURITIUS
Port Louis
Curepipe
Rose Hill
Vacoas
Mahébourg
RÉUNION
Saint-Denis
Saint-Pierre
MASCARENE ISLANDS
© R. M©N.

Australia

INDONESIA
JAWA
Yogyakarta
Surakarta
Madiun
Kediri
Malang
Jember
Denpasar
BALI
LOMBOK
SUMBAWA
NUSA TENGGARA
LESSER SUNDA ISLANDS
SUMBA
Waingapu
TIMOR
Kupang
Timor Sea
INDIAN OCEAN
ASHMORE ISLANDS
HIBERNIA REEF
CARTIER ISLAND (Austl.)
SCOTT REEF
BROWSE ISLAND
BONAPARTE ARCHIPELAGO
CAPE LONDONDERRY
Joseph Bonaparte Gulf
ADÈLE ISLAND
BUCCANEER ARCHIPELAGO
CAPE LEVEQUE
Yampi Sound
KIMBERLEY PLATEAU
KING LEOPOLD RANGES
DURACK RANGE
Wyndham
Kununurra
Derby
Broome
Fitzroy Crossing
Halls Creek
Gordon Downs
ROWLEY SHOALS
CAPE LATOUCHE TREVILLE
La Grange
EIGHTY MILE BEACH
Port Hedland
Shay Gap
GREAT SANDY DESERT
DAMPIER ARCHIPELAGO
MONTEBELLO ISLANDS
BARROW ISLAND
Roebourne
Dampier
Marble Bar
Nullagine
MUIRON ISLANDS
NORTH WEST CAPE
Onslow
Pannawonica
HAMERSLEY RANGE
Wittenoom
Mount Brockman 1129
1235 Mount Bruce
Tom Price
Paraburdoo
Newman
POINT CLOATES
CAPE CUVIER
Tropic of Capricorn
Mount Augustus 1105
Carnarvon
BERNIER ISLAND
DORRE ISLAND
DIRK HARTOG ISLAND
STEEP POINT
Wooramel
ROBINSON RANGES
Peak Hill
906 Mount Essendon
WESTERN AUSTRALIA
GIBSON DESERT
Lake Disappointment
Lake Mackay
Lake Carnegie
Wiluna
Meekatharra
Nannine
Cue
Sandstone
Mount Magnet
Agnew
Mount Redcliffe 576
Laverton
Malcolm
Leonora
Menzies
Kanowna
Kalgoorlie
Boulder
Coolgardie
Southern Cross
Bullfinch
Bencubbin
Bonnie Rock
Dalwallinu
HOUTMAN ABROLHOS
Northampton
Mullewa
Geraldton
Yalgoo
Dongara
Three Springs
GREEN HEAD
Moora
DARLING RANGE
Muchea
Stirling
Perth
Fremantle
Pinjarra
Northam
York
Merredin
Kellerberrin
Beverley
Brookton
Hyden
Lake Johnston
Narrogin
Newdegate
Wagin
Nyabing
Katanning
Gnowangerup
Bunbury
Collie
Busselton
Bridgetown
CAPE NATURALISTE
Manjimup
Augusta
CAPE LEEUWIN
Pemberton
Bluff Knoll 1096
Mount Barker
Albany
Denmark
POINT D'ENTRECASTEAUX
WEST CAPE HOWE
CAPE VANCOUVER
CAPE KNOB
HOOD POINT
Ravensthorpe
Hopetoun
Esperance
ARCHIPELAGO OF THE RECHERCHE
CAPE ARID
Norseman
POINT CULVER
Zanthus
Rawlinna
Haig
Forrest
Deakin
NULLARBOR PLAIN
Eucla
Eyre
GREAT VICTORIA DESERT
Great Australian Bight
Maralinga
Ooldea
CAPE ADIEU
SAINT PETER ISLAND
Mount Aloysius 1085
Mount Olga 1069
Ayers Rock 867
1439 Mount Woodroffe
Mount Leisler 901
Mount Zeil 1511
Lake Amadeus
TANAMI DESERT
NORTHERN TERRITORY
Wave Hill
Victoria River Downs
Daly Waters
Darwin
Rum Jungle
Pine Creek
Katherine
ARNHEM L
MELVILLE ISLAND
BATHURST ISLAND
POINT BLAZE
CAPE CROKER
Barrow
Newcastle Waters

Kilometers 0 200 400 600 Km.
Statute Miles 0 200 400 600 Mi.

Scale 1:12,000,000
One centimeter represents 120 kilometers.
One inch represents approximately 190 miles.
Lambert Conformal Conic Projection

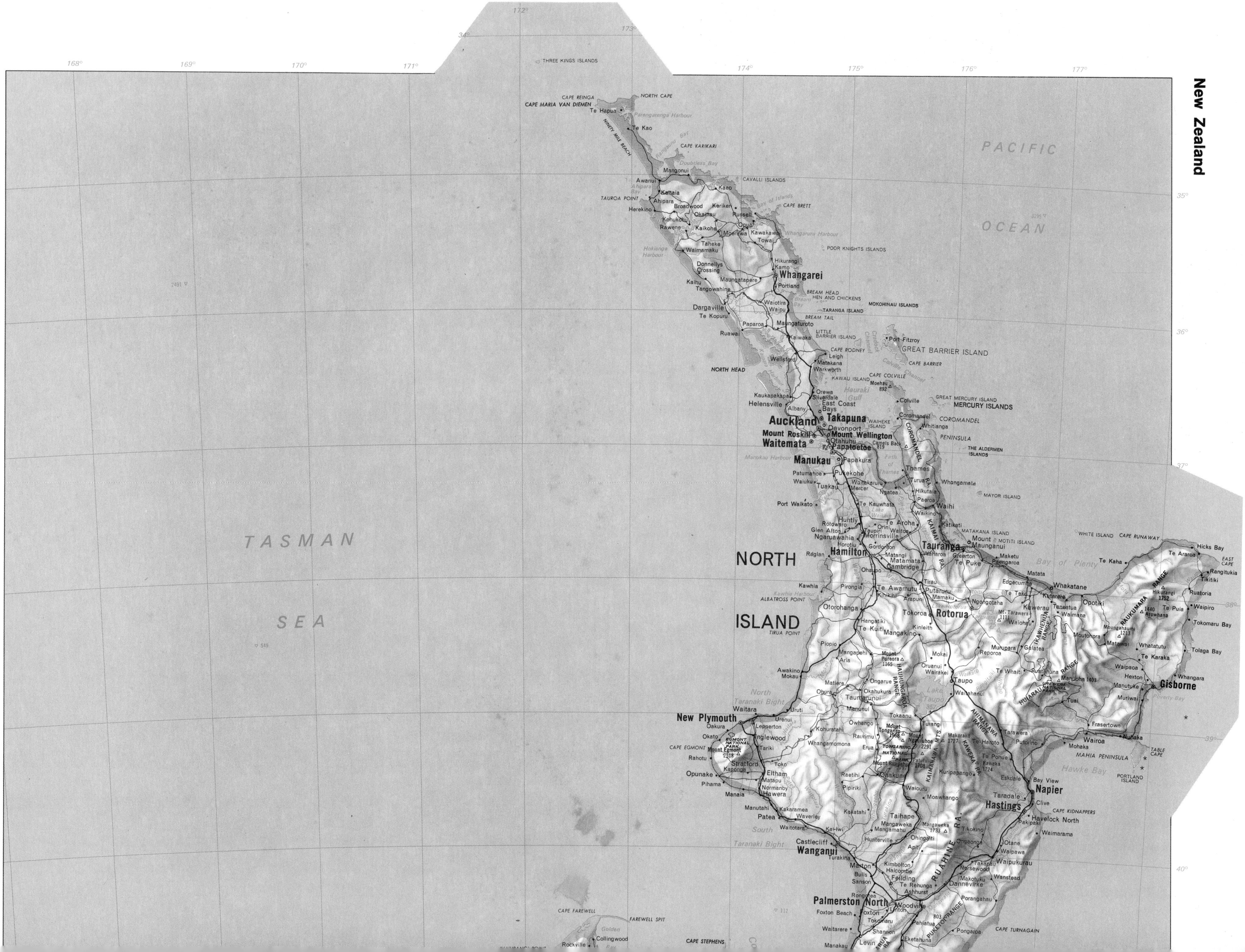
PACIFIC
OCEAN
TASMAN
SEA
NORTH
ISLAND
THREE KINGS ISLANDS
CAPE REINGA
CAPE MARIA VAN DIEMEN
NORTH CAPE
Te Hapua
Parengarenga Harbour
NINETY MILE BEACH
Te Kao
CAPE KARIKARI
Doubtless Bay
Mangonui
CAVALLI ISLANDS
Awanui
Kaitaia
TAUROA POINT
Ahipara
Herekino
Kaeo
Kerikeri
Russell
CAPE BRETT
Bay of Islands
Kohukohu
Rawene
Kaikohe
Moerewa
Kawakawa
Towai
Whangaruru Harbour
Taheke
Waimamaku
Hokianga Harbour
POOR KNIGHTS ISLANDS
Donnellys Crossing
Hikurangi
Kamo
Whangarei
Portland
Kaihu
Tangowahine
Maungatapere
BREAM HEAD
HEN AND CHICKENS
MOKOHINAU ISLANDS
Dargaville
Te Kopuru
Waiotira
Waipu
TARANGA ISLAND
BREAM TAIL
Paparoa
Maungaturoto
Ruawai
Kaiwaka
LITTLE BARRIER ISLAND
Port Fitzroy
GREAT BARRIER ISLAND
CAPE RODNEY
Leigh
Matakana
Warkworth
Wellsford
CAPE BARRIER
NORTH HEAD
KAWAU ISLAND
CAPE COLVILLE
Moehau 892
Hauraki Gulf
Orewa
Silverdale
East Coast Bays
Kaukapakapa
Helensville
Albany
Colville
GREAT MERCURY ISLAND
MERCURY ISLANDS
Auckland
Takapuna
WAIHEKE ISLAND
Coromandel
COROMANDEL PENINSULA
Whitianga
Devonport
Mount Roskill
Mount Wellington
Otahuhu
Waitemata
Papatoetoe
Camels Back 819
THE ALDERMEN ISLANDS
Manukau Harbour
Manukau
Papakura
Firth of Thames
Thames
Patumahoe
Pukekohe
Waiuku
Tuakau
Waitakaruru
Mercer
Ngatea
Turua
Hikutaia
Whangamata
MAYOR ISLAND
Port Waikato
Te Kauwhata
Paeroa
Waihi
Waikino
Huntly
Rotowaro
Glen Afton
Ngaruawahia
Te Aroha
Orini
Waitoa
Tauplri
Morrinsville
Katikati
MATAKANA ISLAND
Mount Maunganui
MOTITI ISLAND
WHITE ISLAND
CAPE RUNAWAY
Hicks Bay
Te Araroa
EAST CAPE
Rangitukia
Tikitiki
Raglan
Horotiu
Hamilton
Gordonton
Tauranga
Matangi
Matamata
Cambridge
Greerton
Te Puke
Maketu
Pongaroa
Bay of Plenty
Te Kaha
Ohaupo
Matata
Whakatane
Edgecumbe
Te Teko
Kutarere
Opotiki
RAUKUMARA RANGE
Hikurangi 1752
Ruatoria
Kawhia
Kawhia Harbour
ALBATROSS POINT
Pirongia
Te Awamutu
Kihikihi
Tirau
Putaruru
Arapuni
Mamaku
Ngongotaha
Kawerau
Taneatua
Waimana
Te Puia
Waipiro
Tokomaru Bay
Otorohanga
Tokoroa
Rotorua
Mt. Tarawera 1111
Waiohau
Toatoa
Hangatiki
Te Kuiti
TIRUA POINT
Kinleith
Mangakino
Motuhora
Moungahaumi 1213
Matawai
Whatatutu
Tolaga Bay
Piopio
Mangapehi
Aria
Mount Pureora 1165
HAUHUNGAROA RANGE
Mokai
Murupara
Reporoa
Galatea
IKAWHENUA RANGE
Te Karaka
Waipaoa
Hexton
Manutuke
Gisborne
Whangara
Poverty Bay
Awakino
Mokau
Oruanui
Wairakei
Te Whaiti
Manuoha 1403
Muriwai
North Taranaki Bight
Matiere
Ohura
Ongarue
Okahukura
Taumarunui
Taupo
Lake Taupo
Waitahanui
HUIARAU RANGE
Tuai
Waitara
Uruti
Manunui
Tokaanu
New Plymouth
Oakura
Lepperton
Urenui
Kohuratahi
Owhango
Mount Tongariro 1968
Turangi
Frasertown
Okato
EGMONT NATIONAL PARK
Mount Egmont 2518
Inglewood
Raurimu
TONGARIRO NATIONAL PARK
Makorako 1727
KAWEKA RA.
Te Haroto
Tarawera
Putorino
Wairoa
Nuhaka
Mohaka
TABLE CAPE
MAHIA PENINSULA
CAPE EGMONT
Rahotu
Stratford
Tariki
Whangamomona
Erua
Mount Ruapehu
KAIMANAWA MTS.
Te Pohue
Kaweka 1724
Toko
Kaponga
Opunake
Eltham
Matapu
Normanby
Hawera
Pihama
Manaia
Raetihi
Pipiriki
Ohakune
Waiouru
Kuripapango
Eskdale
Bay View
Napier
Hawke Bay
PORTLAND ISLAND
Moawhango
Taradale
Hastings
Clive
CAPE KIDNAPPERS
Manutahi
Kakaramea
Patea
Waverley
Kakatahi
Taihape
Mangaweka
Mangamahu
Pakipaki
Havelock North
Waimarama
South Taranaki Bight
Waitotara
Kai-Iwi
Hunterville
Ohingaiti
Apiti
RUAHINE RA.
Otane
Waipawa
Waipukurau
Castlecliff
Wanganui
Turakina
Marton
Kimbolton
Halcombe
Bulls
Sanson
Feilding
Te Rehunga
Ashhurst
Makotuku
Dannevirke
Wanstead
Palmerston North
Rongotea
Foxton Beach
Foxton
Woodville
Linton
Tokomaru
PUKETOI RANGE
Porangahau
Pahiatua
Shannon
Pongaroa
CAPE TURNAGAIN
Waitarere
Manakau
Levin
Eketahuna
CAPE FAREWELL
FAREWELL SPIT
Golden Bay
Collingwood
Rockville
CAPE STEPHENS
168°
169°
170°
171°
172°
173°
174°
175°
176°
177°
34°
35°
36°
37°
38°
39°
40°

Kilometers 0 50 100 150 Km.

Statute Miles 0 50 100 150 Mi.

Scale 1:3,000,000

One centimeter represents 30 kilometers.

One inch represents approximately 47 miles.

Lambert Conformal Conic Projection

Islands of the Pacific

a

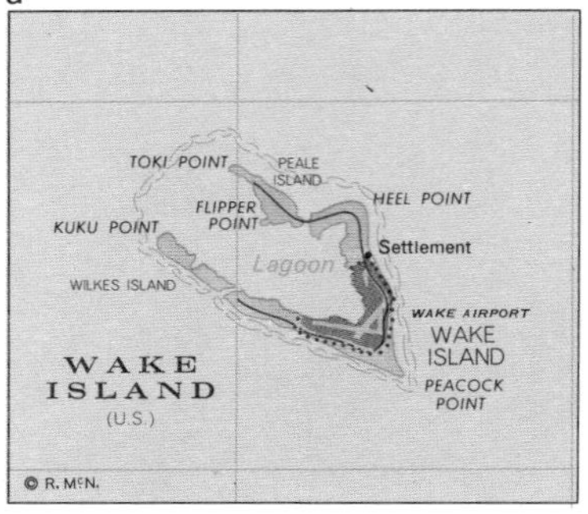

b

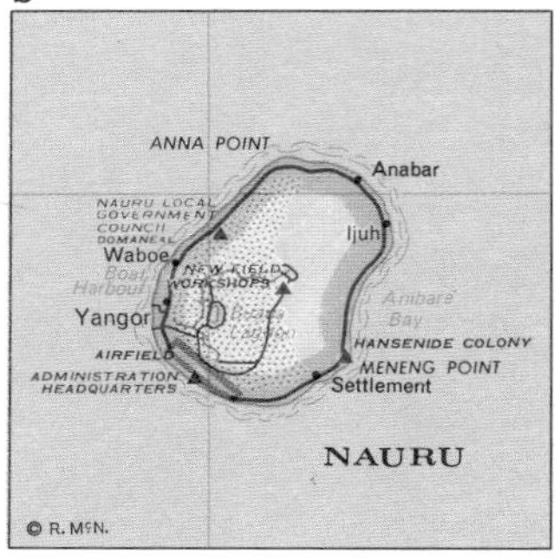

c

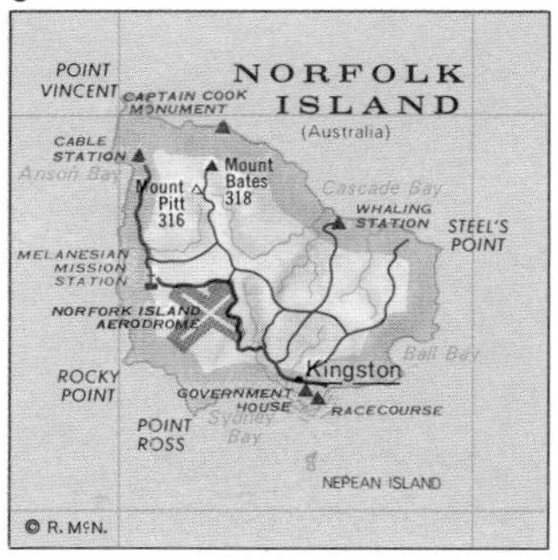

d

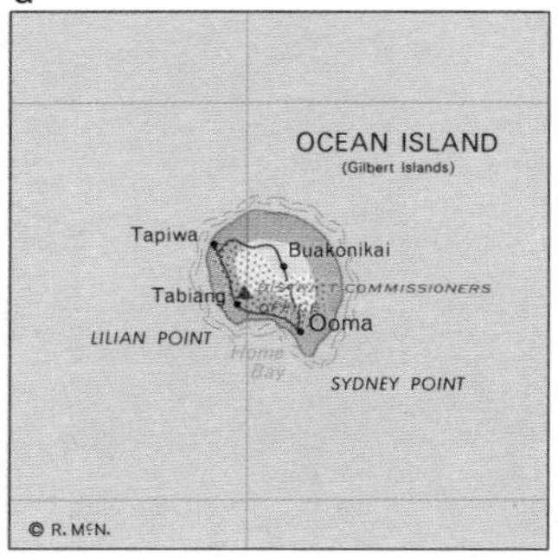

e

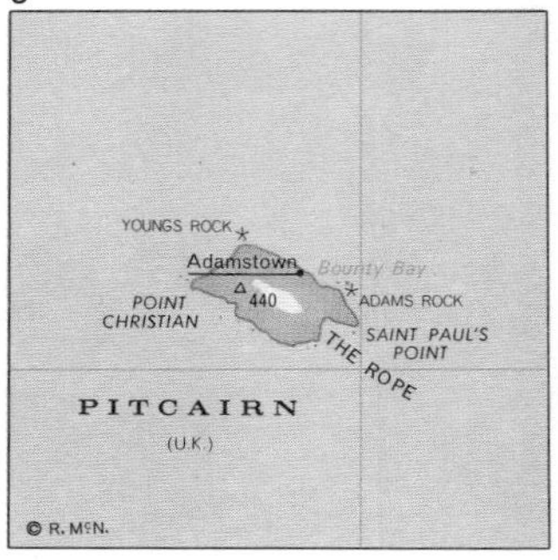

f

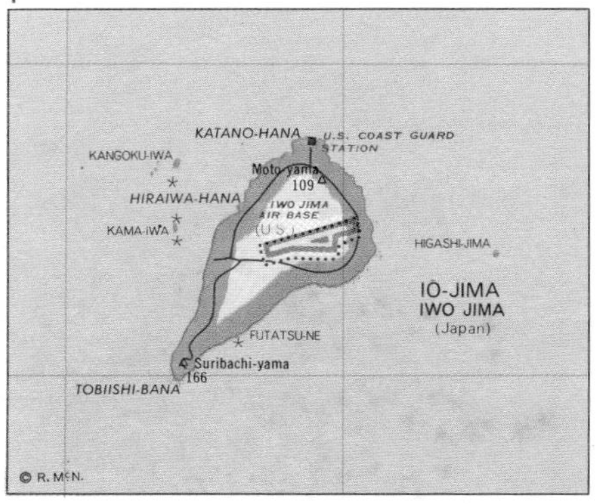

g

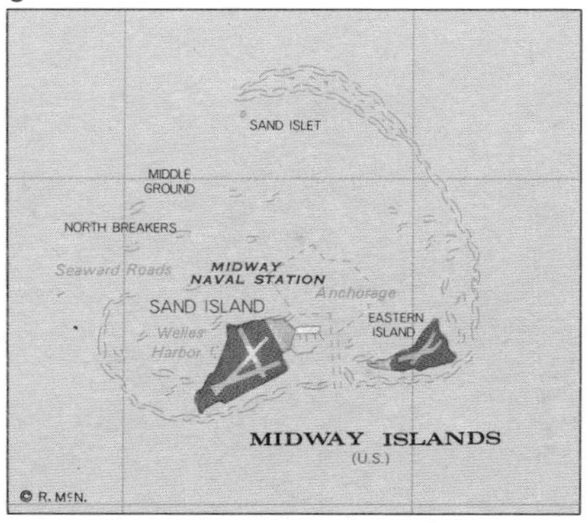

h

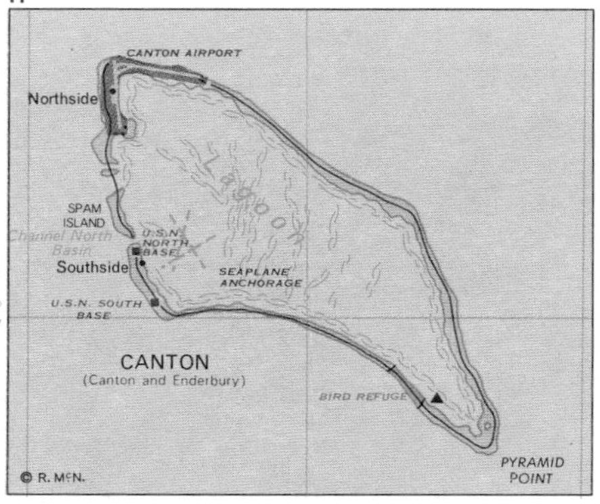

k

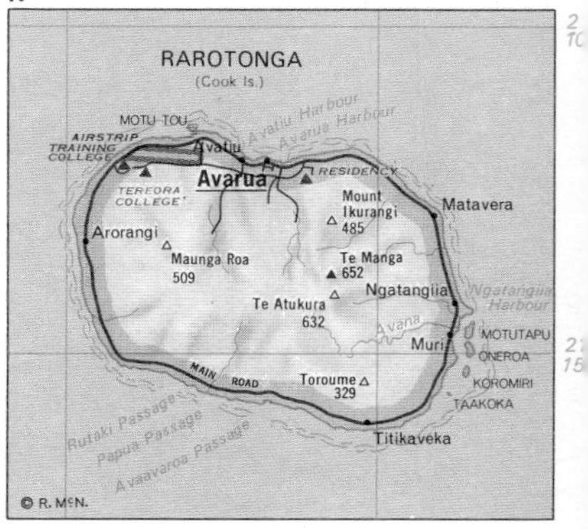

Kilometers 0 5 10 15 Km.
Statute Miles 0 5 10 15 Mi.

Scale 1:300,000
One centimeter represents 3 kilometers.
One inch represents approximately 4.7 miles.

m

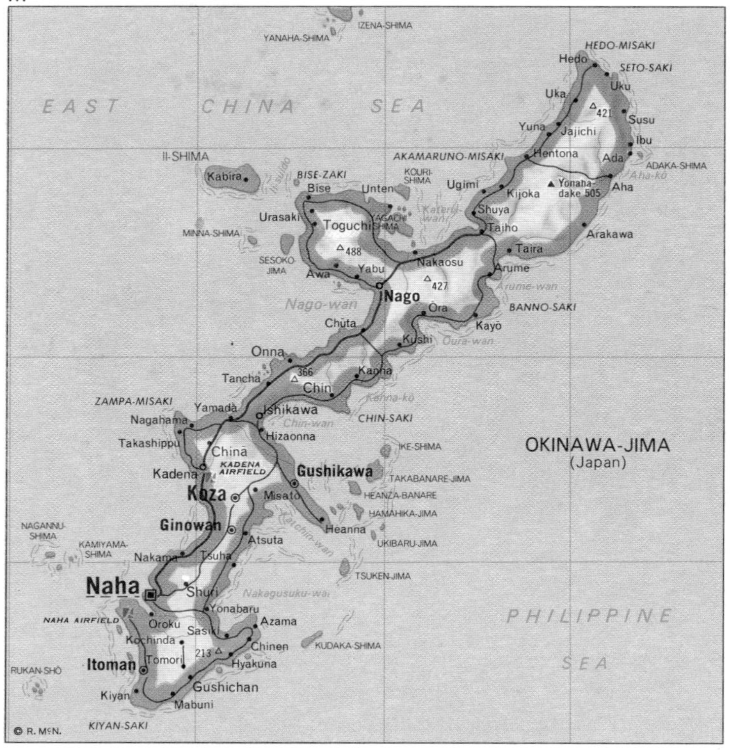

n

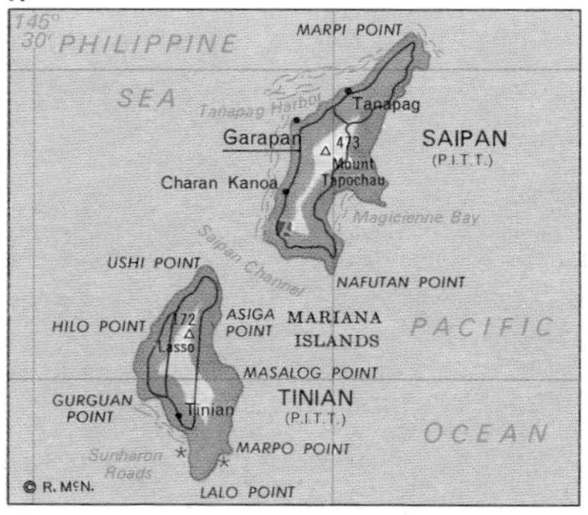

o

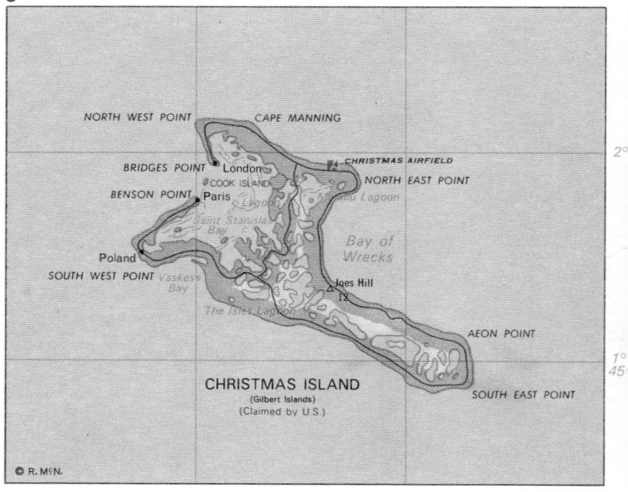

p

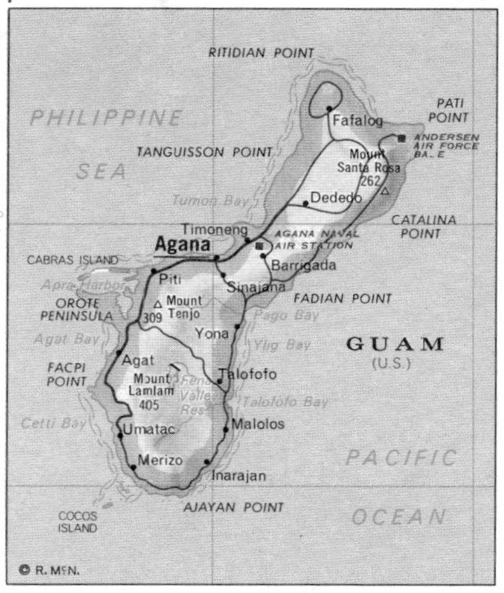

q

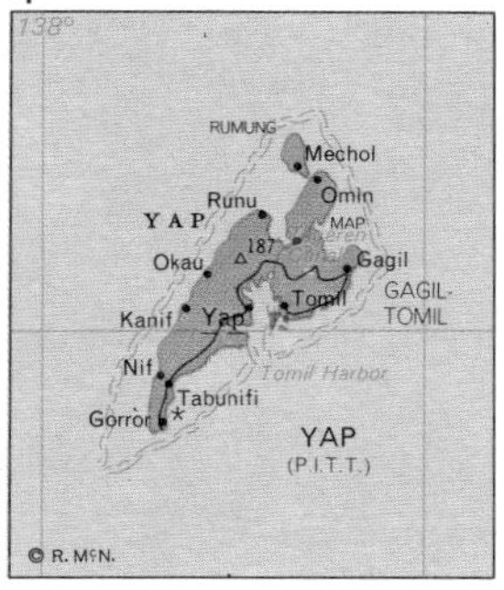

r

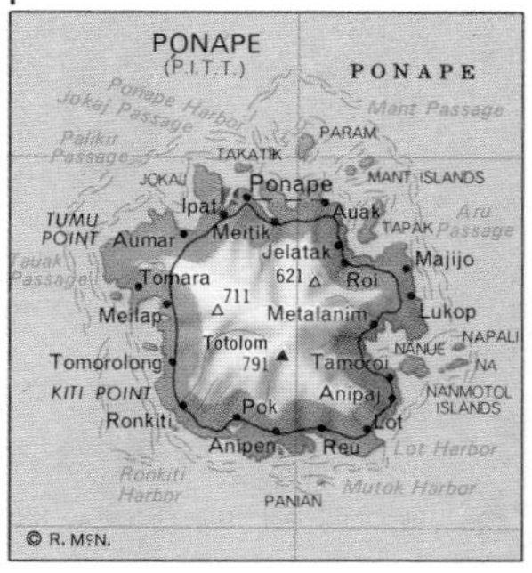

s

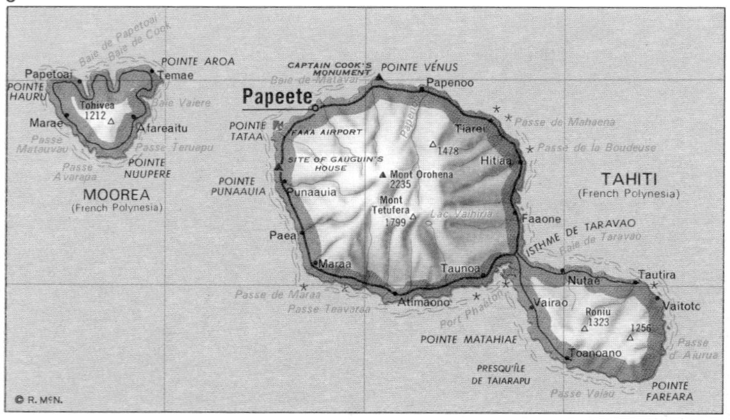

t

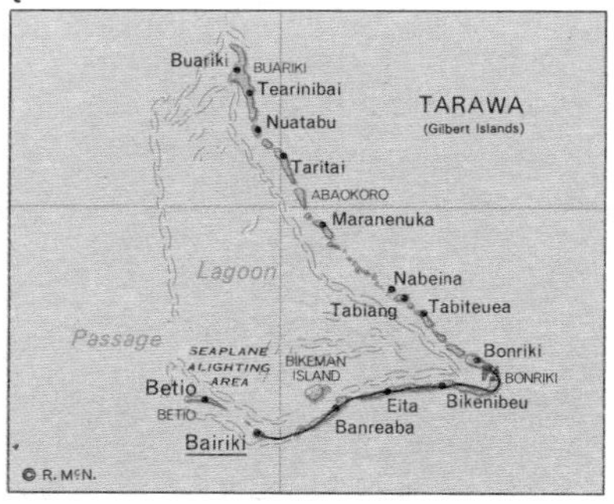

u

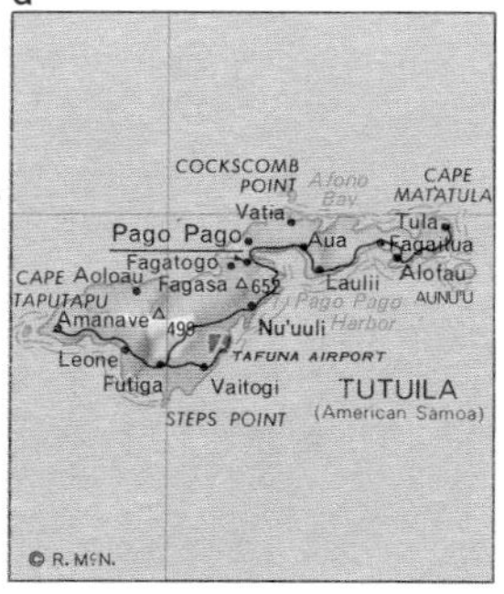

v

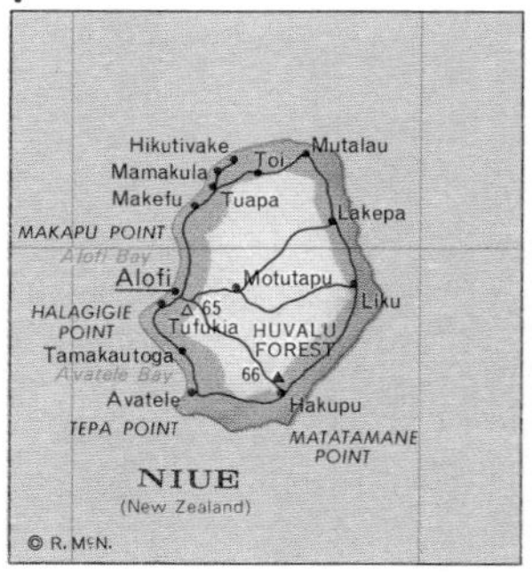

w

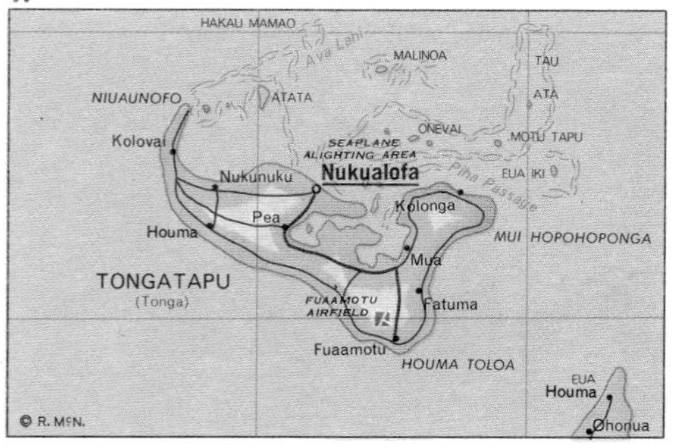

x

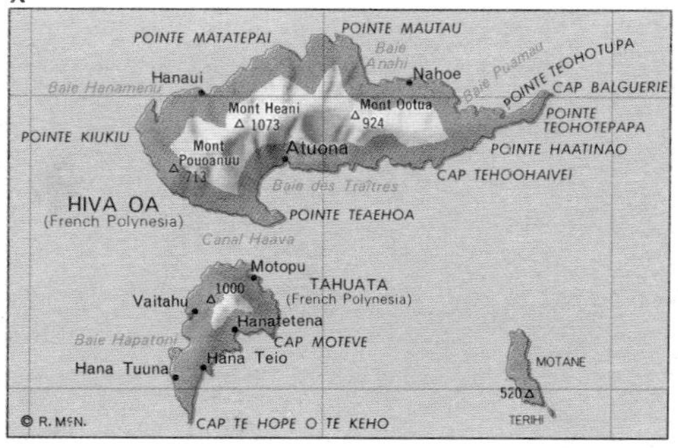

y

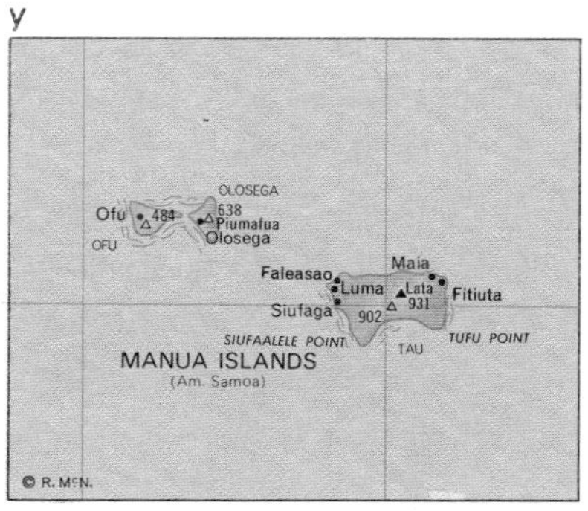

z

Kilometers 0 10 20 30 40 50 Km.
Statute Miles 0 10 20 30 40 50 Mi.

Scale 1:1,000,000
One centimeter represents 10 kilometers.
One inch represents approximately 16 miles.
Transverse Mercator Projection

a

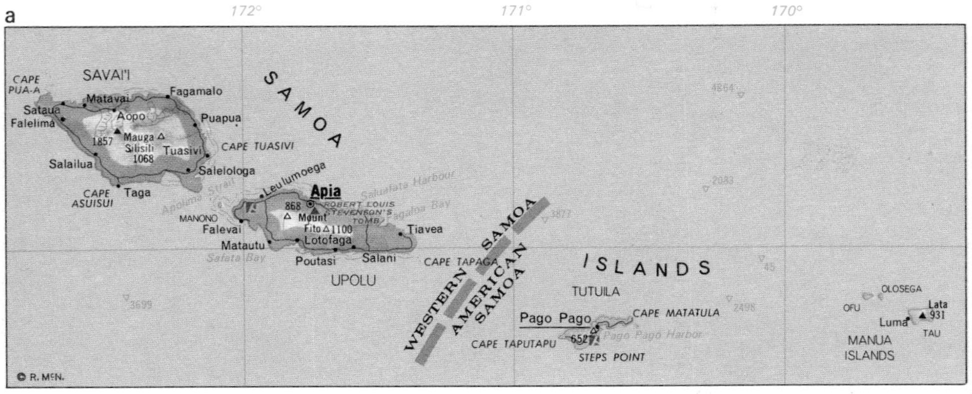

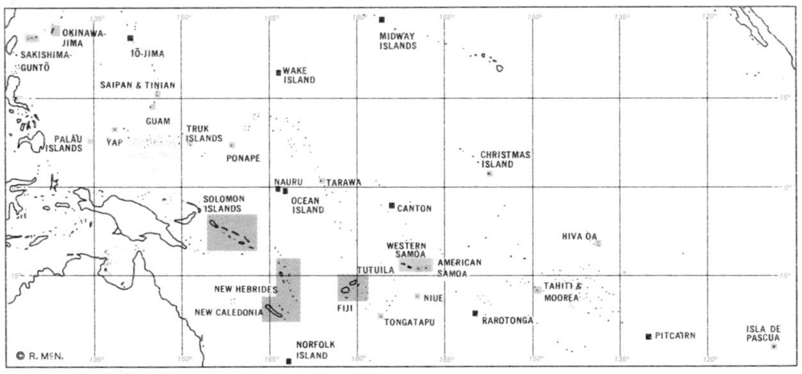

b

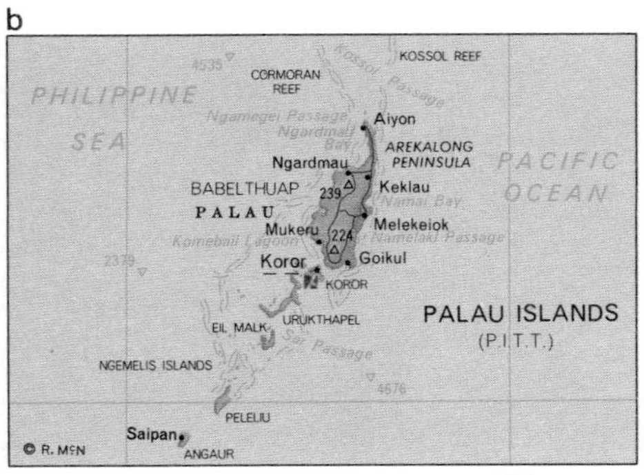

c

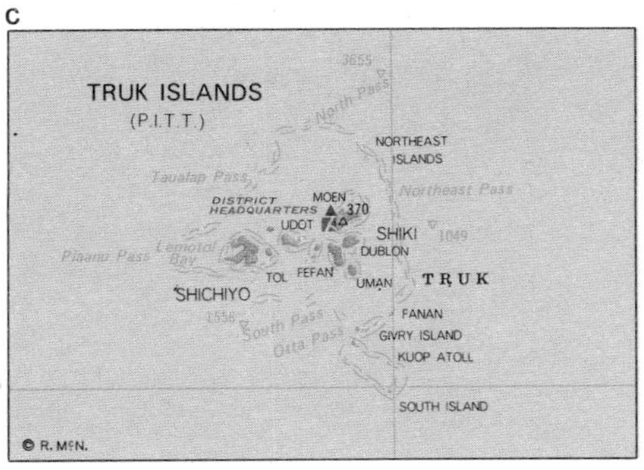

d

Kilometers 0 50 100 150 Km.
Statute Miles 0 50 100 150 Mi.

Scale 1:3,000,000

One centimeter represents 30 kilometers.
One inch represents approximately 47 miles.
Lambert Conformal Conic Projection

e

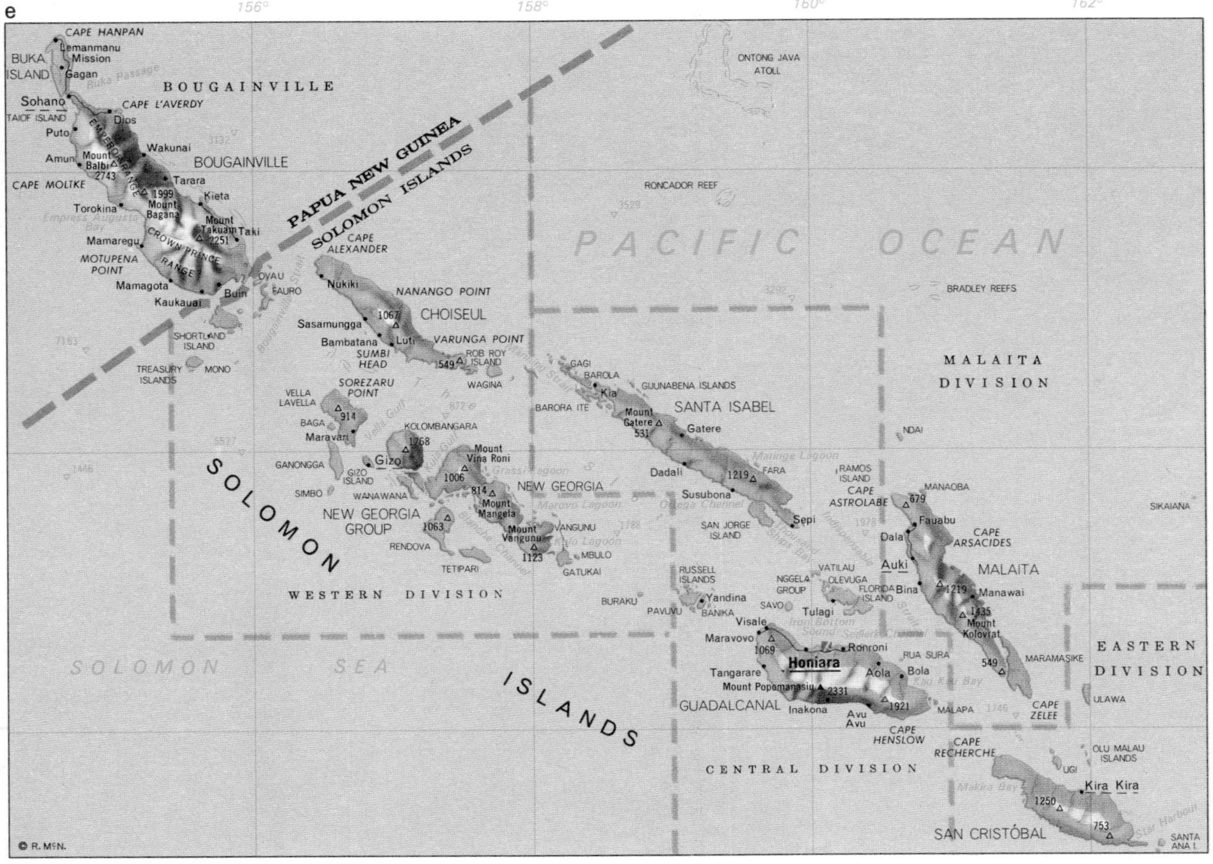

f

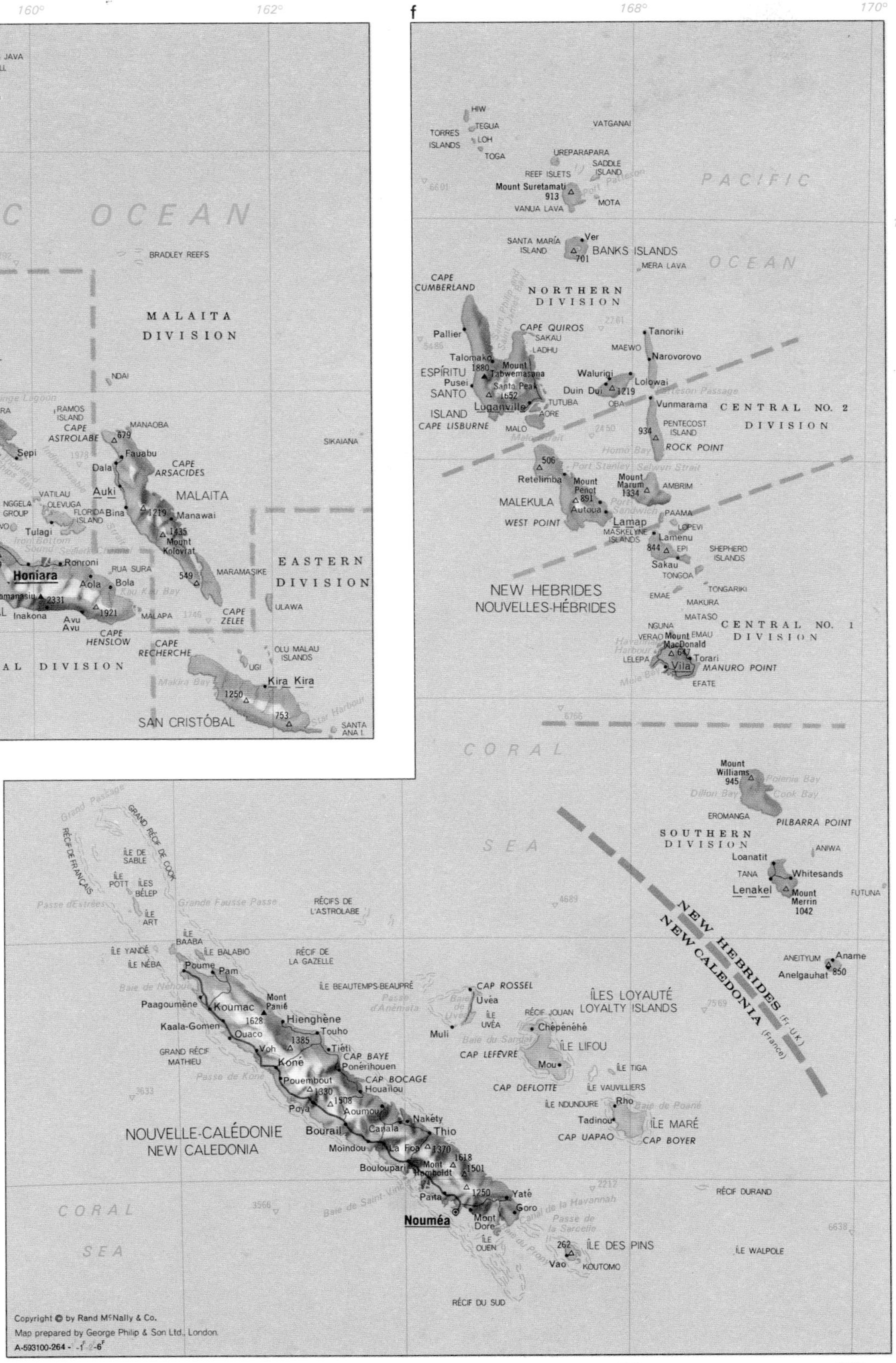

g

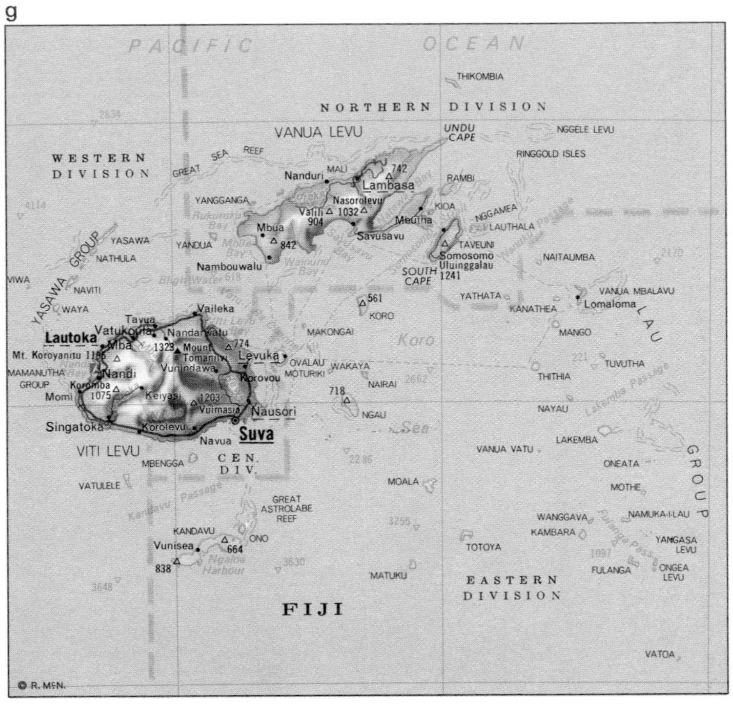

Kilometers 0 100 200 300 Km.
Statute Miles 0 100 200 300 Mi.

Scale 1:6,000,000

One centimeter represents 60 kilometers.
One inch represents approximately 95 miles.
Lambert Conformal Conic Projection

a

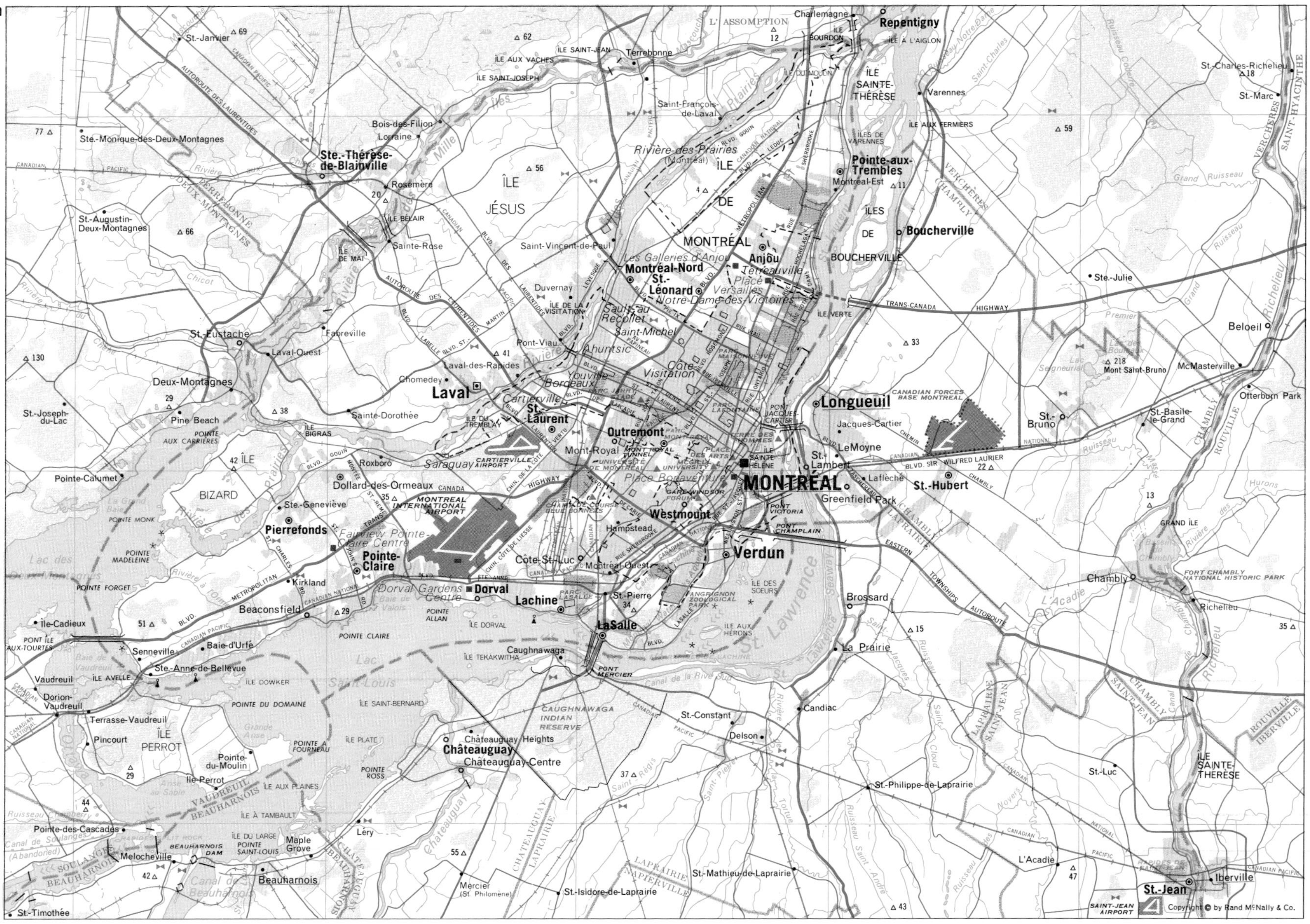

b

Scale 1:300,000

One centimeter represents 3 kilometers.
One inch represents approximately 4.7 miles.

Kilometers 0 5 10 15 Km.
Statute Miles 0 5 10 15 Mi.

Scale 1:300,000

One centimeter represents 3 kilometers.
One inch represents approximately 4.7 miles.

Kilometers 0 5 10 15 Km.
Statute Miles 0 5 10 15 Mi.

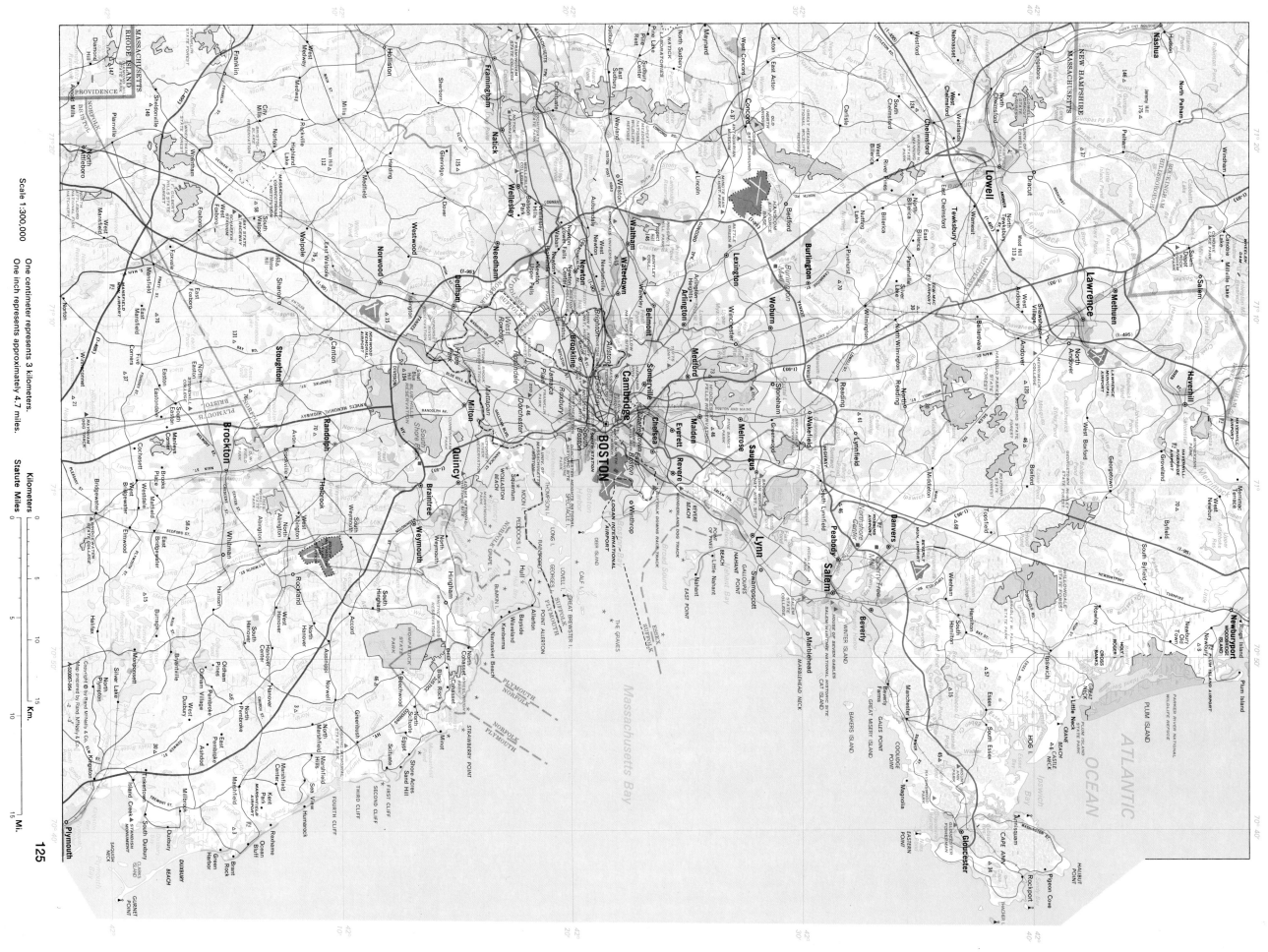

74°40'
74°30'
74°20'
74°10'
74°
41° 10'
41°
40° 50'
40° 40'
40° 30'
40° 20'
NEW YORK
Jersey City
Newark
Elizabeth
Paterson
Passaic
Clifton
Hackensack
Paramus
Hoboken
Bayonne
Kearny
Irvington
Orange
East Orange
West Orange
Bloomfield
Montclair
Nutley
Belleville
Union City
West New York
North Bergen
Fort Lee
Teaneck
Englewood
Bergenfield
Ridgewood
Fair Lawn
Garfield
Lodi
Wayne
Morristown
Summit
Millburn
Livingston
Union
Westfield
Cranford
Linden
Rahway
Plainfield
Piscataway
Edison
New Brunswick
East Brunswick
Sayreville
Perth Amboy
Somerville
Princeton
Princeton Township
Red Bank
STATEN ISLAND
Yonkers
New City
Suffern
Ramapo
Dover
Brooklyn
Manhattan
Queens
Bronx
Long Island City
Jamaica
Flatbush
Coney Island
Raritan Bay
Lower New York Bay
Sandy Hook
Sandy Hook Bay
GATEWAY NATIONAL RECREATION AREA
GREAT SWAMP NATIONAL WILDLIFE REFUGE
WATCHUNG MOUNTAIN
RAMAPO MTS.
HAMBURG MTS.
KANOUSE MOUNTAIN
COPPERAS MOUNTAIN
GERMANY FLATS
SOURLAND MTN.
NEW YORK
NEW JERSEY
SUSSEX
MORRIS
PASSAIC
BERGEN
ESSEX
HUDSON
UNION
MIDDLESEX
MONMOUTH
SOMERSET
MERCER
ROCKLAND
ORANGE
WESTCHESTER
RICHMOND
KINGS
QUEENS
Lake Hopatcong
Newark International Airport

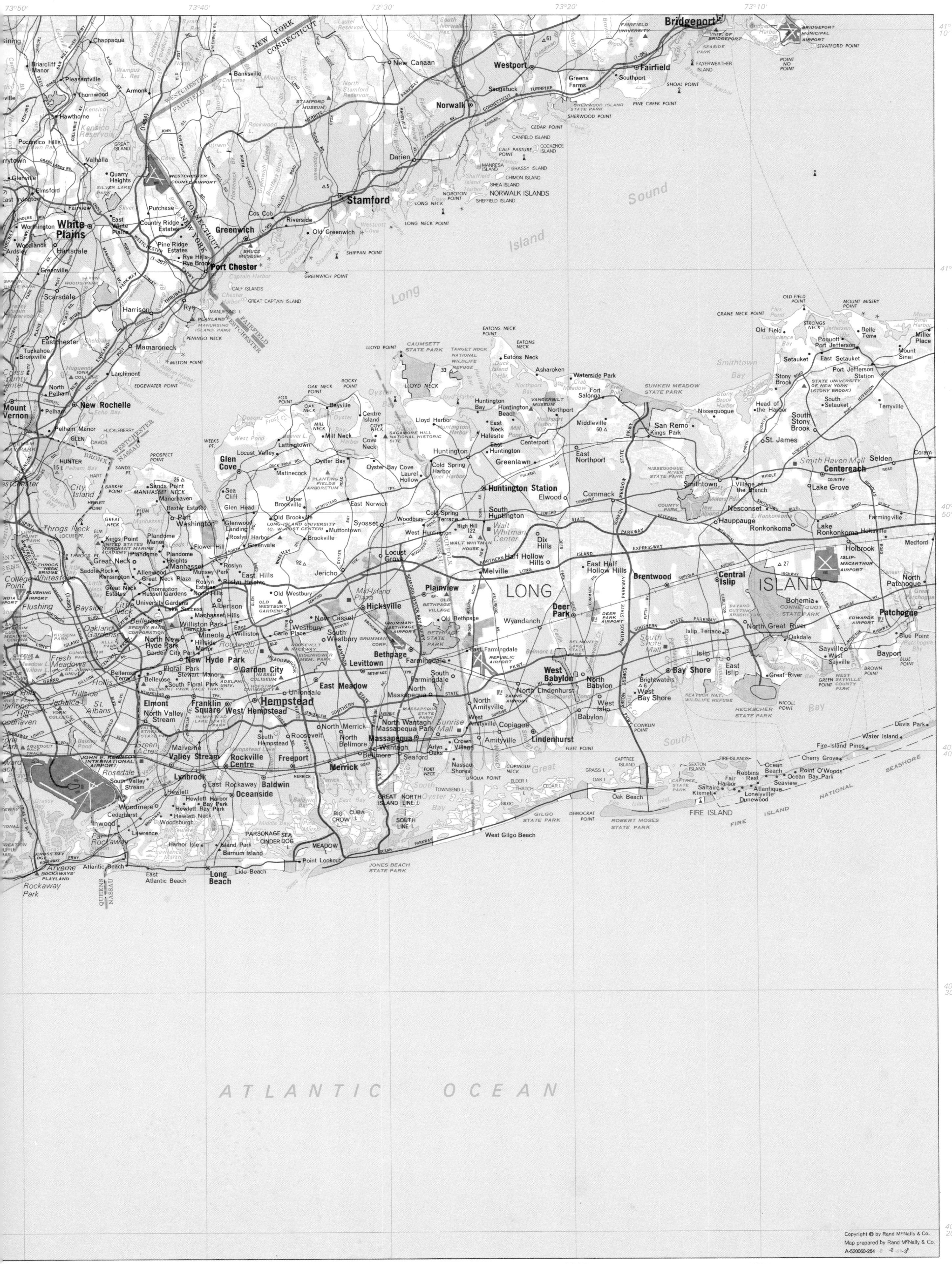

Scale 1:300,000

One centimeter represents 3 kilometers.
One inch represents approximately 4.7 miles.

Kilometers 0 5 10 15 Km.
Statute Miles 0 5 10 15 Mi.

Philadelphia

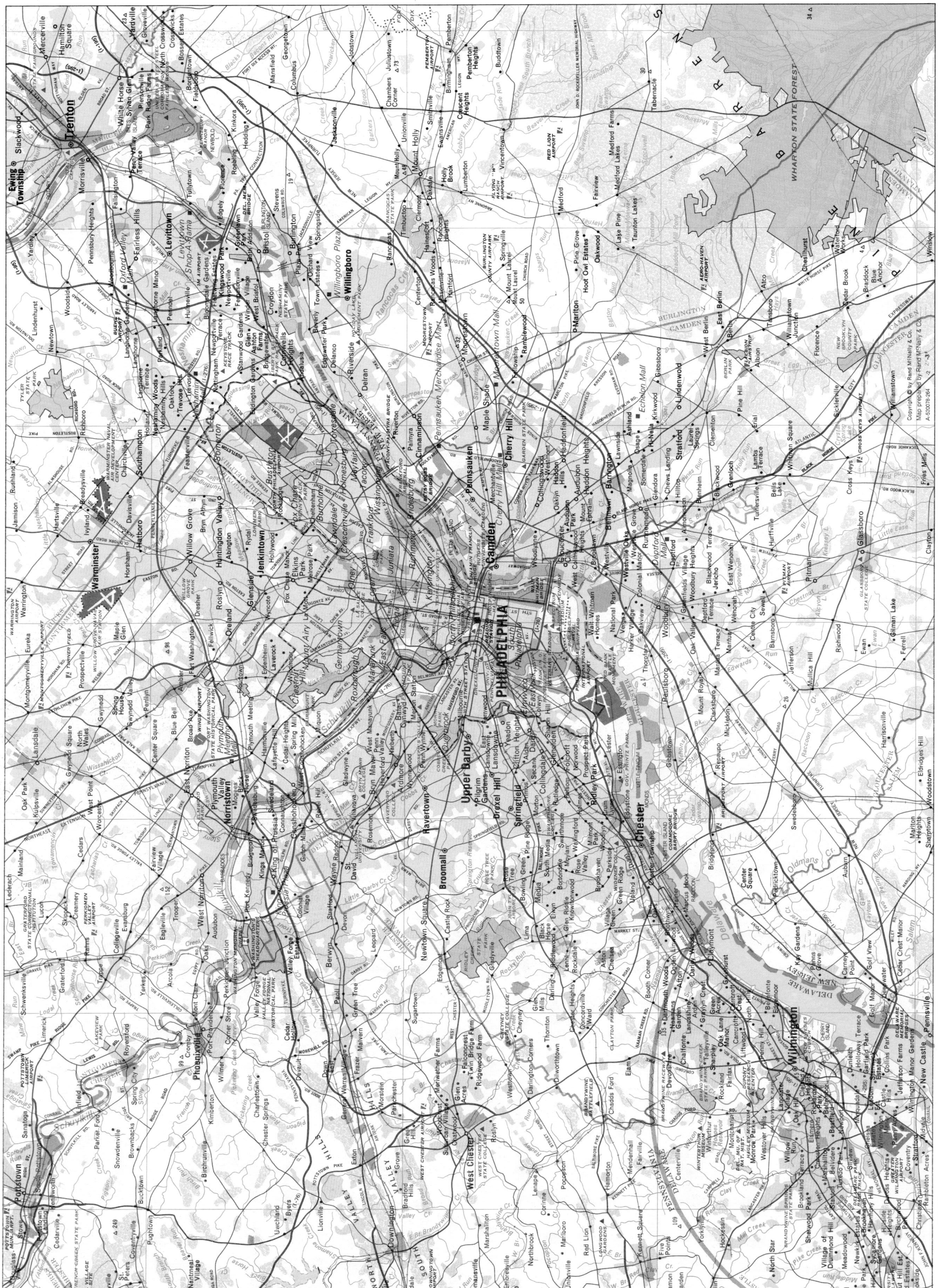

Scale 1:300,000

One centimeter represents 3 kilometers.
One inch represents approximately 4.7 miles.

Kilometers 0 5 10 15 Km.
Statute Miles 0 5 10 15 Mi.

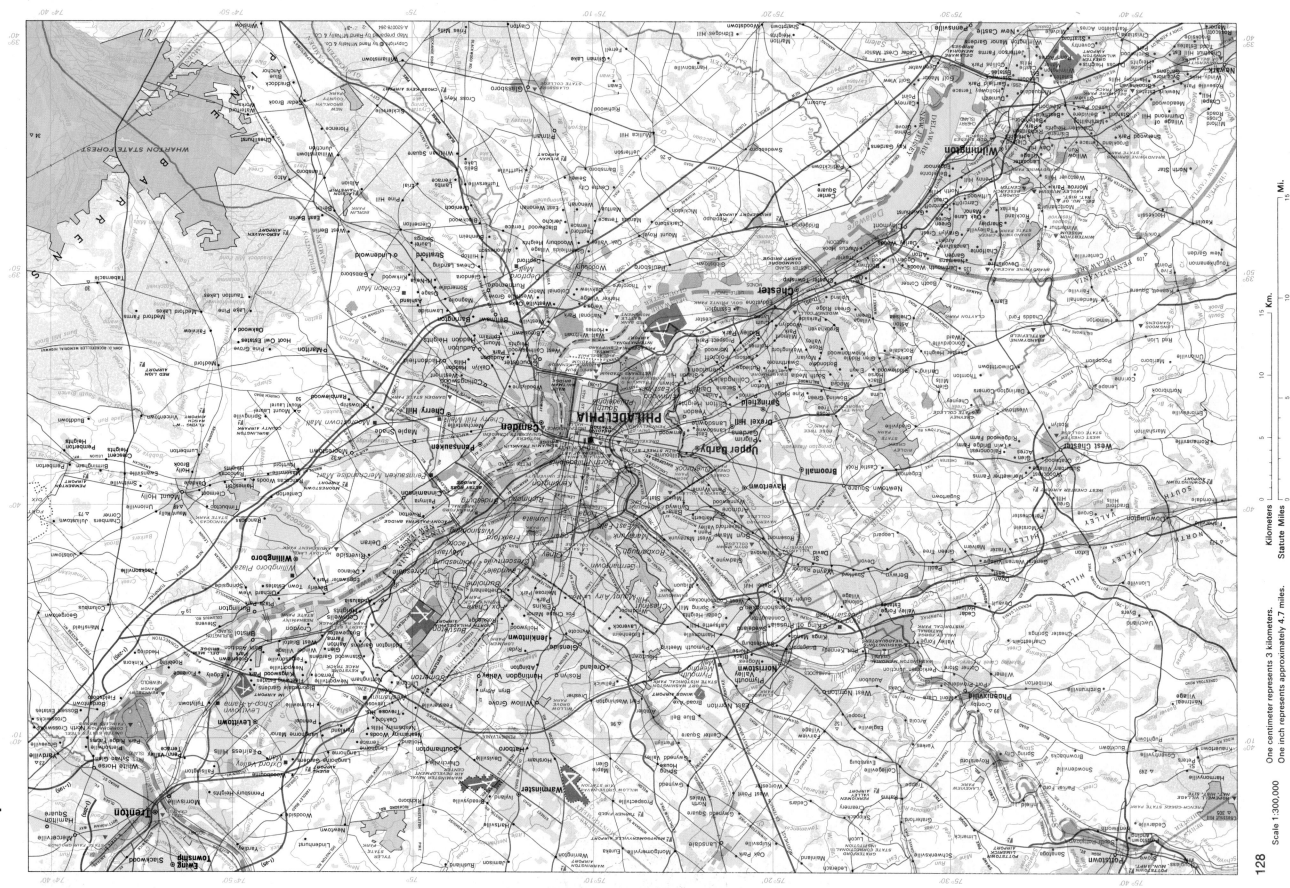

Buffalo—Niagara Falls · Baltimore · Washington

Scale 1:300,000

One centimeter represents 3 kilometers.
One inch represents approximately 4.7 miles.

Kilometers
Statute Miles

a

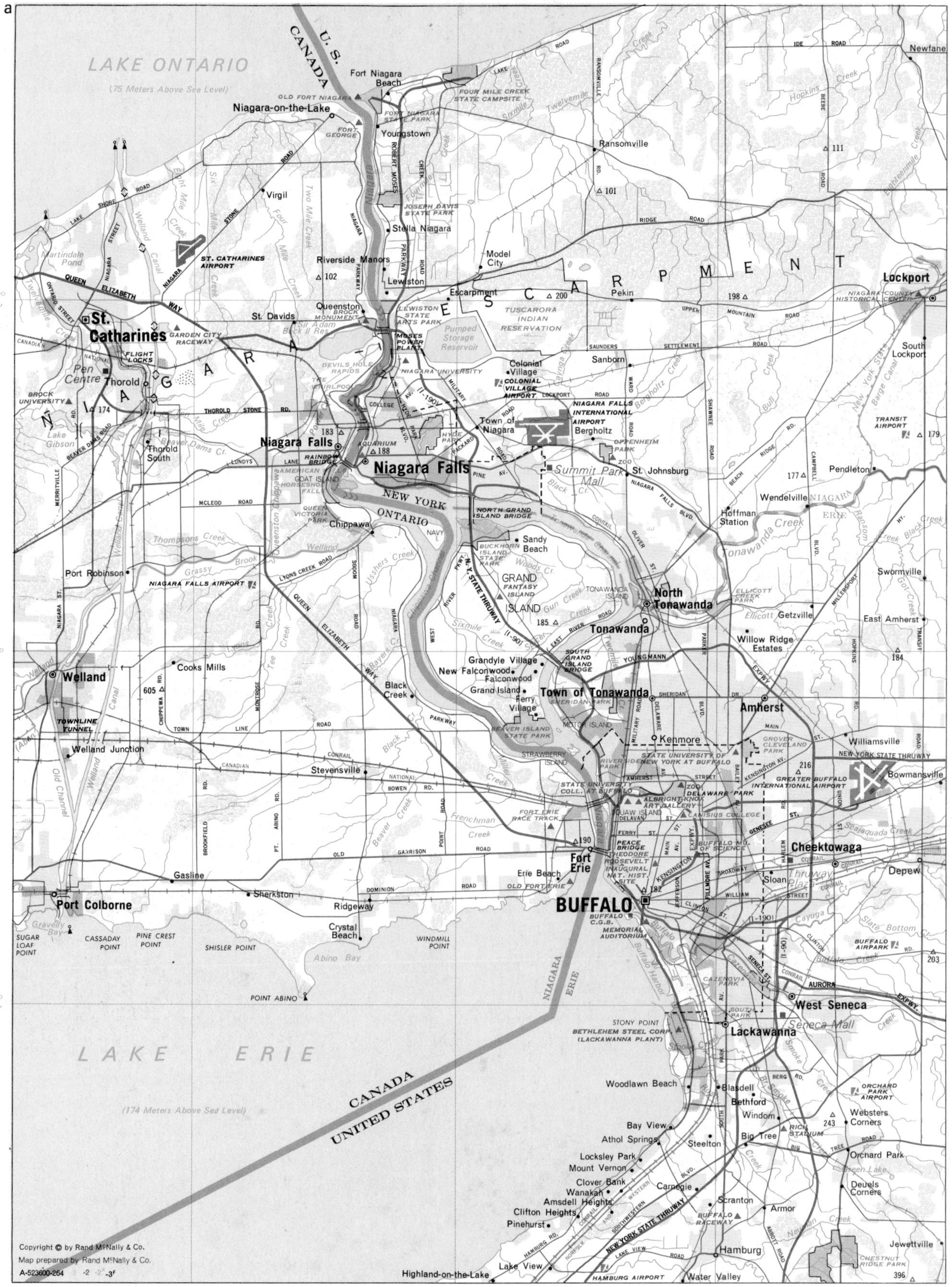

b

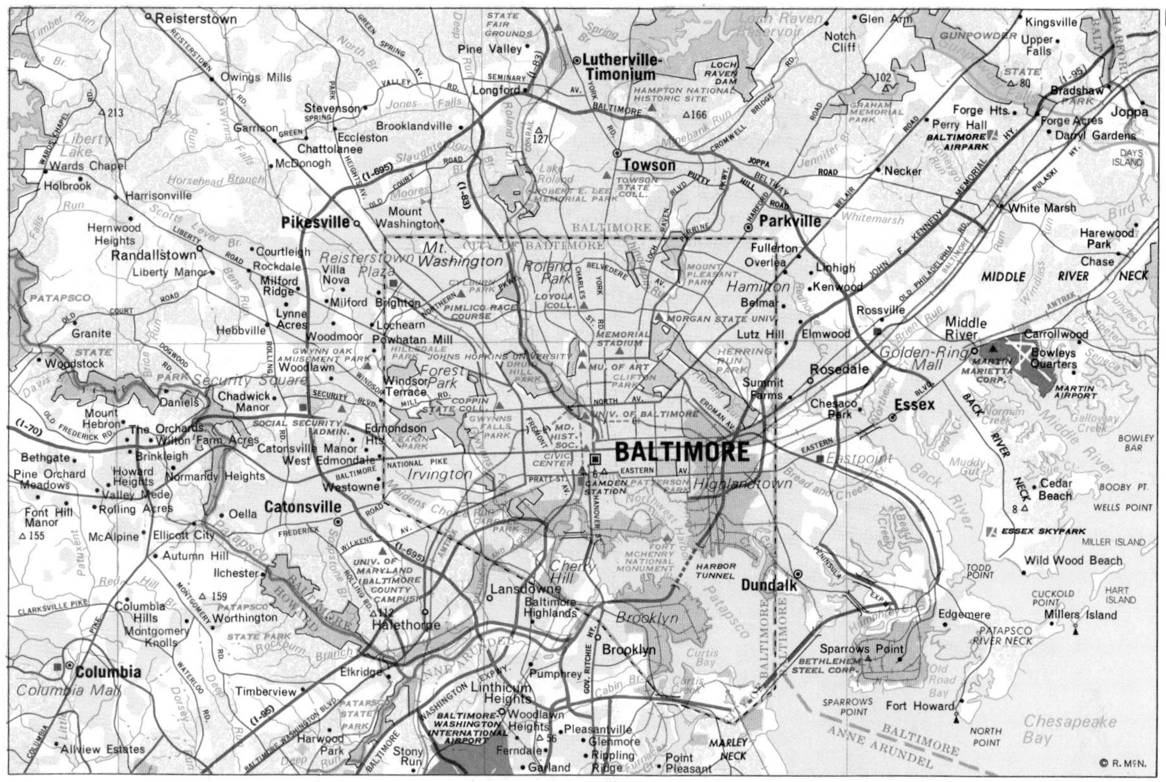

c

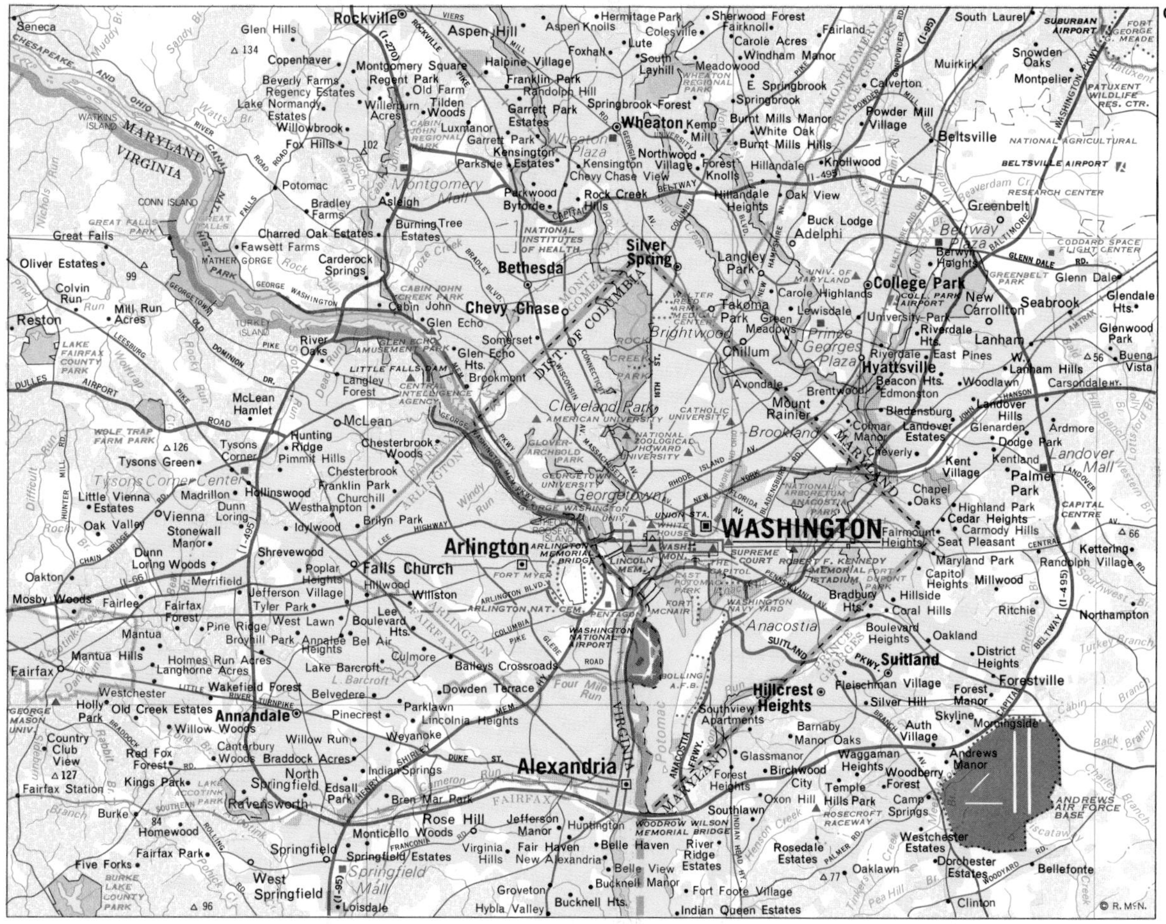

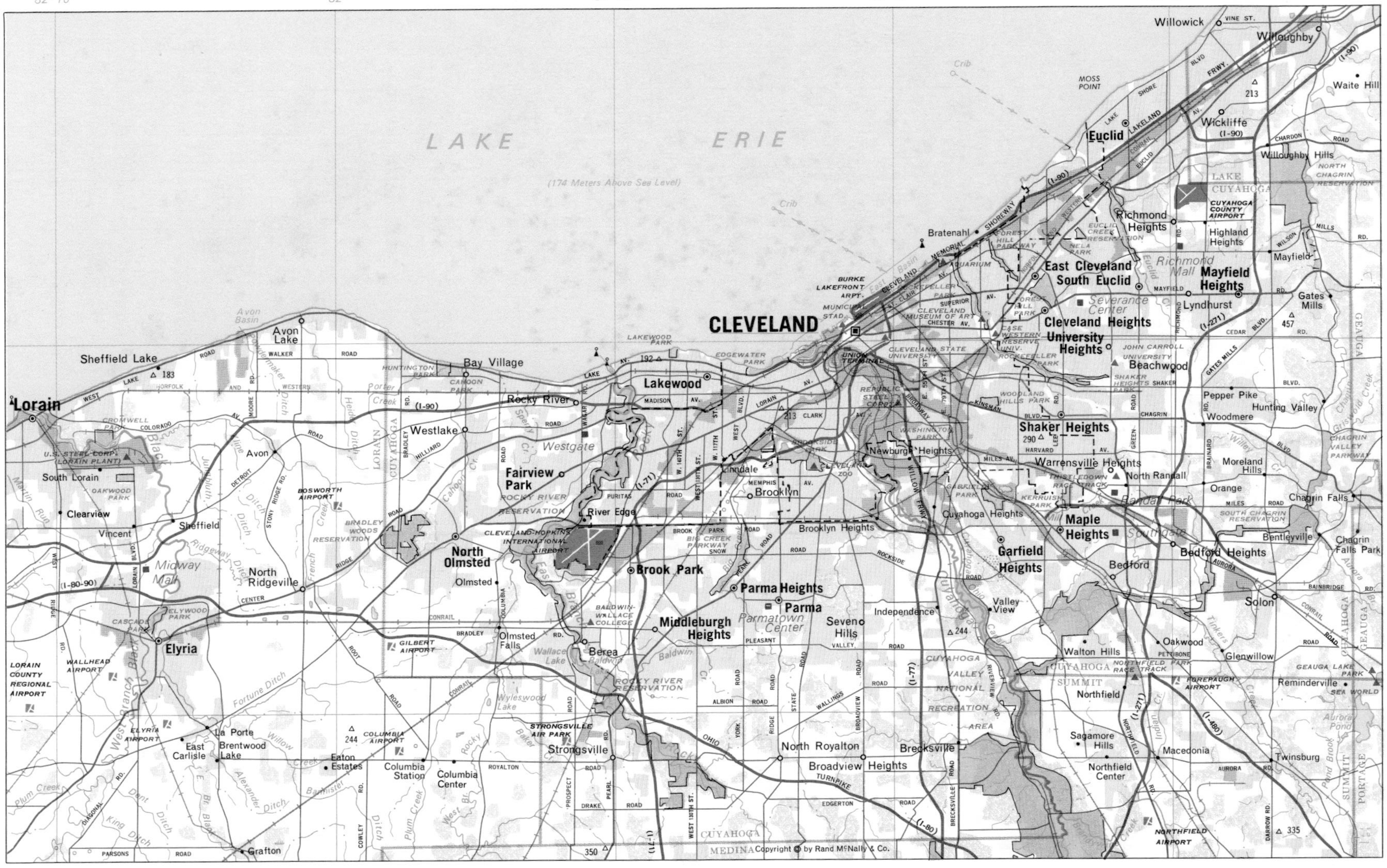

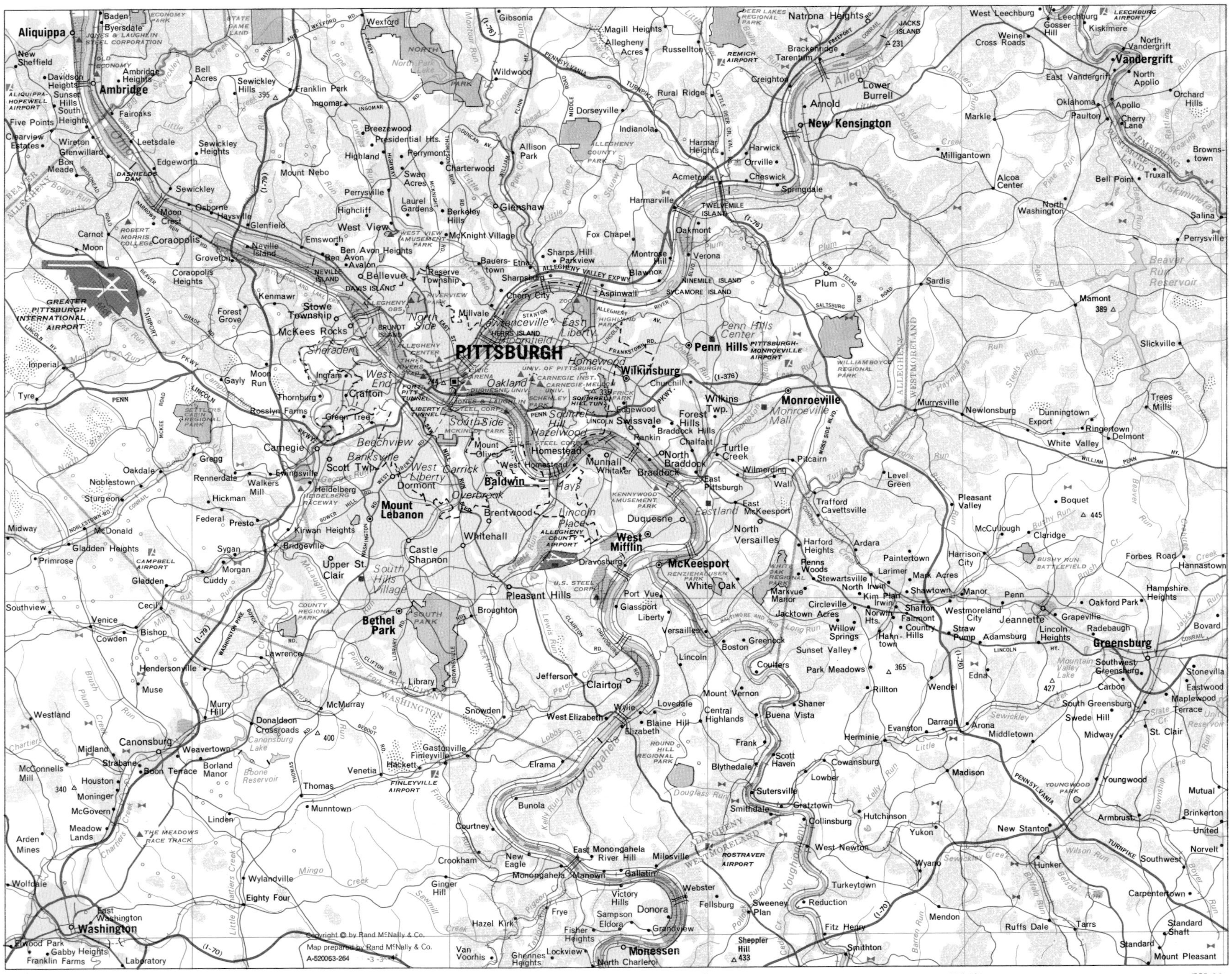

Scale 1:300,000

One centimeter represents 3 kilometers.
One inch represents approximately 4.7 miles.

Kilometers 0 5 10 15 Km.
Statute Miles 0 5 10 15 Mi.

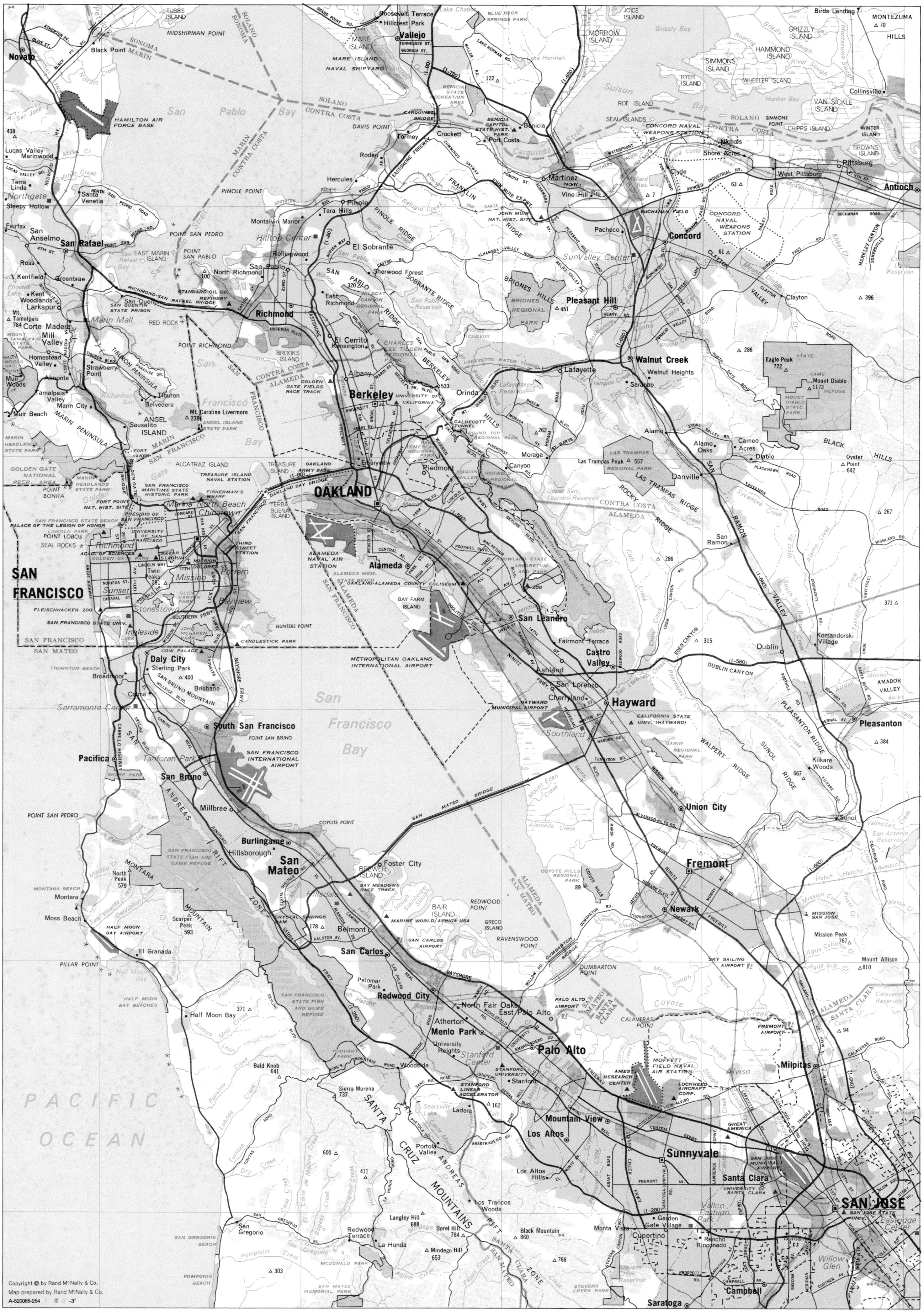

Scale 1:300,000

One centimeter represents 3 kilometers.
One inch represents approximately 4.7 miles.

Kilometers 0 5 10 15 Km.
Statute Miles 0 5 10 15 Mi.

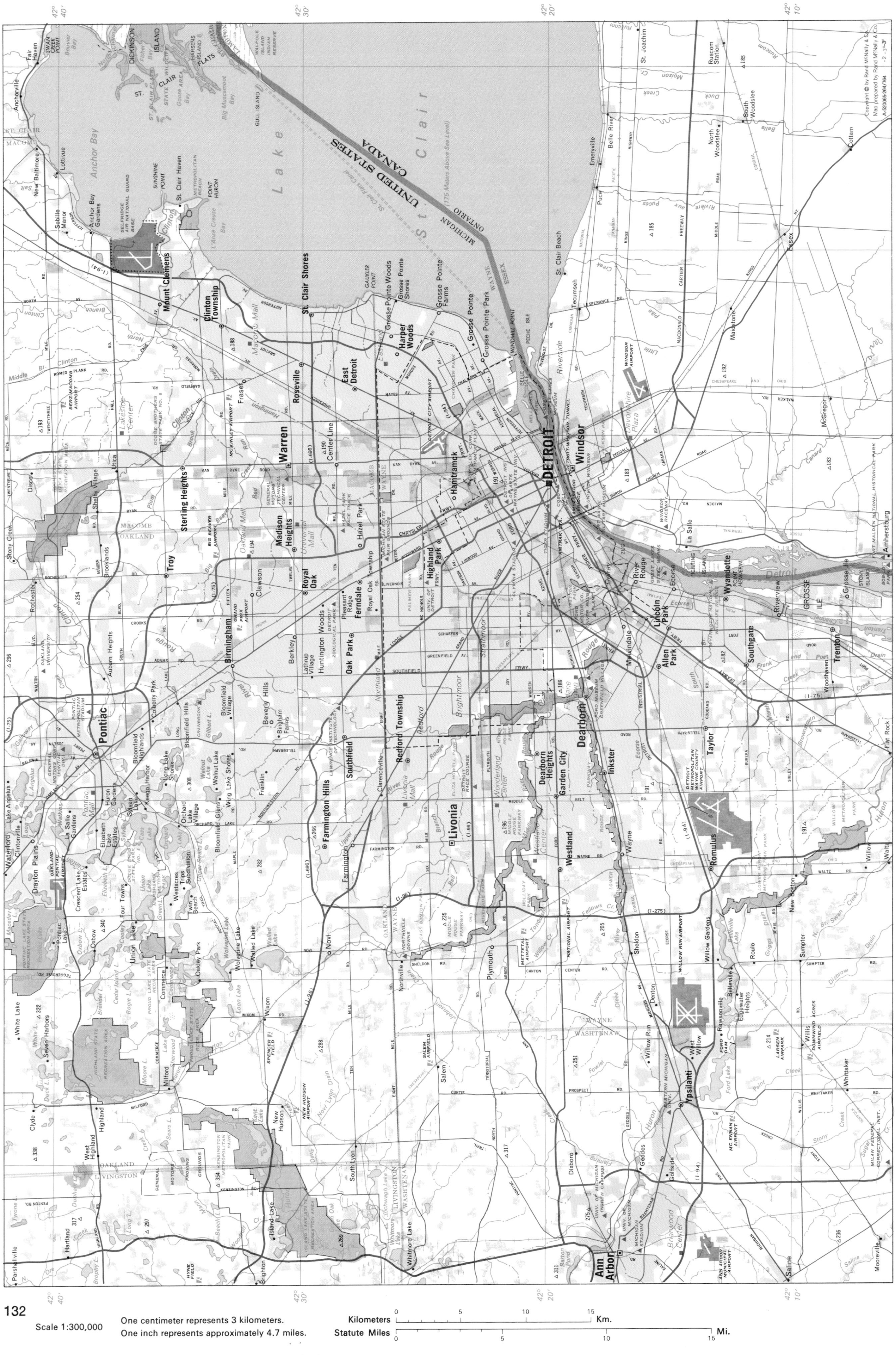

Scale 1:300,000

One centimeter represents 3 kilometers.
One inch represents approximately 4.7 miles.

Kilometers 0 5 10 15 Km.
Statute Miles 0 5 10 15 Mi.

Scale 1:300,000

One centimeter represents 3 kilometers.
One inch represents approximately 4.7 miles.

Kilometers 0 5 10 15 Km.
Statute Miles 0 5 10 15 Mi.

Scale 1:300,000

One centimeter represents 3 kilometers.
One inch represents approximately 4.7 miles.

Kilometers 0 5 10 15 Km.
Statute Miles 0 5 10 15 Mi.

a

b

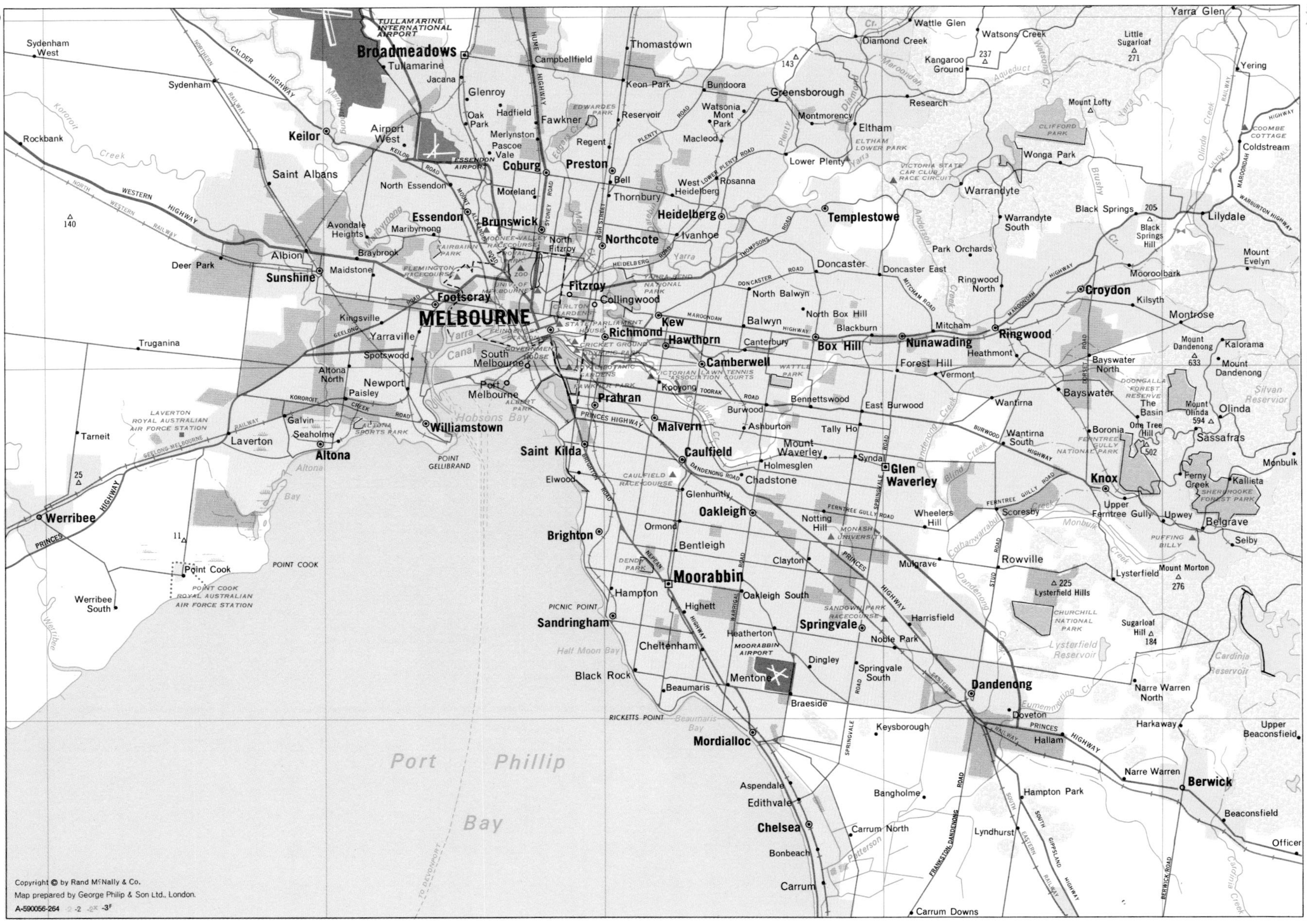

Scale 1:300,000

One centimeter represents 3 kilometers.
One inch represents approximately 4.7 miles.

Kilometers 0 5 10 15 Km.
Statute Miles 0 5 10 15 Mi.

a

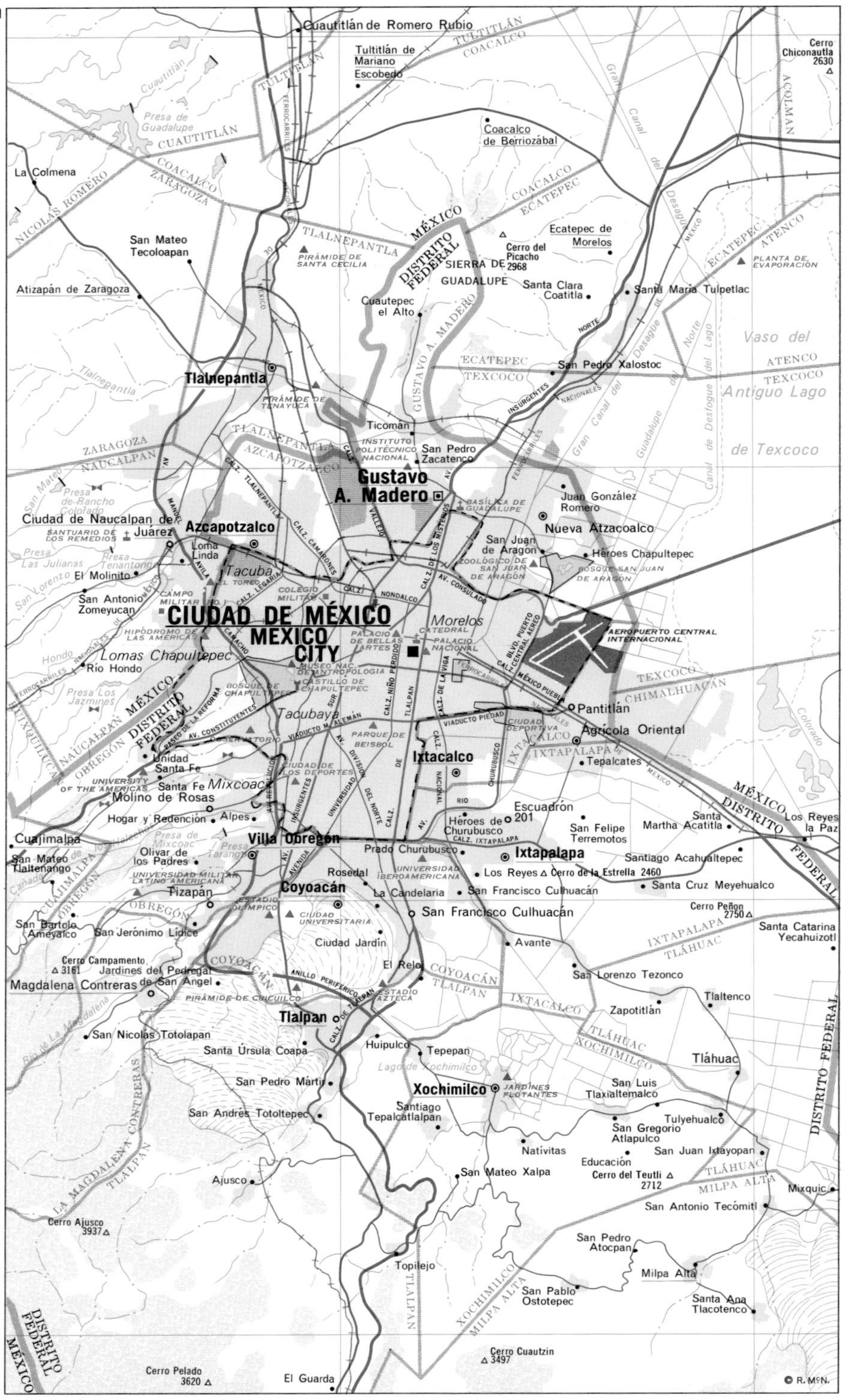

b

c

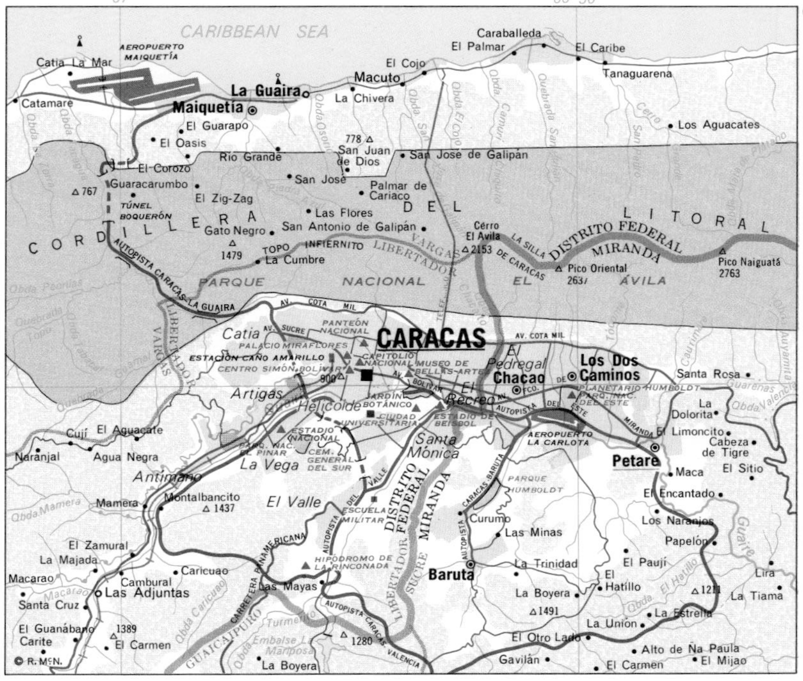

d

e

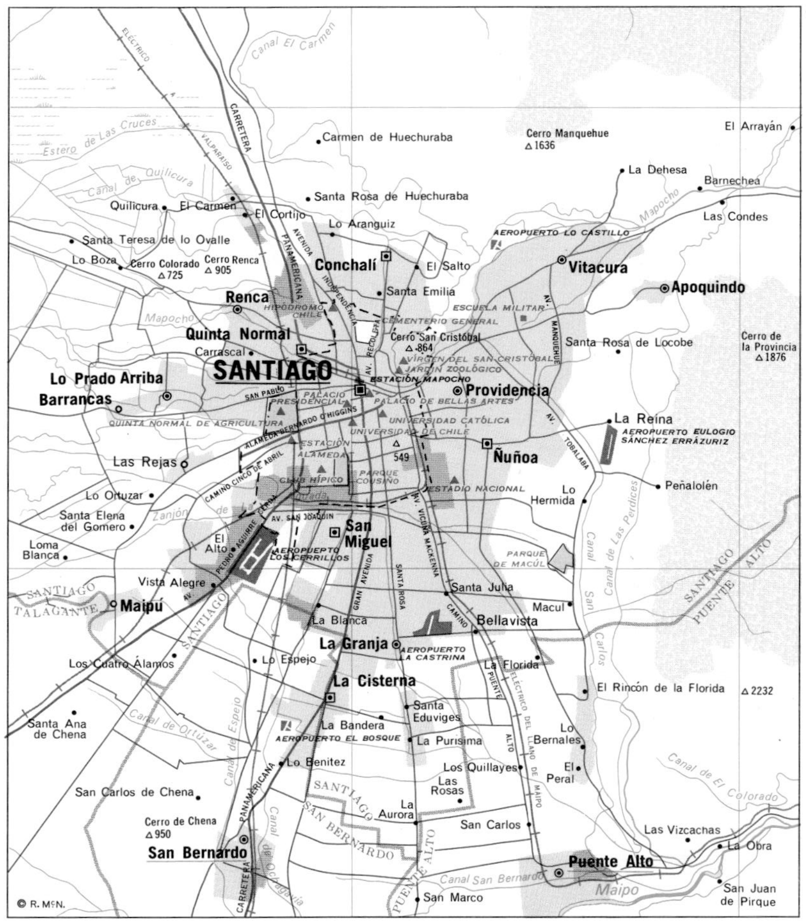

Scale 1:300,000

One centimeter represents 3 kilometers.
One inch represents approximately 4.7 miles.

Kilometers 0 5 10 15 Km.
Statute Miles 0 5 10 15 Mi.

a

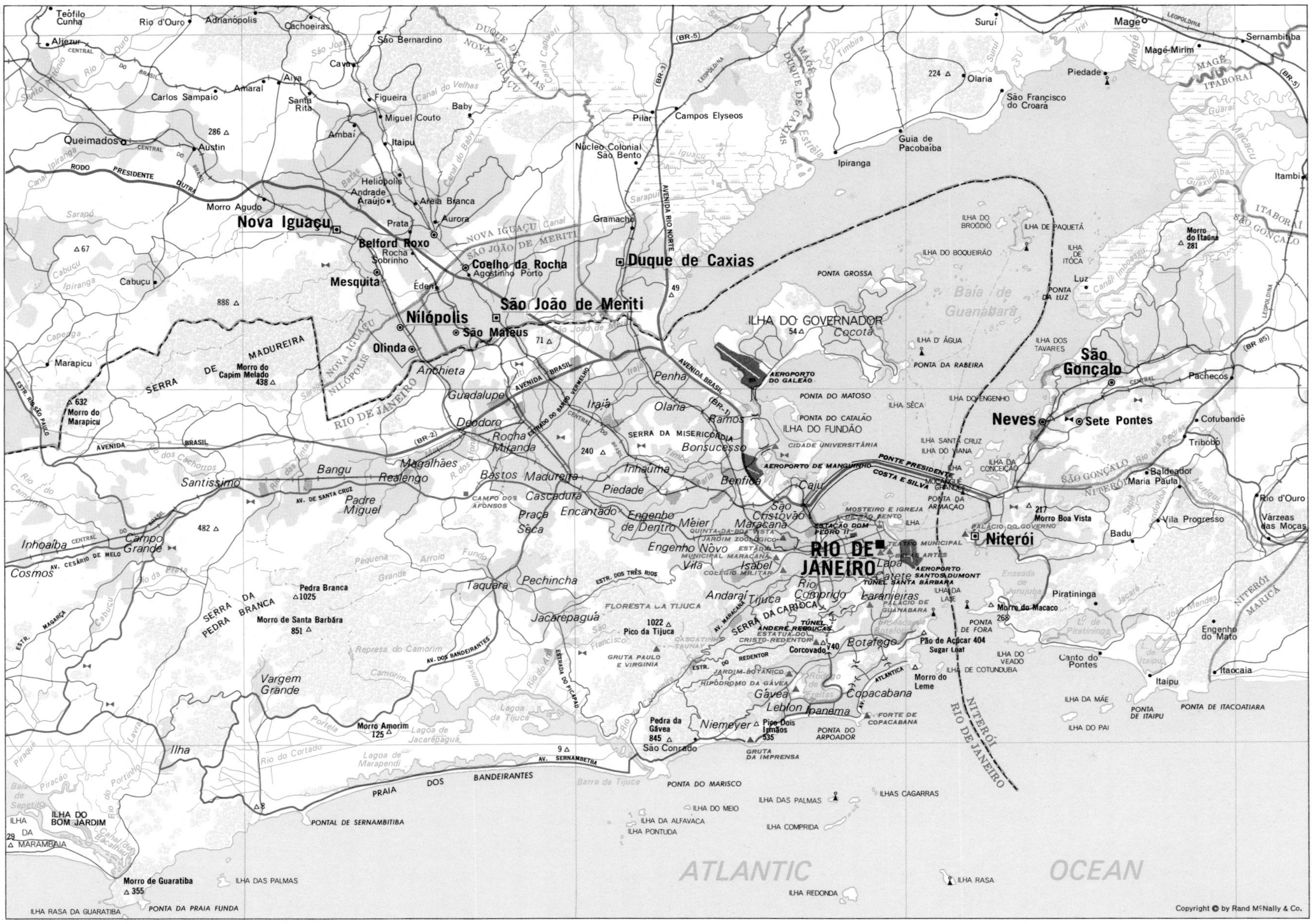

b

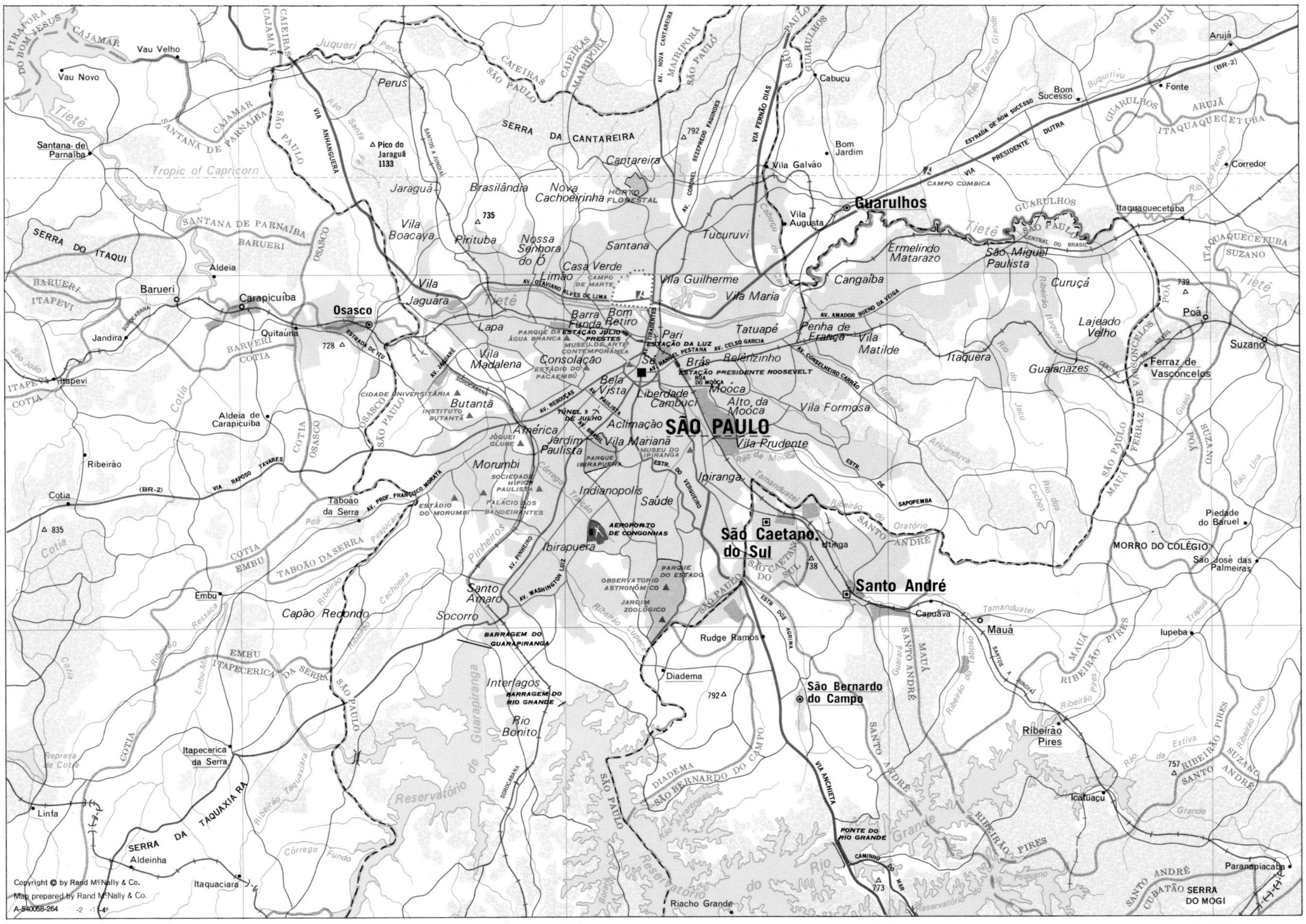

Scale 1:300,000

One centimeter represents 3 kilometers.
One inch represents approximately 4.7 miles.

Kilometers 0 5 10 15 Km.
Statute Miles 0 5 10 15 Mi.

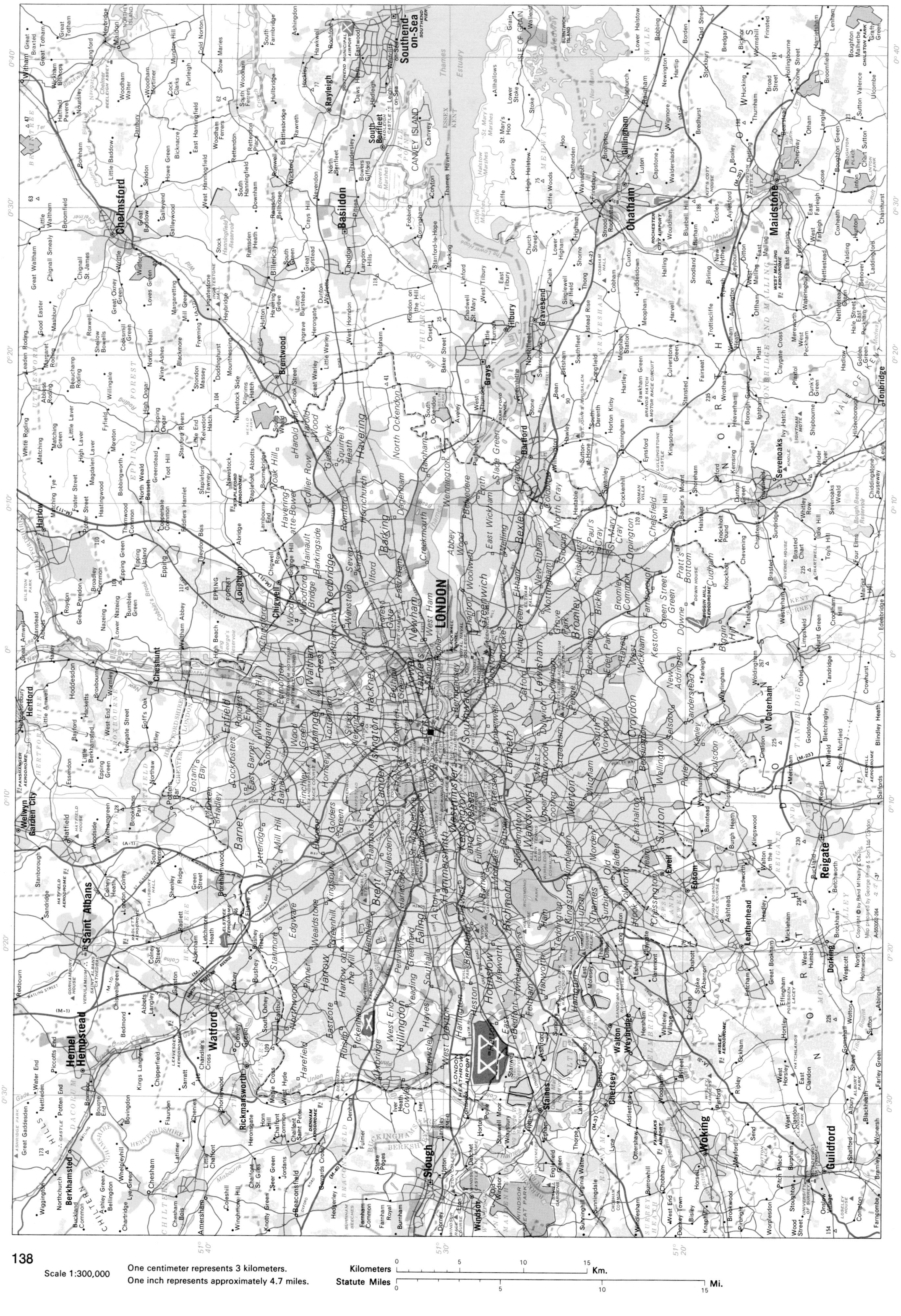

Scale 1:300,000

One centimeter represents 3 kilometers.
One inch represents approximately 4.7 miles.

Kilometers 0 5 10 15 Km.
Statute Miles 0 5 10 15 Mi.

Scale 1:300,000

One centimeter represents 3 kilometers.
One inch represents approximately 4.7 miles.

Kilometers
Statute Miles

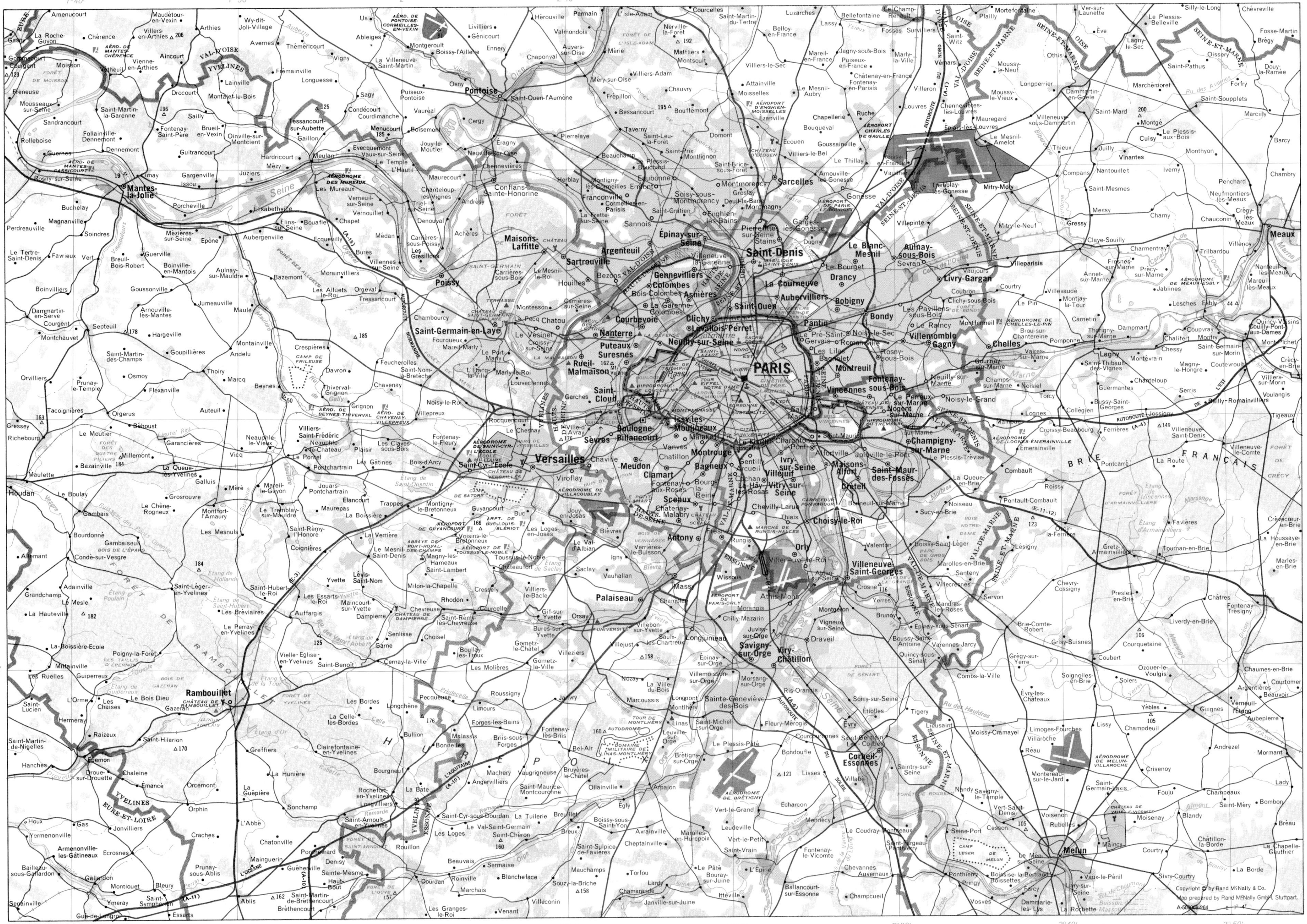

Paris

Berlin · Vienna · Budapest

a
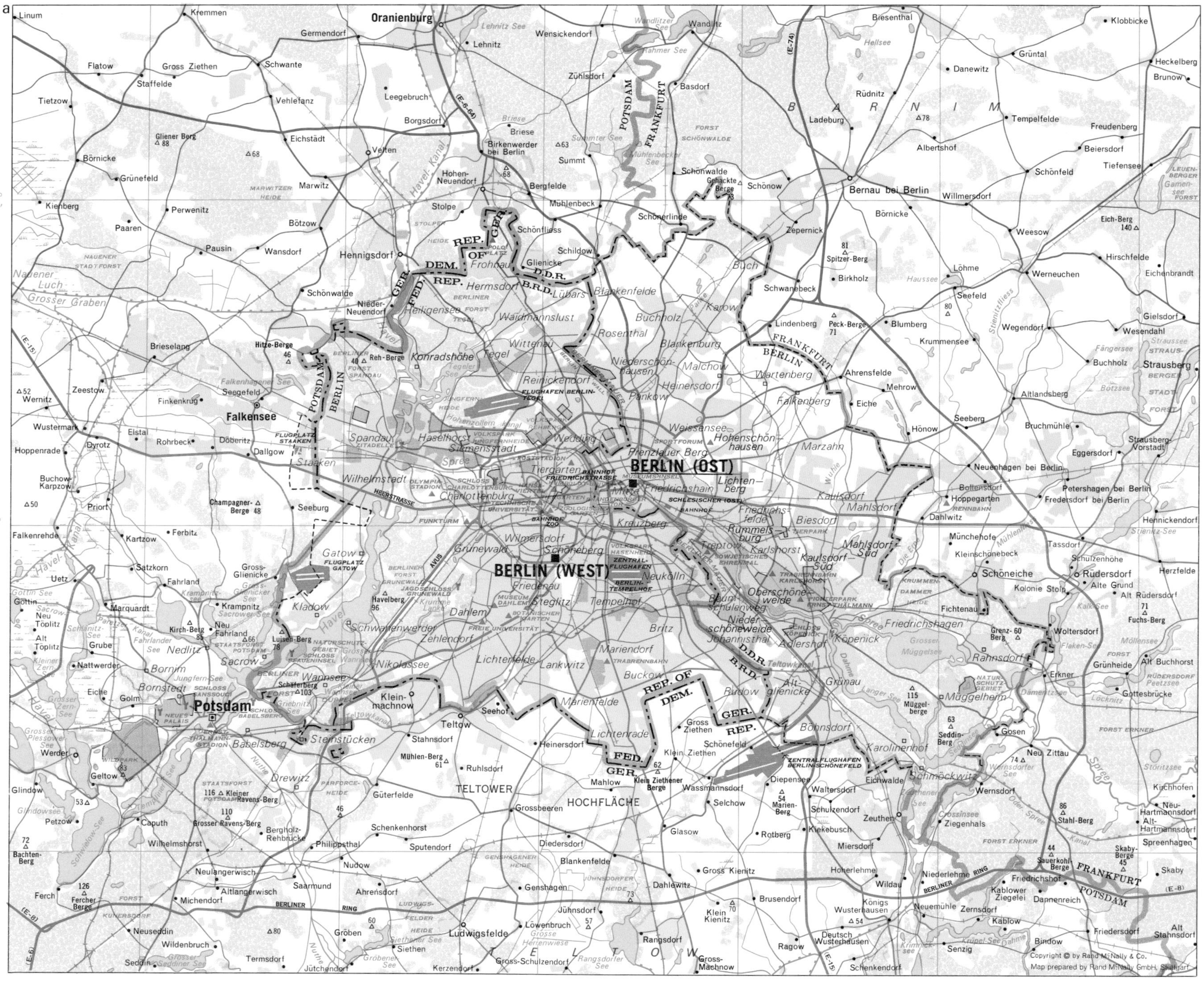

b
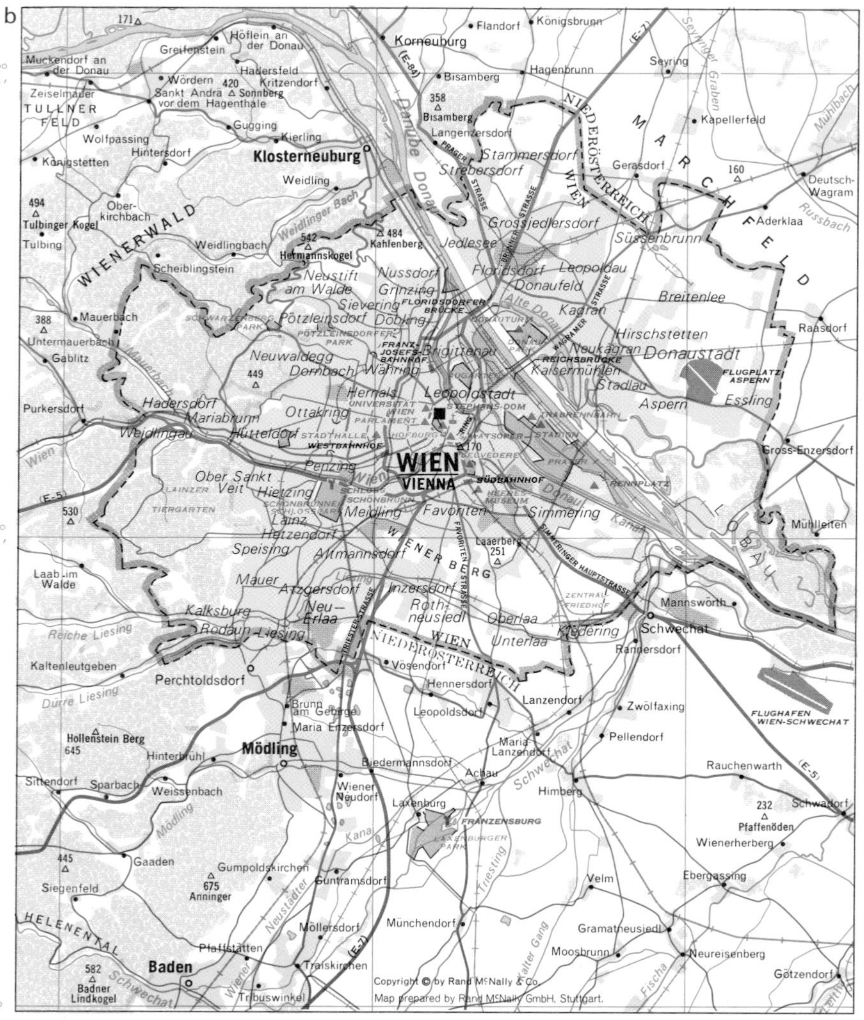

c
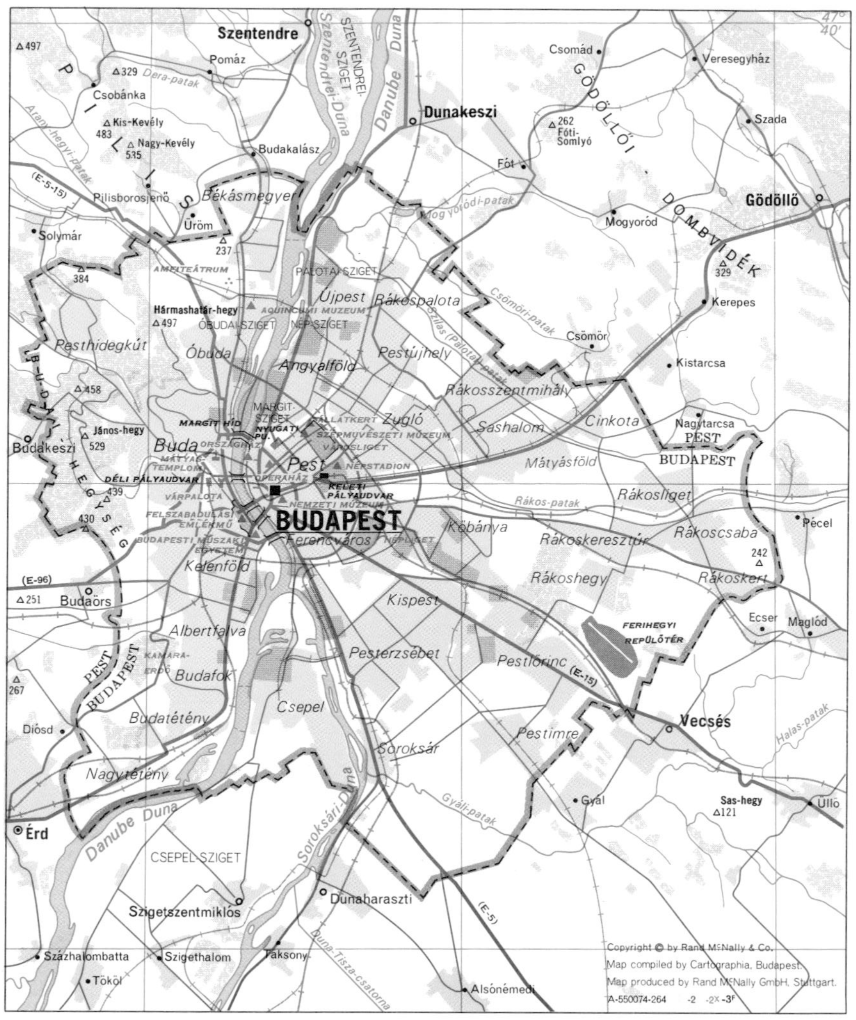

Scale 1:300,000

One centimeter represents 3 kilometers.
One inch represents approximately 4.7 miles.

Kilometers 0 5 10 15 Km.
Statute Miles 0 5 10 15 Mi.

a

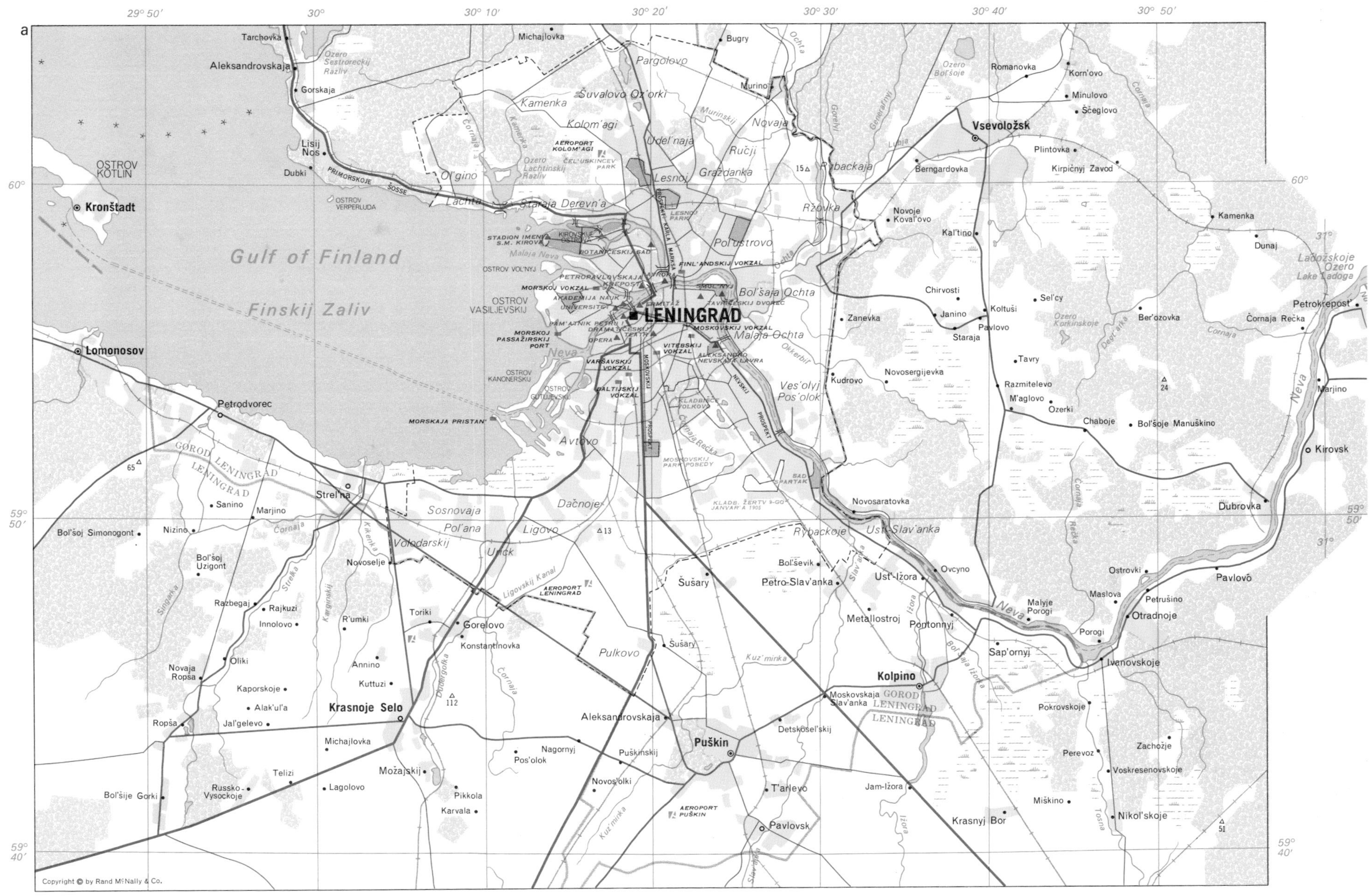

b

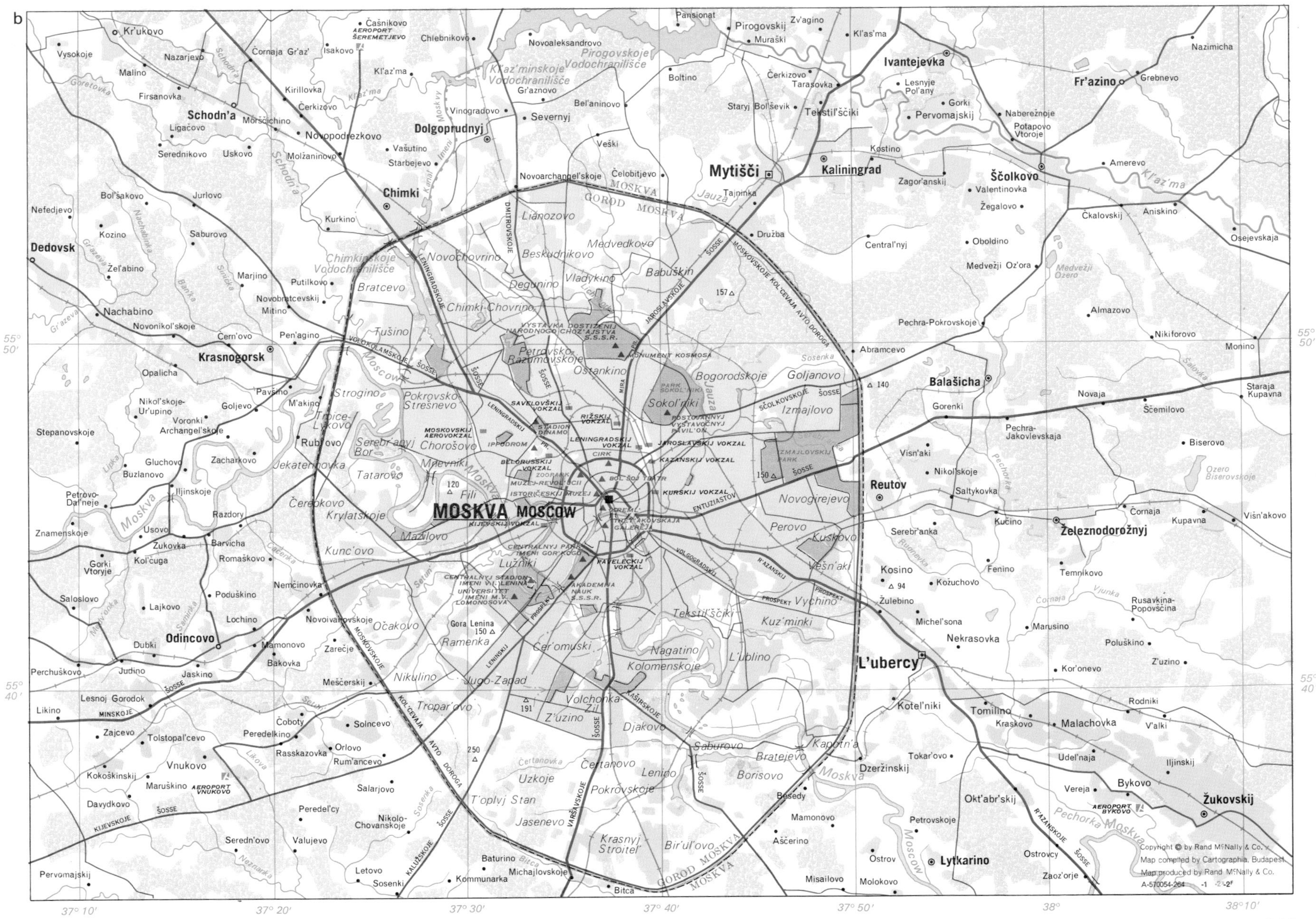

Scale 1:300,000

One centimeter represents 3 kilometers.
One inch represents approximately 4.7 miles.

Kilometers 0 5 10 15 Km.
Statute Miles 0 5 10 15 Mi.

Rome · Athens · Istanbul · Tehran

b

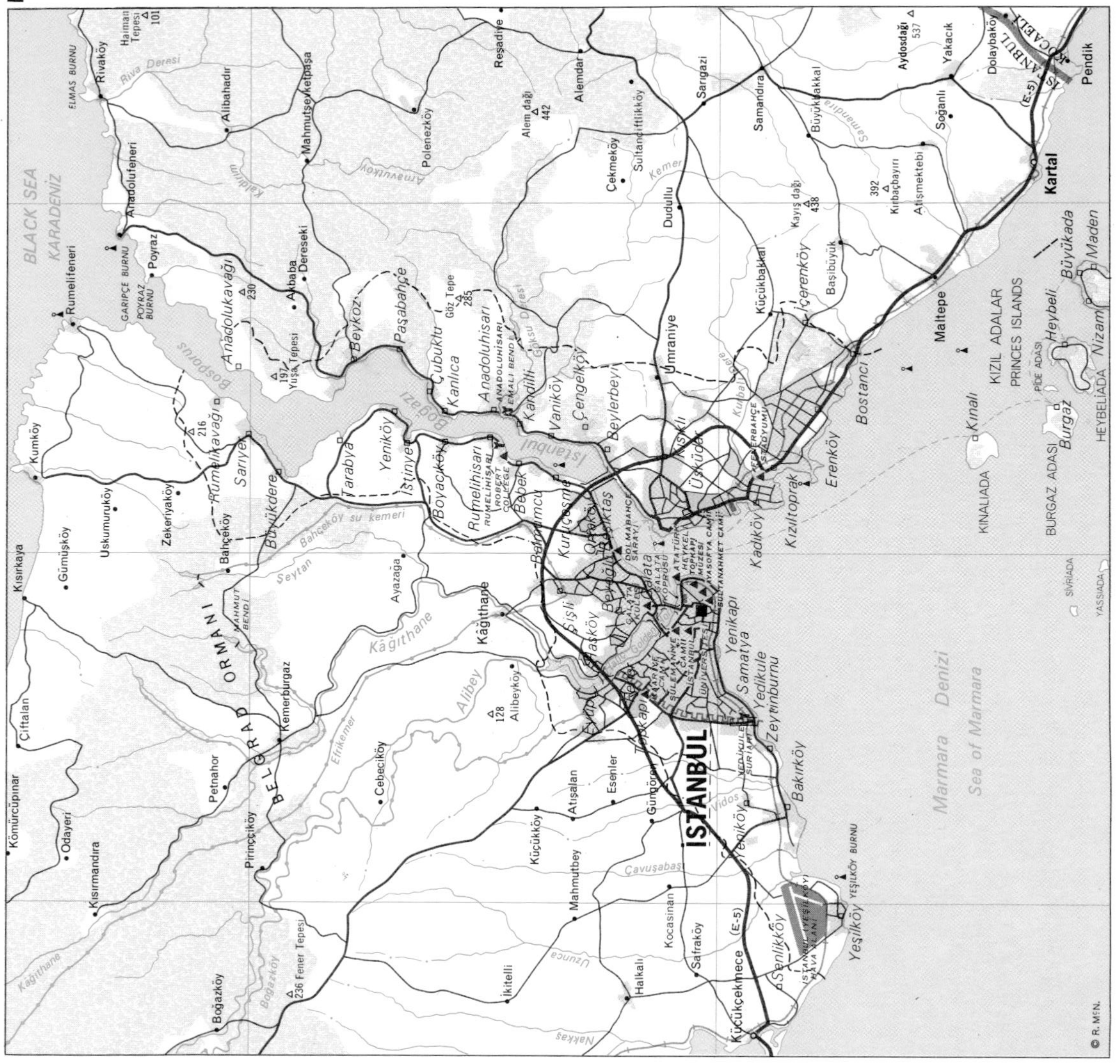

d

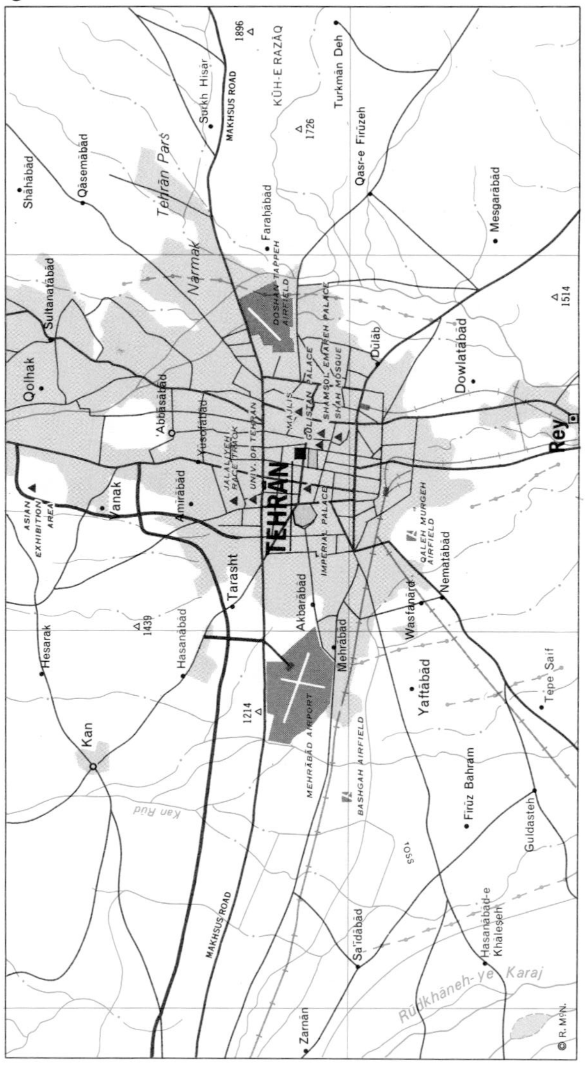

a

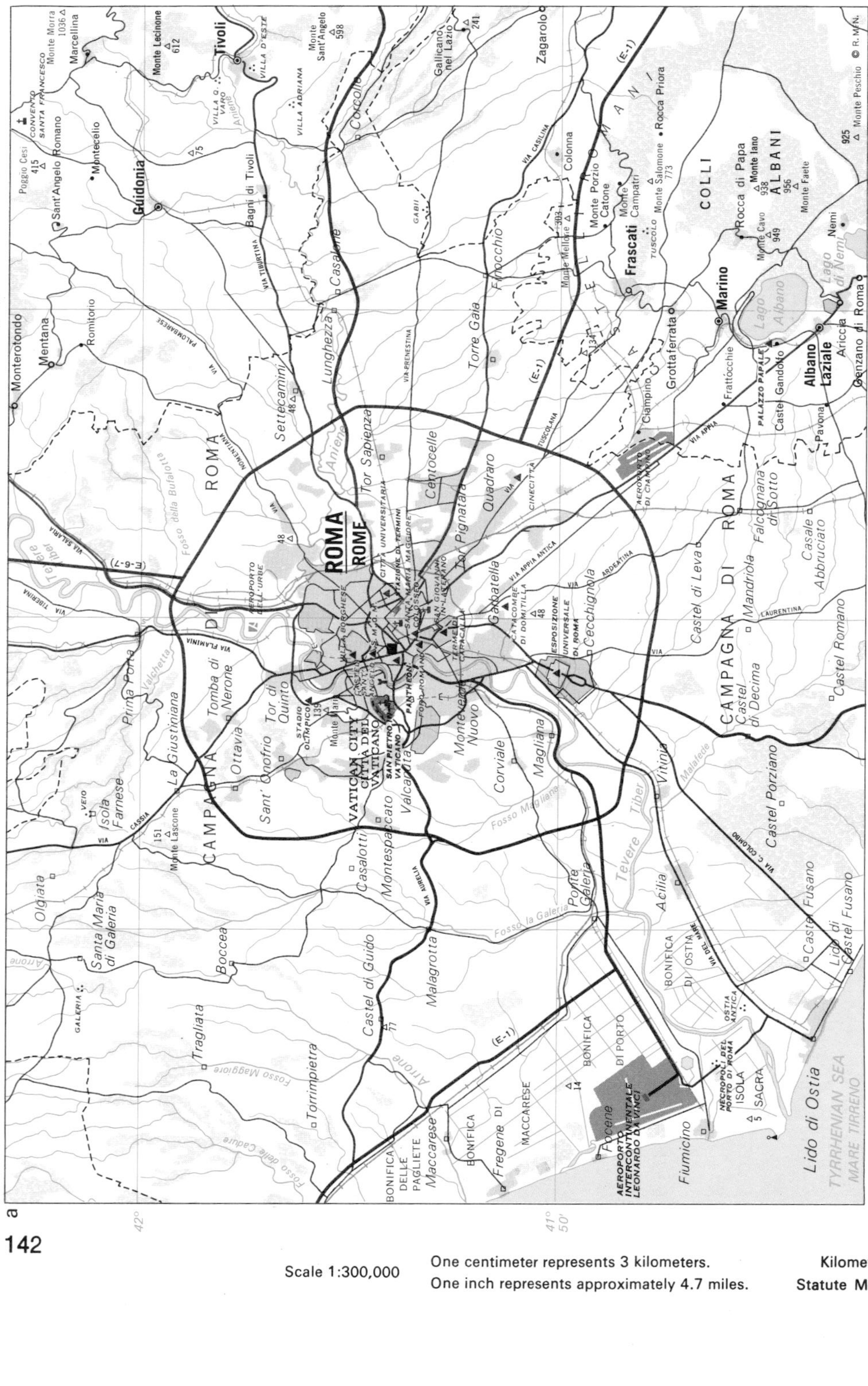

c

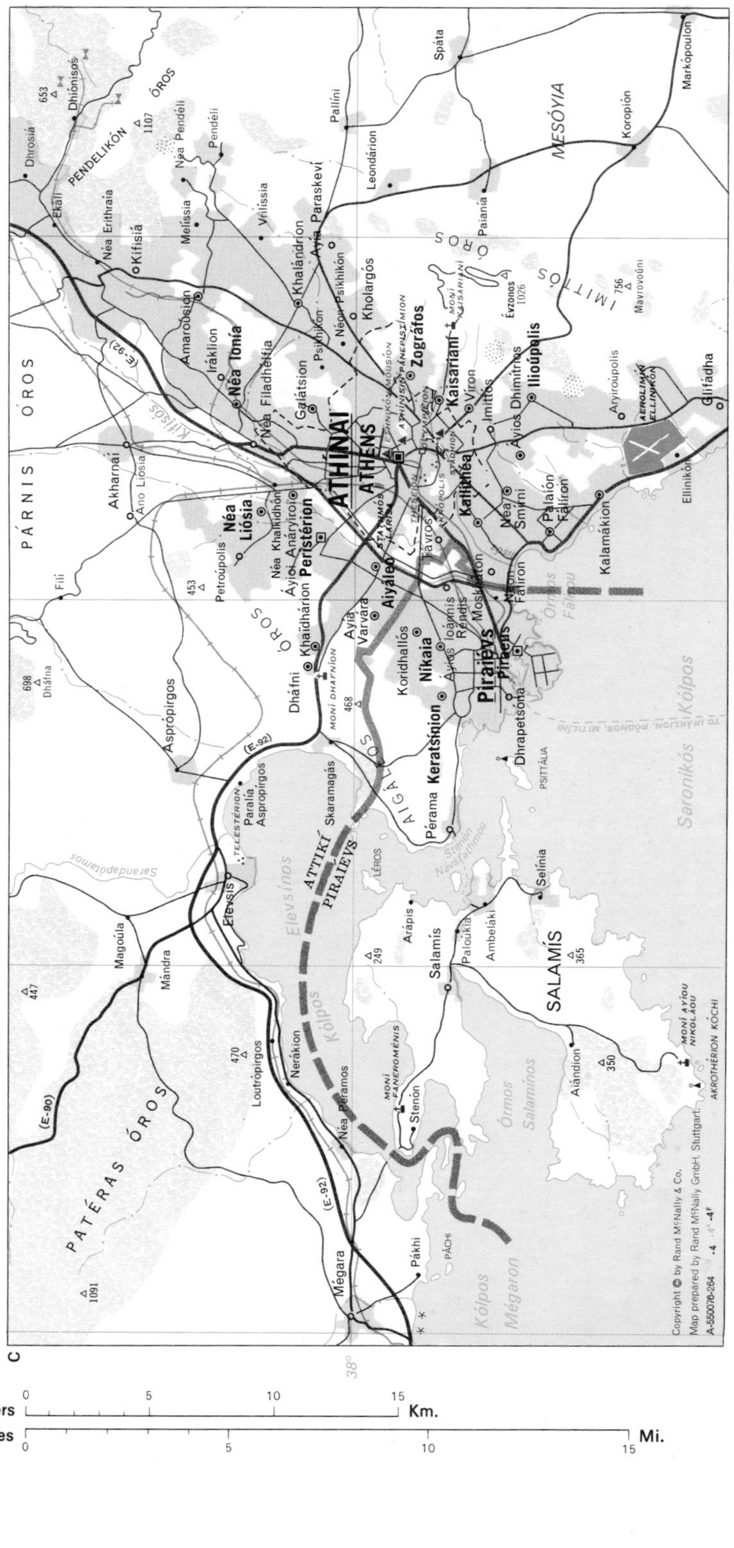

Scale 1:300,000

One centimeter represents 3 kilometers.
One inch represents approximately 4.7 miles.

Kilometers 0 5 10 15 Km.
Statute Miles 0 5 10 15 Mi.

Peking · Seoul · Singapore · Hong Kong

Scale 1:300,000
One centimeter represents 3 kilometers.
One inch represents approximately 4.7 miles.

Kilometers 0 5 10 15 Km.
Statute Miles 0 5 10 Mi.

a
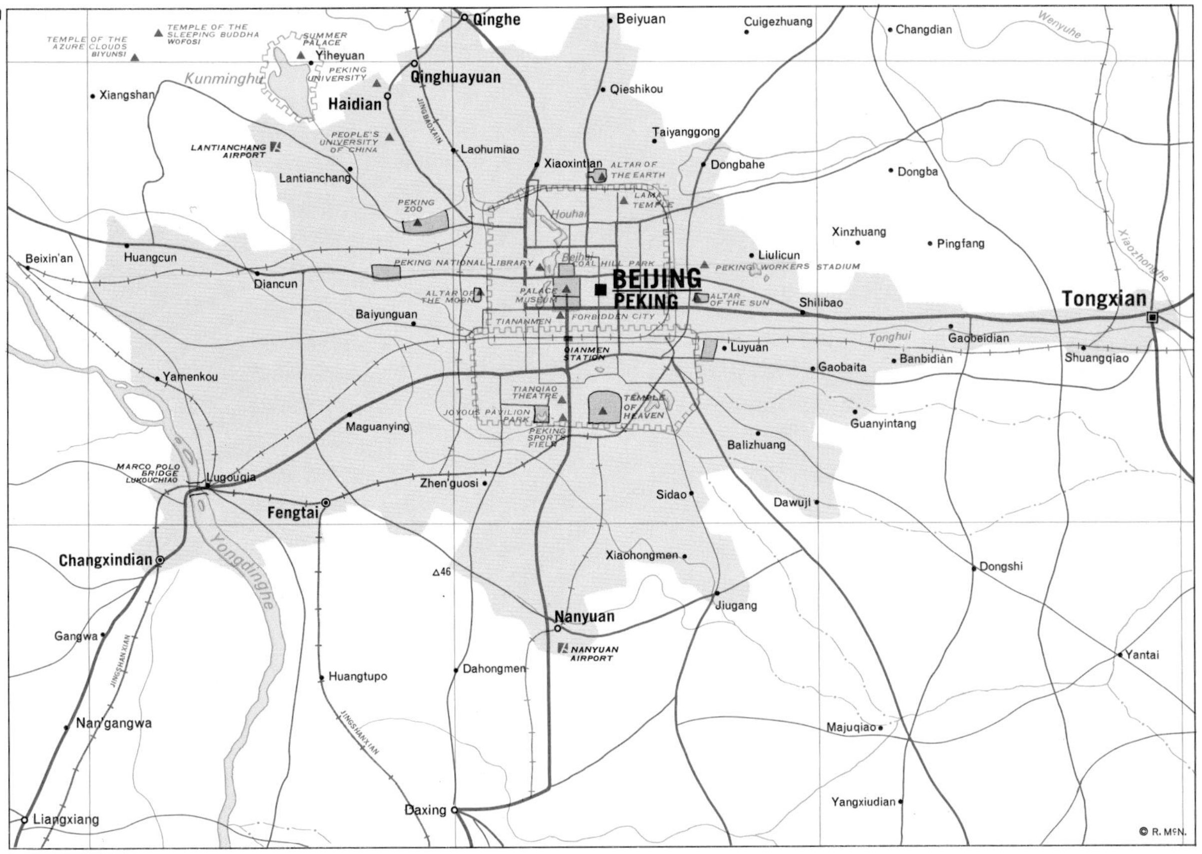

b
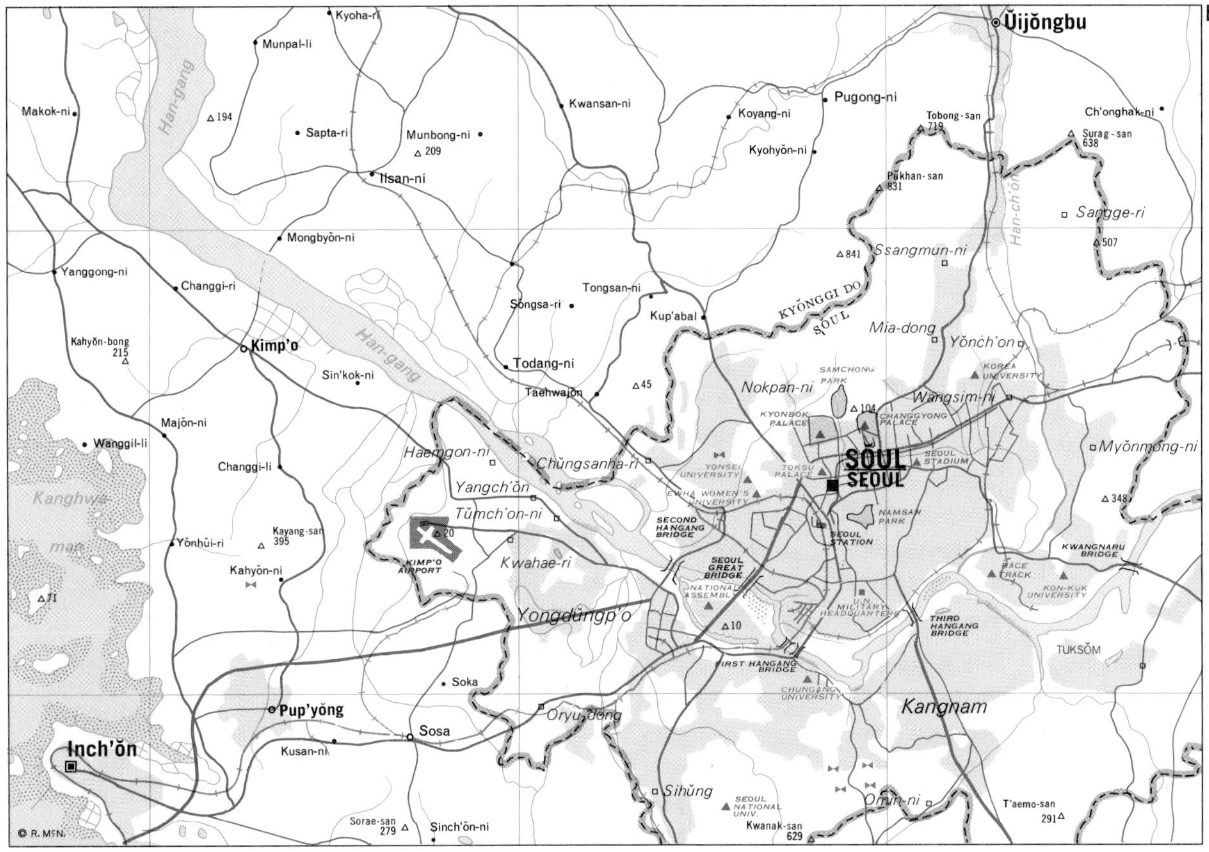

c
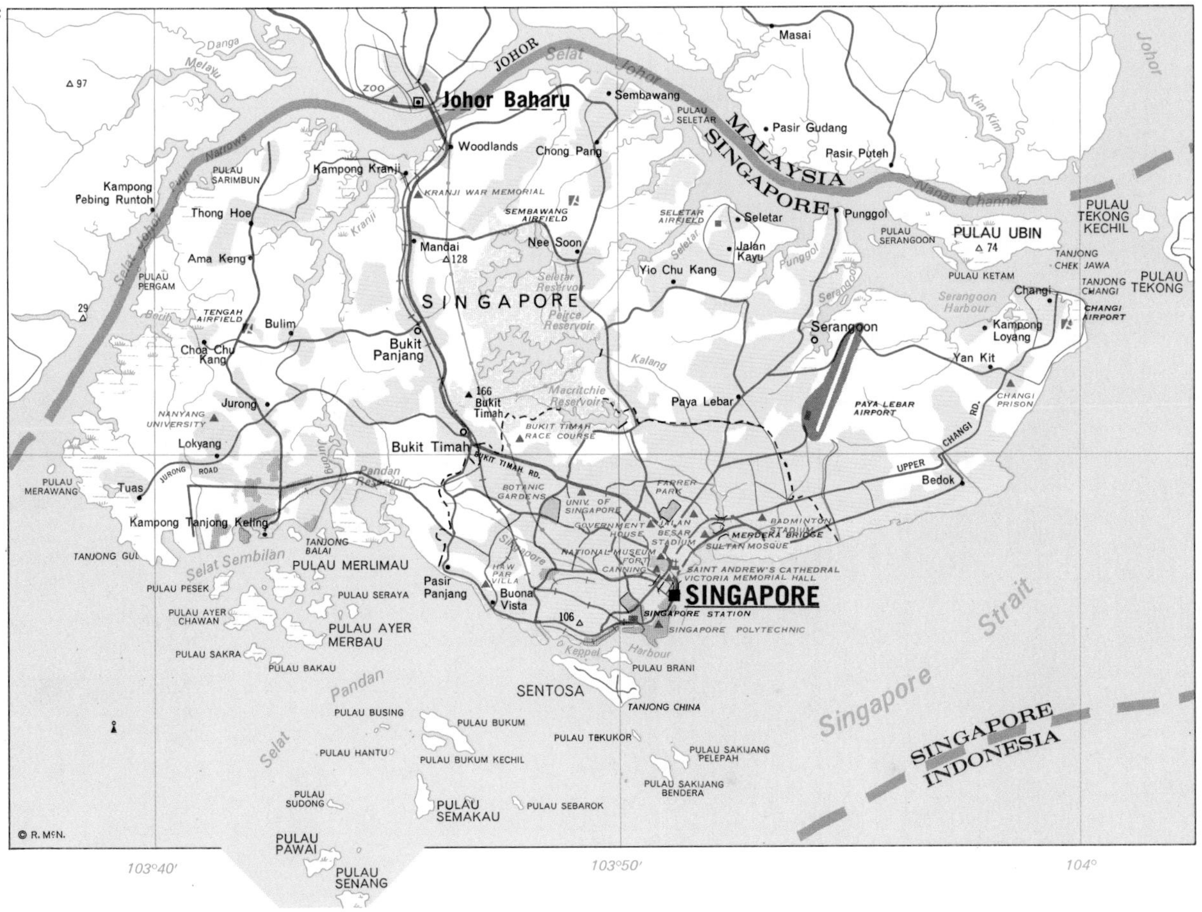

d
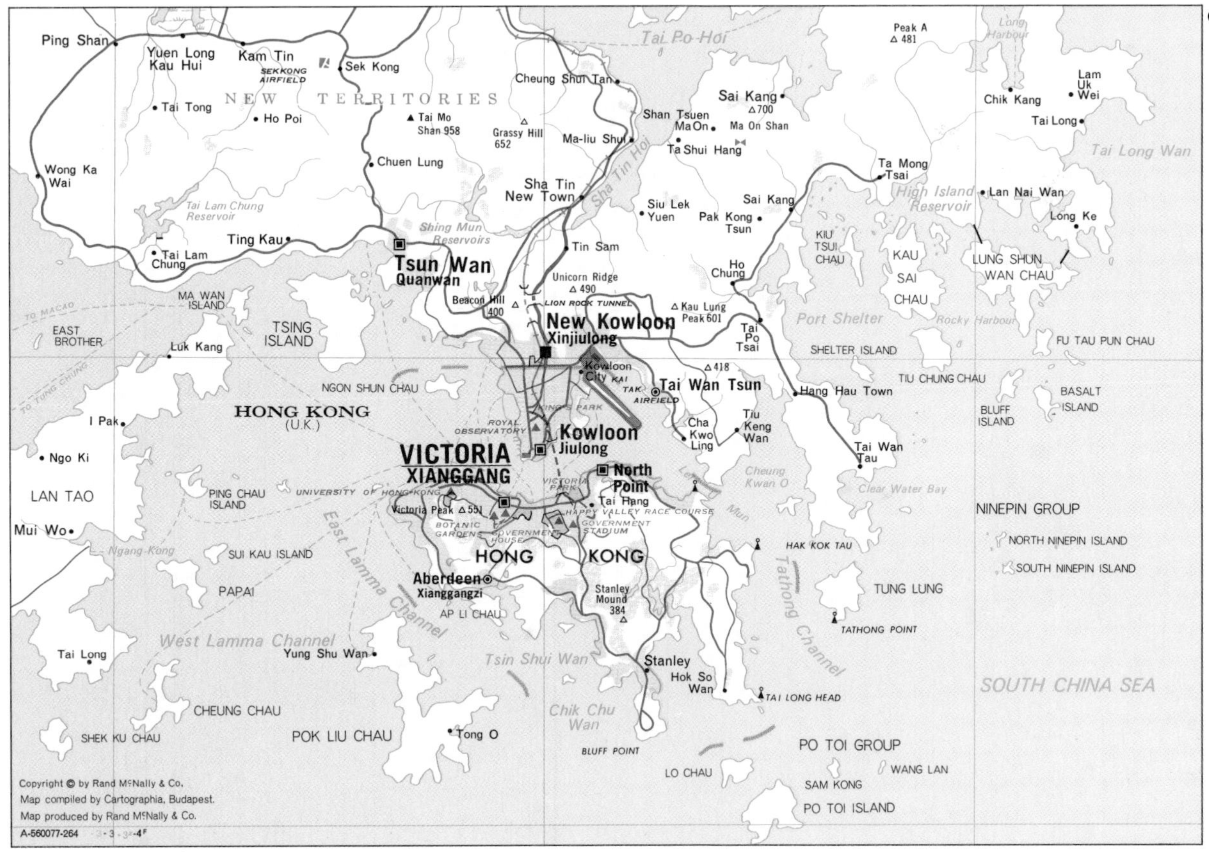

Tokyo—Yokohama

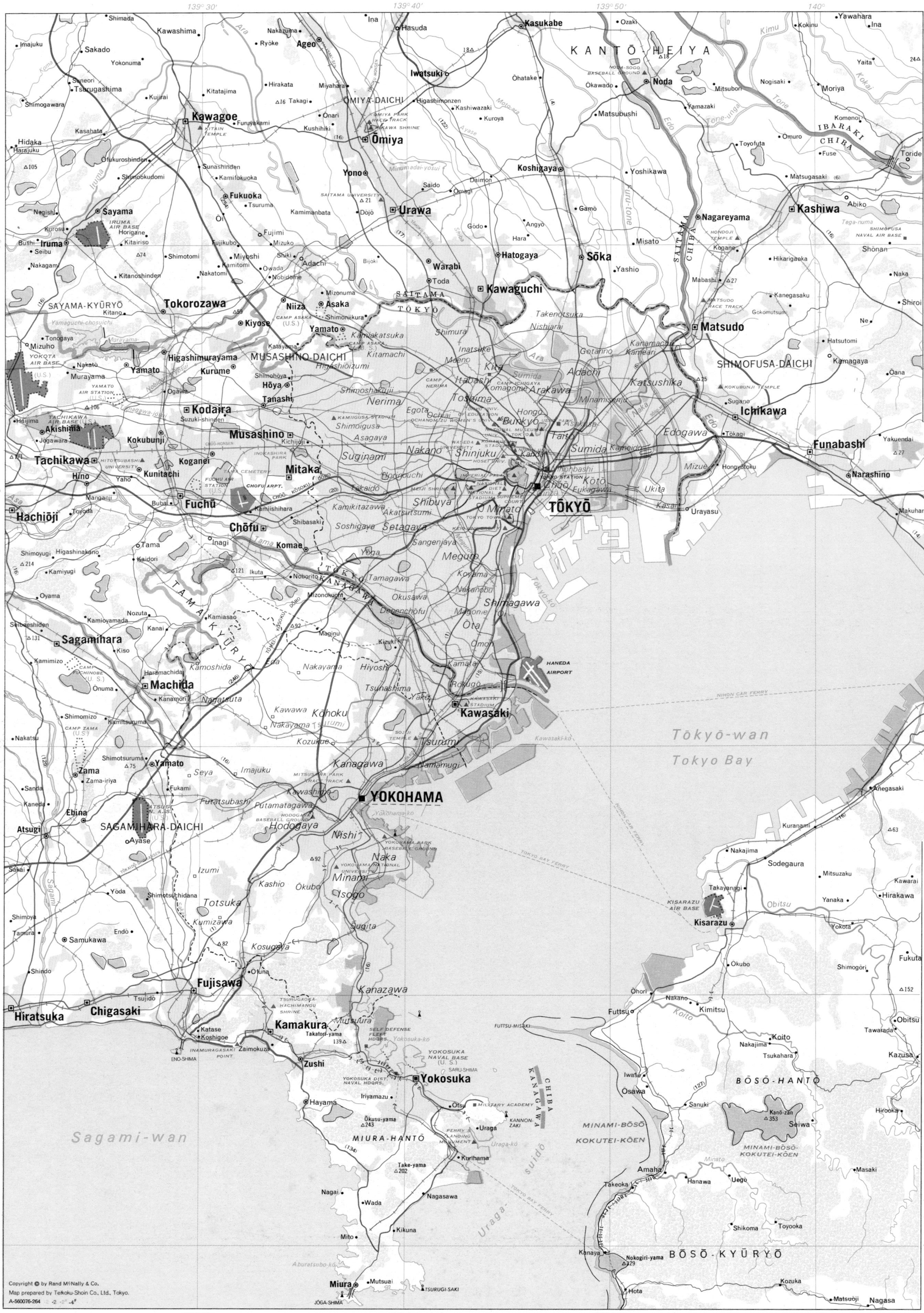

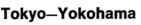

Scale 1:300,000

One centimeter represents 3 kilometers.
One inch represents approximately 4.7 miles.

Kilometers 0 5 10 15 Km.
Statute Miles 0 5 10 15 Mi.

The World in Theme Maps

Page

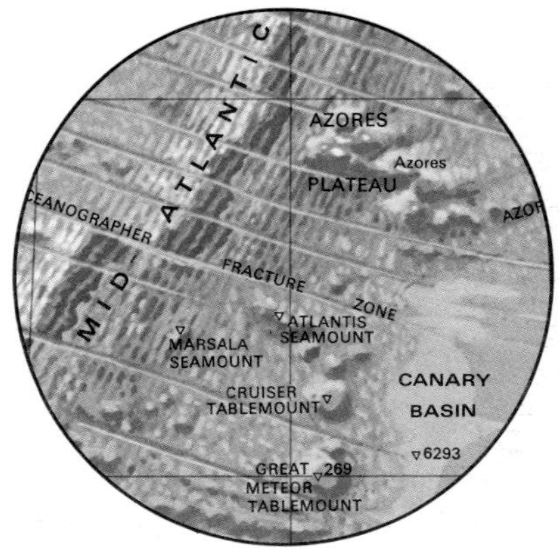

The Earth and Space 146–151

A spacecraft carrying us in orbit around the nearest star, Earth is one of nine planets circling the Sun—itself but one of 100,000 million stars in a single galaxy, the Milky Way. Space probes of the 1960's and 1970's have taught us much about our satellite, the Moon.

Environmental Maps 152–167

Ten major environments, natural or modified by man, are depicted in this series. The colors and patterns for each category (inset legend, shown on each map) depict natural features and illustrate the results of man's activity. Hill shading is used to show land configuration. Together, these design elements create a striking visual impression of the earth's surface. The appearance and/or general activity of an area dictate its classification; boundaries are never absolute but mark the center of transitional zones; gradations of meaning exist within a single category—thus "grassland/grazing land" identifies the lush pampas of Argentina and the savanna of Africa as well as the Soviet Union's steppes. Actual urban shapes are shown for only the largest metropolitan areas; red dots indicate smaller urban concentrations; black dots, selected reference points. From this series, at least two startling observations can be made: (1) although severely limited in extent, the red urban areas represent 40 percent of the world's population; (2) man has had but slight impact on vast areas of each continent—as shown by the extent of barren lands, wasteland, tundra, forests, and swamps.

World View 168–189

Easy-to-read charts show the world's politically related areas, population, languages, religions, natural resources, energy production and consumption, wealth and trade, climate, geology, time zones, drainage regions and ocean currents.

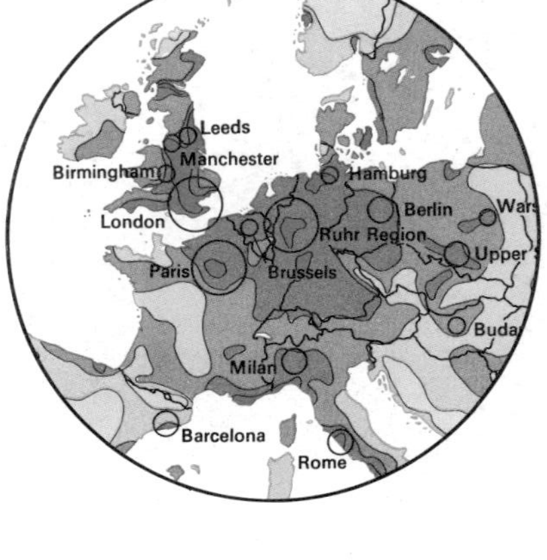

Ocean Floor Maps 190–195

These maps (with land areas in grayish-white) convey an impression of the physical nature of the world's ocean floors. In general, colors used are those thought to exist on the ocean floors: for continental shelves or shallow inland seas, grayish-green corresponding to sediments washed from continental areas; in deeper parts, white for the chalky ooze derived from the skeletons of marine life and red for the fine mud from land. Relief shading reveals many different features on the ocean floor: towering mountain ranges, vast canyons, broad plains, and a variety of other physiographic forms exceeding in magnitude those found on the continents. Note, for example, the Mid-Atlantic Ridge, a chain of mountains bisected by a trough that produces twin ridgelines. Away from the center there are parallel and lower crests, while at right angles to the crests are numerous fracture zones. Measurements of temperatures and magnetism indicate that the troughs in the Mid-Atlantic Ridge are younger than the paralleling crests, whose ages increase with distance from the center. It is believed that the central troughs mark a line where molten materials from the earth's interior rise to the ocean floor to form gigantic plates that move slowly apart. This theory suggests that continents, having been a single landmass in ancient times, are slowly moving away from each other. The matching curves of the Atlantic shorelines of South America and Africa have long been cited as support for such conjecture. Where the subsea plates meet certain continental areas or island chains, they plunge downward to replenish inner-earth materials and form trenches of profound depths. Along the northern and western edges of the Pacific Ocean are several lines of such gutters, including some of the world's deepest known spots—Mariana Trench, Tonga Trench, Kuril Trench. Other identifiable features include: the great submarine canyons that lead from the edges of the continents; seamounts that rise above the ocean floors; and the continental shelves, which appear to be underwater extensions of landmasses, varying in shape from narrow fringes to broad plains.

The Planet Earth in Space

THE OTHER PLANETS

New Mexico State University Observatory

MERCURY

Closest planet to the Sun, with a mean distance of 36 million miles, Mercury has little atmosphere to shield it. Temperatures can thus range from 700° F during the day to 300° F below zero at night. It was long believed that Mercury's rotational and orbital periods were the same—88 days—which would keep one face of the planet always toward the Sun. In 1965, however, radio astronomers at Arecibo, Puerto Rico, discovered that it rotates once every 58.6 days, or two-thirds of its period of revolution around the Sun. Mercury, 53 million miles from Earth at its closest, can occasionally be seen with the unaided eye as a morning star before sunrise and as an evening star after sunset. The unmanned spacecraft Mariner 10 flew to within 460 miles of Mercury in 1974, recording a crater-marked, moonlike surface with thick layers of lava and many ridges and valleys.

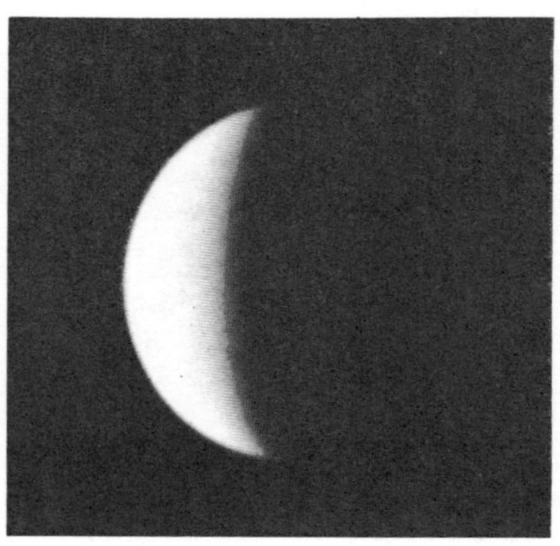

New Mexico State University Observatory

VENUS

The brightest body in the heavens, aside from the Sun and Moon, Venus is also the nearest planet to Earth and the most like our planet in terms of size and mass. U.S. and Soviet spacecraft have transmitted invaluable data on the planet that would otherwise be unavailable, since most of its atmosphere is composed of a thick layer of carbon dioxide, which prevents a clear view of Venus' surface from Earth. In December 1978 Pioneer Venus 2 sent back the information that clouds 40 miles from the surface were hotter at the poles than at the equator and that Venusian atmosphere contains large amounts of argon. It is now thought that Venus is inhospitable to life: its atmospheric pressure is 100 times that of Earth's, and temperatures on the surface can reach as much as 900° F. The intense heat is most likely due to the fact that Venus' dense atmosphere traps the Sun's rays, thus creating a "greenhouse effect."

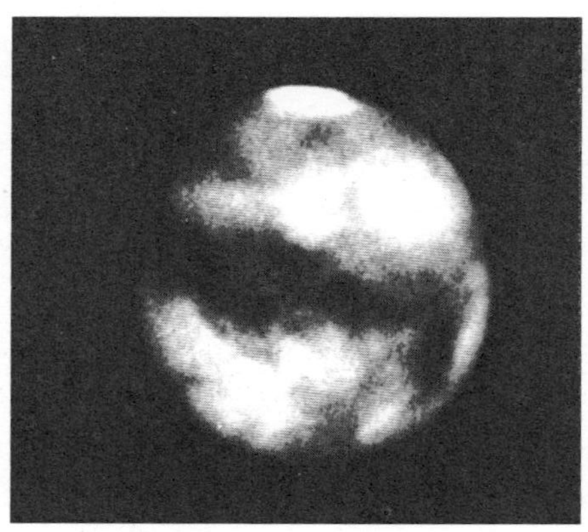

Hale Observatories

MARS

For years the "canals" of Mars were thought to be the work of intelligent beings, and the dark patches appearing on the planet were attributed to vegetation. But four Mariner flybys and the 1976 landings on Mars by Vikings 1 and 2 showed that, in fact, the surface was heavily crater-scarred, much like our Moon, both from meteor impact and volcanic eruption. Many of the craters showed marks of erosion by the strong winds that blow around the planet, some of them capable of creating giant dust storms. Channels do exist on Mars' surface, but they appear to be dry stream beds. Even more striking was the conclusion drawn by scientists that the permanent polar caps are most probably water ice, overlaid with a thick stratum of carbon dioxide during the long Martian winters. Carbon dioxide makes up 95 per cent of the planet's atmosphere. However, tests conducted on the surface of Mars have so far failed to reveal the presence of life. Mars has two small satellites, both also cratered by meteor impact.

Lunar and Planetary Laboratory, University of Arizona

JUPITER

This giant of planets, eleven times the diameter of Earth, has only about one-fourth the density of our planet. Its surface is gaseous, composed of hydrogen and helium; methane and ammonia, which form when hydrogen, carbon and nitrogen unite, are also present in its atmosphere. If water were present as well, there would be all the ingredients necessary for living cells to be created once catalyzed by a strong electrical discharge or ultraviolet radiation. Jupiter emits bursts of intense radio energy at random—next to the Sun it is the strongest radio-emitting body in the solar system. A thirteenth satellite of the planet was discovered in 1974, the same year that Pioneer 11 transmitted data indicating that Jupiter has a magnetic field 20,000 times stronger than Earth's. In 1979 the Voyager spacecraft sent back close-up pictures of Jupiter's four major satellites and also discovered a ring of debris orbiting the planet.

THE EARTH AND THE UNIVERSE

The planet Earth is a spacecraft carrying all of us about 18.5 miles a second in orbit around the nearest star, the Sun. Nine planets are held captive by the gravitational grasp of this star, and Earth is the third in distance from it. In addition, a profusion of small bodies called asteroids orbit in a belt between Mars and Jupiter. And still much smaller bodies, the meteoroids, hurtle within the solar system. When meteoroids enter Earth's atmosphere, they flame up and are called meteors, or shooting stars. If they survive the passage through the atmosphere and land on Earth, they are known as meteorites. Comets also orbit the Sun, and some of them may go out as far as 2 light-years from Earth.

The Sun is a star in the Milky Way Galaxy, a loose spiral star system of about 100,000 million stars. Somewhat like a mammoth pin-wheel, it has a bulbous nucleus with thinner arms extending from it. Its overall diameter is estimated to be 100,000 light-years, and its maximum breadth at the nucleus is about 20,000 light-years. The Sun lies close to the main plane, about 30,000 light-years from the galactic center. A light-year is the distance light travels in one year at a speed of 186,000 miles a second. The Galaxy rotates, and the Sun makes one revolution around its center in 225 million years.

But the Milky Way Galaxy is not the entire universe. The astronomer Edwin Hubble calculated, after an extensive survey, that there were nearly 100 million galaxies within the range of the Mount Wilson 100-inch telescope. This would mean one billion galaxies within the range of the 200-inch Hale telescope on Mount Palomar.

With so many galaxies, the law of probability indicates that there are other stars with orbiting planets, and among these there are quite probably some with the conditions to support life.

MAN GOES TO THE MOON

Unmanned spacecraft blazed the trail—taking close-up photographs, testing the soil for its chemical composition, and mapping the surfaces. After Earth orbit by one-man Mercurys and two-man Geminis, the three-man Apollos were ready to go, and on December 25, 1968, Apollo 8 orbited the Moon. Then, with Apollo 11, Neil Armstrong and Edwin Aldrin, Jr. stepped onto the Moon on July 20, 1969, while Michael Collins remained in Moon orbit aboard the command ship. Seven Apollo missions followed in the next three years—five landing men on the Moon, one aborting, the seventh docking in space with the Soviet Union's Soyuz 19. The last manned flight to the Moon, Apollo 17, took place on December 7–19, 1972.

THE SOLAR SYSTEM CHART

Tracing the solar system on an actual astronomical photograph, taken at the Harvard College Observatory's Southern Station, makes this a unique chart. The position of the planets and their orbits have been accurately placed against the background of stars in the constellation Ara, as if viewed from a point in space 2700 astronomical units (almost 251 billion miles) from the Sun, in the general direction of the star Capella in the constellation Auriga. The chart actually consists of two parts: the relatively nearby solar system and the remote background of stars which forms a part of the Southern Milky Way.

The position of each planet on its orbit is shown for January 1, 1970. Tick marks on the orbital paths indicate the positions of the far outer planets at each succeeding one-year interval through the year 1980, except for Neptune where space did not permit the entire decade.

The scale of the solar system is by custom based on the astronomical unit (AU), which is the mean distance of the Earth from the Sun. On this map, one astronomical unit equals about one centimeter, disregarding the foreshortening caused by the viewpoint. Thus the Earth's nearly circular orbit is two centimeters in diameter. The orbits appear elliptical because from the vantage point chosen the solar system is tilted 26° from edge-on. A tilt of 90° would be required to look "straight down" on the plane of the ecliptic. To indicate which side of the orbit is closer to us, it has been drawn wider than the far side. Each orbital path is shown in the characteristic color of the planet. A non-existent short tail is attached to each planet to visualize its forward movement. The Sun is not drawn to scale; to show its correct relative size would have made it as large as the orbit of Jupiter.

Lunar and Planetary Laboratory, University of Arizona

SATURN

With its brilliant white rings orbiting around a dull yellowish banded body, Saturn is the jewel of the solar system. The rings are composed of small particles of ice and ice-covered space debris. There are four: the two outer ones, separated by a gap called Cassini's Division, are bright; the next one, the Crepe Ring, is much fainter and more transparent; and the fourth, discovered in 1969, is quite faint and so close to the planet that it is observable only under the best telescopic conditions. The rings surround Saturn's equatorial plane, and at some points during the planet's orbit around the Sun they are almost invisible because they are edge on to Earth. Although Saturn is the second largest planet, its density is so low that it would float in water. Voyagers 1 and 2, having passed Jupiter, will fly by Saturn in 1980 and 1981.

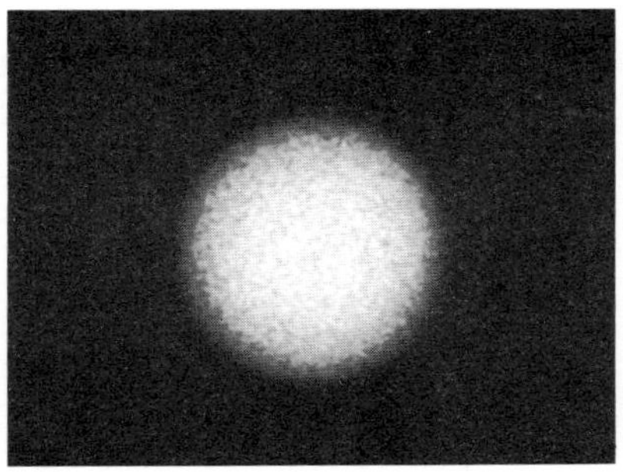

Project Stratoscope of Princeton University.

URANUS

In 1781 astronomer William Herschel found what he believed to be a comet in the course of a routine telescopic sky survey; it was not until several months later that he concluded that what he had come upon was a new planet, the first to be discovered by telescope. In 1977 a further discovery was made—the five-moon planet is now known to have five rings as well. The rings had not been seen before because Uranus' distance from the Sun (and from Earth—it is never less than 1.6 billion miles from us) makes it difficult to observe. In addition, the rings are very narrow. Like Saturn's, they are probably composed of ice particles. Uranus is unique in that its equatorial plane is inclined about 82° to its orbital plane; thus, its 84-year revolution around the Sun is accomplished with one or the other of its poles nearly always facing the Sun.

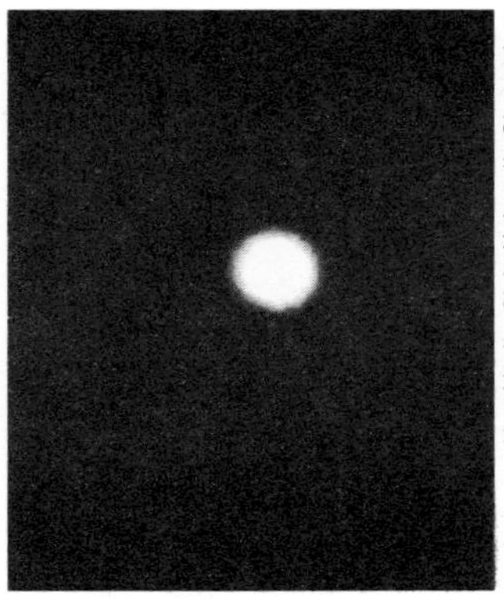

New Mexico State University Observatory sponsored by NSF, NASA, and ONR

NEPTUNE

The discovery of Neptune was a triumph of mathematics and of gravitational theory. Soon after the sighting of Uranus, it was found that the planet wandered from its calculated orbit. Two astronomers, Adams of England and Leverrier of France, suspected that the deviation was due to the pull of another planet and proceeded to calculate the orbit such a body would need to influence Uranus in this manner. The telescope at Berlin Observatory was set to Leverrier's predicted position on September 23, 1846, and Neptune was sighted that night. Both Adams and Leverrier are credited with the discovery. Of Neptune's two satellites, Triton is slightly larger than our Moon; Nereid, the smaller, has the most eccentric orbit of any known satellite. Its distance from Neptune can vary by as much as 12.8 million miles.

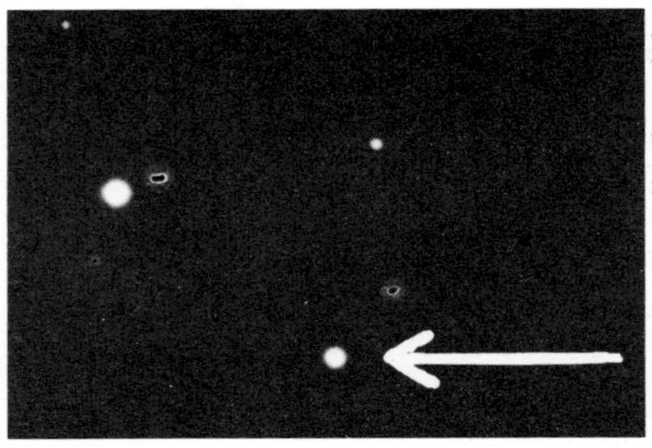

Hale Observatories

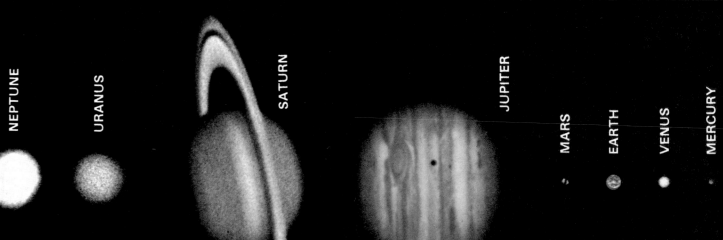

PLUTO

The most distant of the known planets, Pluto has an orbit of such eccentricity that at times it comes closer to the Sun than does its inner neighbor, Neptune. It was discrepancies in Uranus' orbit, still unexplained by the discovery of Neptune, however, that led astronomers to believe in the existence of a ninth planet as early as 1909. American astronomers Percival Lowell and W. H. Pickering calculated the orbit of a theoretical ninth planet and in 1930 it was discovered—within 6° of the predicted position—by Clyde W. Tombaugh at the Lowell Observatory. In 1978 astronomers at the U.S. Naval Observatory made an additional discovery: Pluto has a moon. The satellite's diameter is calculated to be about 500–700 miles; since Pluto itself is only about 1300 miles across, this is the largest satellite in relation to its planet yet known in the solar system. Pluto has a density only slighter greater than that of water and is roughly the same size as Mars.

Our Solar System

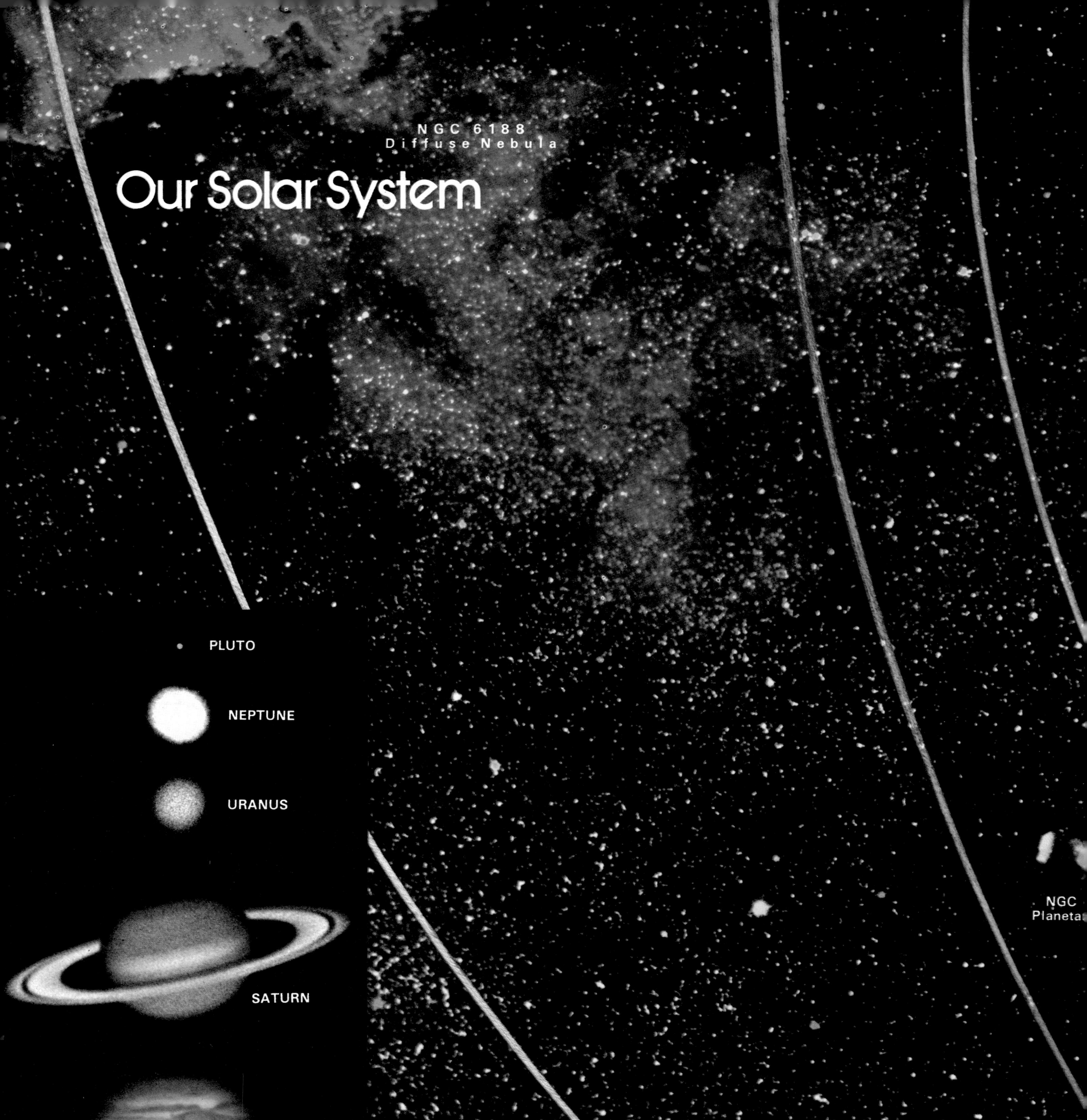

SOLAR SYSTEM DATA	Sun ☉	Mercury ☿	Venus ♀	Earth ⊕	Mars ♂
Equatorial Diameter (Earth = 1 or 7,926.4 miles)	109.2	0.38	0.95	1	0.53
Mass (Earth = 1)	333,000	0.06	0.82	1	0.11
Mean Density (Water = 1)	1.5*	5.50	5.27	5.52	3.95
Oblateness	~0	?	probably <1/30,000	1/298.25	1/190.
Albedo	—	0.06	0.76	0.39	0.15
Visual Magnitude at Maximum Light from Earth	−26.5	−1.9	−4.4	—	−2.8
Visual Magnitude at Maximum Light from 2700 AU	−9.3	+14.6	+11.7	+13.9	+16.7
Number of Satellites	—	0	0	1	2
Mean Distance from Sun (Earth = 1 or 92,957,000 miles)	—	0.39	0.72	1	1.52
Sidereal Period of Revolution Around Sun	—	88 days	224.7 days	1 year	1.88 yea
Mean Orbital Velocity (miles/sec)	—	29.7	21.7	18.5	15.0
Eccentricity of Orbit	—	0.206	0.007	0.017	0.093
Inclination of Orbit to Ecliptic	—	7°00′	3°24′	—	1°51′
Sidereal Period of Rotation on Axis	Equator, 25 days; 75° Lat., 33 days	58.6 days	243 days	$23^h56^m04^s$	24^h37^m2
Inclination of Equator	7°	less than 28°	between 170° & 180°	23°.45	24°.9
Escape Velocity (miles/sec)	384	2.7	6.4	7.0	3.2

*Varies greatly with depth.

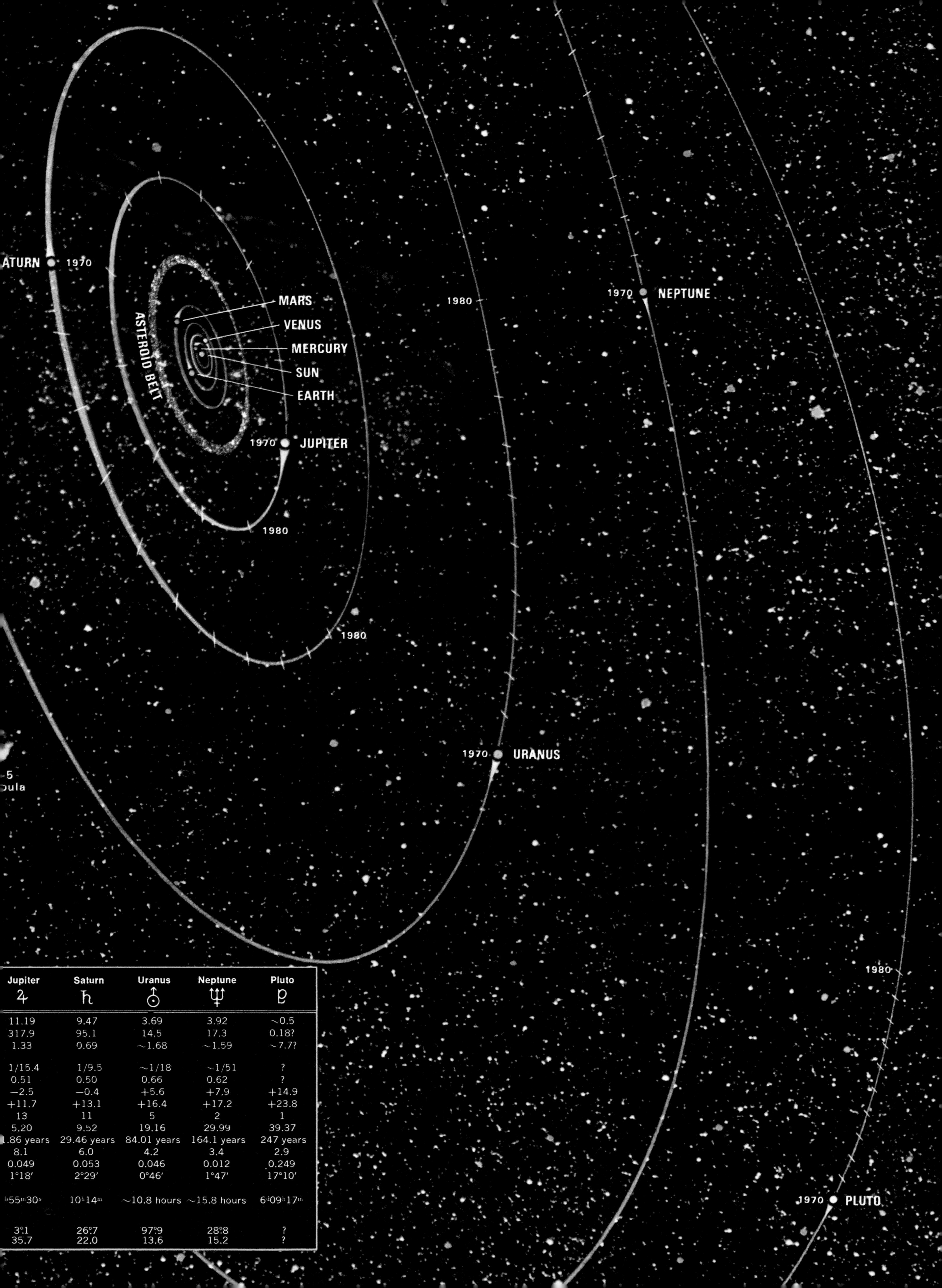

Jupiter ♃	Saturn ♄	Uranus ♅	Neptune ♆	Pluto ♇
11.19	9.47	3.69	3.92	~0.5
317.9	95.1	14.5	17.3	0.18?
1.33	0.69	~1.68	~1.59	~7.7?
1/15.4	1/9.5	~1/18	~1/51	?
0.51	0.50	0.66	0.62	?
−2.5	−0.4	+5.6	+7.9	+14.9
+11.7	+13.1	+16.4	+17.2	+23.8
13	11	5	2	1
5.20	9.52	19.16	29.99	39.37
.86 years	29.46 years	84.01 years	164.1 years	247 years
8.1	6.0	4.2	3.4	2.9
0.049	0.053	0.046	0.012	0.249
1°18′	2°29′	0°46′	1°47′	17°10′
$^{h}55^{m}30^{s}$	$10^{h}14^{m}$	~10.8 hours	~15.8 hours	$6^{d}09^{h}17^{m}$
3°1	26°7	97°9	28°8	?
35.7	22.0	13.6	15.2	?

The Moon

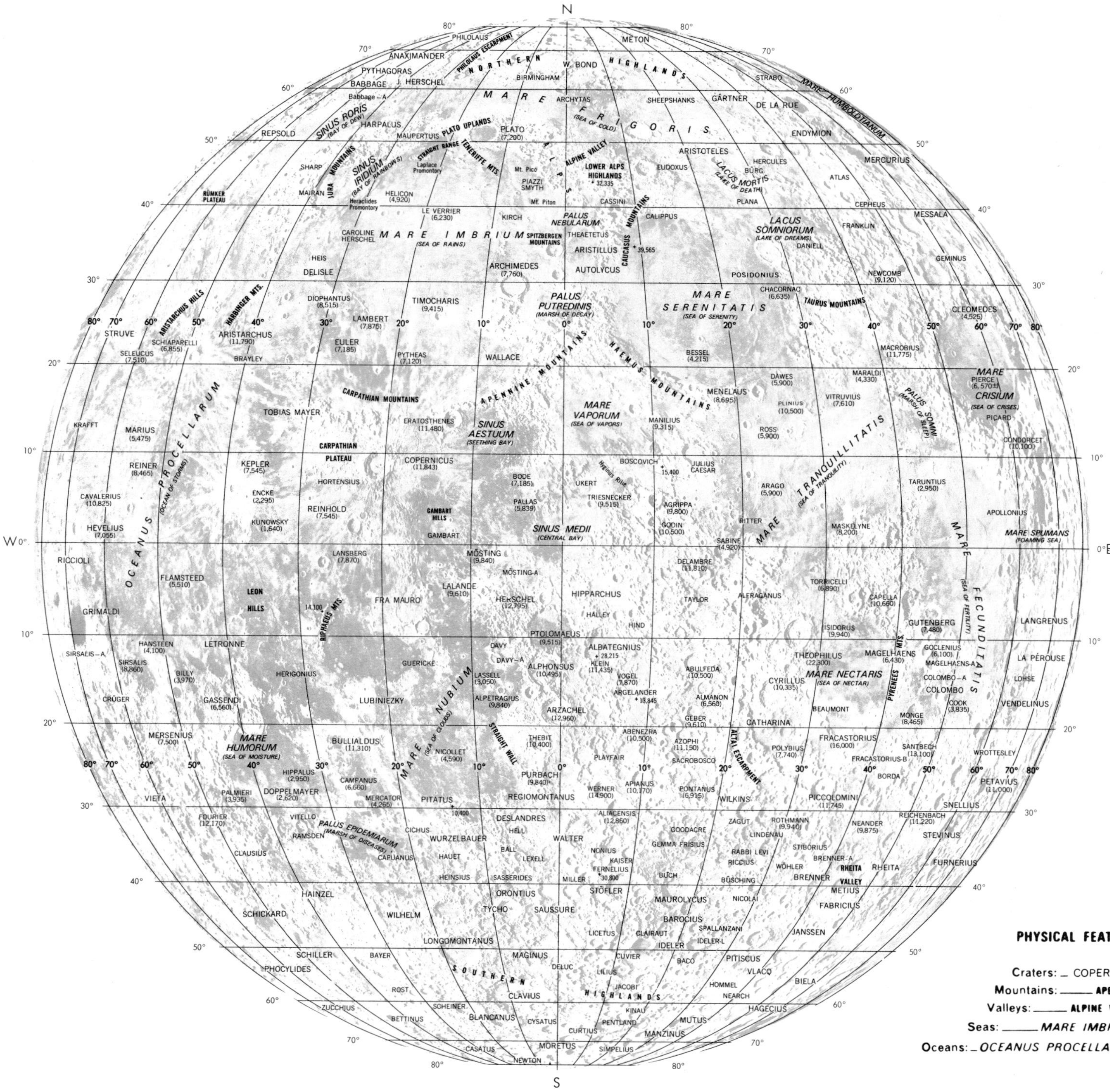

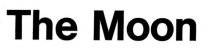

PHYSICAL FEATURES

Craters: _ COPERNICUS
Mountains: _____ APENNINE
Valleys: _____ ALPINE VALLEY
Seas: _____ *MARE IMBRIUM*
Oceans: _ *OCEANUS PROCELLARUM*

INDEX

Abenezra, crater	21°S	12°E
Abulfeda, crater	14°S	14°E
*Aestuum, Sinus; bay	12°N	9°W
Albategnius, crater	11°S	4°E
Alfraganus, crater	5°S	19°E
Aliacensis, crater	31°S	5°E
Alphonsus, crater	14°S	3°W
Alpine Valley	49°N	2°E
Altai Escarpment	24°S	22°E
Anaximander crater	69°N	53°W
Apennine Mountains	20°N	2°W
Archimedes, crater	30°N	4°W
Archytas, crater	59°N	5°E
Argelander, crater	17°S	6°E
Aristarchus, crater	24°N	47°W
Aristarchus Hills	27°N	53°W
Aristillus, crater	34°N	2°E
Aristoteles, crater	50°N	18°E
Arzachel, crater	19°S	2°W
Atlas, crater	46°N	45°E
Babbage, crater	59°N	57°W
Baco, crater	51°S	20°E
Barocius, crater	45°S	18°E
Beaumont, crater-ring	18°S	29°E
Biela, crater	55°S	53°E
Billy, crater	14°S	50°W
Birmingham, crater	65°N	9°W
Blancanus, crater-basin	64°S	23°W
Bode, crater	7°N	3°W
Brenner, crater-ring	39°S	40°E
Büsching, crater	38°S	21°E
Campanus, crater	28°S	28°W
Capella, crater	6°S	35°E
Caroline Herschel, crater	35°N	31°W
Carpathian Plateau	10°N	25°W
Carpathian Mountains	15°N	24°W
Casatus, crater	72°S	21°W
Catharina, crater	18°S	24°E
Caucasus Mountains	36°N	8°E
Cavalerius, crater	5°N	67°W
Clairaut, crater	47°S	15°E
Clavius, crater	59°S	15°W
Cleomedes, crater	27°N	55°E
Colombo, crater	15°S	46°E
Condorcet, crater	12°N	70°E
Cook, crater	18°S	49°E
Copernicus, crater	10°N	20°W
*Crisium, Mare; sea	18°N	58°E
Curtius, crater	67°S	6°E
Cuvier, crater	50°S	11°E
Cyrillus, crater	13°S	24°E
Davy, crater	12°S	8°W
De la Rue, crater	58°N	46°E
Diophantus, crater	28°N	34°W
Doppelmayer, crater-ring	29°S	41°W
Endymion, crater	54°N	58°E
*Epidemiarum, Palus; marsh	32°S	29°W
Eratosthenes, crater	15°N	11°W
Eudoxus, crater	45°N	17°E
Fabricius, crater	43°S	42°E
*Fecunditatis, Mare; sea	4°S	51°E
Flamsteed, crater	5°S	44°W
Fourier, crater	31°S	53°W
Fracastorius, crater-ring	21°S	34°E
Fra Mauro, crater	6°S	17°W
Franklin, crater	38°N	48°E
*Frigoris, Mare; sea	56°N	4°E
Furnerius, crater	36°S	61°E
Gambart, crater	1°N	15°W
Gambart Hills	4°N	17°W
Gärtner, crater	59°N	35°E
Gassendi, crater	17°S	40°W
Geminus, crater	34°N	57°E
Goclenius, crater-ring	10°S	45°E
Grimaldi crater	6°S	68°W
Guericke, crater	11°S	14°W
Gutenberg, crater-basin	9°S	41°E
Haemus Mountains	16°N	14°E
Hagecius, crater	60°S	50°E
Harbinger Mountains	27°N	42°W
Heraclides Promontory	41°N	33°W
Hercules, crater	47°N	40°E
Hippalus, crater-ring	25°S	32°W
Hipparchus, crater	6°S	6°E
*Humboldtianum, Mare; sea	57°N	80°E
*Humorum, Mare; sea	23°S	38°W
Hyginus Rille	8°N	6°E
*Imbrium, Mare; sea	36°N	16°W
*Iridum, Sinus; bay	45°N	32°W
Isidorus, crater	8°S	33°E
Jacobi, crater	57°S	12°E
Janssen, crater	47°S	43°E
John Herschel, crater	62°N	40°W
Julius Caesar, crater	9°N	15°E
Jura Mountains	46°N	38°W
Kaiser, crater	37°S	7°E
Kepler, crater	8°N	38°W
Lalande, crater	5°S	9°W
Lambert, crater	26°N	21°W
Langrenus, crater	9°S	61°E
Lansberg, crater	0°	27°W
LaPérouse, crater	11°S	76°E
Laplace Promontory	46°N	26°W
Leon Hills	6°S	38°W
Letronne, crater	11°S	43°W
Le Verrier, crater	40°N	21°W
Lilius, crater	55°S	6°E
Lohse, crater	14°S	60°E
Lower Alps, highlands	47°N	6°E
Lubiniezky, crater-ring	18°S	24°W
Macrobius, crater	22°N	46°E
Mairan, crater	42°N	43°W
Manilius, crater	14°N	9°E
Maraldi, crater	20°N	35°E
Marius, crater	12°N	51°W
Maurolycus, crater	42°S	16°E
*Medii, Sinus; bay	0°	0°
Mercurius, crater	47°N	67°E
Mersenius, crater	22°S	49°W
Messala, crater	39°N	60°E
Meton, crater	76°N	24°E
*Mortis, Lacus; lake	44°N	27°E
Mösting, crater	1°S	6°W
Mutus, crater	64°S	31°E
Nearch, crater	58°S	40°E
*Nebularum, Palus; marsh	38°N	1°E
*Nectaris, Mare; sea	14°S	34°E
Newcomb, crater	30°N	44°E
Northern Highlands	69°N	10°W
*Nubium, Mare; sea	19°S	14°W
Pallas, crater	5°N	2°W
Pentland, crater	65°S	13°E
Petavius, crater	26°S	60°E
Philolaus Escarpment	69°N	27°W
Philolaus, crater	74°N	35°W
Pico, Mount	46°N	8°W
Pitatus, crater	29°S	13°W
Pitiscus, crater	51°S	31°E
Piton, Mount	41°N	1°W
Plato, crater	52°N	10°W
Plato Uplands	53°N	20°W
Plinius, crater	16°N	24°E
Polybius, crater	23°S	26°E
Pontanus, crater	29°S	15°E
Posidonius, crater	32°N	30°E
*Procellarum, Oceanus ocean	10°N	47°W
Ptolemaeus, crater	9°S	2°W
Purbach, crater	26°S	2°W
*Putredinis, Palus; marsh	27°N	1°W
Pyrenees Mts.	14°S	41°E
Pythagoras, crater	64°N	66°W
Pytheas, crater	20°N	20°W
Regiomontanus, crater	28°S	1°W
Reiner, crater	7°N	55°W
Reinhold, crater	3°N	23°W
Rheita Valley	39°S	47°E
Riccius, Crater	37°S	27°E
Riphaeus Mountains	8°S	27°W
Ritter, crater	·2°N	19°E
*Roris, Sinus; bay	54°N	46°W
Ross, crater	12°N	22°E
Rothmann, crater	30°S	28°E
Rümker Plateau	40°N	57°W
Sacrobosco, crater-basin	23°S	17°E
Santbech, crater	21°S	44°E
Schiaparelli, crater	23°N	59°W
Schickard, crater	44°S	53°W
Schiller, crater	52°S	40°W
*Serenitatis, Mare; sea	30°N	17°E
Simpelius, crater	73°S	17E°
Sirsalis, crater	13°S	60°W
Snellius, crater	29°S	57°E
*Somnii, Palus; marsh	15°N	46°E
*Somniorum, Lacus; lake	37°N	35°E
Southern Highlands	58°S	5°W
Spitzbergen Mountains	35°N	5°W
*Spumans, Mare; sea	1°N	65°E
Stevinus, crater	33°S	55°E
Stöfler crater,	41°S	5°E
Straight, range	49°N	20°W
Straight Wall	22°S	8°W
Struve, crater	23°N	70°W
Taruntius, crater	5°N	47°E
Taurus Mountains	28°N	35°E
Taylor, crater	5°S	17°E
Teneriffe Mountains	48°N	14°W
Theophilus, crater	11°S	27°E
Tobias Mayer, crater-ring	16°N	29°W
*Tranquillitatis, Mare; sea	9°N	30°E
Triesnecker, crater	4°N	3°E
Tycho, crater	43°S	11°W
Ukert, crater	8°N	1°E
*Vaporum, Mare; sea	14°N	5°E
Vendelinus, crater	17°S	62°E
Vieta, crater	29°S	56°W
Vitruvius, crater	18°N	32°E
Vlacq, crater	54°S	39°E
Wallace, crater-ring	20°N	9°W
Walter, crater	33°S	0°
Wilkins, crater-basin	29°S	20°E
W. Bond, crater	66°N	3°E
Zagut, crater	32°S	22°E

*Lowlands

Shortly after Commander Neil A. Armstrong of Apollo 11 first set foot on the Moon, he took this picture of Lunar Module Pilot Edwin E. Aldrin, Jr. descending the ladder to join him.

Earth's only satellite, the Moon, is so large in relation to its planet—with a diameter one-quarter that of Earth's—that the two bodies are sometimes considered a "double planet." Scientists long believed that the Moon broke away from Earth 4 billion years ago. However, the presence of unknown minerals in samples collected during Apollo landings between 1969 and 1972 suggest that the satellite was never a part of Earth, despite the chemical similarity of both bodies. The Moon's enormous seas and craters were caused by meteoric impact; there is no existing volcanic activity. This remarkably detailed view of the Moon was photographed from aboard the Apollo 11 spacecraft when it was only 10,000 nautical miles away on its homeward-bound course to Earth.

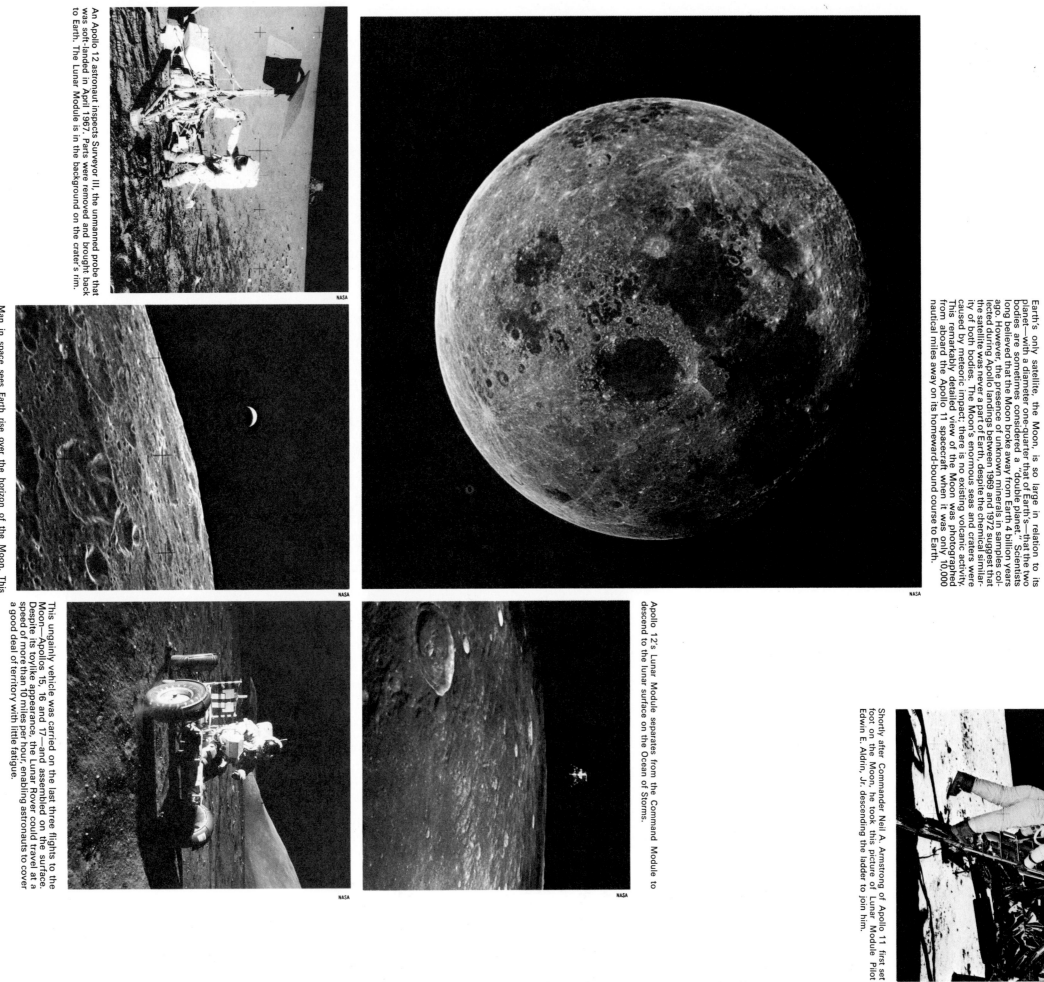

Apollo 12's Lunar Module separates from the Command Module to descend to the lunar surface on the Ocean of Storms.

An Apollo 12 astronaut inspects Surveyor III, the unmanned probe that was soft-landed in April 1967. Parts were removed and brought back to Earth. The Lunar Module is in the background on the crater's rim.

Man in space sees Earth rise over the horizon of the Moon. This spectacular photograph was taken by the Apollo 12 astronauts on their way down to the second successful lunar landing.

This ungainly vehicle was carried on the last three flights to the Moon—Apollos 15, 16 and 17—and assembled on the surface. Despite its toylike appearance, the Lunar Rover could travel at a speed of more than 10 miles per hour, enabling astronauts to cover a good deal of territory with little fatigue.

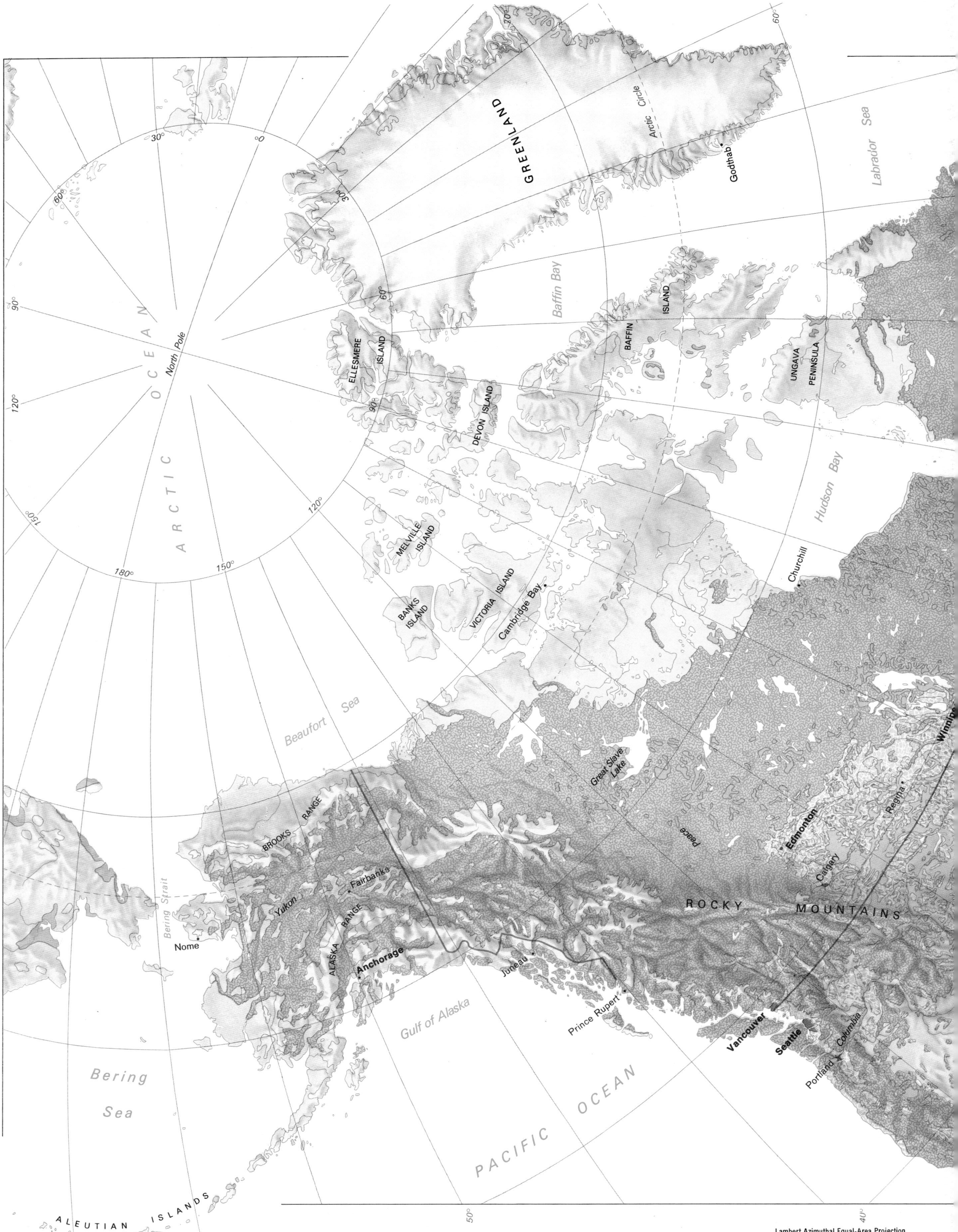

Lambert Azimuthal Equal-Area Projection

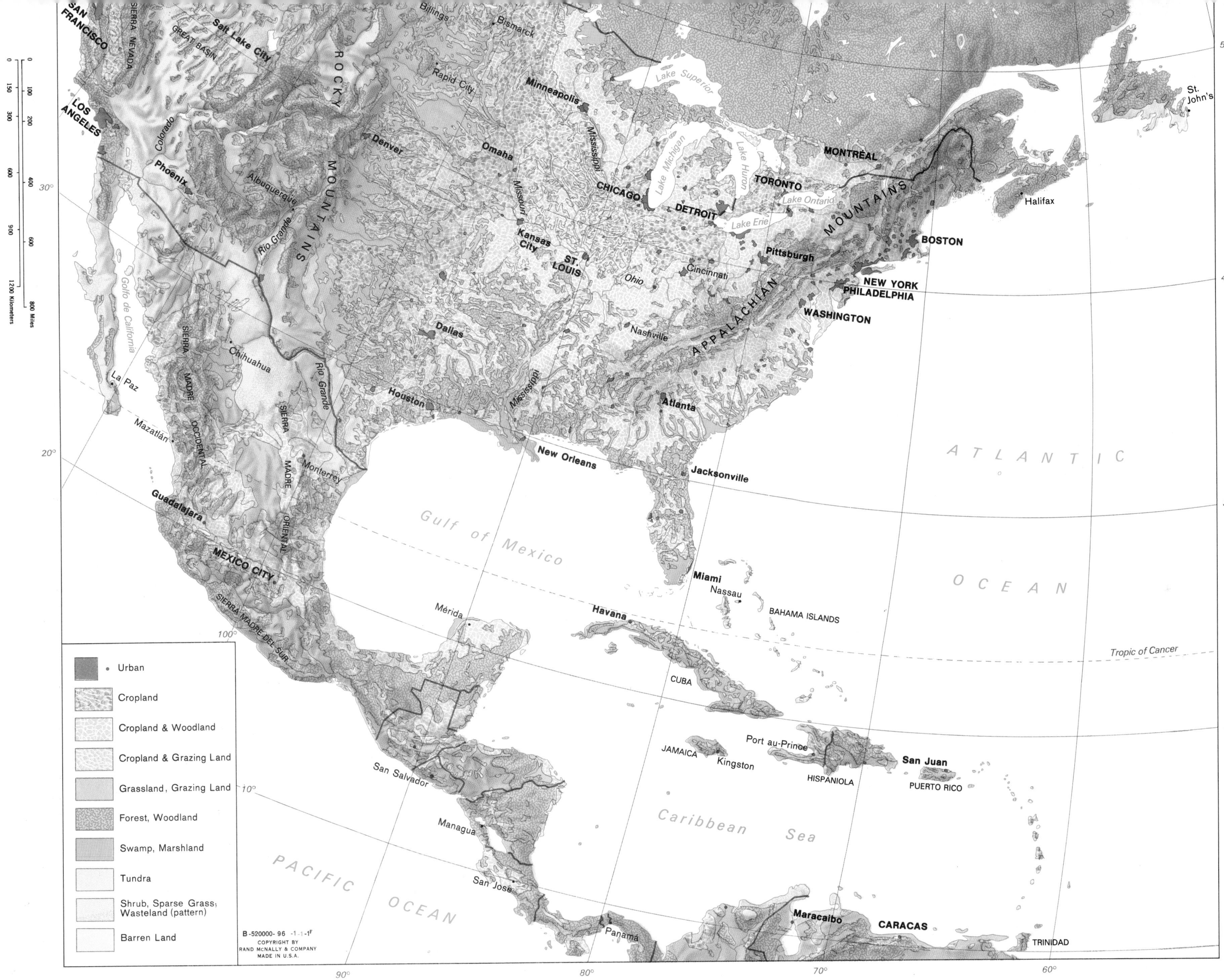

SAN FRANCISCO
SIERRA NEVADA
GREAT BASIN
Salt Lake City
Billings
Bismarck
ROCKY MOUNTAINS
Rapid City
Minneapolis
Lake Superior
St. John's
LOS ANGELES
Colorado
Denver
Omaha
Mississippi
Lake Michigan
Lake Huron
MONTREAL
Phoenix
Albuquerque
Missouri
CHICAGO
TORONTO
Lake Ontario
Halifax
DETROIT
Lake Erie
Rio Grande
Kansas City
ST. LOUIS
Pittsburgh
BOSTON
Cincinnati
Ohio
NEW YORK
PHILADELPHIA
WASHINGTON
APPALACHIAN MOUNTAINS
Golfo de California
Dallas
Nashville
SIERRA MADRE OCCIDENTAL
Chihuahua
La Paz
Houston
Atlanta
Mazatlán
SIERRA MADRE ORIENTAL
Monterrey
New Orleans
Jacksonville
ATLANTIC OCEAN
Guadalajara
Gulf of Mexico
MEXICO CITY
Miami
Nassau
BAHAMA ISLANDS
Mérida
Havana
SIERRA MADRE DEL SUR
Tropic of Cancer
CUBA
Port au-Prince
JAMAICA
Kingston
HISPANIOLA
San Juan
PUERTO RICO
San Salvador
Caribbean Sea
Managua
PACIFIC OCEAN
San José
Maracaibo
CARACAS
Panamá
TRINIDAD
50°
40°
30°
20°
10°
100°
90°
80°
70°
60°
0 100 200 400 600 800 Miles
0 150 300 600 900 1200 Kilometers
Urban
Cropland
Cropland & Woodland
Cropland & Grazing Land
Grassland, Grazing Land
Forest, Woodland
Swamp, Marshland
Tundra
Shrub, Sparse Grass, Wasteland (pattern)
Barren Land
B-520000-96 -1-1-1
COPYRIGHT BY RAND McNALLY & COMPANY
MADE IN U.S.A.

PACIFIC OCEAN
Vancouver
Seattle
Spokane
Portland
Columbia
CASCADE RANGE
Medford
ROCKY MOUNTAINS
Calgary
Regina
Winnipe
Lake Winnipeg
Bismarck
Billings
Boise
Rapid City
Missouri
Casper
Great Salt Lake
Salt Lake City
Reno
GREAT BASIN
SAN FRANCISCO
SIERRA NEVADA
Fresno
Omaha
Denver
Las Vegas
Wichita
LOS ANGELES
San Diego
Colorado
Phoenix
Albuquerque
Amarillo
Oklahoma City
Red
Dallas
El Paso
Odessa
Hermosillo
Gulf of California
Rio Grande
San Antonio
Chihuahua
SIERRA MADRE OCCIDENTAL
SIERRA MADRE ORIENTAL
Torreón
Monterrey
50°
45°
40°
35°
30°
25°
125°
120°
115°
110°
105°
100°
B-520500-96 -1-1-1
COPYRIGHT BY
RAND McNALLY & COMPANY
MADE IN U.S.A.

Moosonee
James Bay
Gulf of St. Lawrence
St. Lawrence
Quebec
Halifax
Thunder Bay
Lake Superior
Sudbury
MONTRÉAL
Bangor
Duluth
Lake Huron
Minneapolis
Mississippi
TORONTO
Lake Ontario
BOSTON
Buffalo
Lake Michigan
Milwaukee
DETROIT
Lake Erie
Cleveland
NEW YORK
CHICAGO
Pittsburgh
PHILADELPHIA
APPALACHIAN MOUNTAINS
WASHINGTON
Indianapolis
Cincinnati
Kansas City
Missouri
ST. LOUIS
Ohio
Roanoke
Norfolk
OZARK PLATEAU
Nashville
Charlotte
Memphis
Arkansas
Little Rock
ATLANTIC OCEAN
Atlanta
Birmingham
Charleston
Red
Jacksonville
Tallahassee
New Orleans
Houston
Tampa
Gulf of Mexico
Miami
Nassau
Urban
Cropland
Cropland & Woodland
Cropland & Grazing Land
Grassland, Grazing Land
Forest, Woodland
Swamp, Marshland
Shrub, Sparse Grass, Wasteland (pattern)
Barren Land
Polyconic Projection
0 50 100 200 300 400 Miles
0 75 150 300 450 600 Kilometers

Lambert Azimuthal Equal-Area Projection

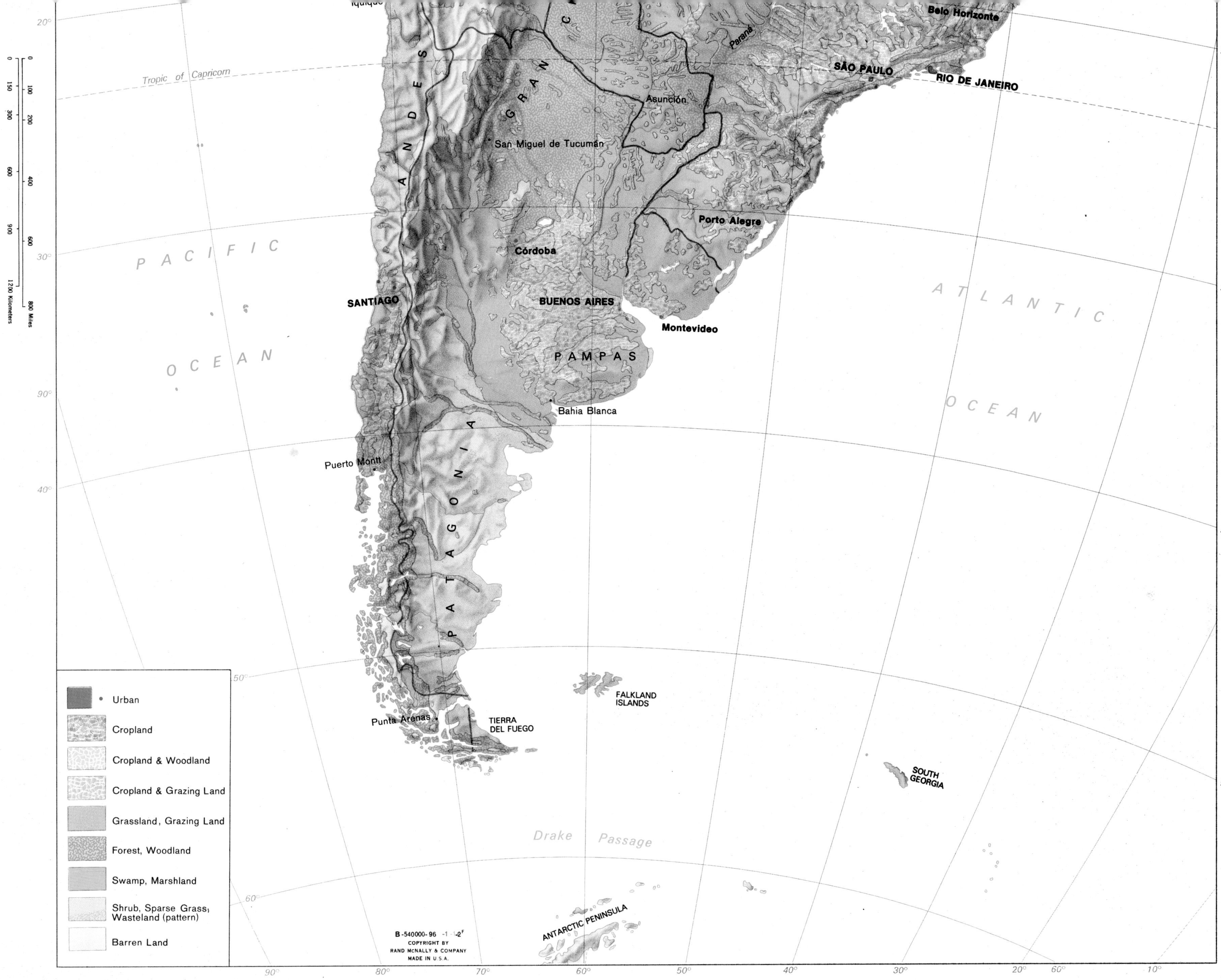
Iquique
Belo Horizonte
Paraná
SÃO PAULO
RIO DE JANEIRO
Tropic of Capricorn
Asunción
GRAN C
San Miguel de Tucumán
ANDES
Porto Alegre
PACIFIC
OCEAN
Córdoba
SANTIAGO
BUENOS AIRES
Montevideo
ATLANTIC
OCEAN
PAMPAS
Bahia Blanca
Puerto Montt
PATAGONIA
FALKLAND ISLANDS
Punta Arenas
TIERRA DEL FUEGO
SOUTH GEORGIA
Drake Passage
ANTARCTIC PENINSULA
0 100 200 400 600 800 Miles
0 150 300 600 900 1200 Kilometers
Urban
Cropland
Cropland & Woodland
Cropland & Grazing Land
Grassland, Grazing Land
Forest, Woodland
Swamp, Marshland
Shrub, Sparse Grass, Wasteland (pattern)
Barren Land
20°
30°
40°
50°
60°
90°
80°
70°
10°

Europe

Urban
Cropland
Cropland & Woodland
Cropland & Grazing Land
Grassland, Grazing Land
Forest, Woodland
Swamp, Marshland
Tundra
Shrub, Sparse Grass, Wasteland (pattern)
Barren Land
Oasis
ATLANTIC OCEAN
North Sea
Baltic Sea
Gulf of Bothnia
Bay of Biscay
Mediterranean Sea
Tyrrhenian Sea
Adriatic Sea
Aegean Sea
Reykjavik
Narvik
Murmansk
Trondheim
Bergen
Oslo
Stockholm
Helsinki
LENINGRAD
Tallinn
Göteborg
Riga
Copenhagen
Kaliningrad
Minsk
Pripyat
Glasgow
Belfast
MANCHESTER
Dublin
LONDON
Amsterdam
Hamburg
Elbe
BERLIN
Oder
Warsaw
Antwerp
Essen
Leipzig
Frankfurt
Brest
PARIS
Seine
Loire
Strasbourg
Prague
Kraków
L'vov
Rhine
Danube
Munich
VIENNA
CARPATHIANS
Dnestr
Zürich
ALPS
Lyon
Bordeaux
Garonne
Rhône
MILAN
Tisza
BUDAPEST
Zagreb
Sava
Venice
Genoa
Belgrade
Bucharest
Sofia
La Coruña
Bilbao
PYRENEES
Ebro
Douro
MADRID
Lisbon
Marseille
BARCELONA
CORSICA
ROME
SARDINIA
Naples
Tirane
ISLAS BALEARES
Sevilla
Tanger
Oran
Algiers
Palermo
SICILY
Athens
Casablanca
ATLAS MOUNTAINS
Tunis
MALTA
CRETE
Ume
20°
10°
0°
30°
60°
50°
40°
Longitude West of Greenwich
Longitude East of Greenwich
Conic Projection
0 50 100 200 300 400 500 Miles
0 100 200 400 600 800 Kilometers

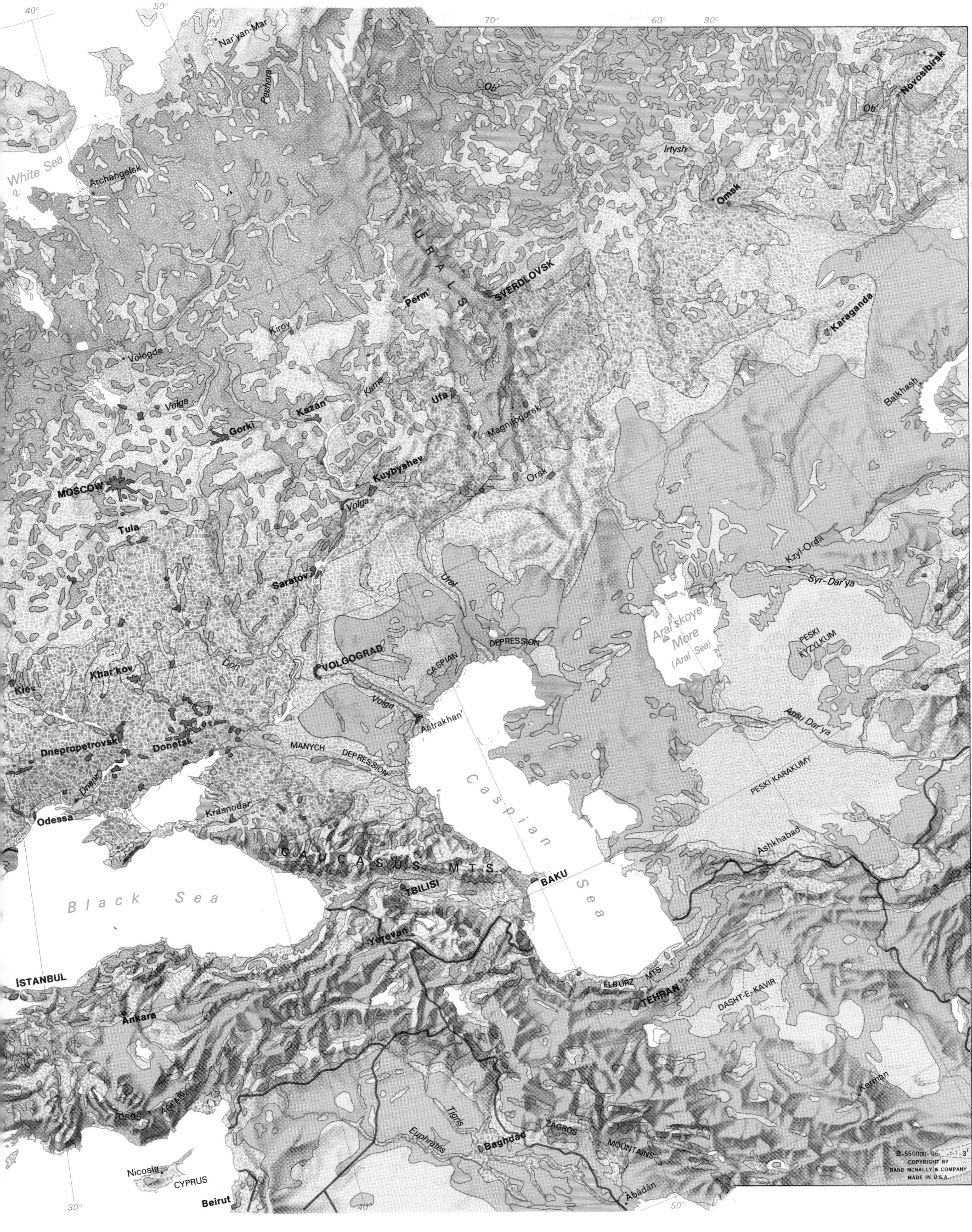

Nar'yan-Mar
Pechora
Ob'
Novosibirsk
Ob'
Irtysh
White Sea
Archangelsk
Omsk
URALS
SVERDLOVSK
Perm'
Karaganda
Kirov
Vologda
Kama
Ufa
Magnitogorsk
Balkhash
Volga
Kazan'
Gorki
Kuybyshev
Orsk
MOSCOW
Volga
Tula
Kzyl-Orda
Syr-Dar'ya
Saratov
Ural
Aral'skoye More (Aral Sea)
PESKI KYZYLKUM
DEPRESSION
VOLGOGRAD
CASPIAN
Don
Khar'kov
Kiev
Volga
Astrakhan'
Amu Dar'ya
Dnepropetrovsk
Donetsk
MANYCH DEPRESSION
Dnepr
PESKI KARAKUMY
Caspian Sea
Odessa
Krasnodar
Ashkhabad
CAUCASUS MTS.
BAKU
TBILISI
Black Sea
Yerevan
İSTANBUL
ELBURZ MTS.
TEHRAN
DASHT-E-KAVIR
Ankara
Kerman
TOROS
AGLARI
Tigris
Euphrates
Baghdad
ZAGROS MOUNTAINS
Nicosia
CYPRUS
Beirut
Abādān
B-550000-96-1-1-3
COPYRIGHT BY RAND MCNALLY & COMPANY
MADE IN U.S.A.

Northern Asia

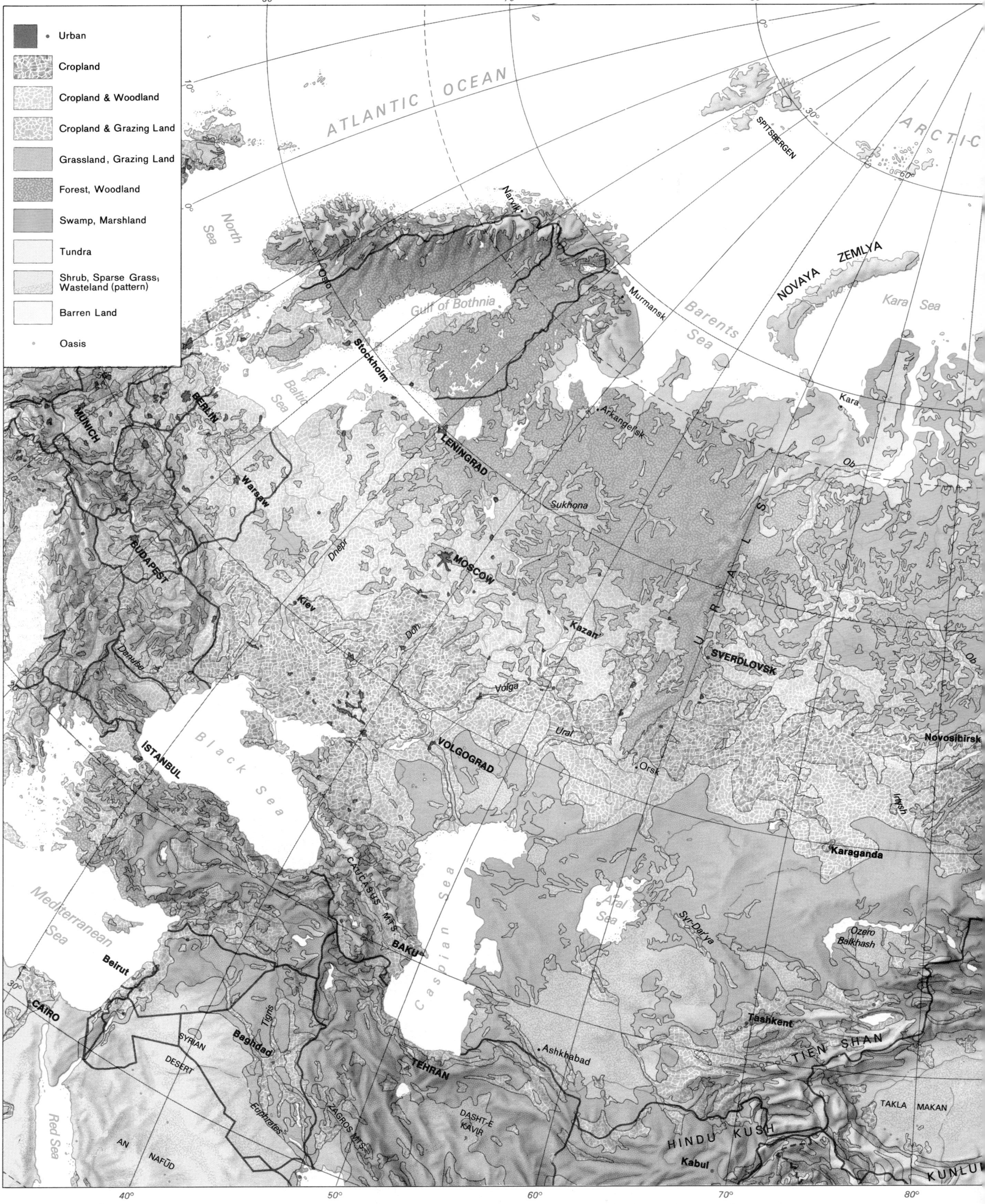

Lambert Azimuthal Equal-Area Projection

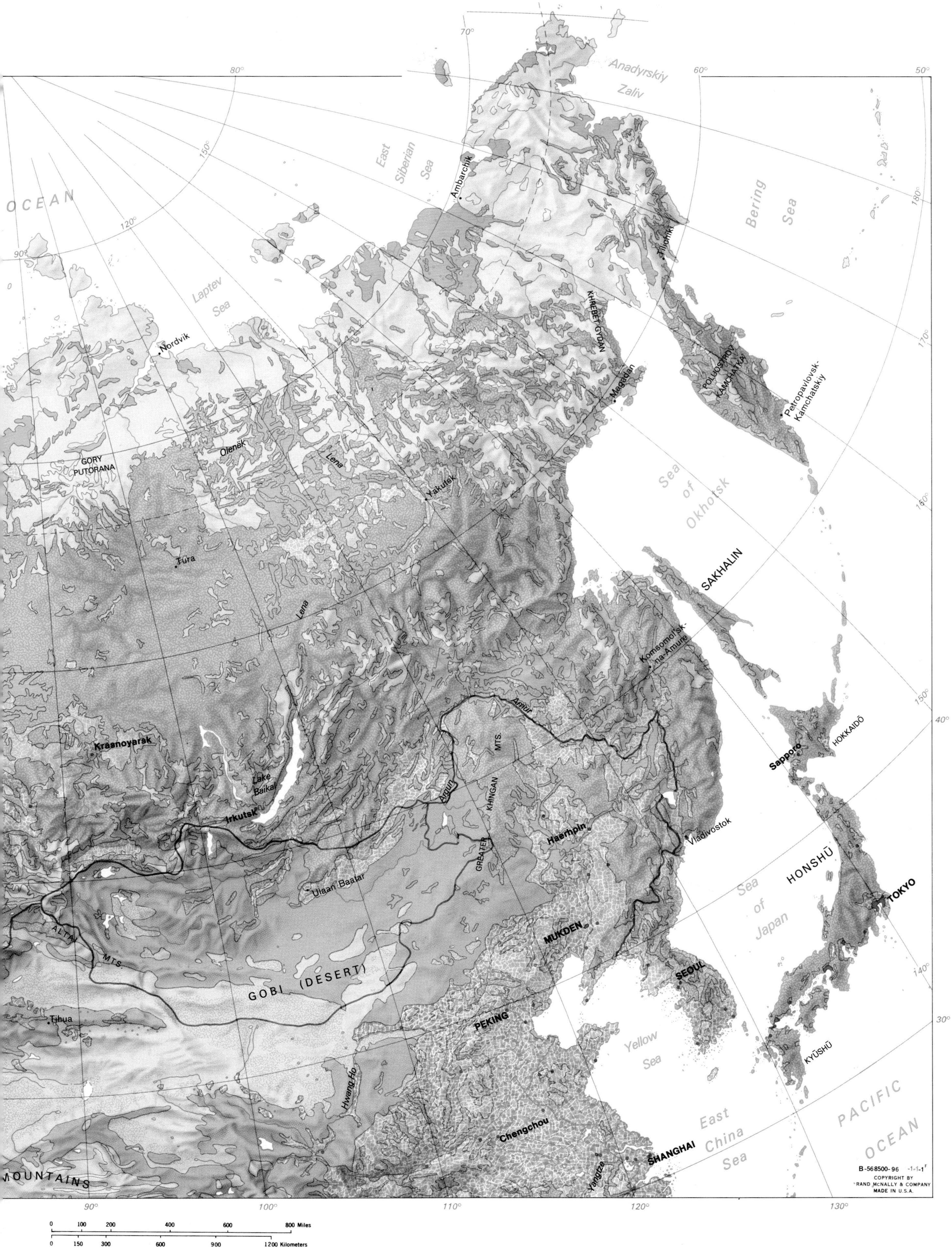
OCEAN
Laptev Sea
Nordvik
East Siberian Sea
Ambarchik
Anadyrskiy Zaliv
Bering Sea
Tilichiki
KHREBET GYDAN
Magadan
POLUOSTROV KAMCHATKA
Petropavlovsk-Kamchatskiy
GORY PUTORANA
Olenëk
Lena
Yakutsk
Sea of Okhotsk
Tura
SAKHALIN
Komsomol'sk-na-Amure
Amur
Krasnoyarsk
Lake Baikal
Irkutsk
Argun
GREATER KHINGAN MTS.
Haerhpin
Vladivostok
HOKKAIDŌ
Sapporo
HONSHŪ
TOKYO
Sea of Japan
Ulaan Baatar
ALTAI MTS.
GOBI (DESERT)
MUKDEN
SEOUL
Tihua
PEKING
Yellow Sea
KYŪSHŪ
Hwang Ho
Chengchou
East China Sea
PACIFIC OCEAN
SHANGHAI
Yangtze
MOUNTAINS
B-568500-96 -1-1-1
COPYRIGHT BY RAND McNALLY & COMPANY
MADE IN U.S.A.
0 100 200 400 600 800 Miles
0 150 300 600 900 1200 Kilometers

30°
40°
50°
60°
70°
80°
20°
10°
Mediterranean Sea
Red Sea
Caspian Sea
Aral Sea
Arabian Sea
Gulf of Aden
INDIAN OCEAN
CAUCASUS MTS.
ZAGROS MTS.
HINDU KUSH
TIEN SHAN
KUNLU
TAKLA MAKAN
PLATEA
WESTERN GHATS
EASTERN GHATS
SYRIAN DESERT
AN NAFŪD
AR RUB' AL KHĀLĪ
DASHT-E KAVĪR
DANAKIL
CEYLON
Beirut
CAIRO
Baghdad
Tigris
Euphrates
BAKU
TEHRAN
Ashkhabad
Tashkent
Karaganda
Ozero Balkhash
Syr-Dar'ya
Kabul
Rawalpindi
Indus
DELHI
Kermān
Mecca
Riyadh
Muscat
KARACHI
Aden
Berbera
BOMBAY
Nāgpur
MADRAS
Calicut
Colombo
Urban
Cropland
Cropland & Woodland
Cropland & Grazing Land
Grassland, Grazing Land
Forest, Woodland
Swamp, Marshland
Tundra
Shrub, Sparse Grass, Wasteland (pattern)
Barren Land
Oasis
Lambert Azimuthal Equal-Area Projection

GOBI (DESERT)
ALTAI MTS.
Ulaan Baatar
GREATER KHINGAN MTS.
Haerhpin
Vladivostok
MUKDEN
SEOUL
TOKYO
HONSHŪ
Sea of Japan
KYŪSHŪ
PEKING
Yellow Sea
Hwang Ho
Tihua
MOUNTAINS
TIBET
Chengchou
SHANGHAI
East China Sea
PACIFIC OCEAN
WUHAN
CHUNGKING
Mekong
T'aipei
Tropic of Cancer
FORMOSA
HIMALAYAS
Brahmaputra
K'unming
CANTON
Philippine Sea
Ganges
CALCUTTA
Mandalay
Salween
Hanoi
HAINAN TAO
MANILA
Bay of Bengal
Rangoon
BANGKOK
South China Sea
Cebu
MINDANAO
HO CHI MINH CITY
Andaman Sea
Kota Kinabalu
Celebes Sea
Manado
Medan
SINGAPORE
Kuching
BORNEO
CELEBES
SUMATRA
Ujung Pandang
Equator
Java Sea
JAKARTA
JAVA
90°
100°
120°
130°
140°
10°
0°
20°
30°
40°
0 100 200 400 600 800 Miles
0 150 300 600 900 1200 Kilometers

Lambert Azimuthal Equal-Area Projection

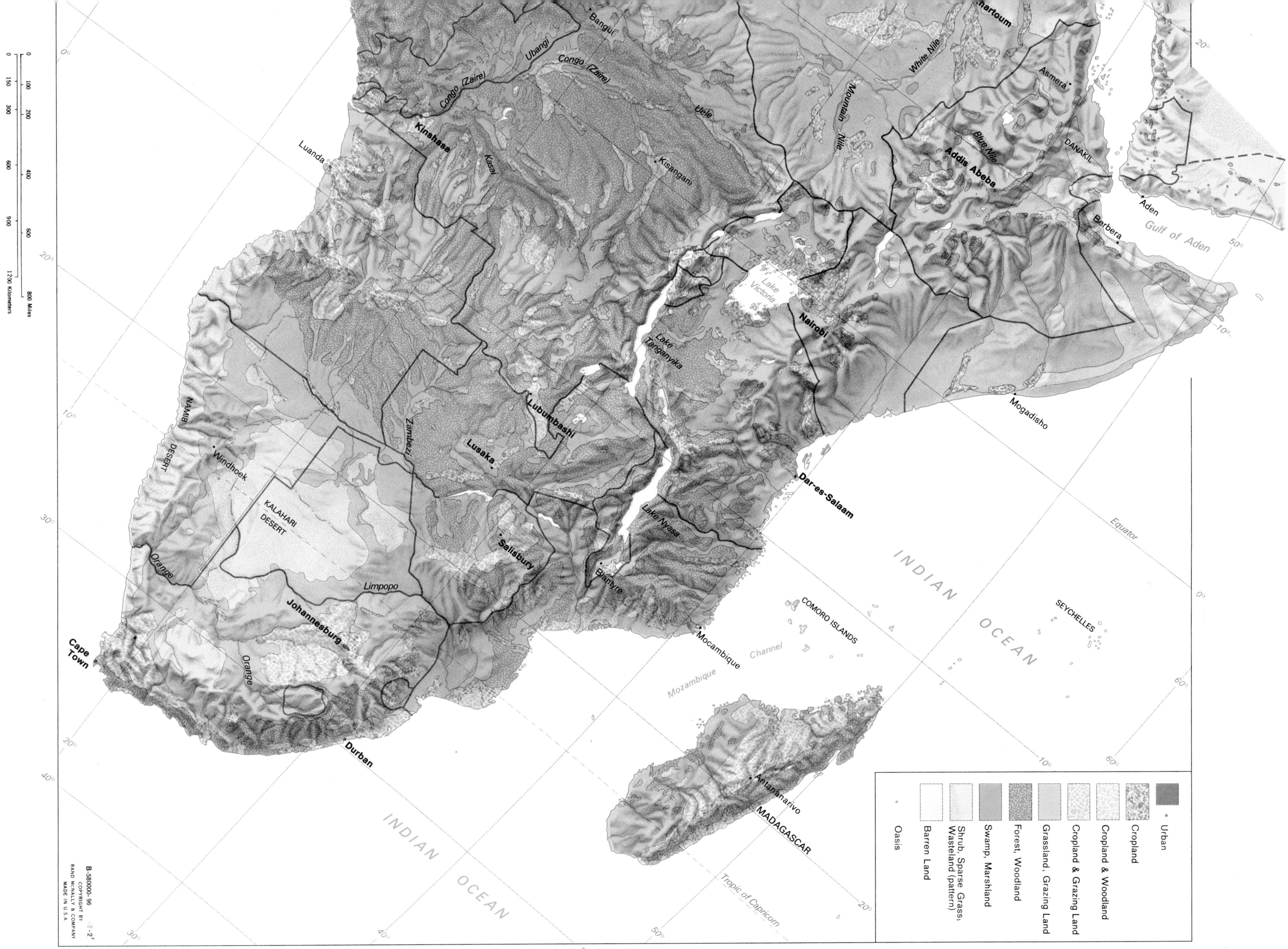

0 100 200 400 600 800 Miles
0 150 300 600 900 1200 Kilometers
Khartoum
Bangui
Ubangi
Congo (Zaire)
Uele
White Nile
Mountain Nile
Asmera
Blue Nile
Addis Abeba
DANAKIL
Aden
Gulf of Aden
Berbera
Kinshasa
Kasai
Luanda
Kisangani
Lake Victoria
Nairobi
Lake Tanganyika
Mogadisho
Lubumbashi
Lusaka
Zambezi
NAMIB DESERT
Windhoek
KALAHARI DESERT
Dar-es-Salaam
Equator
Lake Nyasa
Salisbury
Orange
Limpopo
Blantyre
INDIAN OCEAN
COMORO ISLANDS
SEYCHELLES
Johannesburg
Cape Town
Mocambique
Mozambique Channel
Durban
Antananarivo
MADAGASCAR
Tropic of Capricorn
Urban
Cropland
Cropland & Woodland
Cropland & Grazing Land
Grassland, Grazing Land
Forest, Woodland
Swamp, Marshland
Shrub, Sparse Grass, Wasteland (pattern)
Barren Land
Oasis
B-580000-96
COPYRIGHT BY RAND McNALLY & COMPANY
MADE IN U.S.A.

Lambert Azimuthal Equal-Area Projection

NEW GUINEA
NEW BRITAIN
Port Moresby
SOLOMON ISLANDS
Equator
GILBERT ISLANDS
PACIFIC OCEAN
Coral Sea
Cairns
Townsville
NEW HEBRIDES
SAMOA ISLANDS
Pago Pago
FIJI ISLANDS
Suva
GREAT DIVIDING RANGE
Rockhampton
NEW CALEDONIA
ÎLES LOYAUTÉ
Nouméa
TONGA ISLANDS
Brisbane
Darling
SYDNEY
Canberra
Tasman Sea
MELBOURNE
Auckland
NORTH ISLAND
TASMANIA
Hobart
Wellington
SOUTHERN ALPS
Christchurch
SOUTH ISLAND
Dunedin
STEWART ISLAND
B-590200-96
COPYRIGHT BY
RAND McNALLY & COMPANY
MADE IN U.S.A.
0 100 200 400 600 800 Miles
0 150 300 600 900 1200 Kilometers

The World Jan. 1, 1979

Every political entity that has a separate administration, whether it is independent or dependent, is named here and is distinguished from adjacent units by color. In all, over 200 political units are named. A noncontiguous part of a country has the same color as the country. If it lies at any distance, it is identified (for example, Alaska, a state of the United States), but if it lies close by, it is not (for example, the island of Corsica, which comprises two departments of France).

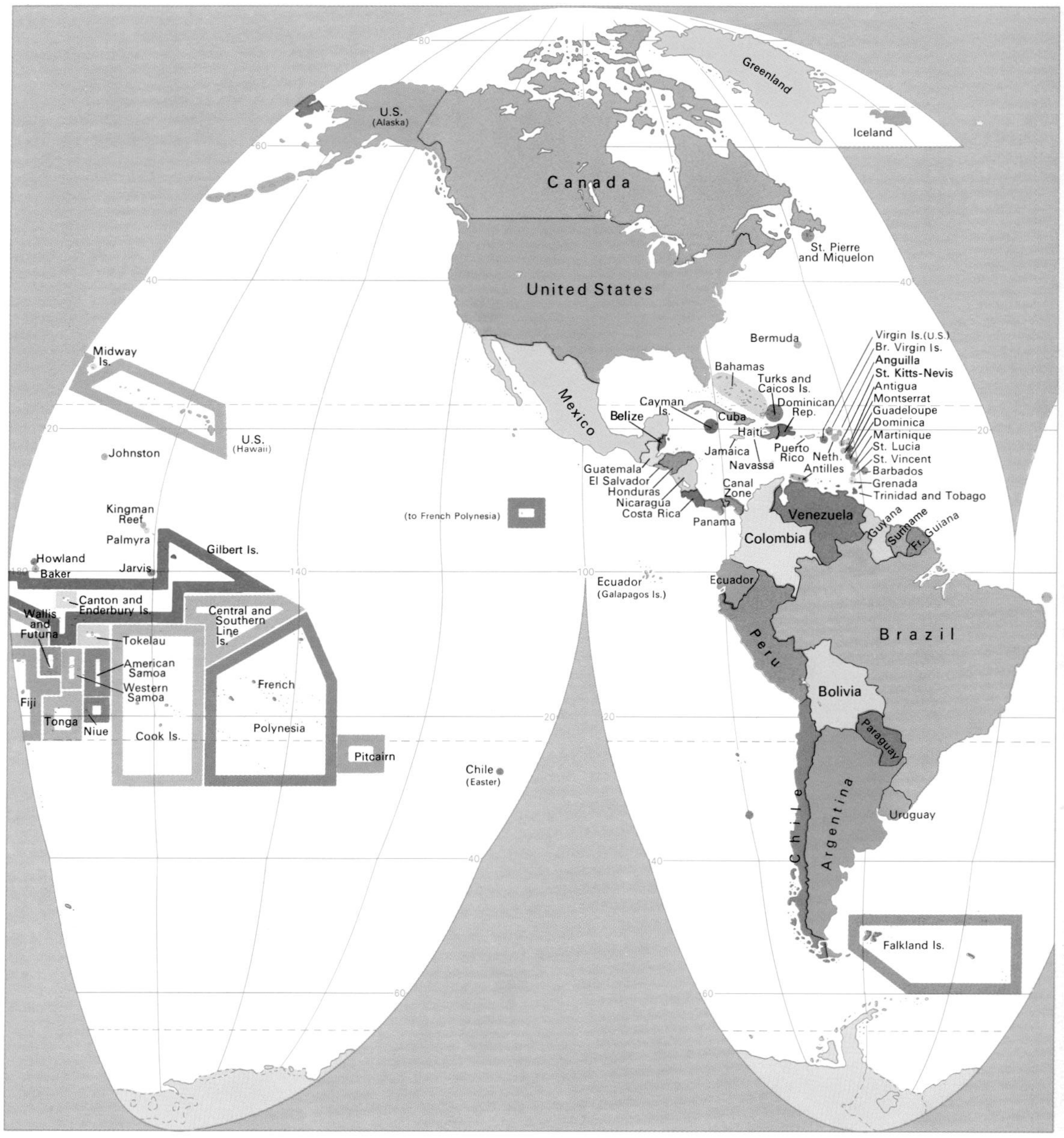

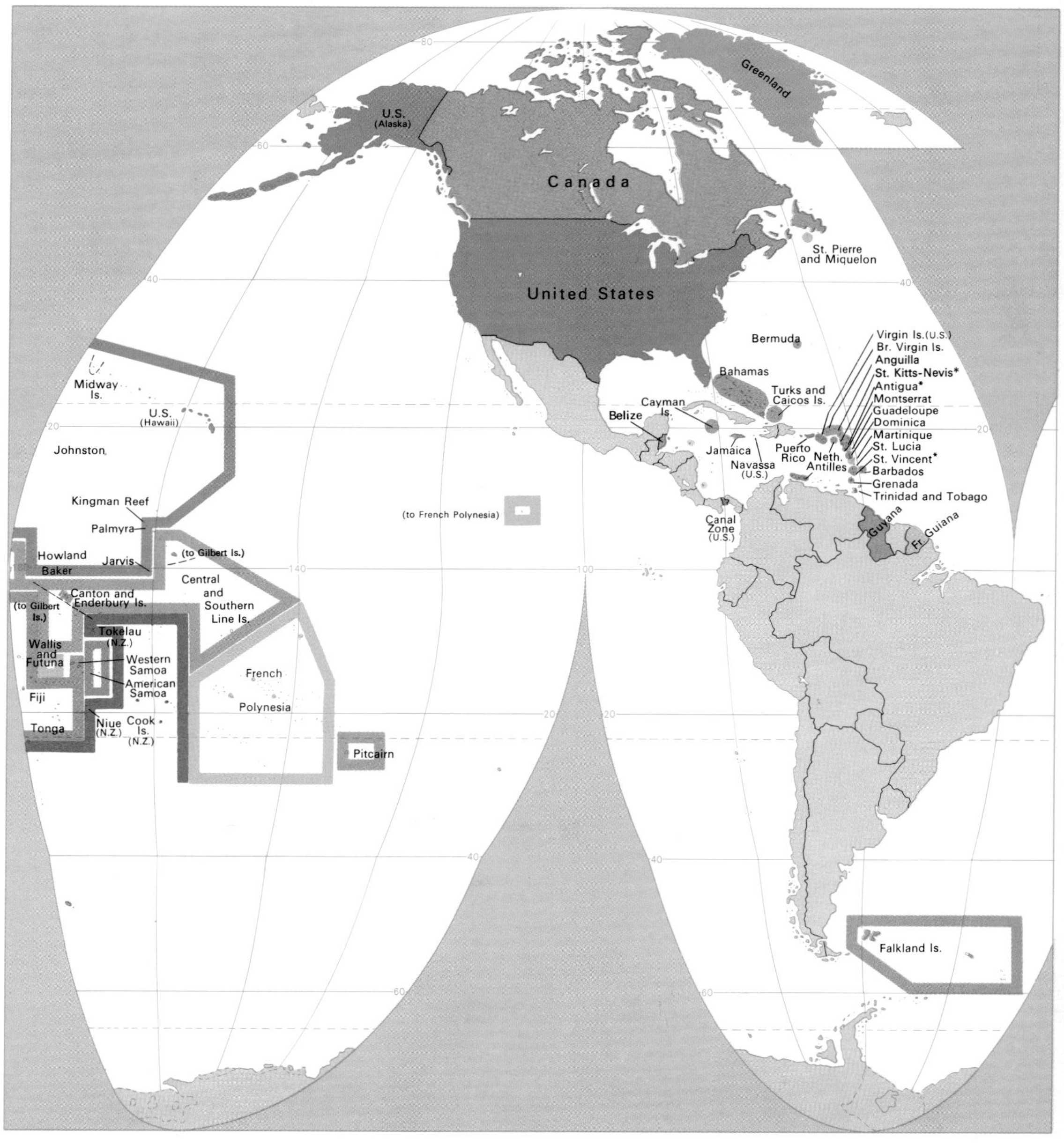

Politically Related Areas

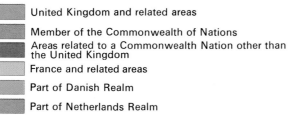

- United Kingdom and related areas
- Member of the Commonwealth of Nations
- Areas related to a Commonwealth Nation other than the United Kingdom
- France and related areas
- Part of Danish Realm
- Part of Netherlands Realm
- United States and related areas

*Virtually independent: major country primarily responsible for foreign relations and defense.

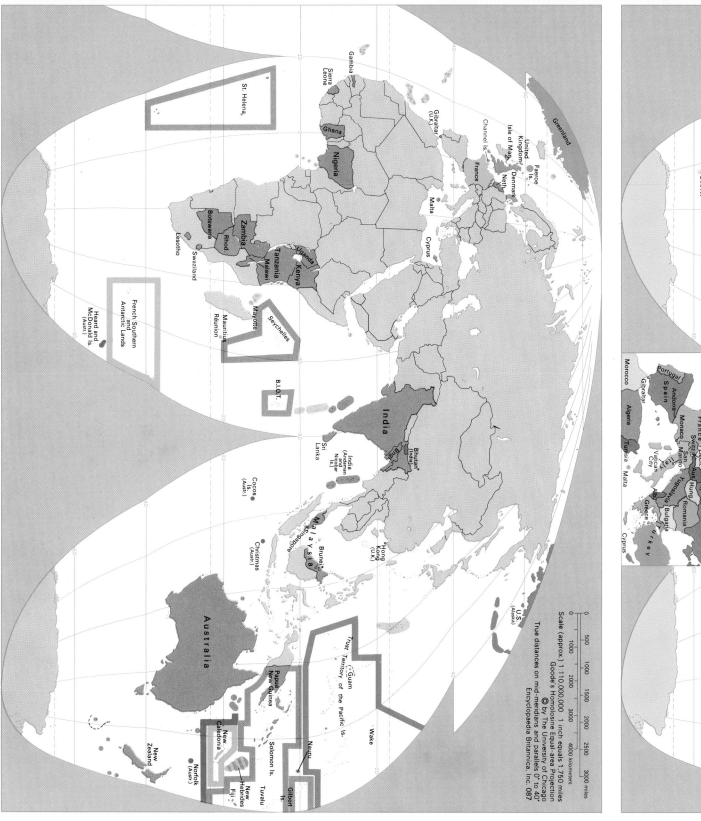

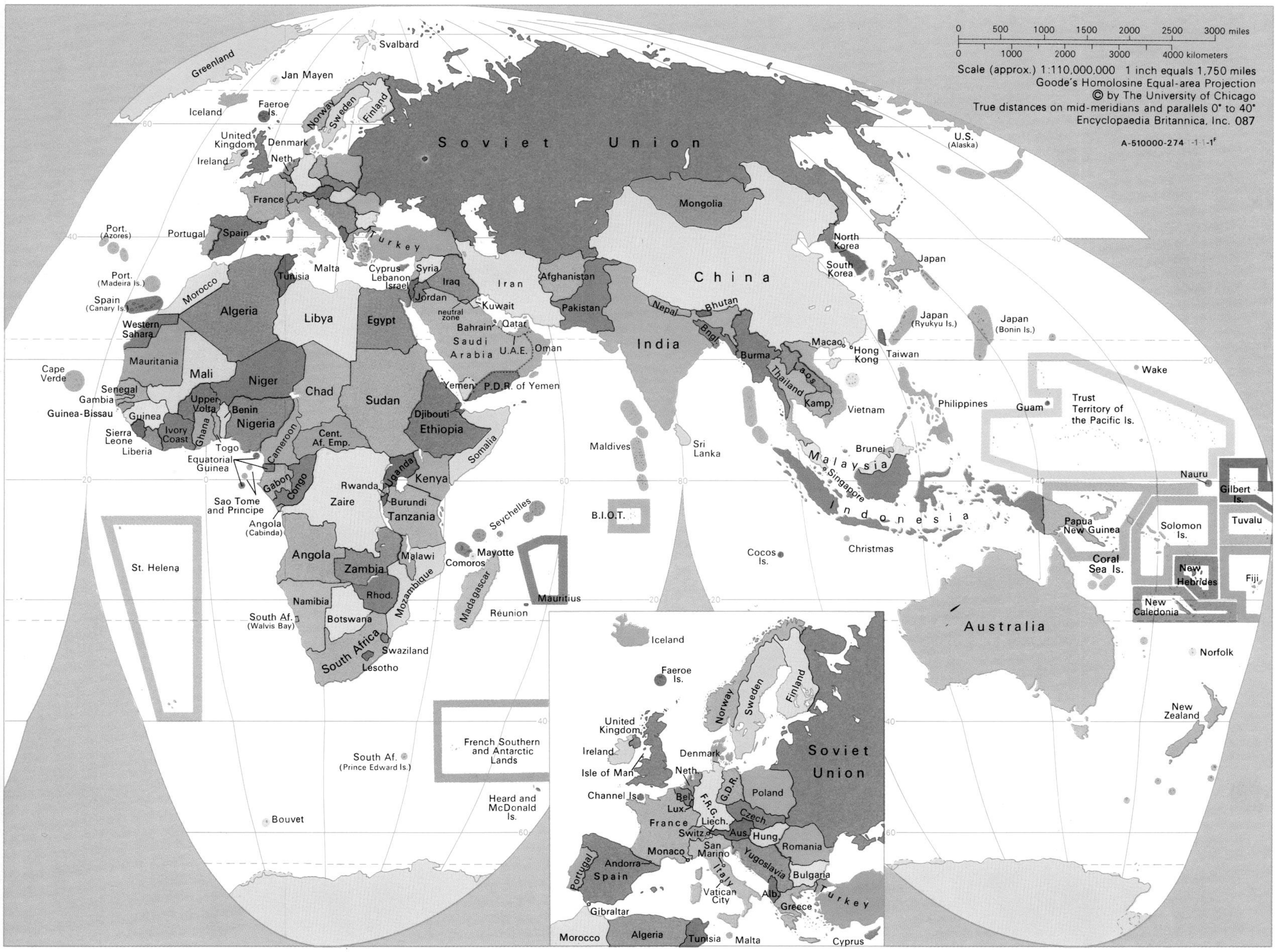
0 500 1000 1500 2000 2500 3000 miles
0 1000 2000 3000 4000 kilometers
Scale (approx.) 1:110,000,000 1 inch equals 1,750 miles
Goode's Homolosine Equal-area Projection
© by The University of Chicago
True distances on mid-meridians and parallels 0° to 40°
Encyclopaedia Britannica, Inc. 087
A-510000-274
Soviet Union
China
India
Mongolia
Australia
Greenland
Iceland
Algeria
Libya
Egypt
Sudan
Chad
Niger
Mali
Nigeria
Ethiopia
Zaire
Angola
Zambia
South Africa
Saudi Arabia
Iran
Japan
Philippines
Indonesia
Malaysia
New Zealand
Trust Territory of the Pacific Is.
St. Helena
French Southern and Antarctic Lands
Heard and McDonald Is.
Bouvet
B.I.O.T.

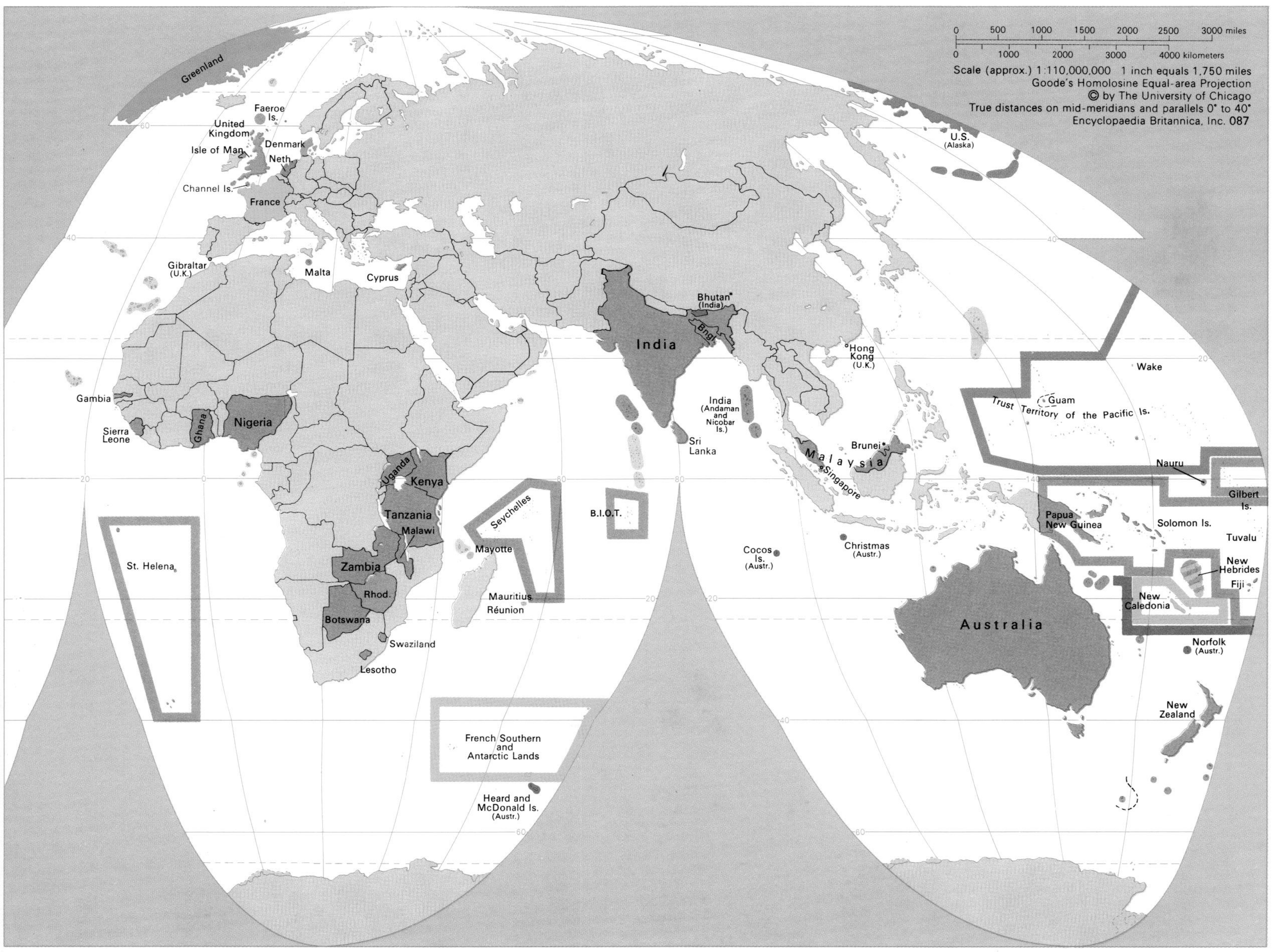
0 500 1000 1500 2000 2500 3000 miles
0 1000 2000 3000 4000 kilometers
Scale (approx.) 1:110,000,000 1 inch equals 1,750 miles
Goode's Homolosine Equal-area Projection
© by The University of Chicago
True distances on mid-meridians and parallels 0° to 40°
Encyclopaedia Britannica, Inc. 087
India
Australia
Nigeria
Ghana
Kenya
Tanzania
Zambia
Malawi
Botswana
Malaysia
Papua New Guinea
Trust Territory of the Pacific Is.
St. Helena
French Southern and Antarctic Lands
Heard and McDonald Is. (Austr.)
New Zealand

Population

Extent of urbanization
Percent of total population urban

- 80% and more
- 60 to 79%
- 40 to 59%
- 20 to 39%
- Less than 20%

Major metropolitan areas

- 5,000,000 and more persons
- 3,000,000 to 4,999,999
- 2,000,000 to 2,999,999

The increase in the proportion of urban to total population reflects the change from a dispersed pattern of human settlement to a concentrated one. In industrialized countries the proportion of people living in cities increases mainly through movement from country to city, due to the attraction of higher wages and greater opportunities, a process which in most cases started about 100 years ago. In the underdeveloped countries, where in recent years the number of people living in cities has risen sharply, the proportion of urban population has not increased appreciably; here the urban growth is generally due not so much to rural-urban migration as it is to the natural population increase in both urban and rural areas, and to the decline in the urban mortality rate.

In population studies the definitions of "urban" differ from country to country, but generally take into account the total number of people in a settlement and the percent of the population engaged in nonagricultural activities. The map shows the degree of urbanization (the proportion of urban to total population), considering as urban those communities having no fewer than 2,000 inhabitants, more than half of them dependent on nonfarm occupations. Also indicated are selected metropolitan areas where cities have expanded beyond their boundaries into the surrounding regions in patterns of continuous settlement oriented toward the central cities.

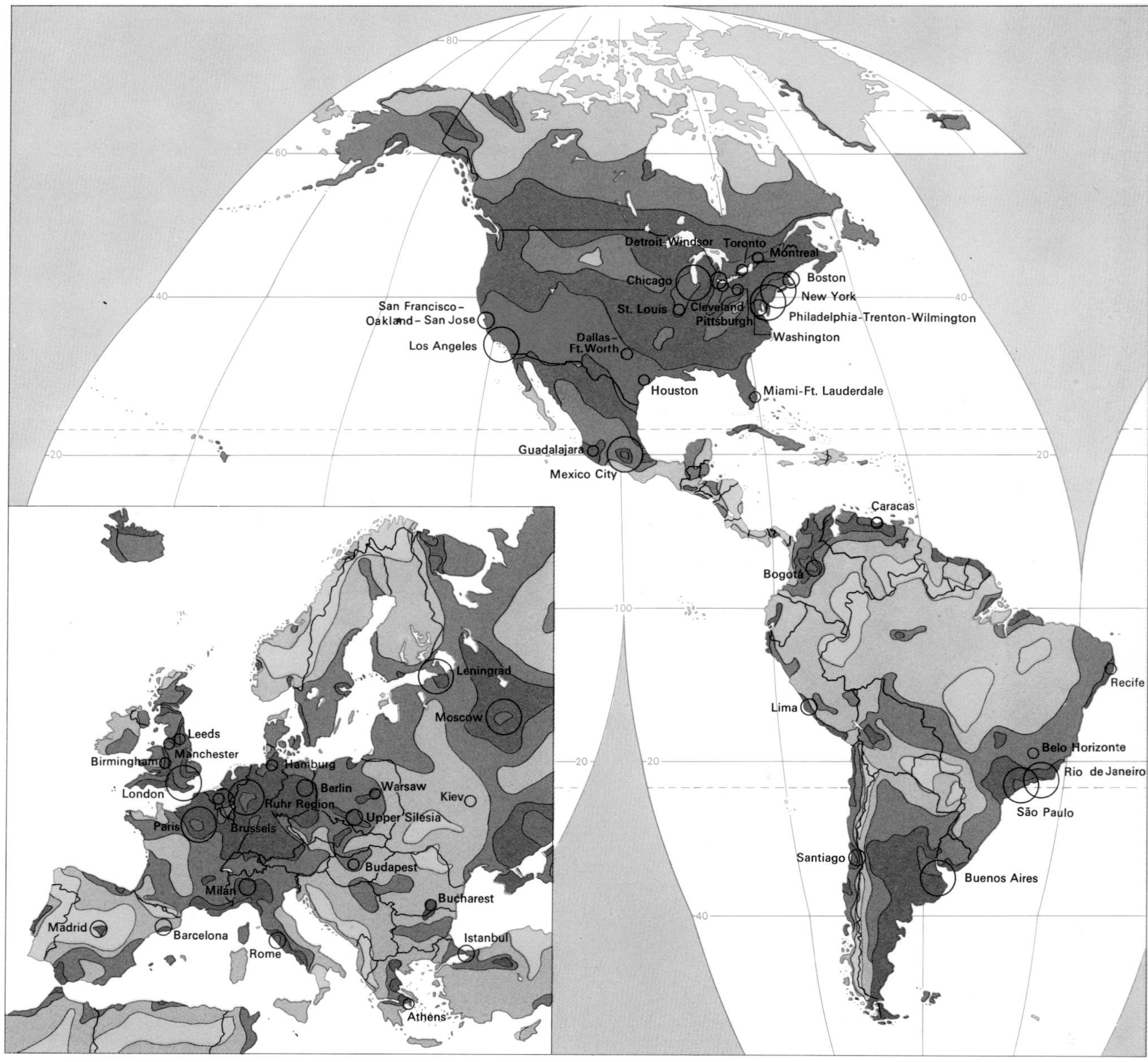

Age and sex composition

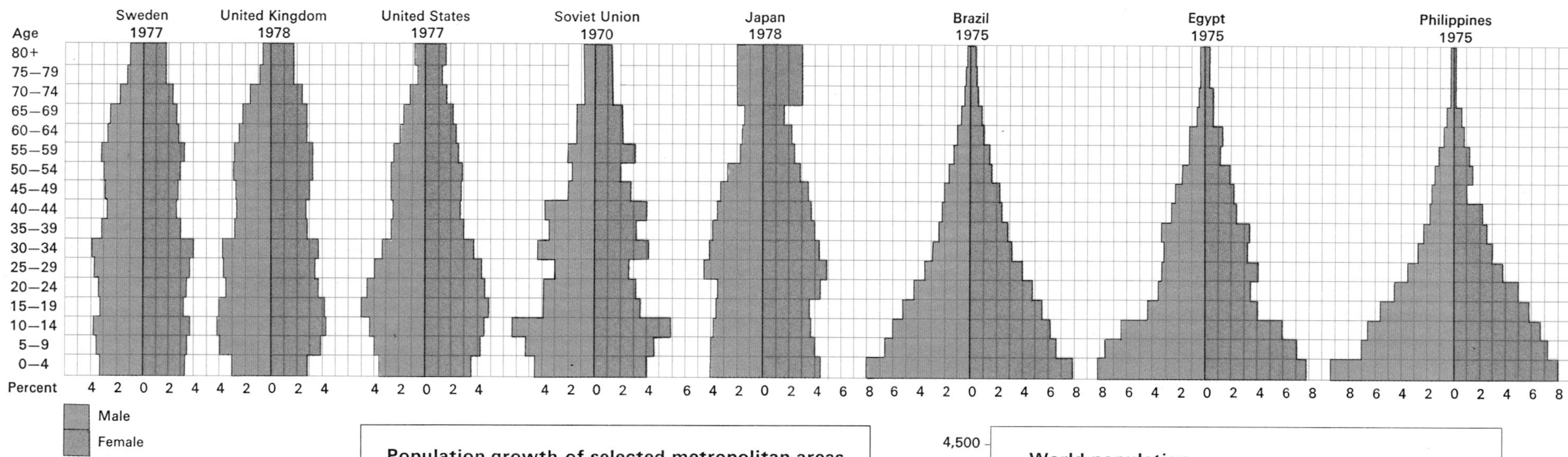

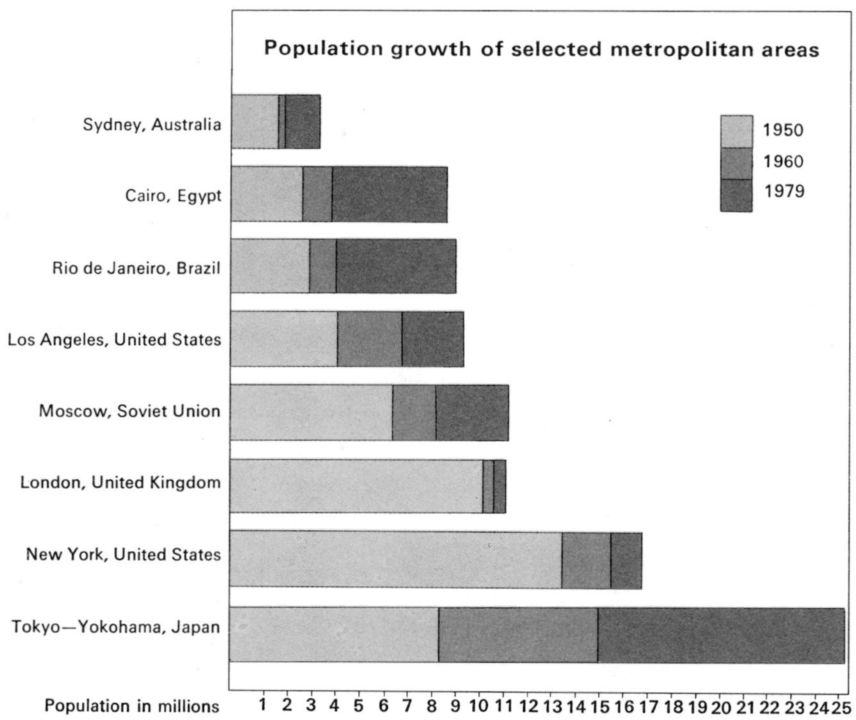

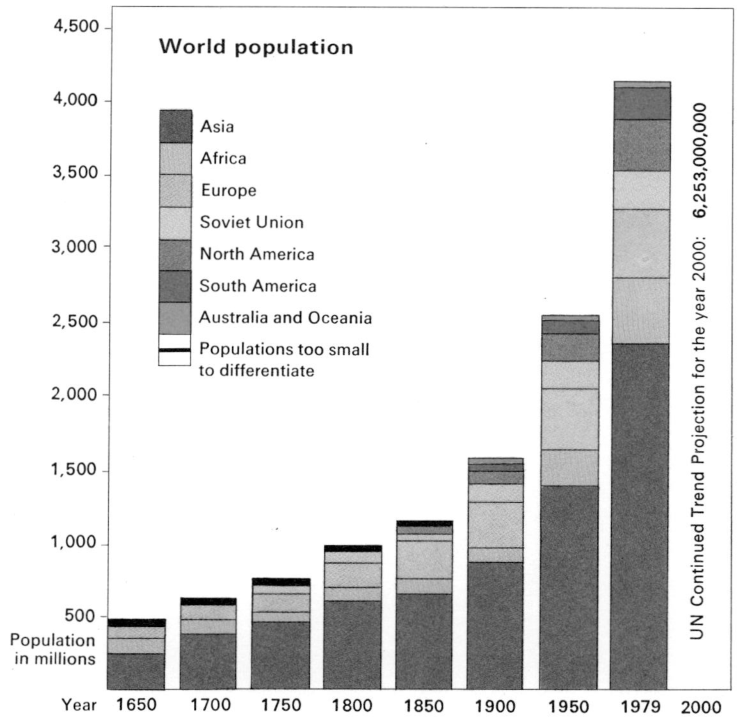

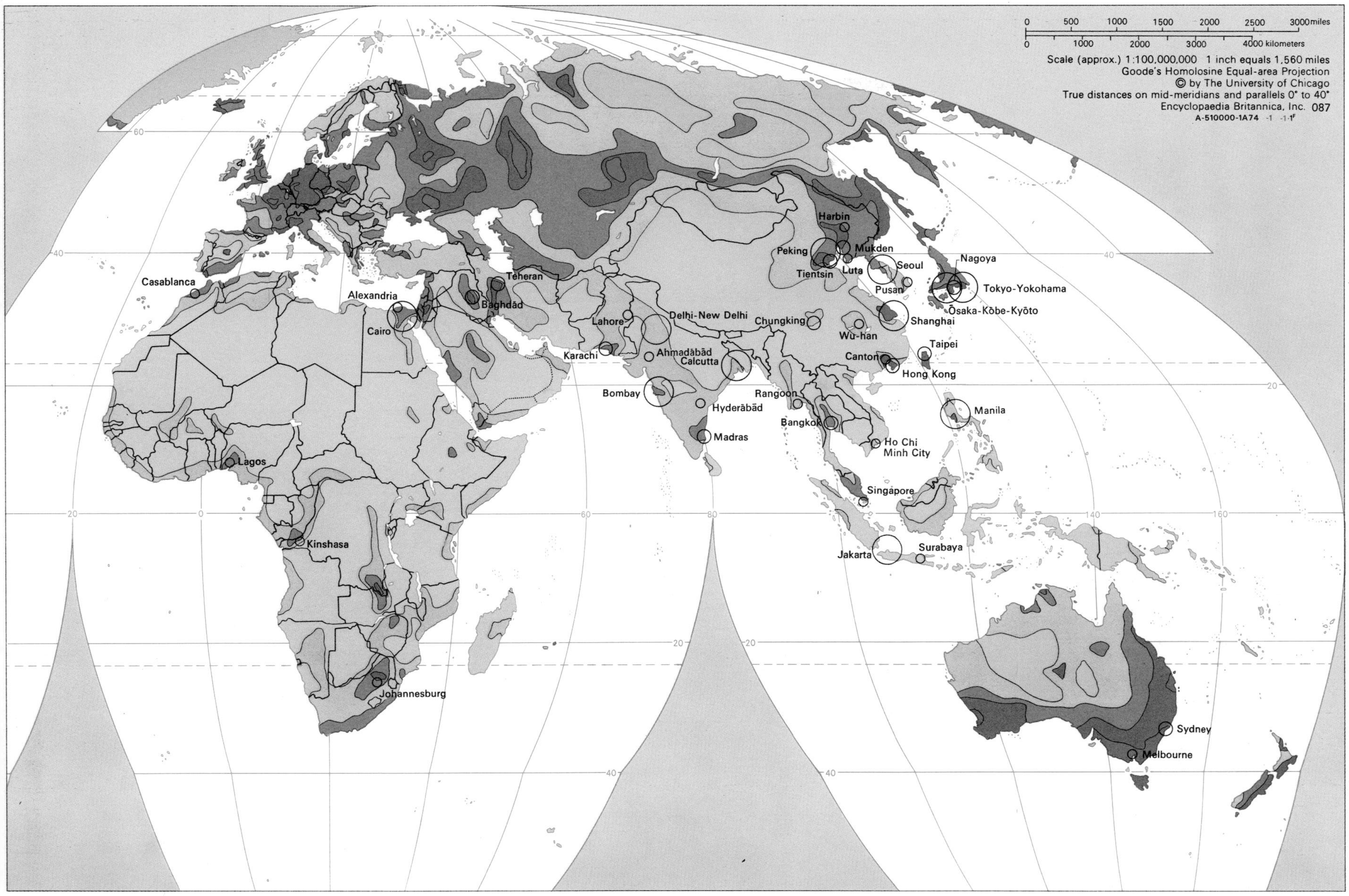

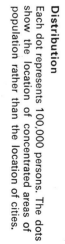

Distribution

Each dot represents 100,000 persons. The dots show the location of concentrated areas of population rather than the location of cities.

Religions

The majority of the inhabitants in each of the areas colored on the map share the religious tradition indicated. Letter symbols show religious traditions shared by at least 25% of the inhabitants within areal units no smaller than one thousand square miles. Therefore minority religions of city-dwellers have generally not been represented.

- R Roman Catholicism
- P Protestantism
- E Eastern Orthodox religions (including Armenian, Coptic, Ethiopian, Greek, and Russian Orthodox)
- M Mormonism
- C Christianity, undifferentiated by branch (chiefly mingled Protestantism and Roman Catholicism, neither predominant)
- I Islam, predominantly Sunni
- Sh Islam, predominantly Shia
- Theravada Buddhism
- L Lamaism
- H Hinduism
- J Judaism
- Ch Chinese religions*
- Ja Japanese religions*
- Korean religions*
- Vietnamese religions*
- T Simple ethnic (tribal) religions
- Sk Sikhism
- Countries under Communist regimes; traditional religions often subject to restraint
- Uninhabited

*In certain Eastern Asian areas, most of the people have plural religious affiliations. Chinese, Korean, and Vietnamese religions include Mahayana Buddhism, Taoism, Confucianism, and folk cults. The Japanese religions include Shinto and Mahayana Buddhism.

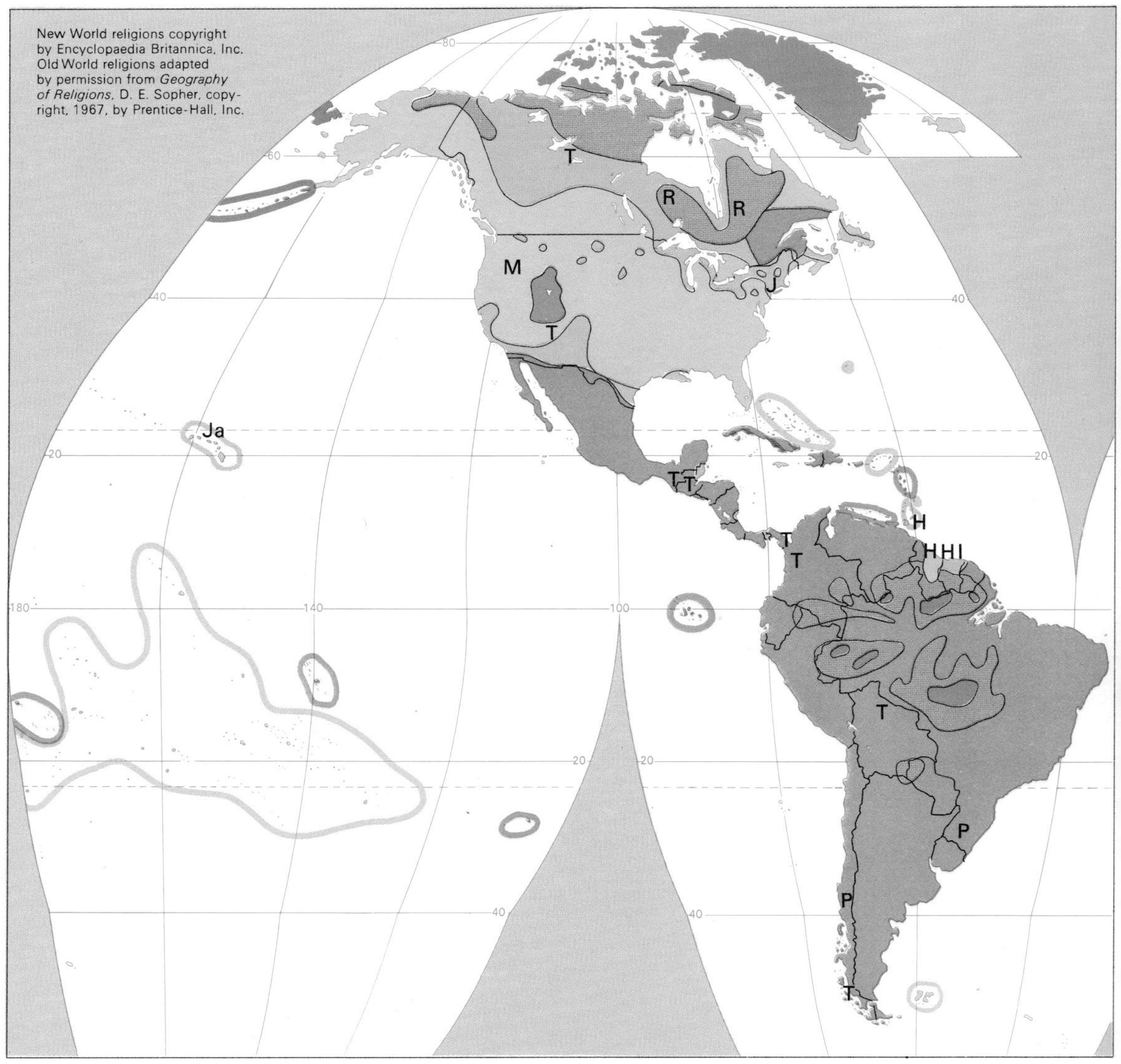

New World religions copyright by Encyclopaedia Britannica, Inc. Old World religions adapted by permission from *Geography of Religions*, D. E. Sopher, copyright, 1967, by Prentice-Hall, Inc.

Languages

Languages of Europe

The following languages are ranked in descending order by number of speakers. Languages spoken by more than 4 million persons are indicated by color. Others listed, spoken by fewer than 4 million persons, are named on the map.

Russian	Lithuanian	Macedonian	Icelandic
German	Albanian	Turkish	Karelian
English	Latvian	Welsh	Lusatian
Italian	Slovenian	Mari	Lappish
French	Chuvash	Romansh	Liv
Ukrainian	Mordvinian	Irish-Gaelic	Frisian
Polish	Basque	Scots-Gaelic	Ladin
Spanish	Breton	Komi	Friulian
Romanian	Estonian	Maltese	Adyge
Dutch-Flemish	Sardinian		
Hungarian			
Serbo-Croatian			
Portuguese			
Czech			
Belorussian			
Swedish			
Greek			
Bulgarian			
Catalan			
Danish			
Finnish			
Norwegian			
Slovak			
All others			

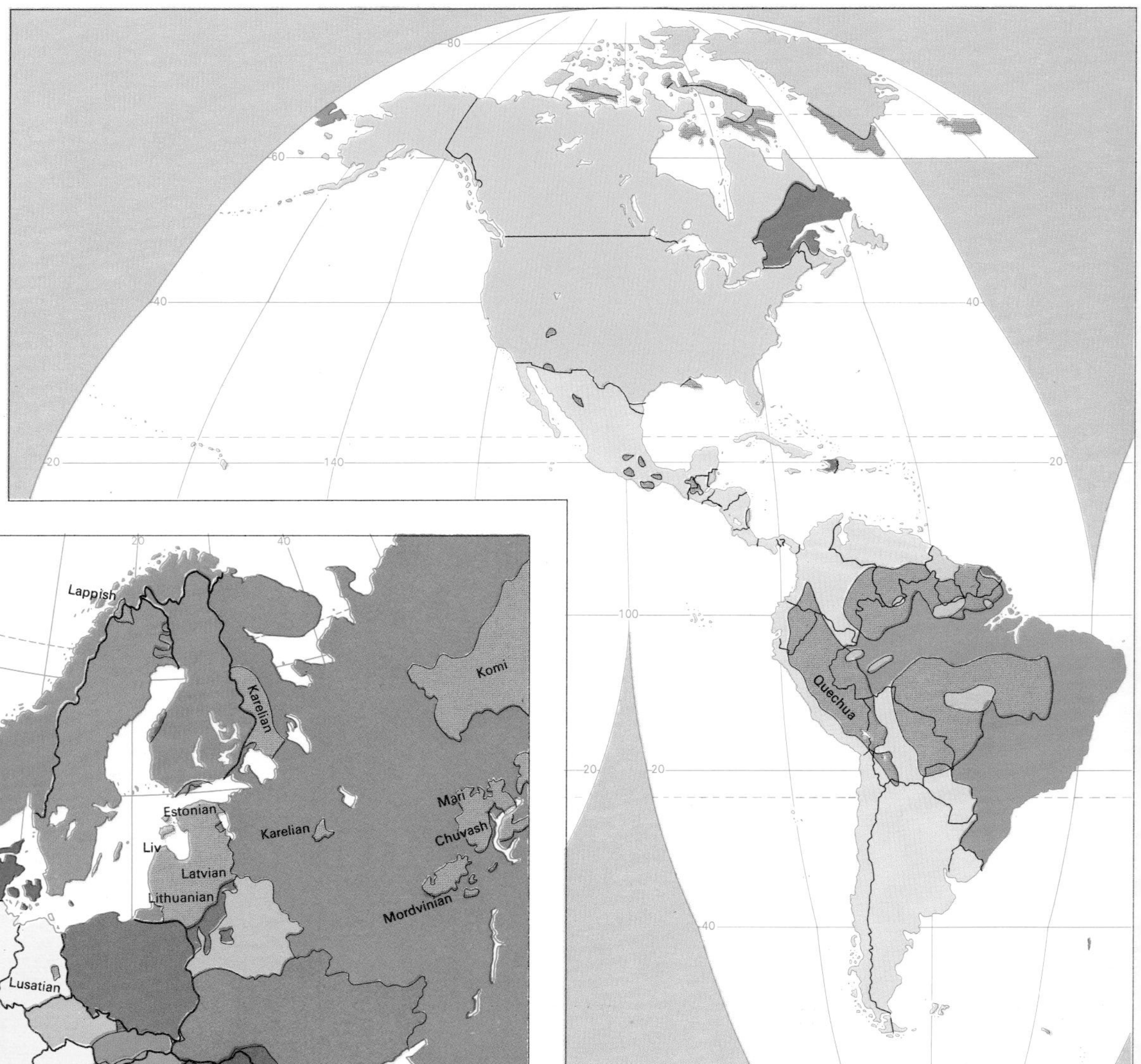

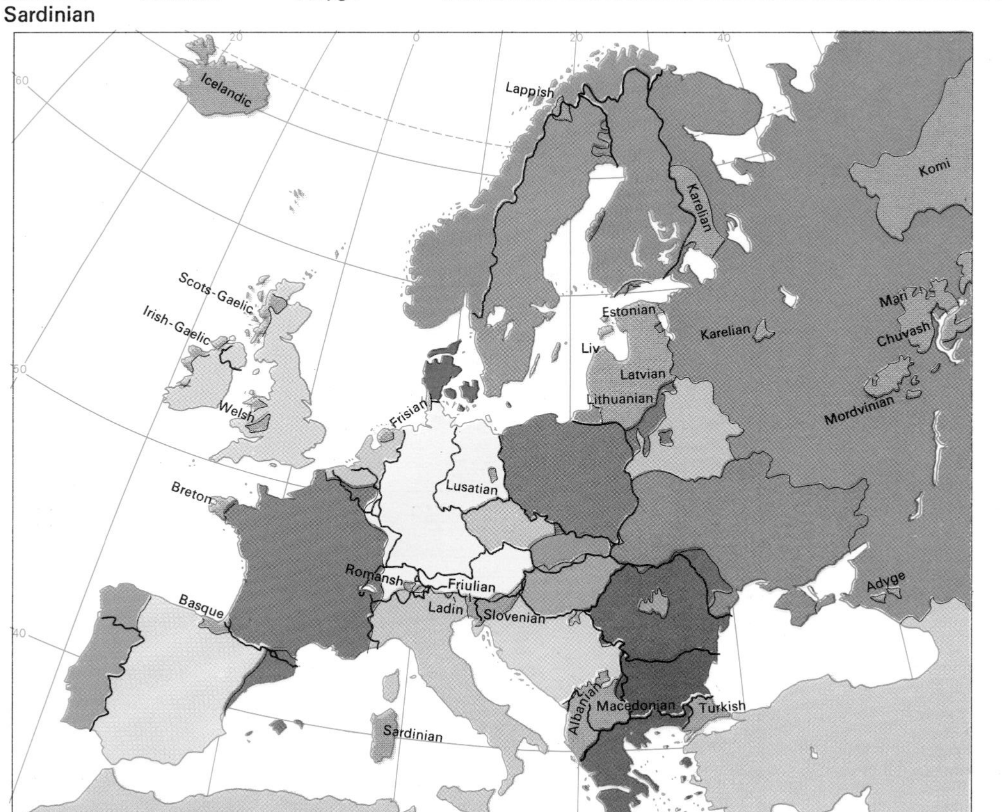

Scale (approx.) 1:36,700,000 1 inch equals 580 miles
Encyclopaedia Britannica, Inc. 086
Compiled by Philip L. Wagner.

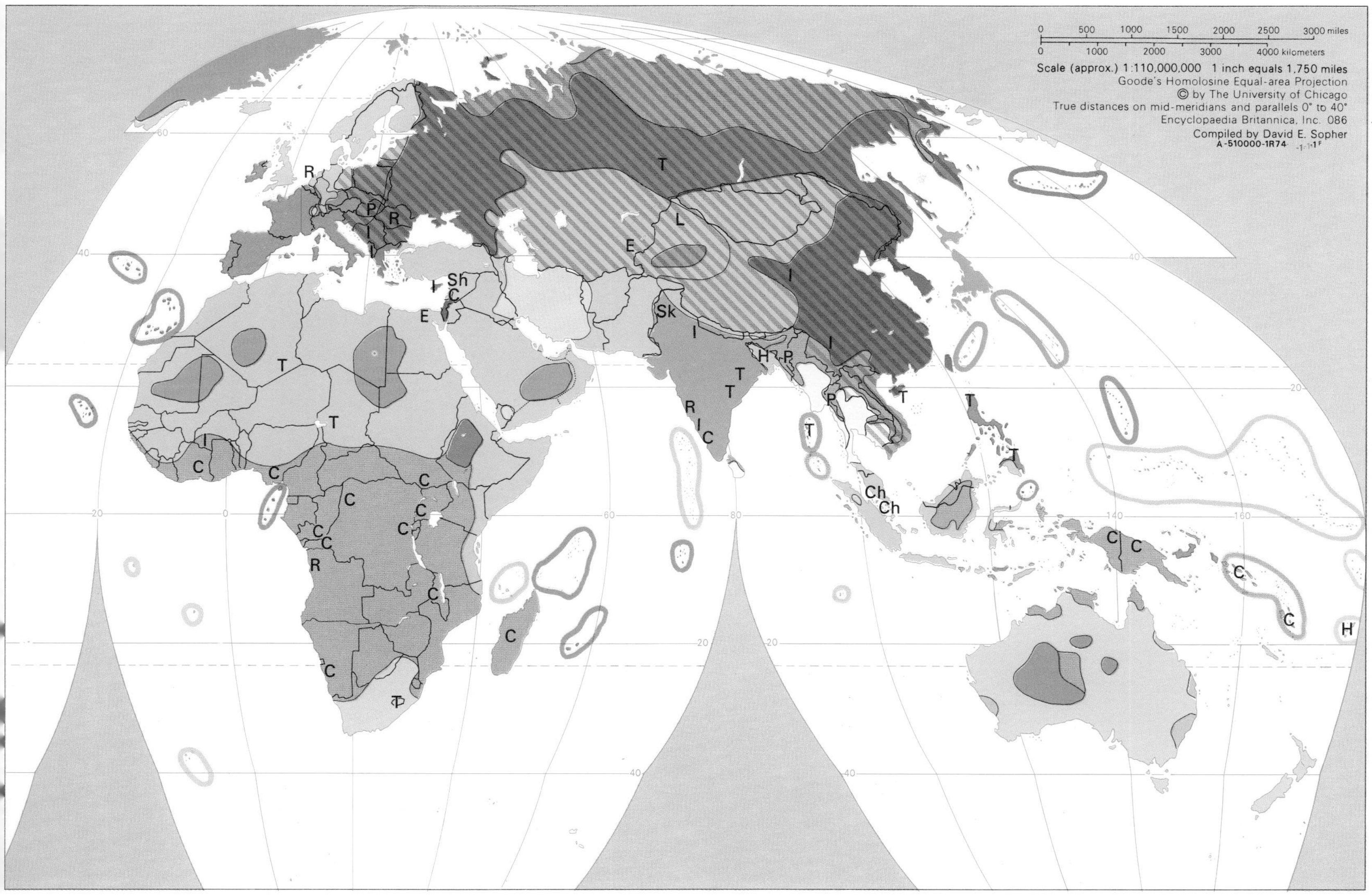

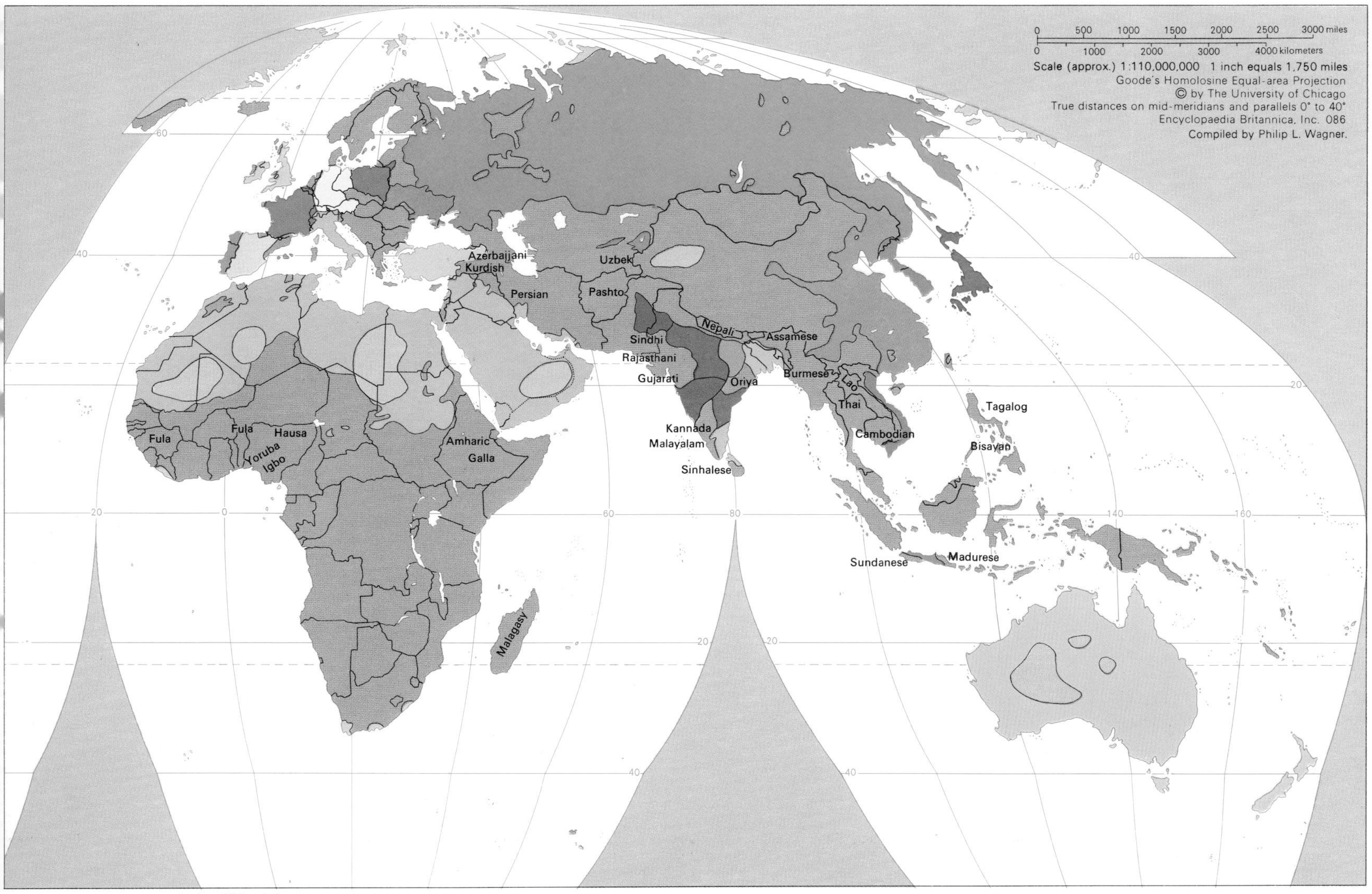

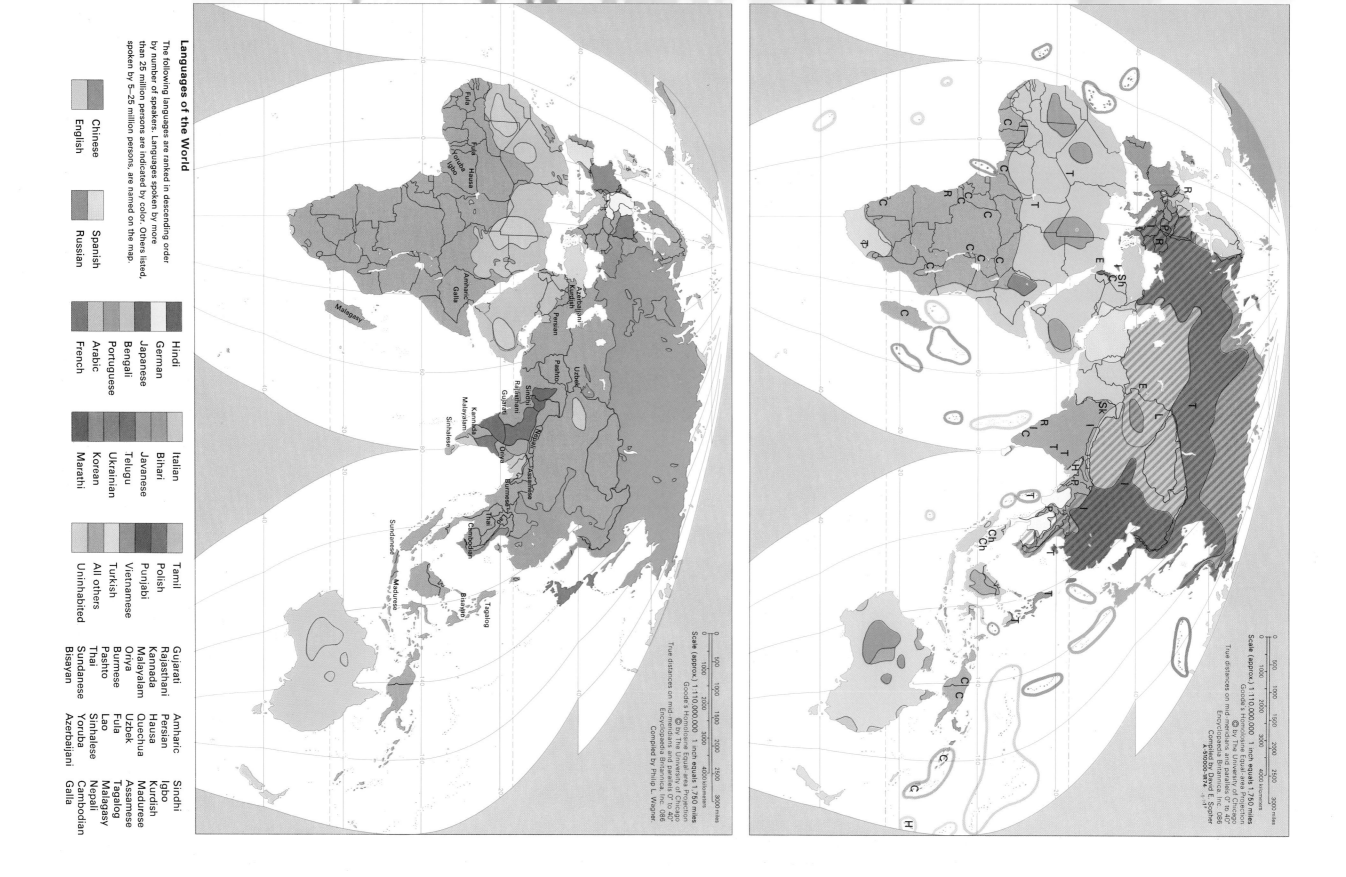

Languages of the World

The following languages are ranked in descending order by number of speakers. Languages spoken by more than 25 million persons are indicated by color. Others listed, spoken by 5–25 million persons, are named on the map.

Chinese
English
Spanish
Russian
Hindi
German
Japanese
Bengali
Portuguese
Arabic
French
Italian
Bihari
Javanese
Telugu
Ukrainian
Korean
Marathi
Tamil
Polish
Punjabi
Vietnamese
Turkish
All others
Uninhabited

Gujarati
Rajasthani
Kannada
Malayalam
Oriya
Burmese
Pashto
Thai
Sundanese
Bisayan
Amharic
Persian
Hausa
Quechua
Uzbek
Fula
Lao
Sinhalese
Yoruba
Azerbaijani
Sindhi
Igbo
Kurdish
Madurese
Assamese
Tagalog
Malagasy
Nepali
Cambodian
Galla

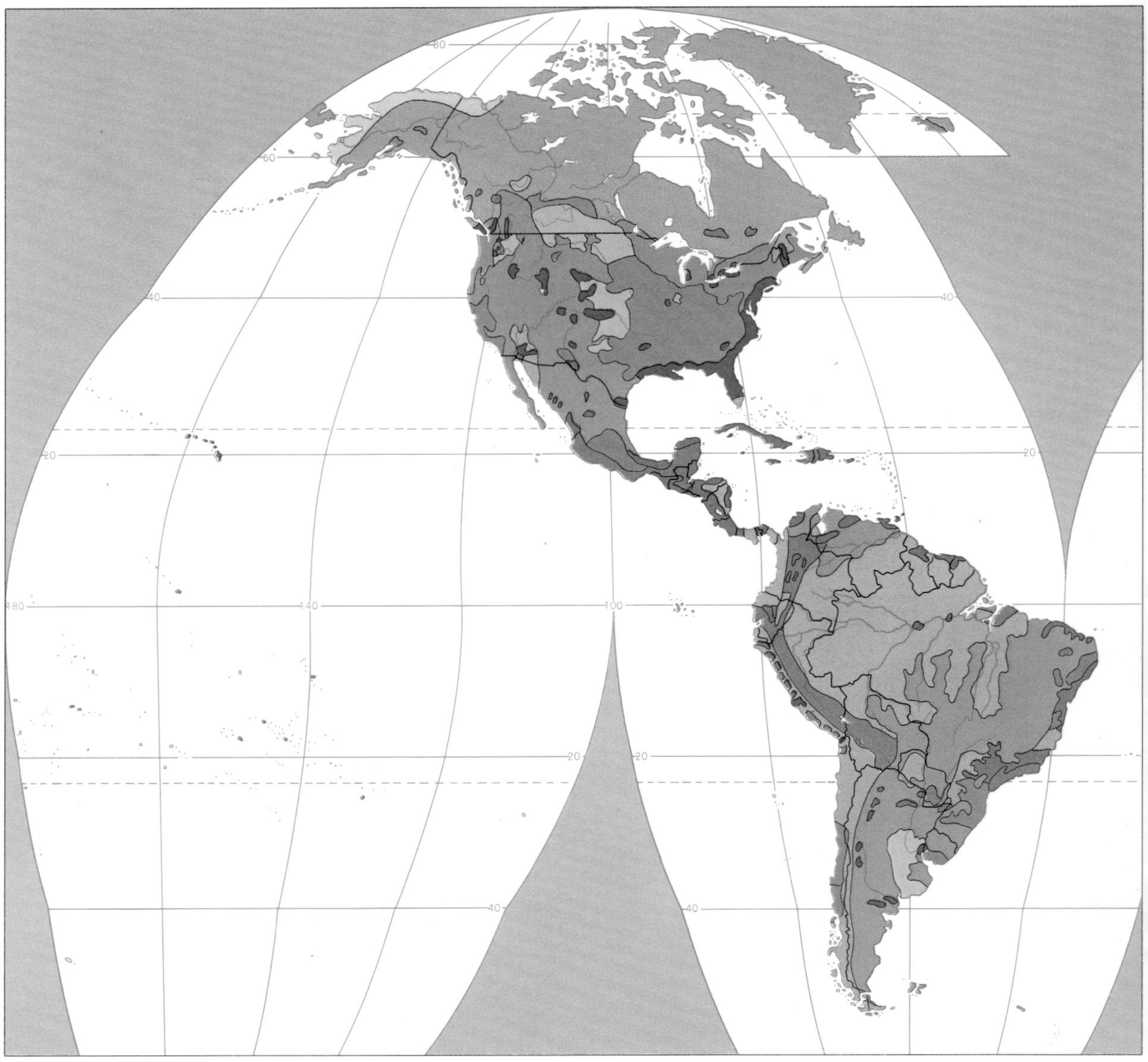

Agricultural Regions

- Cash crop and livestock farming
- Cash crop farming, grain or cotton dominant
- Crop and livestock farming with cash products minor
- Livestock ranching
- Dairying
- Mediterranean agriculture
- Specialized horticulture
- Plantation agriculture
- Intensive subsistence tillage, rice dominant
- Intensive subsistence tillage, with no dominant crop
- Rudimental sedentary farming
- Shifting cultivation
- Nomadic herding
- No agriculture

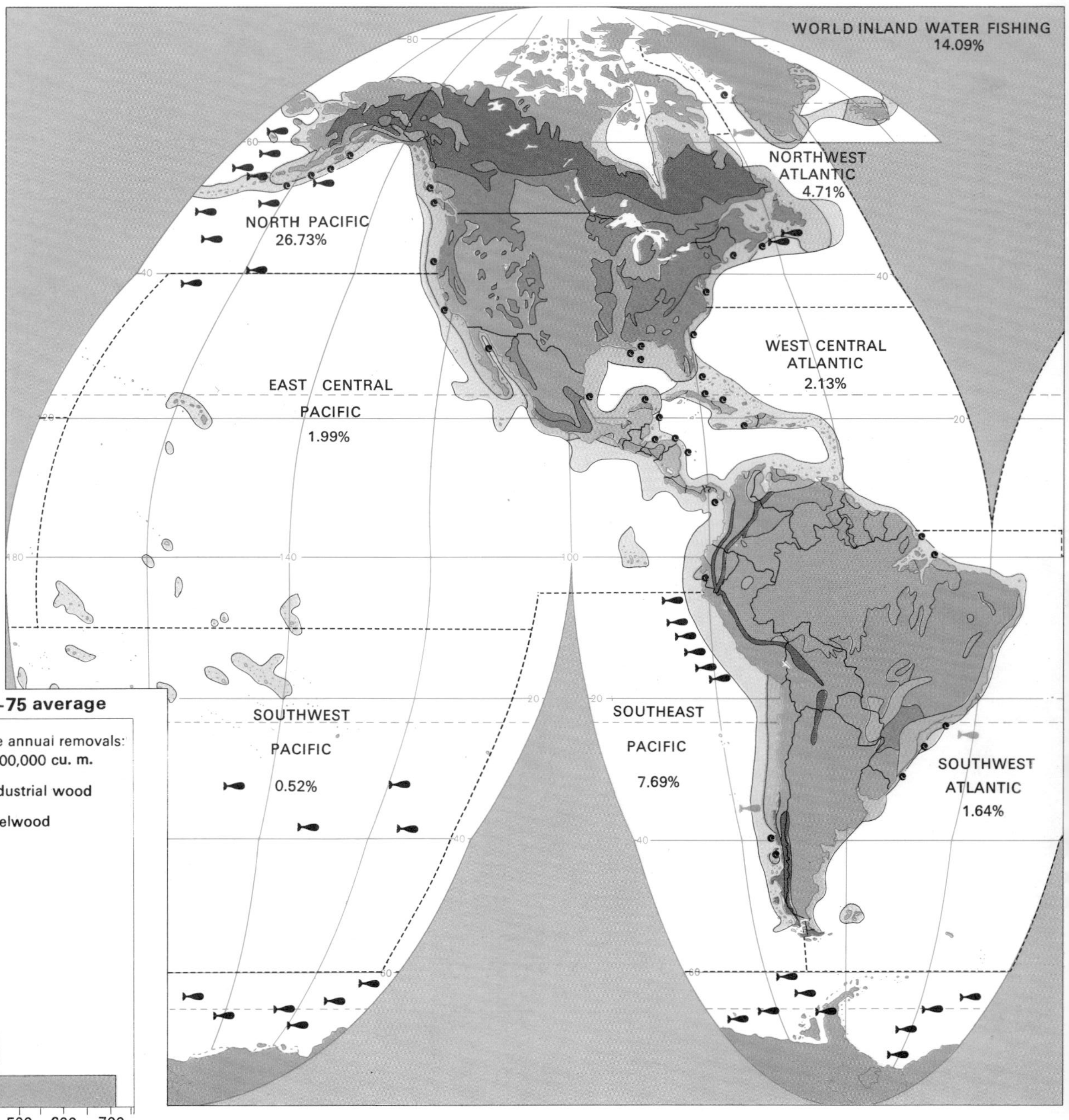

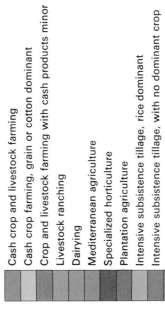

Forests and Fisheries

Forests

- Conifers: cedar, fir, hemlock, pine, redwood, spruce
- Regions of exploitation
- Tropical hardwoods: ebony, mahogany, rosewood, teak
- Regions of exploitation
- Temperate hardwoods: hickory, maple, oak, poplar, walnut, and some mixed hardwoods and conifers
- Regions of exploitation

Fisheries

- Pelagic fishing regions: anchoveta, anchovy, herring, menhaden, pilchard, sardine, sprat, tuna
- Ground fishing regions: cod, haddock, hake, horse mackerel, mackerel, pollack, redfish
- Mixed ground and pelagic fishing regions
- Shellfish: clam, crab, lobster, mussel, oyster, scallop, shrimp, squid
- Whales: blue, fin, minke, pilot, sei, sperm. Each represents an average annual catch of about 300 whales; Each represents an average annual catch of less than 200 whales
- Fishing regions showing percentage of world catch (excluding whales)

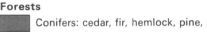

Fishing catch (live weight) 1971-75 average

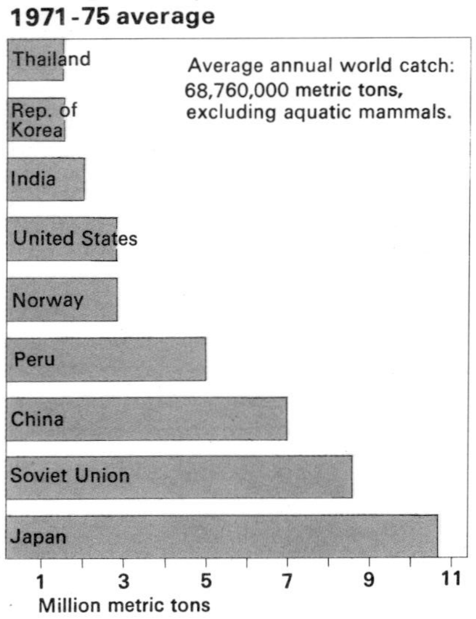

Forest removals 1971-75 average

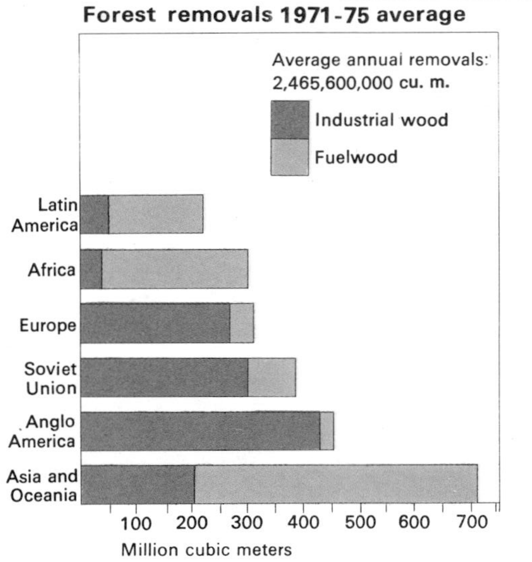

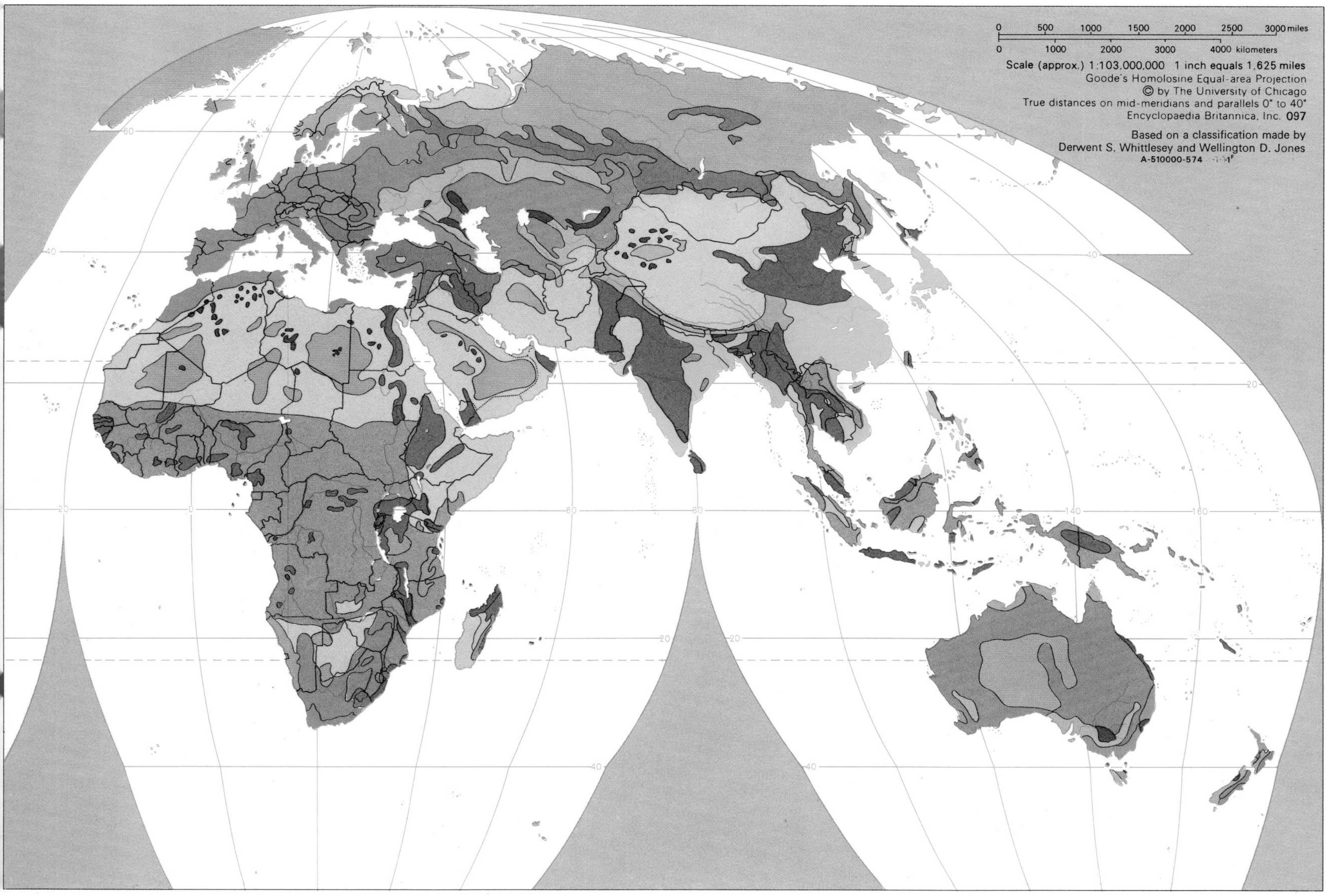
0 500 1000 1500 2000 2500 3000 miles
0 1000 2000 3000 4000 kilometers
Scale (approx.) 1:103,000,000 1 inch equals 1,625 miles
Goode's Homolosine Equal-area Projection
© by The University of Chicago
True distances on mid-meridians and parallels 0° to 40°
Encyclopaedia Britannica, Inc. 097
Based on a classification made by
Derwent S. Whittlesey and Wellington D. Jones
A-510000-574

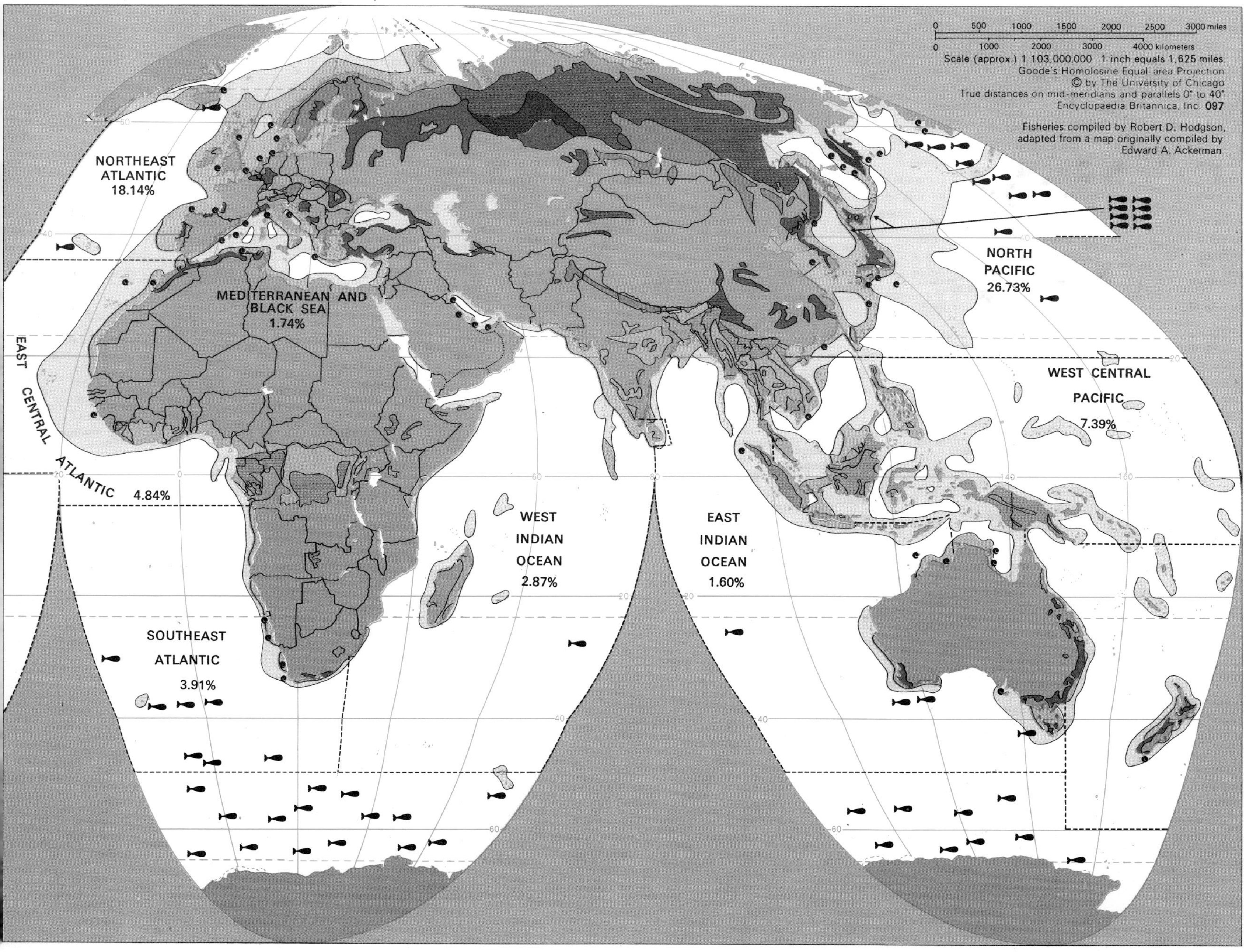
0 500 1000 1500 2000 2500 3000 miles
0 1000 2000 3000 4000 kilometers
Scale (approx.) 1:103,000,000 1 inch equals 1,625 miles
Goode's Homolosine Equal-area Projection
© by The University of Chicago
True distances on mid-meridians and parallels 0° to 40°
Encyclopaedia Britannica, Inc. 097
Fisheries compiled by Robert D. Hodgson,
adapted from a map originally compiled by
Edward A. Ackerman
NORTHEAST ATLANTIC 18.14%
MEDITERRANEAN AND BLACK SEA 1.74%
EAST CENTRAL ATLANTIC 4.84%
SOUTHEAST ATLANTIC 3.91%
WEST INDIAN OCEAN 2.87%
EAST INDIAN OCEAN 1.60%
NORTH PACIFIC 26.73%
WEST CENTRAL PACIFIC 7.39%

Minerals

4-year world average production shown in graphs. Producing areas shown on maps

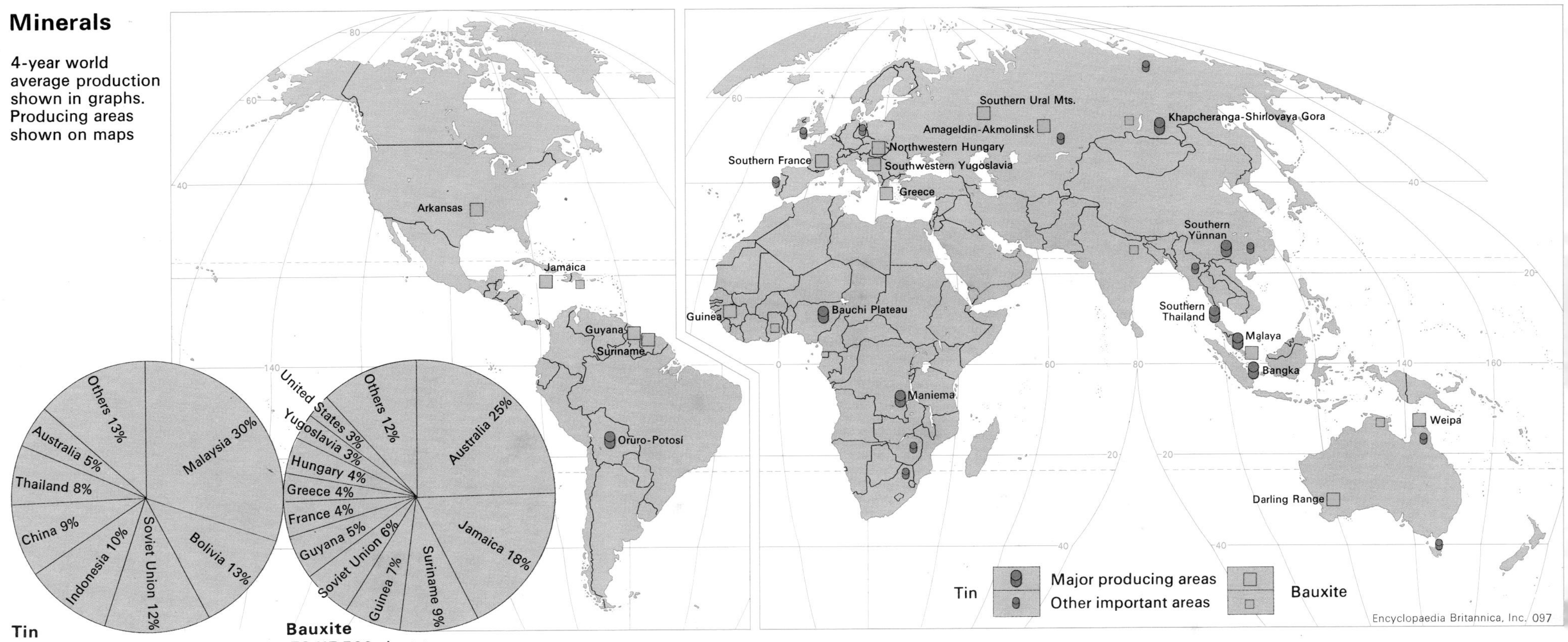

Tin
259,300 short tons

Bauxite
72,117,500 short tons

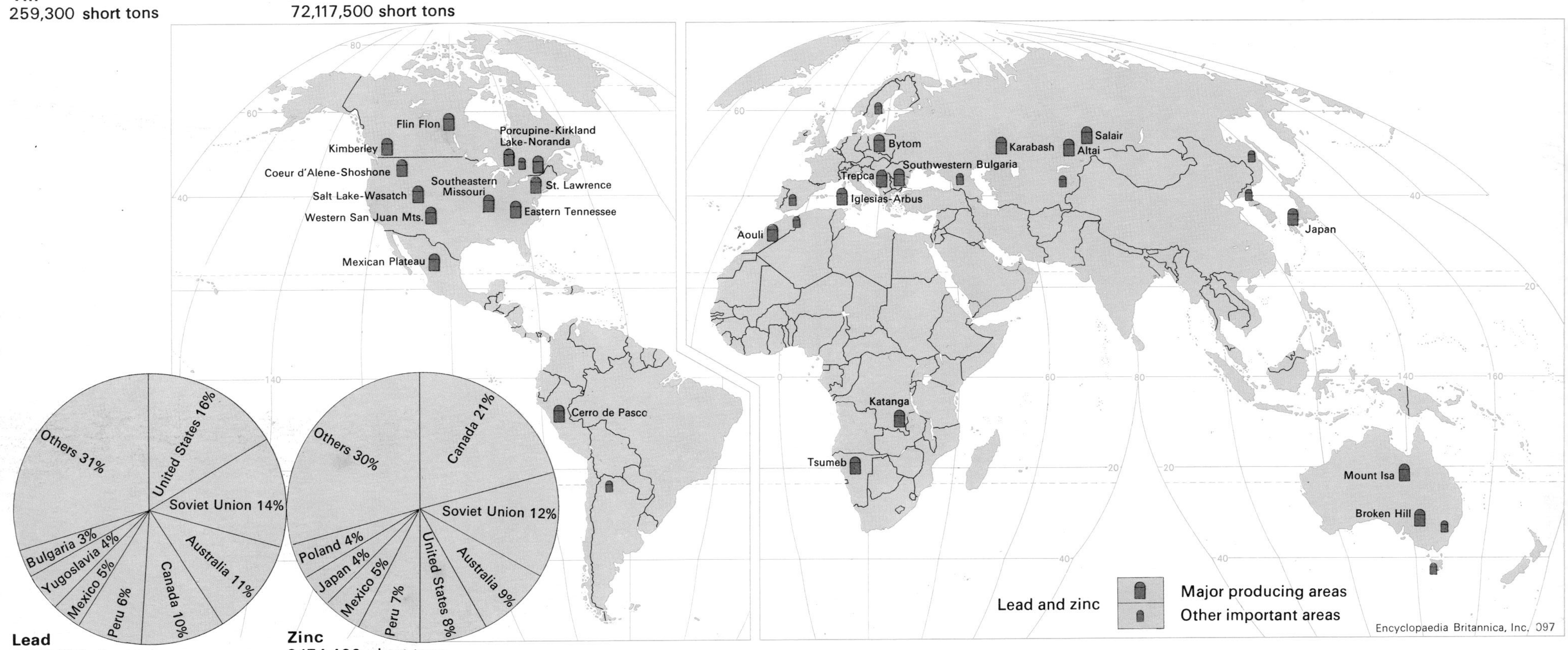

Lead
3,816,300 short tons

Zinc
6,174,400 short tons

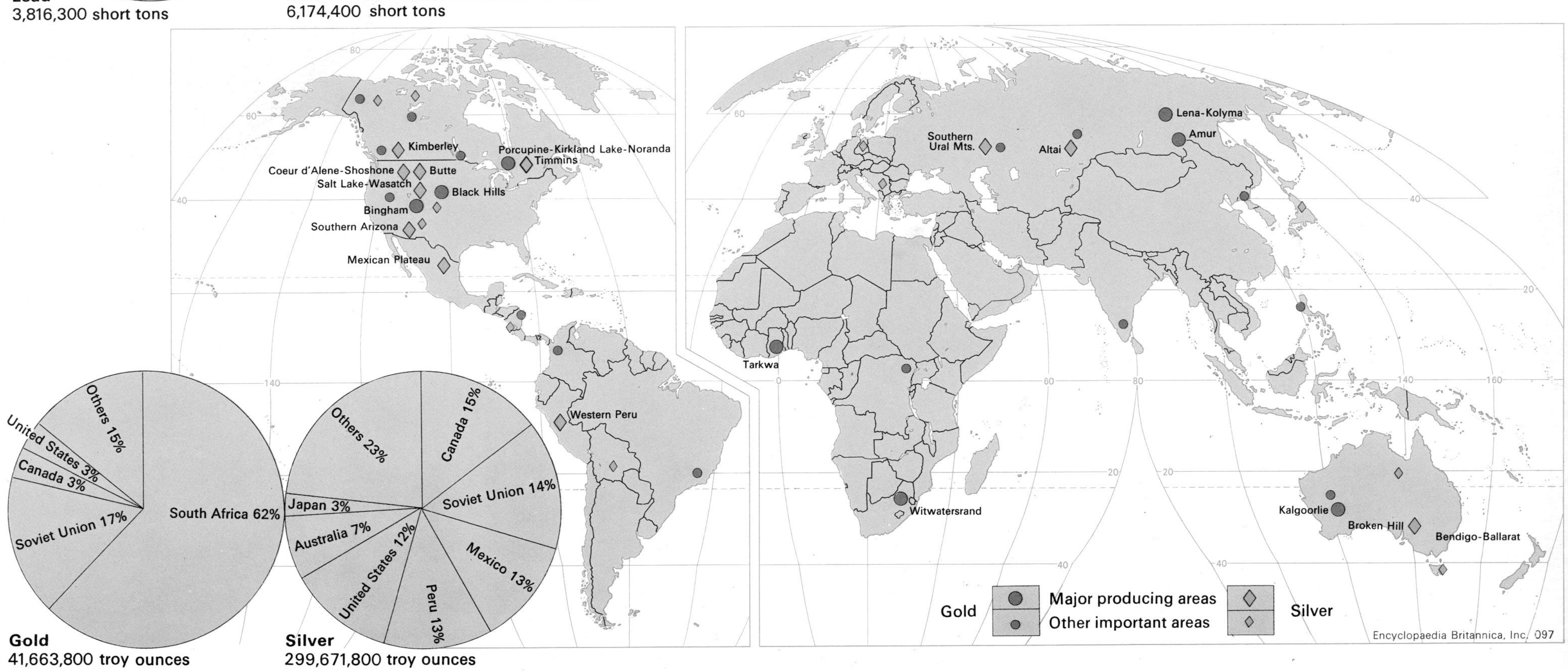

Gold
41,663,800 troy ounces

Silver
299,671,800 troy ounces

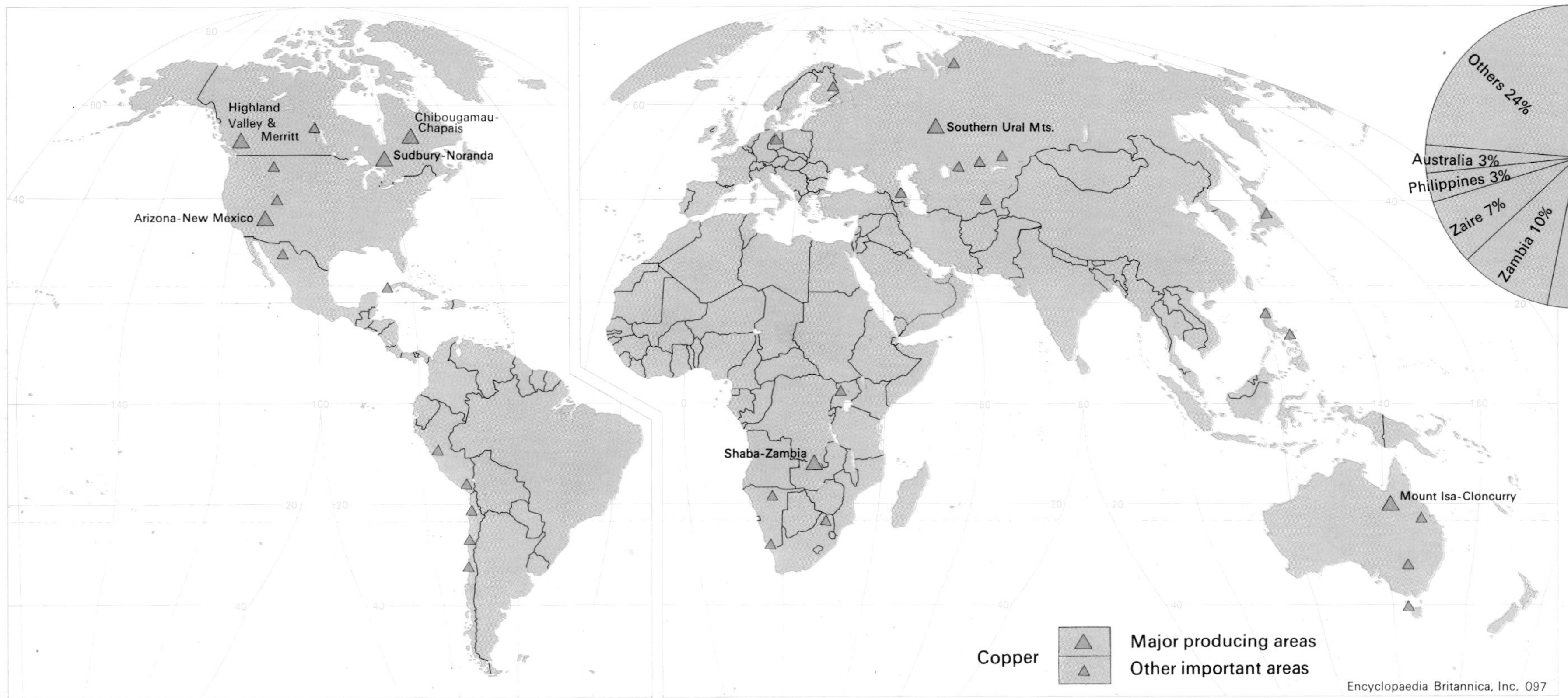

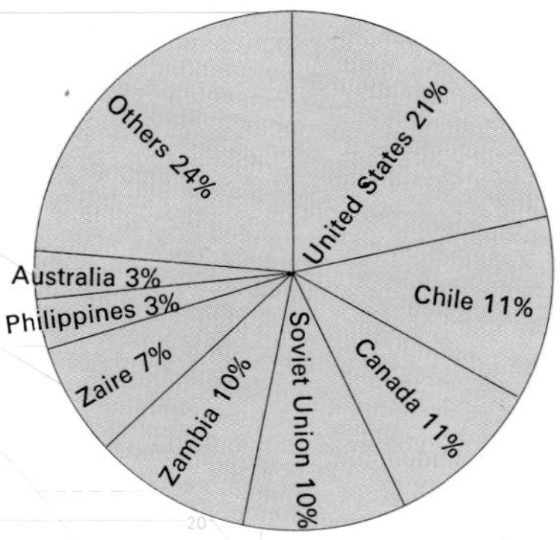

Copper
7,727,300
short tons

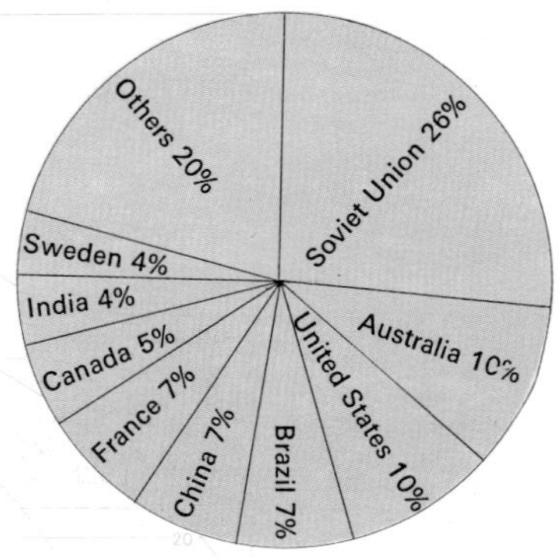

Iron ore
940,636,500
short tons

Ferroalloying Minerals

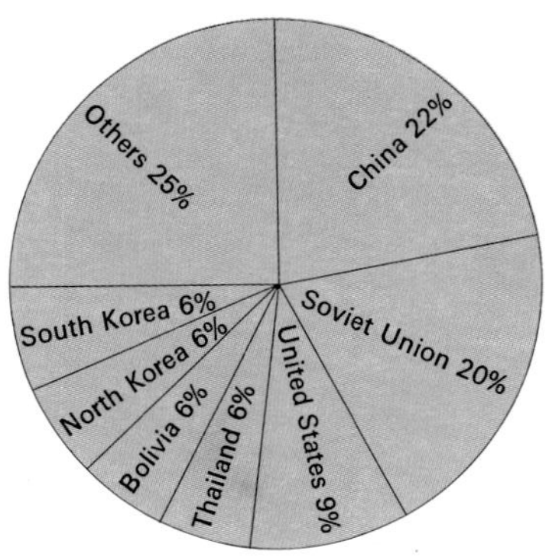

Tungsten
41,600 short tons

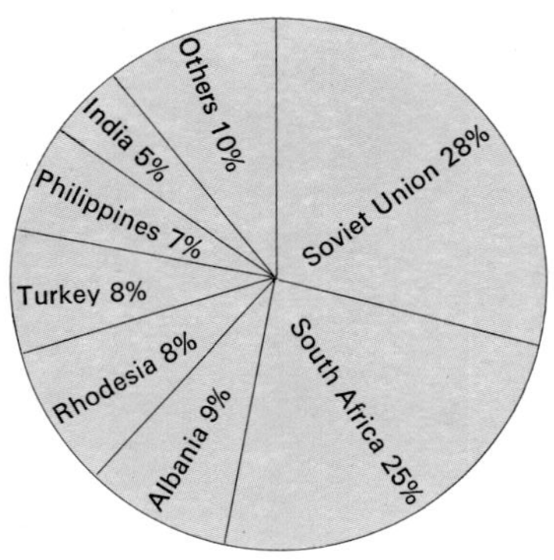

Chromite
7,758,500 short tons

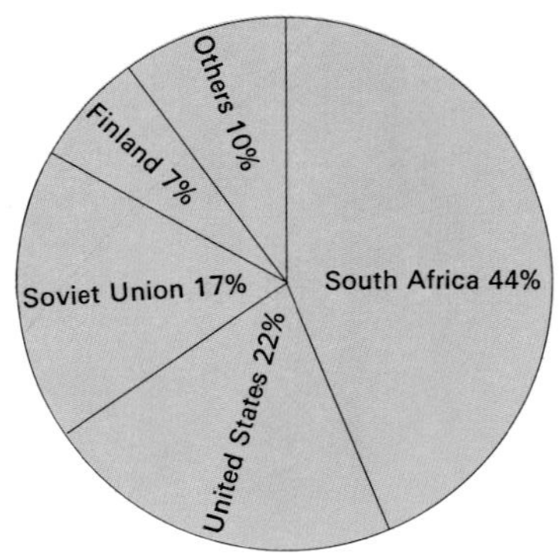

Vanadium
21,700 short tons

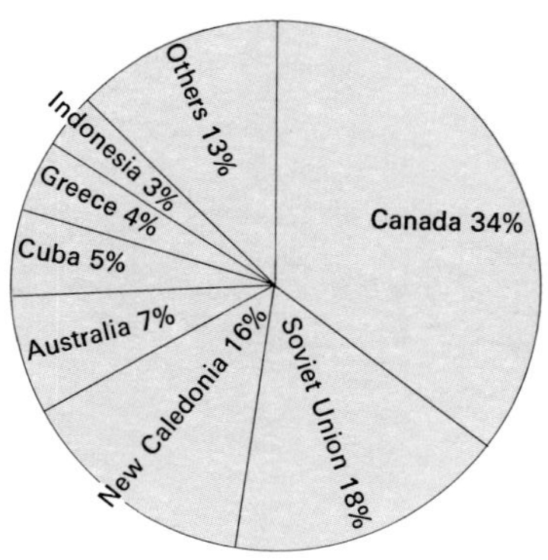

Nickel
806,900 short tons

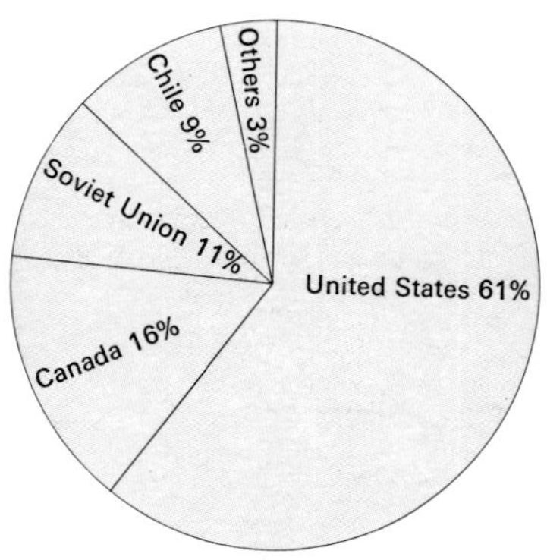

Molybdenum
91,300 short tons

Manganese
24,720,300 short tons

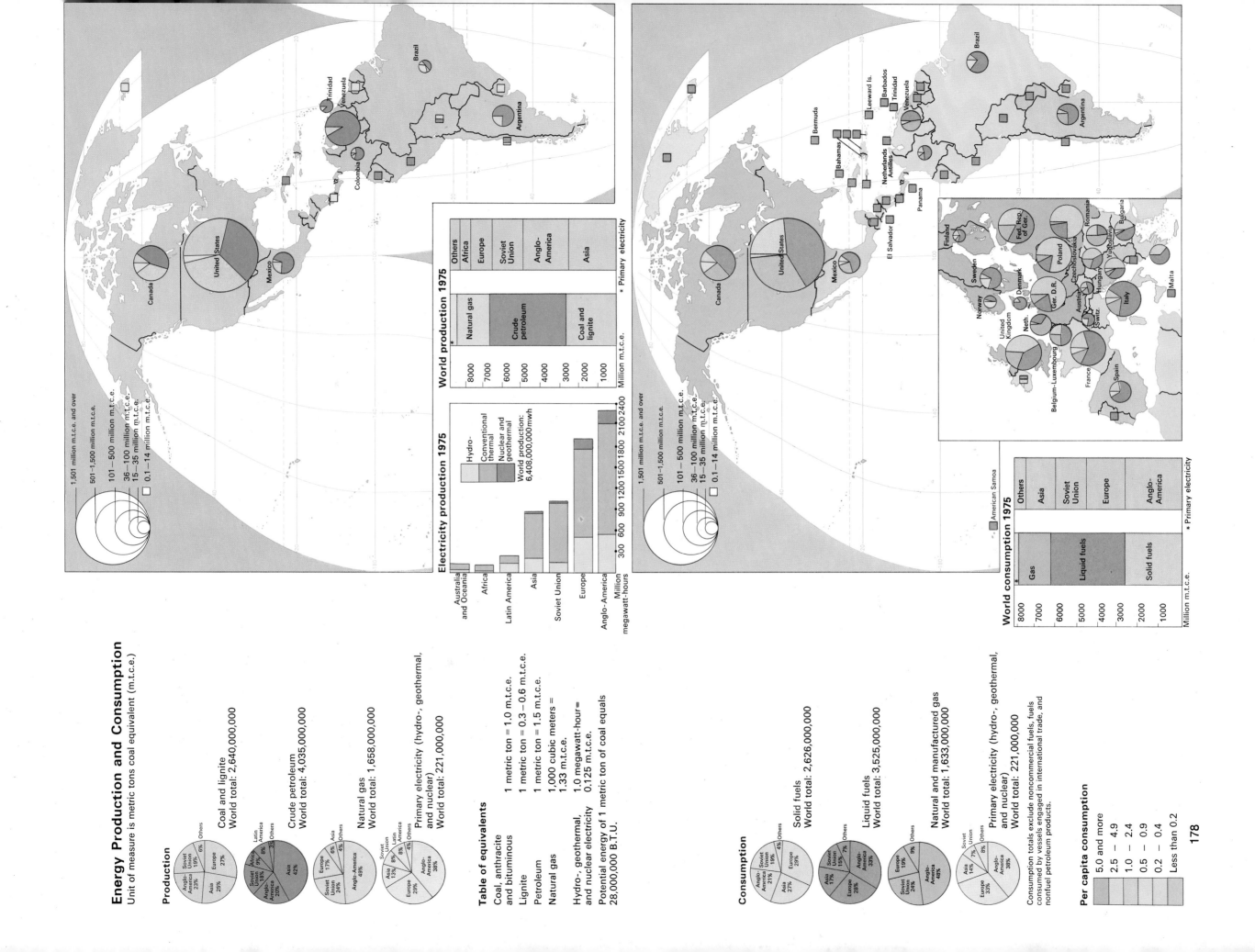

Energy Production and Consumption

Unit of measure is metric tons coal equivalent (m.t.c.e.)

Production

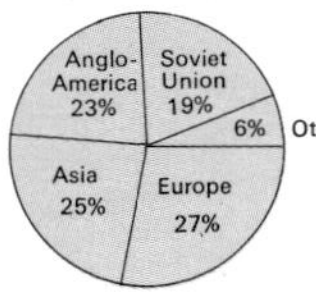

Coal and lignite
World total: 2,640,000,000

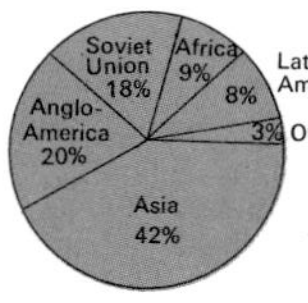

Crude petroleum
World total: 4,035,000,000

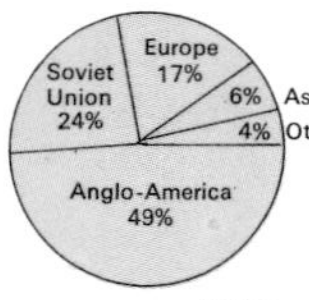

Natural gas
World total: 1,658,000,000

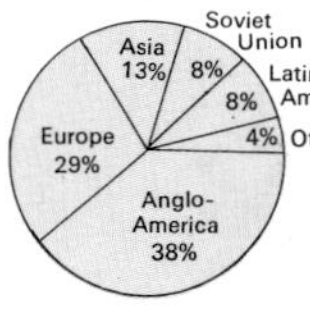

Primary electricity (hydro-, geothermal, and nuclear)
World total: 221,000,000

Table of equivalents

Coal, anthracite and bituminous	1 metric ton = 1.0 m.t.c.e.
Lignite	1 metric ton = 0.3 – 0.6 m.t.c.e.
Petroleum	1 metric ton = 1.5 m.t.c.e.
Natural gas	1,000 cubic meters = 1.33 m.t.c.e.
Hydro-, geothermal, and nuclear electricity	1.0 megawatt-hour= 0.125 m.t.c.e.

Potential energy of 1 metric ton of coal equals 28,000,000 B.T.U.

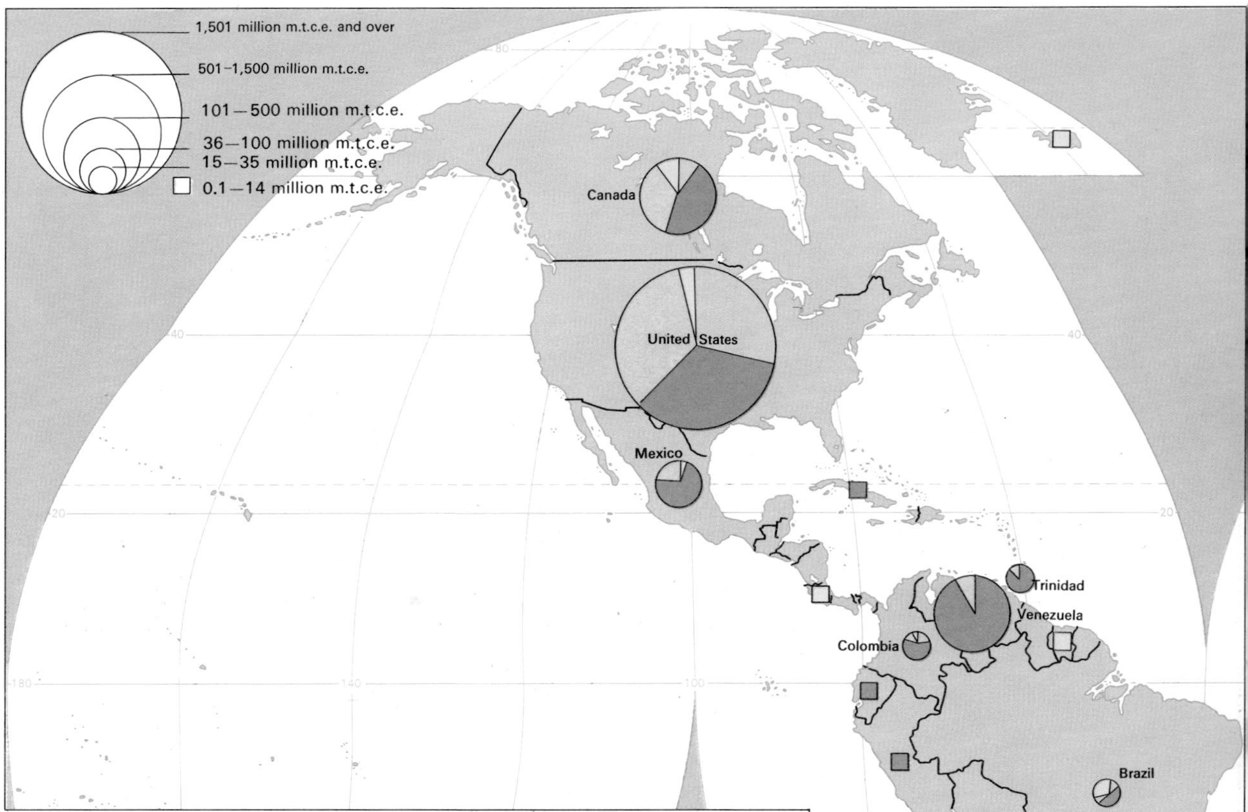

Electricity production 1975

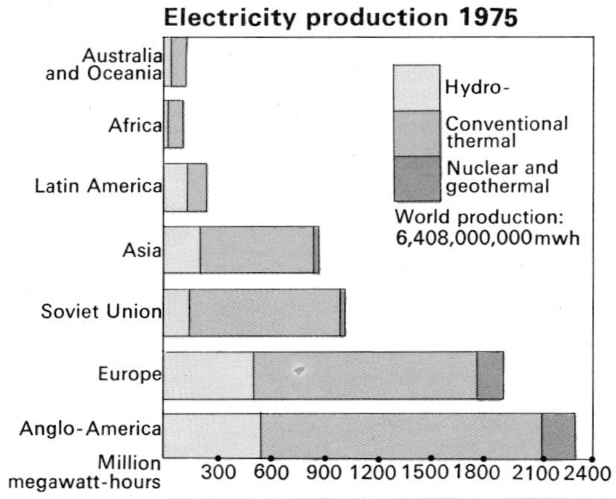

World production 1975

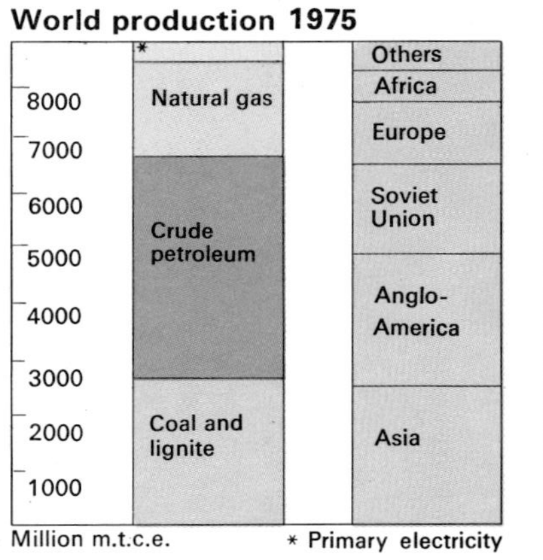

Consumption

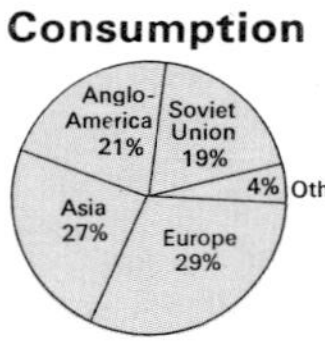

Solid fuels
World total: 2,626,000,000

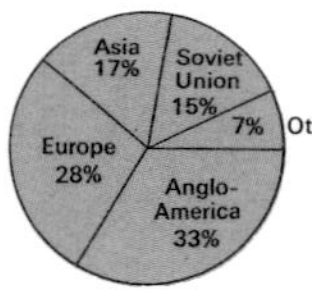

Liquid fuels
World total: 3,525,000,000

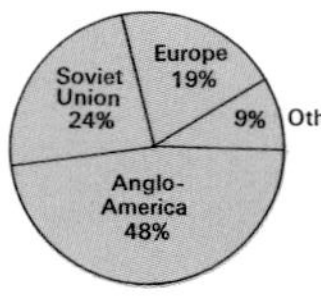

Natural and manufactured gas
World total: 1,633,000,000

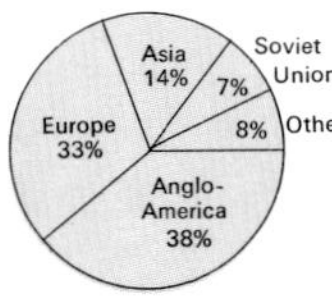

Primary electricity (hydro-, geothermal, and nuclear)
World total: 221,000,000

Consumption totals exclude noncommercial fuels, fuels consumed by vessels engaged in international trade, and nonfuel petroleum products.

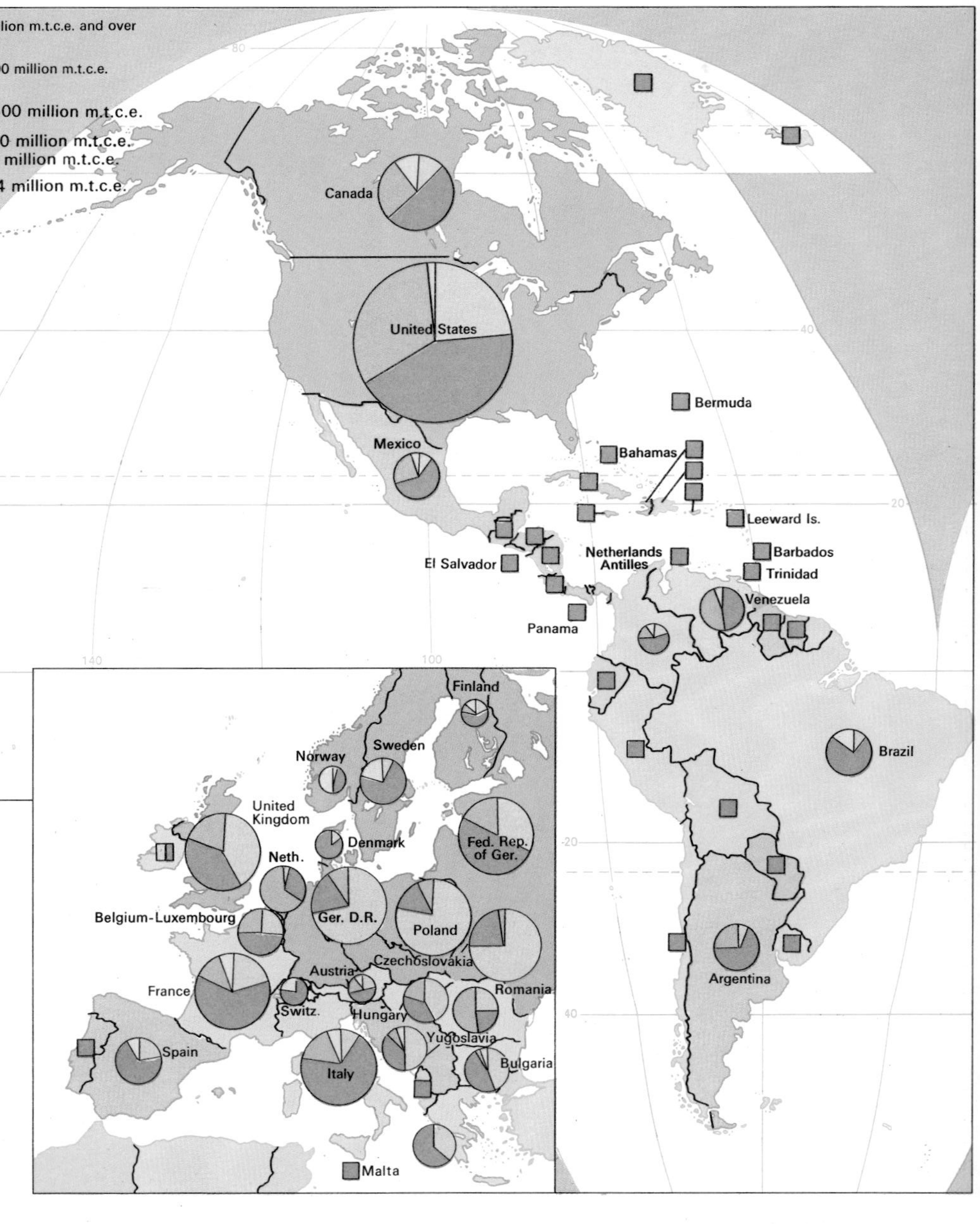

World consumption 1975

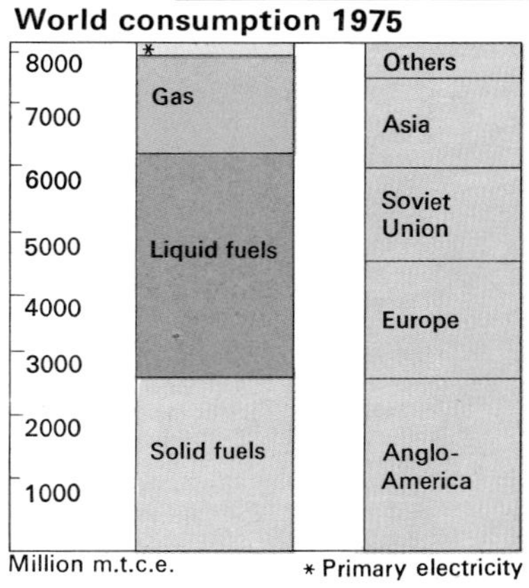

Per capita consumption

- 5.0 and more
- 2.5 – 4.9
- 1.0 – 2.4
- 0.5 – 0.9
- 0.2 – 0.4
- Less than 0.2

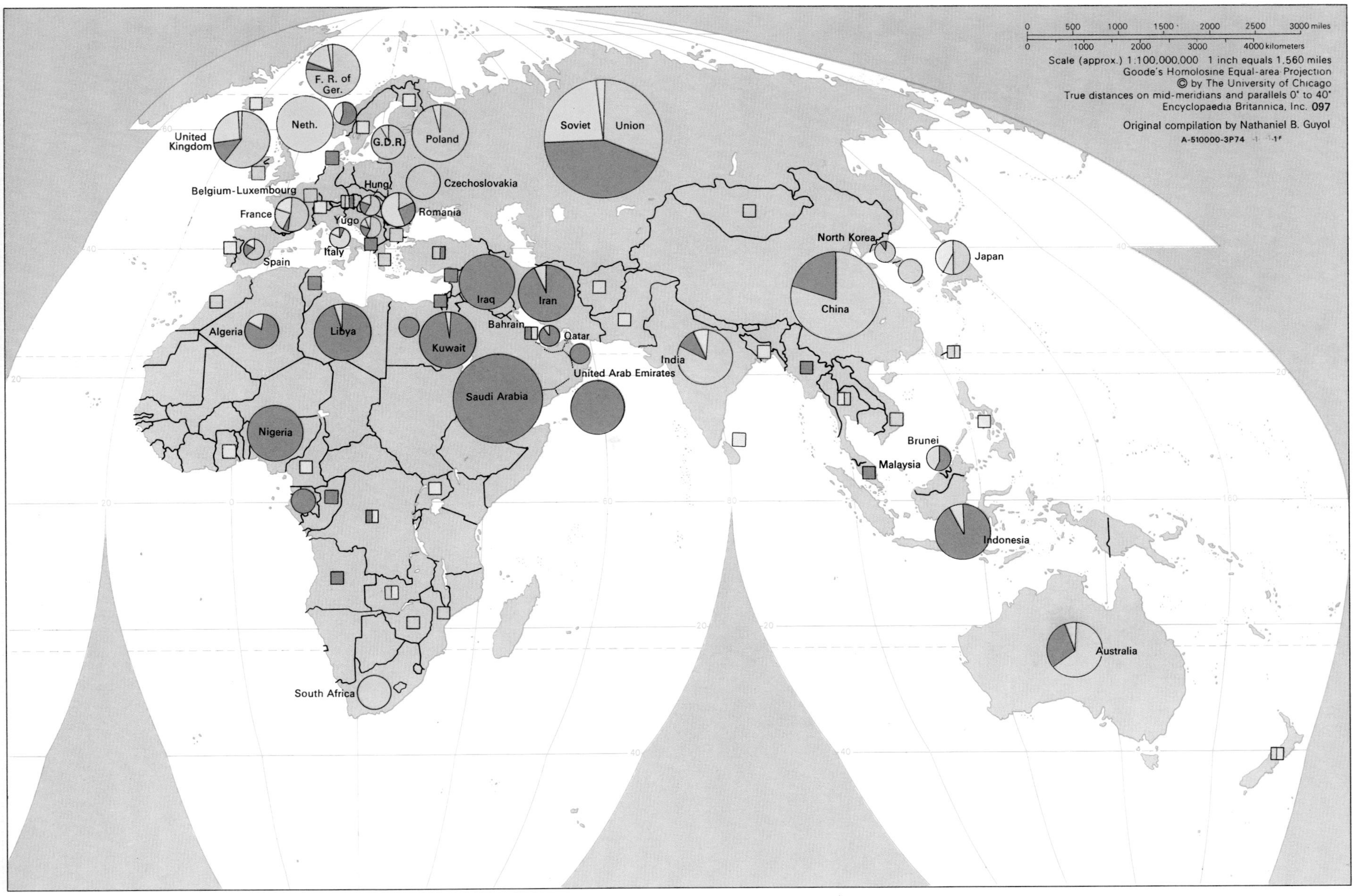
0 500 1000 1500 2000 2500 3000 miles
0 1000 2000 3000 4000 kilometers
Scale (approx.) 1:100,000,000 1 inch equals 1,560 miles
Goode's Homolosine Equal-area Projection
© by The University of Chicago
True distances on mid-meridians and parallels 0° to 40°
Encyclopaedia Britannica, Inc. 097
Original compilation by Nathaniel B. Guyol
A-510000-3P74
F. R. of Ger.
Neth.
United Kingdom
G.D.R.
Poland
Soviet Union
Czechoslovakia
Belgium-Luxembourg
Hung.
France
Yugo.
Romania
Italy
Spain
North Korea
Japan
Iraq
Iran
China
Algeria
Libya
Kuwait
Bahrain
Qatar
India
United Arab Emirates
Saudi Arabia
Nigeria
Brunei
Malaysia
Indonesia
Australia
South Africa

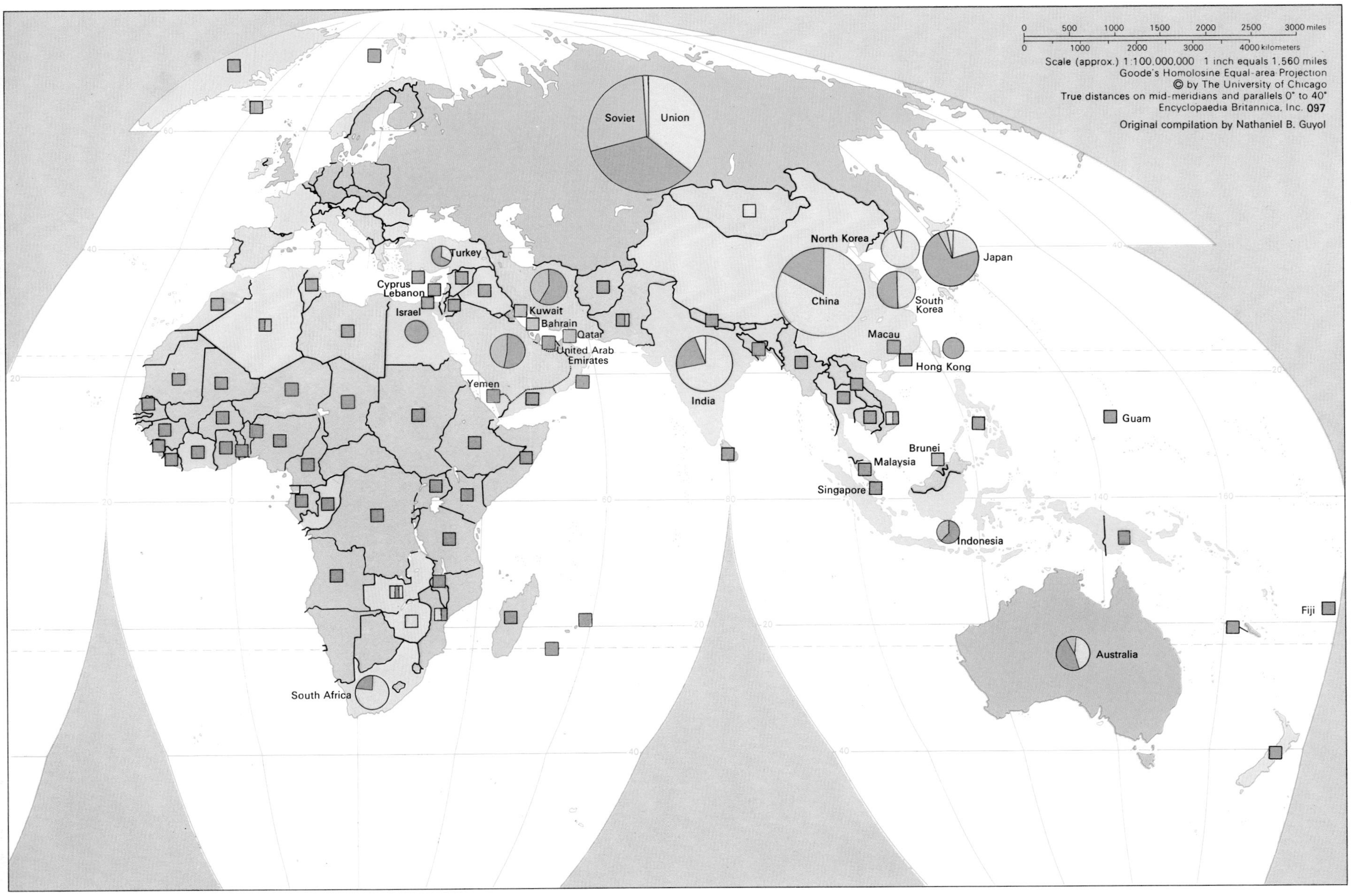
0 500 1000 1500 2000 2500 3000 miles
0 1000 2000 3000 4000 kilometers
Scale (approx.) 1:100,000,000 1 inch equals 1,560 miles
Goode's Homolosine Equal-area Projection
© by The University of Chicago
True distances on mid-meridians and parallels 0° to 40°
Encyclopaedia Britannica, Inc. 097
Original compilation by Nathaniel B. Guyol
Soviet Union
North Korea
Japan
Turkey
Cyprus
Lebanon
Israel
Kuwait
Bahrain
Qatar
United Arab Emirates
China
South Korea
Macau
Hong Kong
Yemen
India
Guam
Brunei
Malaysia
Singapore
Indonesia
Fiji
Australia
South Africa

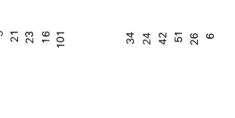

Gross National Product

Total per country at market price In U.S. $000,000	Number of countries
84,000 and more	13
42,000–83,999	9
14,000–41,999	21
4,667–13,999	23
2,334–4,666	16
Less than 2,334	101
No data available	

Per capita In U.S. dollars	Number of countries
■ 3,720 and more	34
॥ 1,860–3,719	24
◗ 620–1,859	42
▲ 207–619	51
♥ 104–206	26
● Less than 104	6

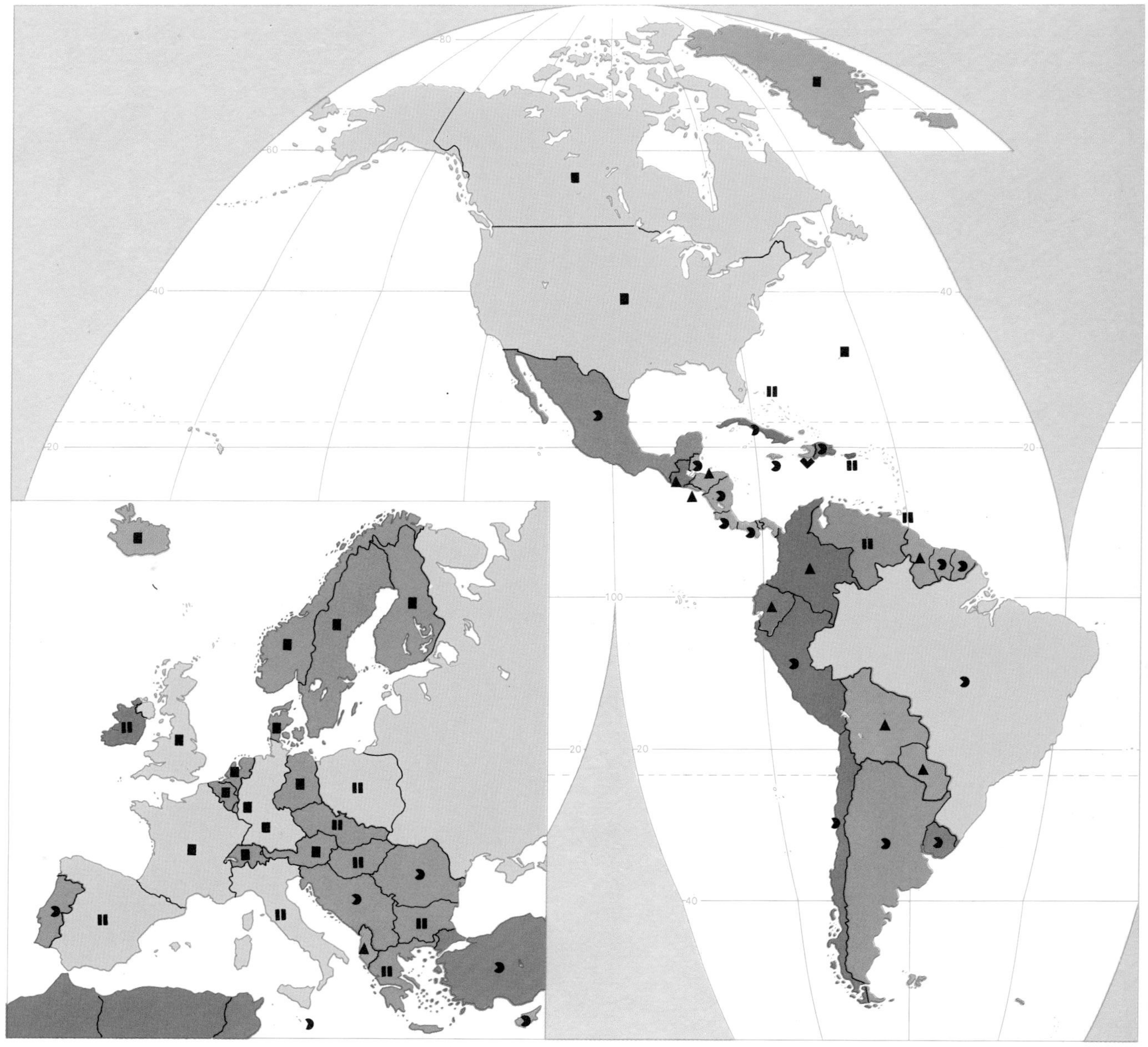

International Trade

Total per country In U.S. $000,000	Number of countries
15,174 and more	25
7,587–15,173	19
2,529–7,586	22
844–2,528	31
423–843	19
Less than 423	41
No data available	

Per capita In U.S. dollars	Number of countries
■ 702 and more	60
॥ 351–701	18
◗ 117–350	39
▲ 40–116	24
♥ 22–39	8
● Less than 22	9

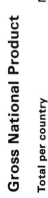

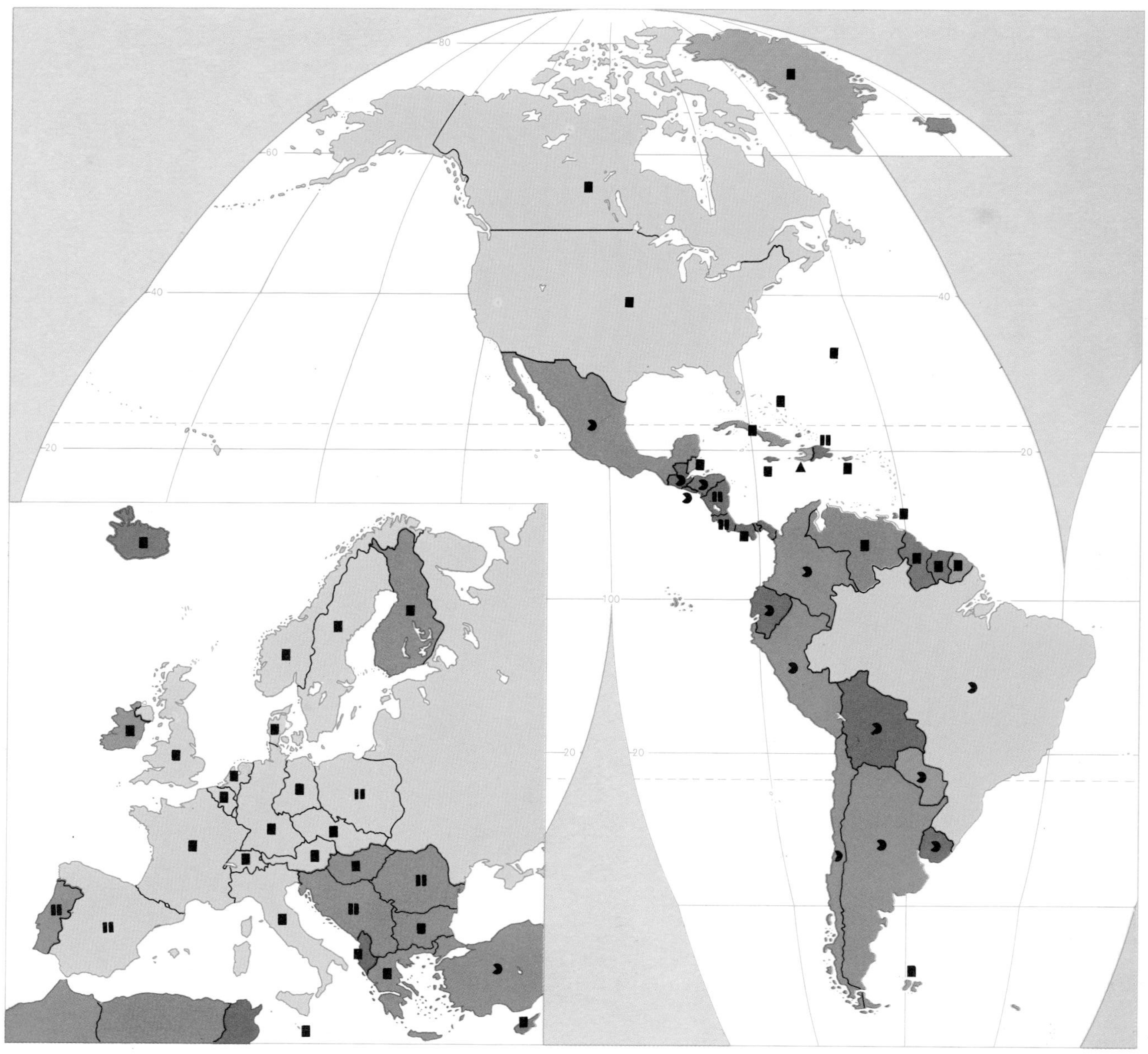

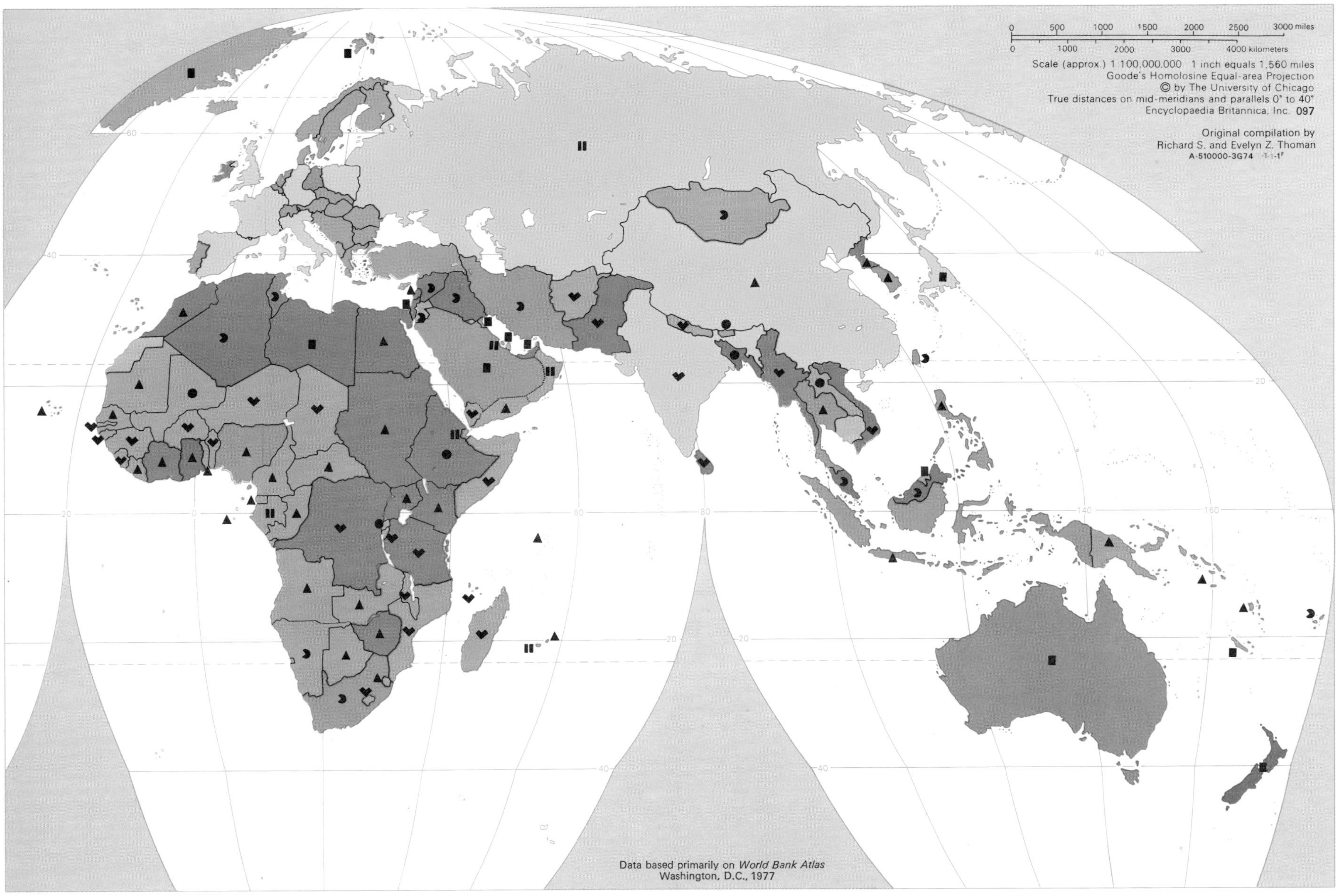
0 500 1000 1500 2000 2500 3000 miles
0 1000 2000 3000 4000 kilometers
Scale (approx.) 1:100,000,000 1 inch equals 1,560 miles
Goode's Homolosine Equal-area Projection
© by The University of Chicago
True distances on mid-meridians and parallels 0° to 40°
Encyclopaedia Britannica, Inc. 097
Original compilation by
Richard S. and Evelyn Z. Thoman
A-510000-3G74
Data based primarily on *World Bank Atlas*
Washington, D.C., 1977

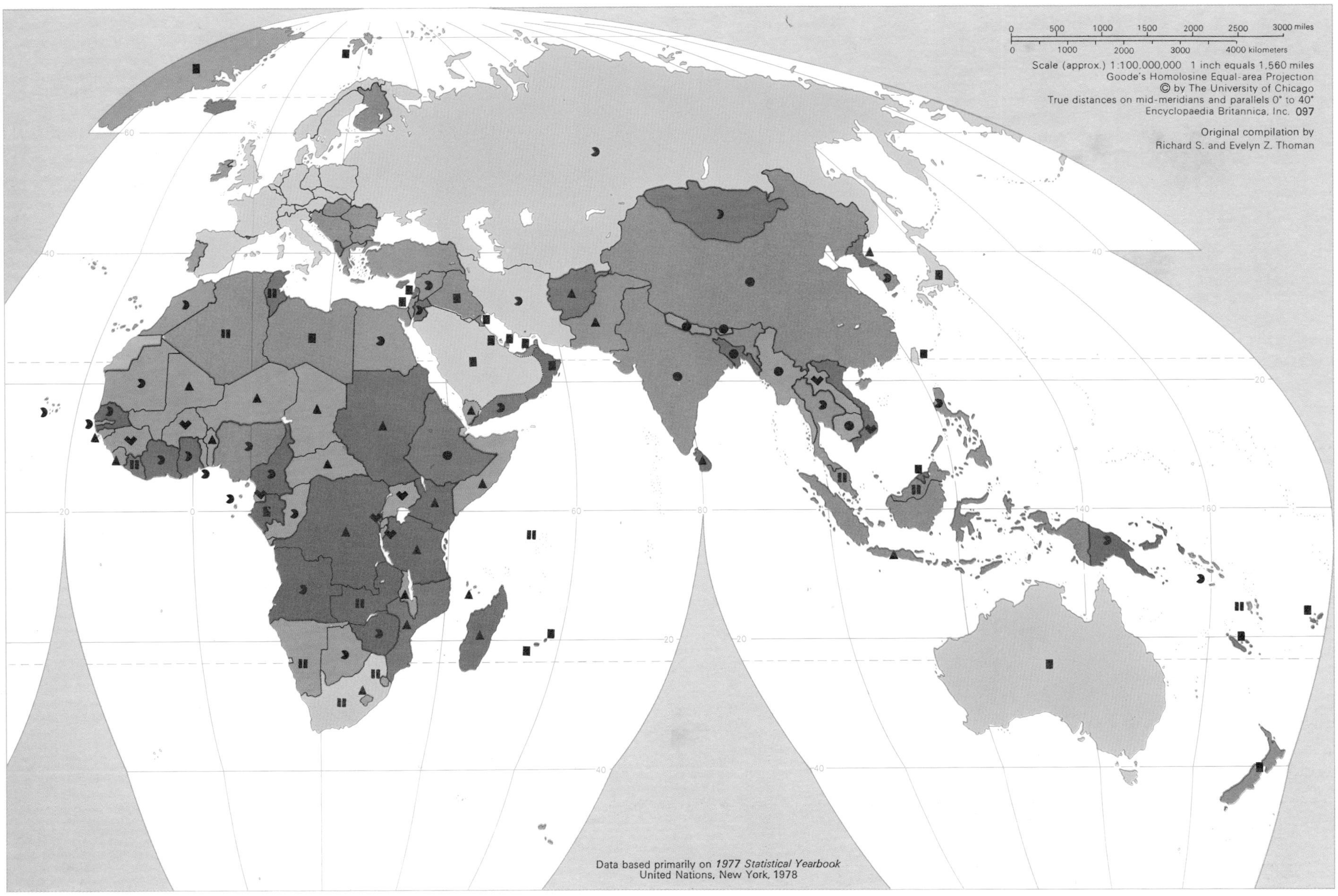
0 500 1000 1500 2000 2500 3000 miles
0 1000 2000 3000 4000 kilometers
Scale (approx.) 1:100,000,000 1 inch equals 1,560 miles
Goode's Homolosine Equal-area Projection
© by The University of Chicago
True distances on mid-meridians and parallels 0° to 40°
Encyclopaedia Britannica, Inc. 097
Original compilation by
Richard S. and Evelyn Z. Thoman
Data based primarily on *1977 Statistical Yearbook*
United Nations, New York, 1978

Climate Graphs

Each graph below shows temperature and rainfall at a weather station that was selected to illustrate one of the climate regions described in the legend at the right. The weather stations are keyed by number to the maps. The elements of the graphs are identified in the sample graph at the top, with a temperature scale in degrees Fahrenheit and Celsius (Centigrade), and a precipitation scale in inches and millimeters.

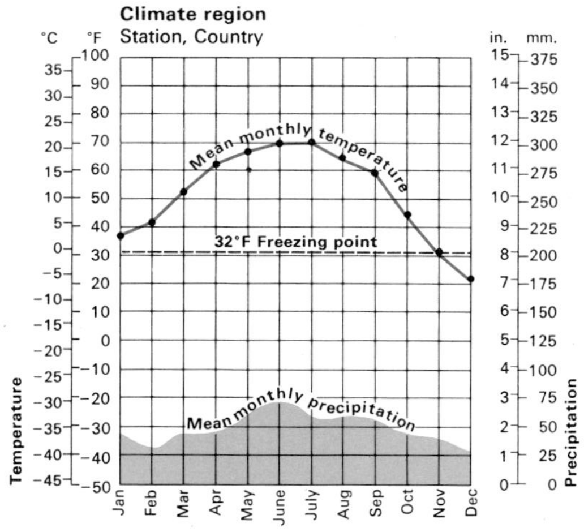

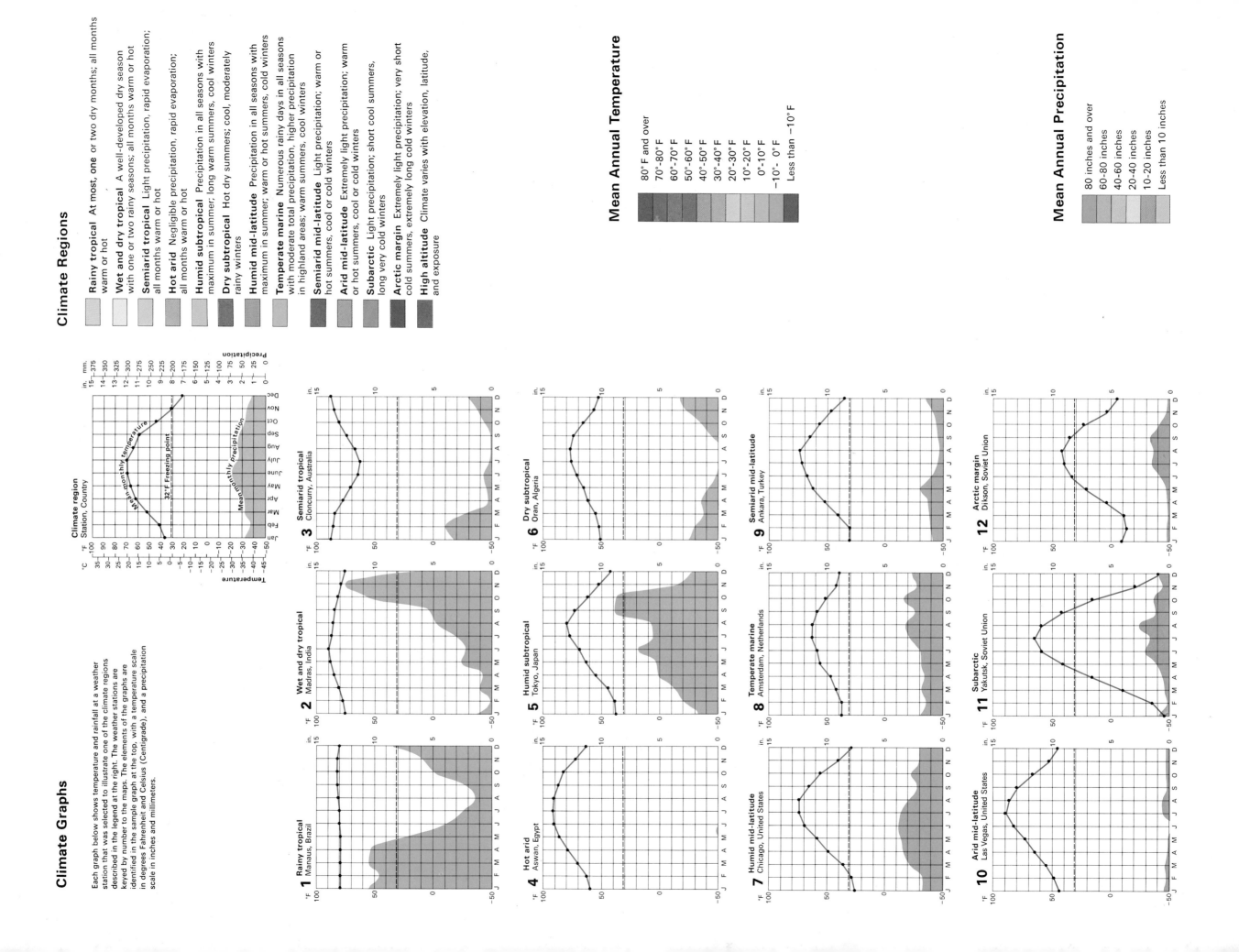

1 Rainy tropical
Manaus, Brazil

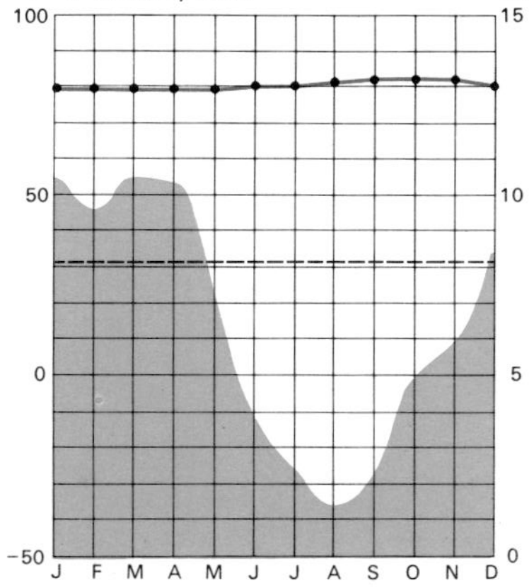

2 Wet and dry tropical
Madras, India

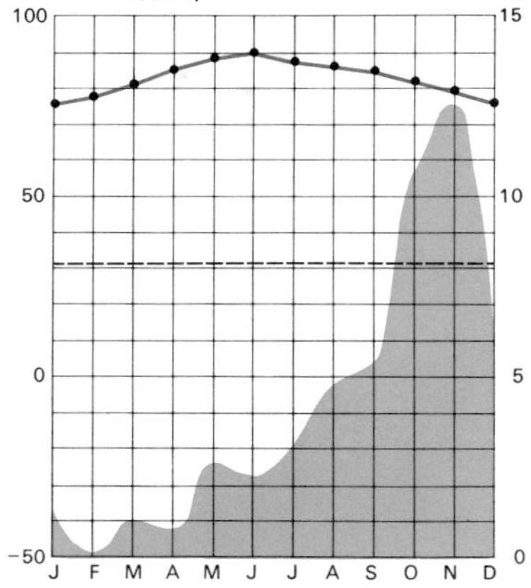

3 Semiarid tropical
Cloncurry, Australia

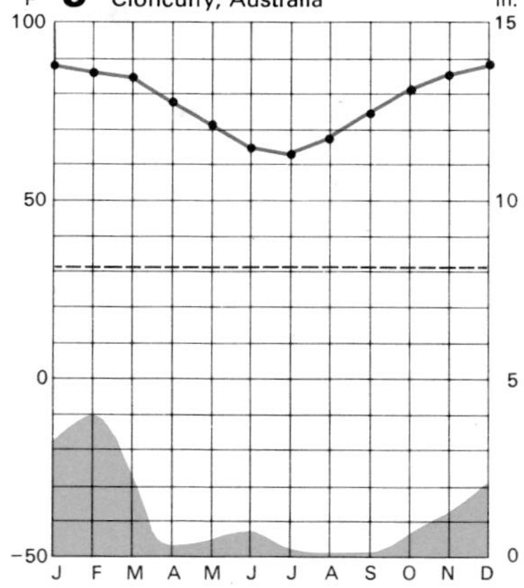

4 Hot arid
Aswan, Egypt

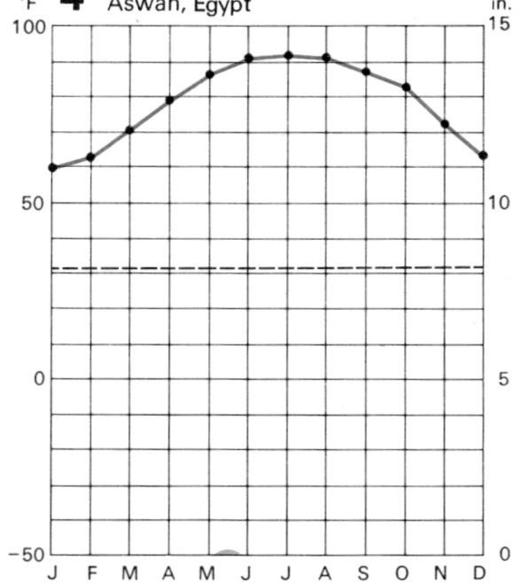

5 Humid subtropical
Tokyo, Japan

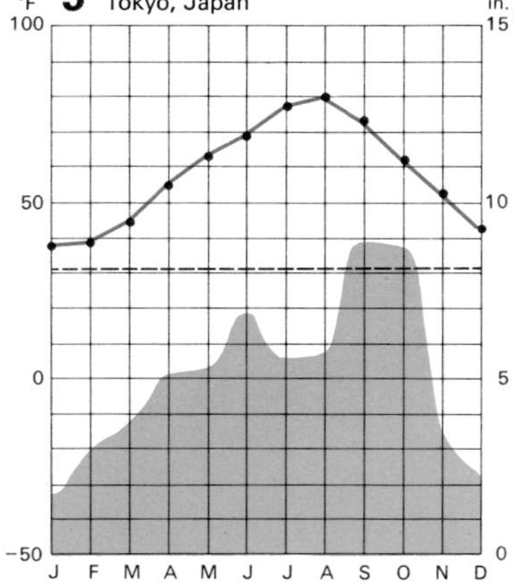

6 Dry subtropical
Oran, Algeria

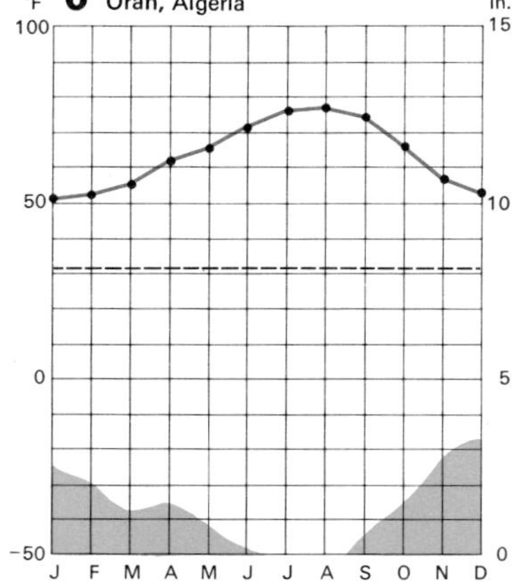

7 Humid mid-latitude
Chicago, United States

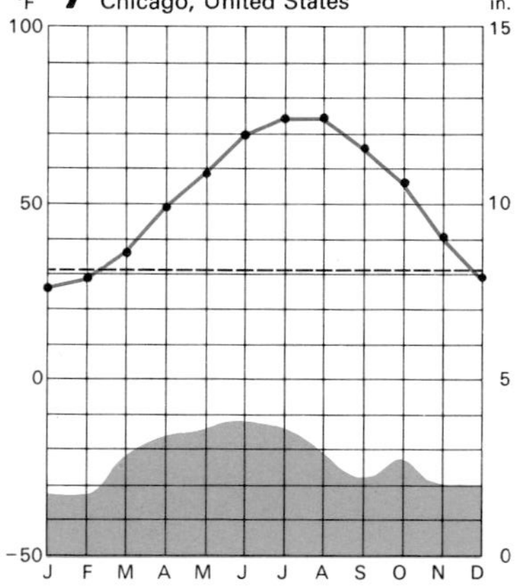

8 Temperate marine
Amsterdam, Netherlands

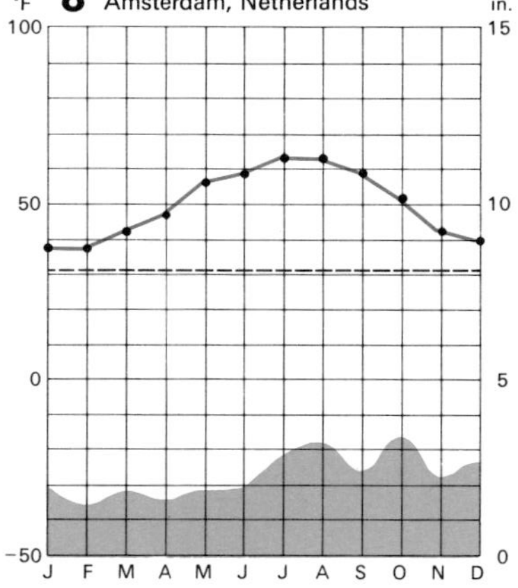

9 Semiarid mid-latitude
Ankara, Turkey

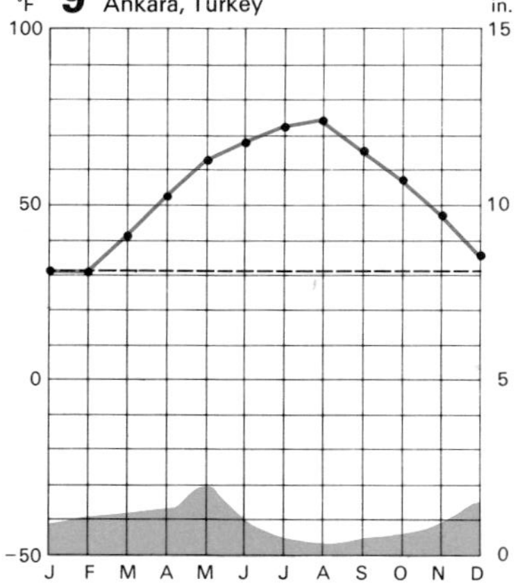

10 Arid mid-latitude
Las Vegas, United States

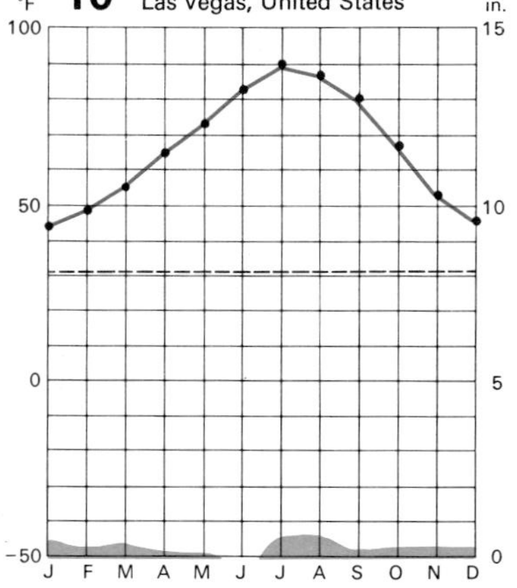

11 Subarctic
Yakutsk, Soviet Union

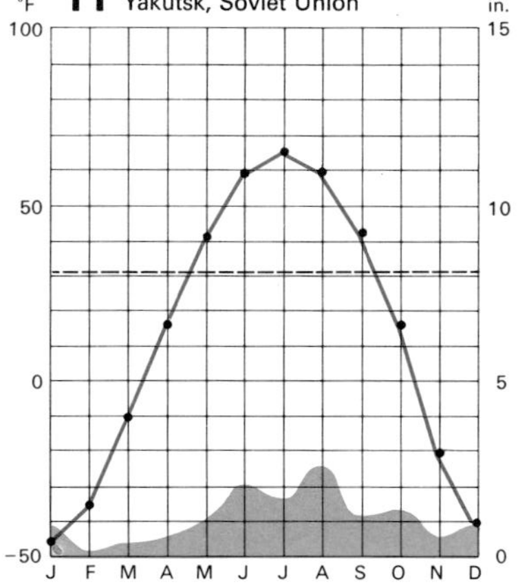

12 Arctic margin
Dikson, Soviet Union

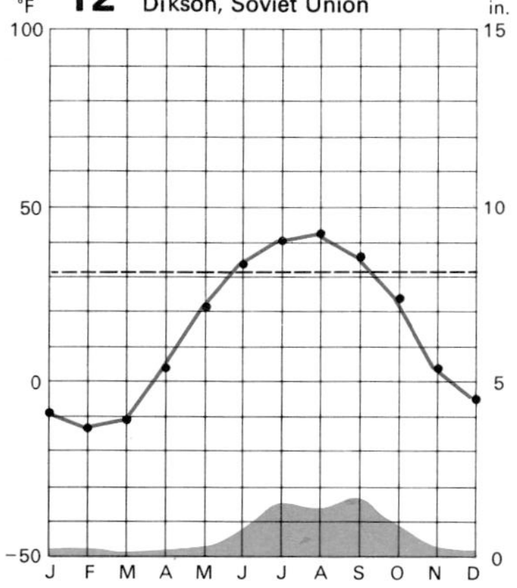

Climate Regions

- **Rainy tropical** At most, one or two dry months; all months warm or hot
- **Wet and dry tropical** A well-developed dry season with one or two rainy seasons; all months warm or hot
- **Semiarid tropical** Light precipitation, rapid evaporation; all months warm or hot
- **Hot arid** Negligible precipitation, rapid evaporation; all months warm or hot
- **Humid subtropical** Precipitation in all seasons with maximum in summer; long warm summers, cool winters
- **Dry subtropical** Hot dry summers; cool, moderately rainy winters
- **Humid mid-latitude** Precipitation in all seasons with maximum in summer; warm or hot summers, cold winters
- **Temperate marine** Numerous rainy days in all seasons with moderate total precipitation, higher precipitation in highland areas; warm summers, cool winters
- **Semiarid mid-latitude** Light precipitation; warm or hot summers, cool or cold winters
- **Arid mid-latitude** Extremely light precipitation; warm or hot summers, cool or cold winters
- **Subarctic** Light precipitation; short cool summers, long very cold winters
- **Arctic margin** Extremely light precipitation; very short cold summers, extremely long cold winters
- **High altitude** Climate varies with elevation, latitude, and exposure

Mean Annual Temperature

- 80° F and over
- 70°-80° F
- 60°-70° F
- 50°-60° F
- 40°-50° F
- 30°-40° F
- 20°-30° F
- 10°-20° F
- 0°-10° F
- −10°- 0° F
- Less than −10° F

Mean Annual Precipitation

- 80 inches and over
- 60-80 inches
- 40-60 inches
- 20-40 inches
- 10-20 inches
- Less than 10 inches

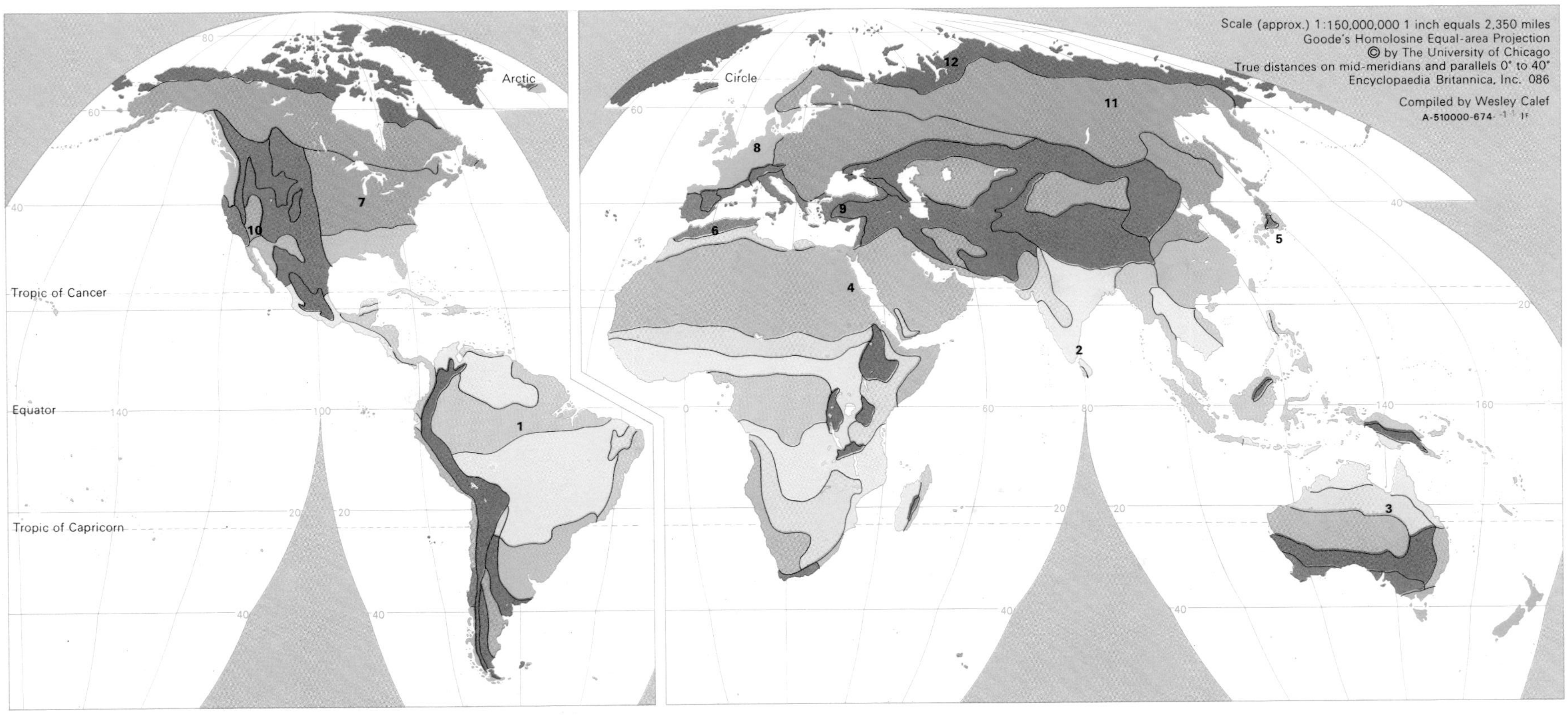
Arctic
Circle
Tropic of Cancer
Equator
Tropic of Capricorn
1
2
3
4
5
6
7
8
9
10
11
12
Scale (approx.) 1:150,000,000 1 inch equals 2,350 miles
Goode's Homolosine Equal-area Projection
© by The University of Chicago
True distances on mid-meridians and parallels 0° to 40°
Encyclopaedia Britannica, Inc. 086
Compiled by Wesley Calef

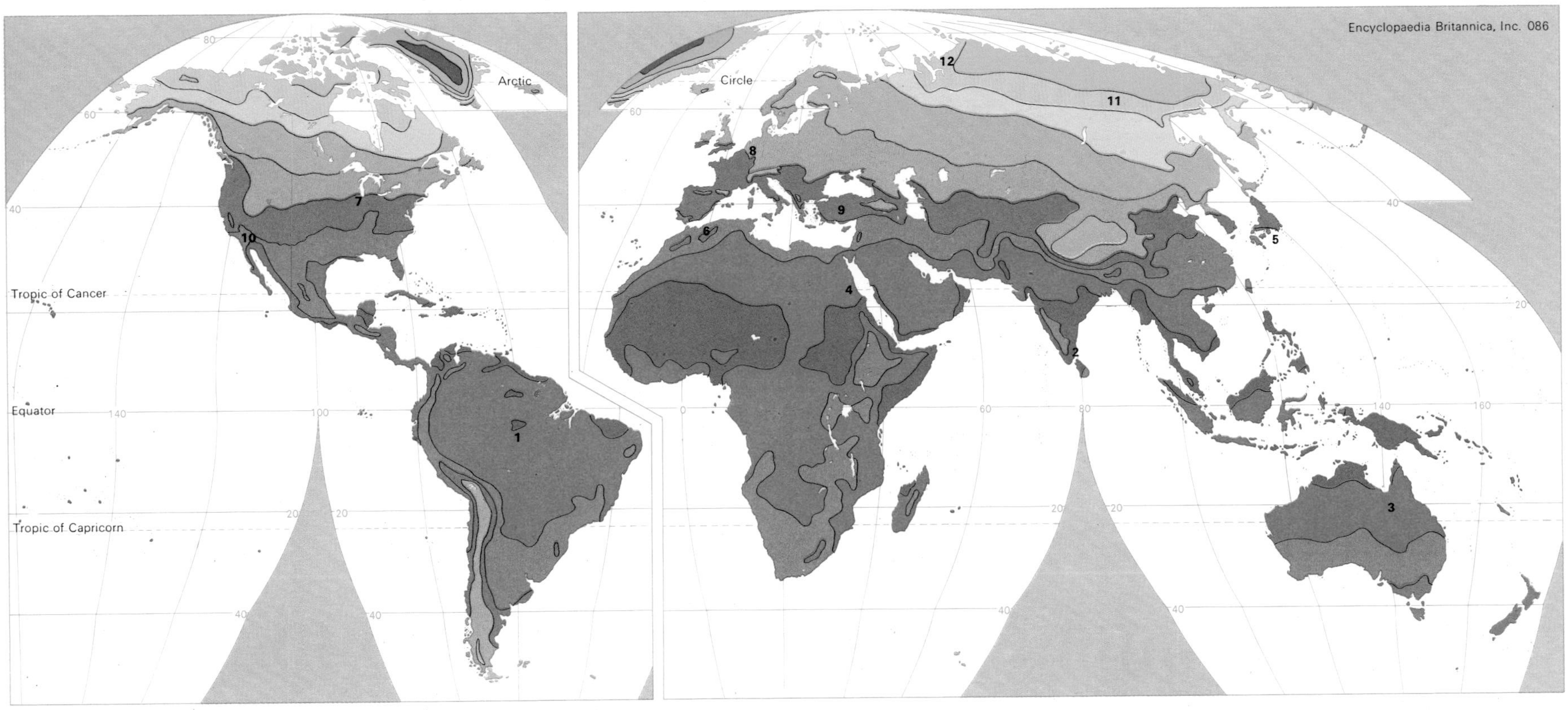
Arctic
Circle
Tropic of Cancer
Equator
Tropic of Capricorn
1
2
3
4
5
6
7
8
9
10
11
12
Encyclopaedia Britannica, Inc. 086

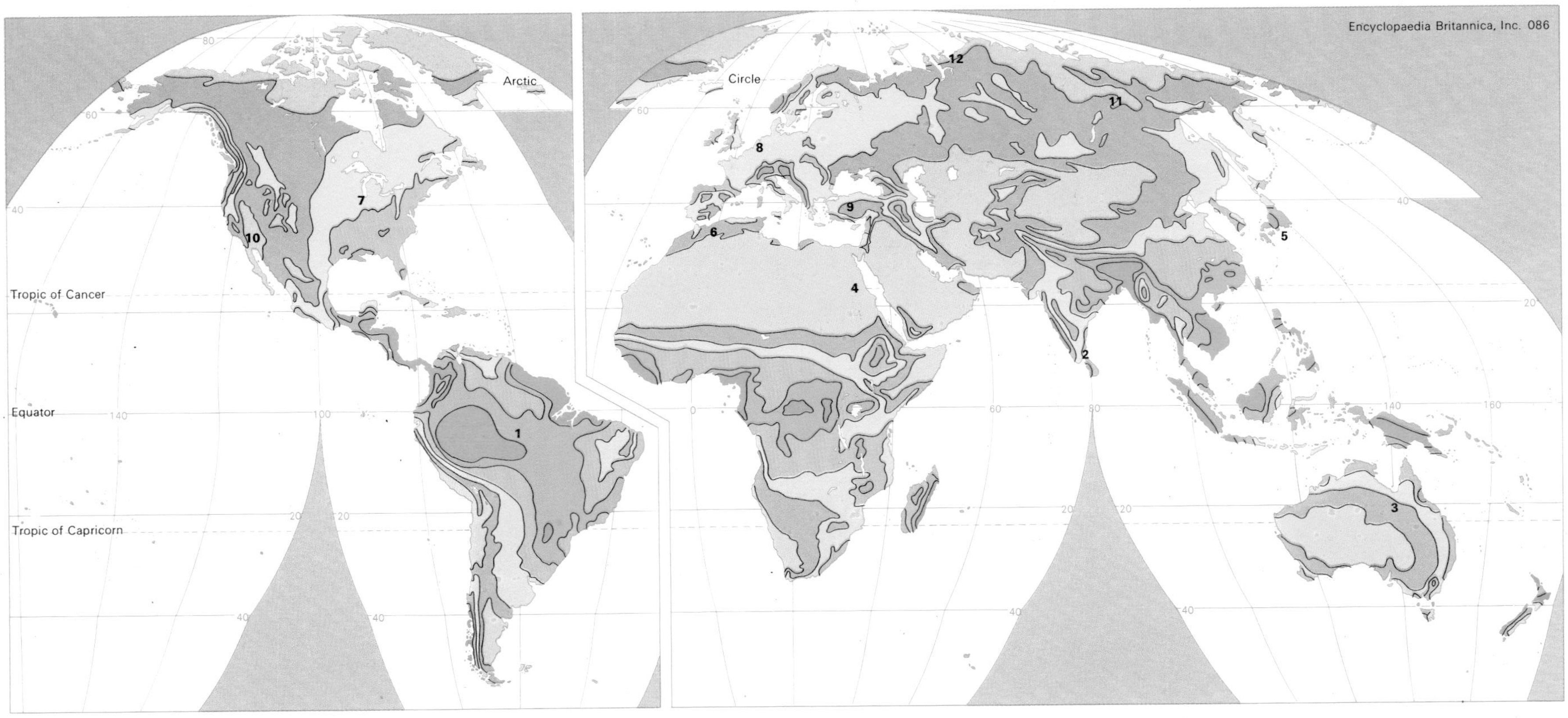
Arctic
Circle
Tropic of Cancer
Equator
Tropic of Capricorn
1
2
3
4
5
6
7
8
9
10
11
12
Encyclopaedia Britannica, Inc. 086

Surface Configuration

Smooth lands

- Level plains: nearly all slopes gentle; local relief less than 100 ft. (30 m.)
- Irregular plains: majority of slopes gentle; local relief 100-300 ft. (30-90 m.)

Broken lands

- Tablelands and plateaus: majority of slopes gentle, with the gentler slopes on the uplands; local relief more than 300 ft. (90 m.)
- Hill-studded plains: majority of slopes gentle, with the gentler slopes in the lowlands; local relief 300-1,000 ft. (90-300 m.)
- Mountain-studded plains: majority of slopes gentle, with the gentler slopes in the lowlands; local relief more than 1,000 ft. (300 m.)

Rough lands

- Hill lands: steeper slopes predominate; local relief less than 1,000 ft. (300 m.)
- Mountains: steeper slopes predominate; local relief 1,000-5,000 ft. (300-1,500 m.)
- Mountains of great relief: steeper slopes predominate; local relief more than 5,000 ft. (1,500 m.)

Other surfaces

- Ice caps: permanent ice
- Maximum extent of glaciation

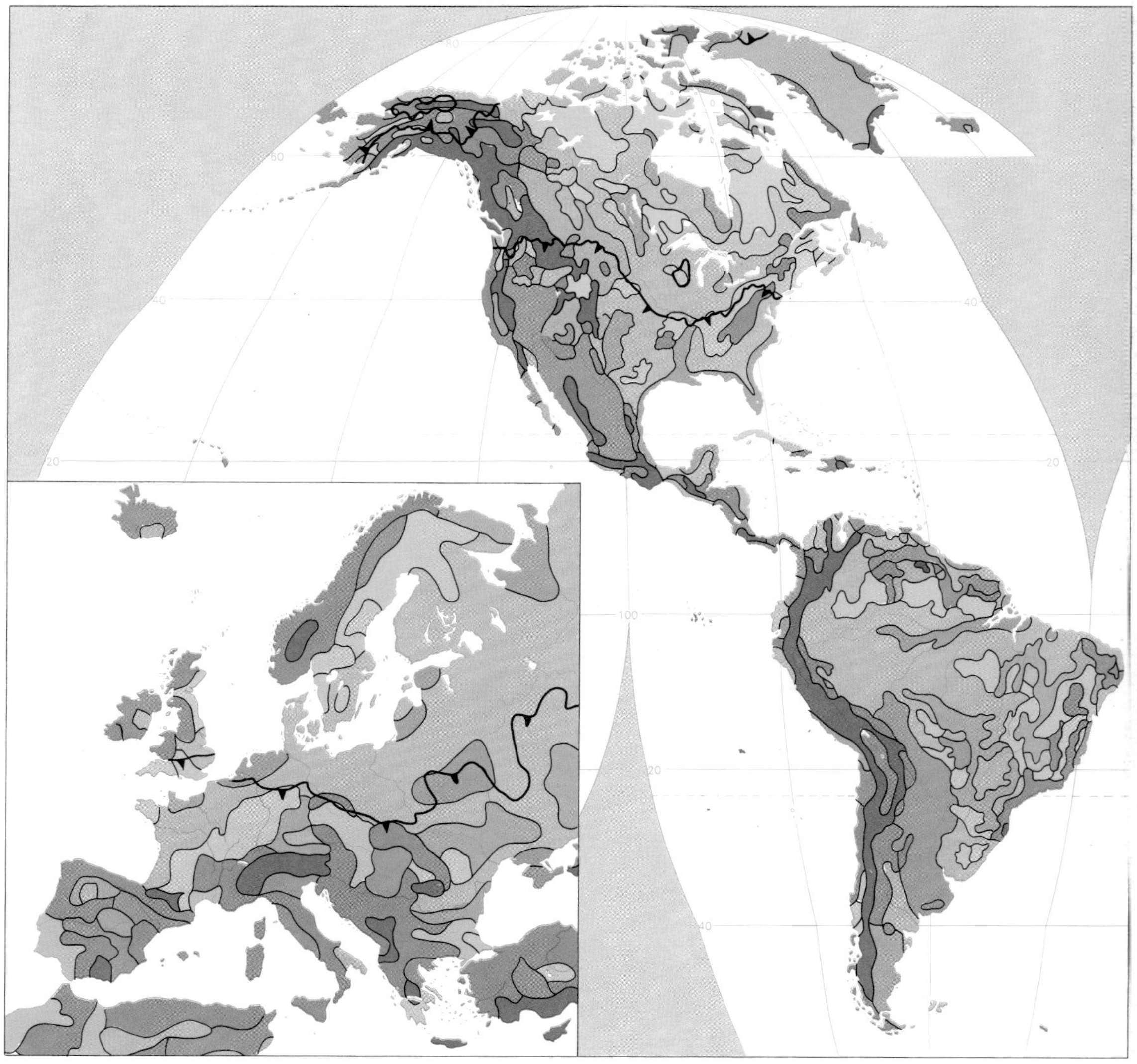

Earth Structure and Tectonics

- Precambrian stable shield areas
- Exposed Precambrian rock
- Paleozoic and Mesozoic flat-lying sedimentary rocks
- Principal Paleozoic and Mesozoic folded areas
- Cenozoic sedimentary rocks
- Principal Cenozoic folded areas
- Lava plateaus
- Major trends of folding

Geologic time chart

Precambrian—from formation of the earth (at least 4 billion years ago) to 600 million years ago

Paleozoic—from 600 million to 200 million years ago

Mesozoic—from 200 million to 70 million years ago

Cenozoic—from 70 million years ago to present time

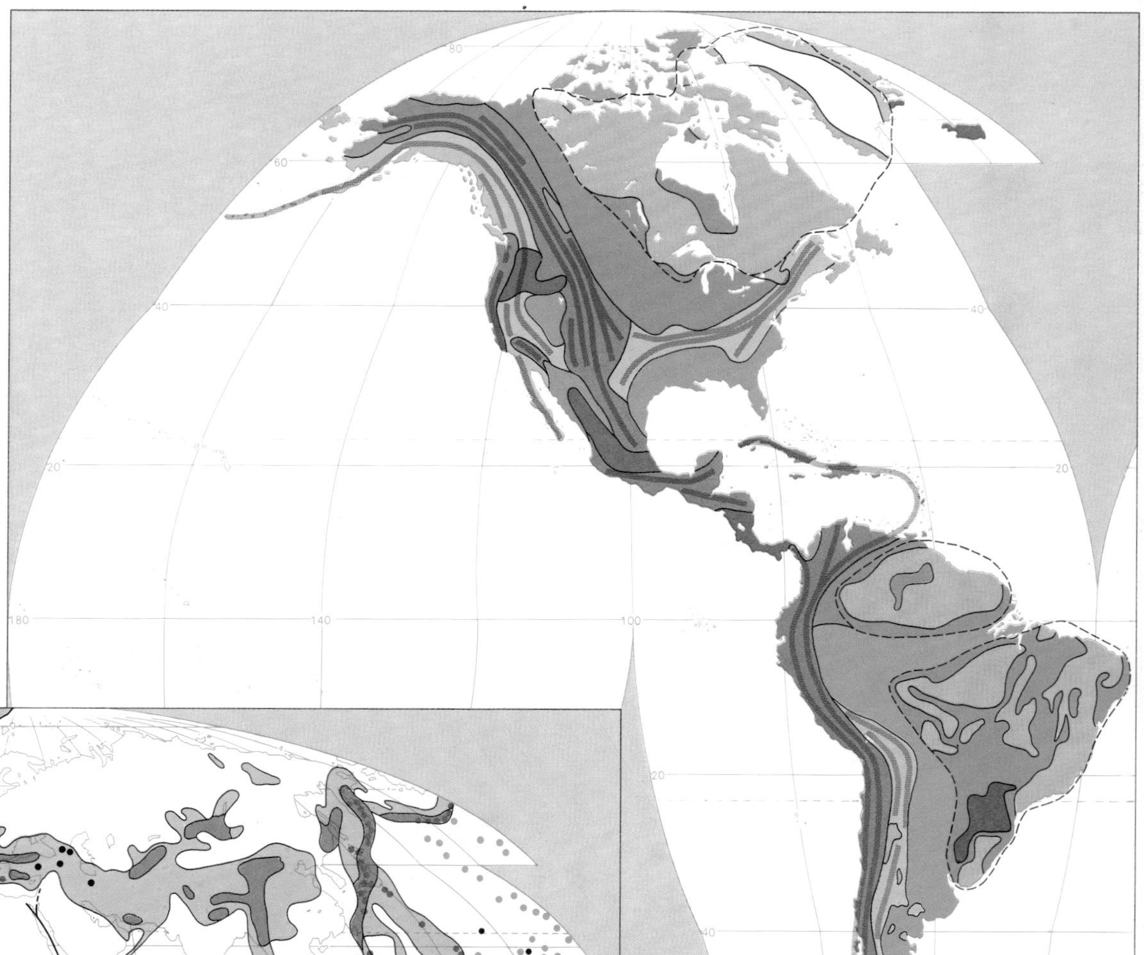

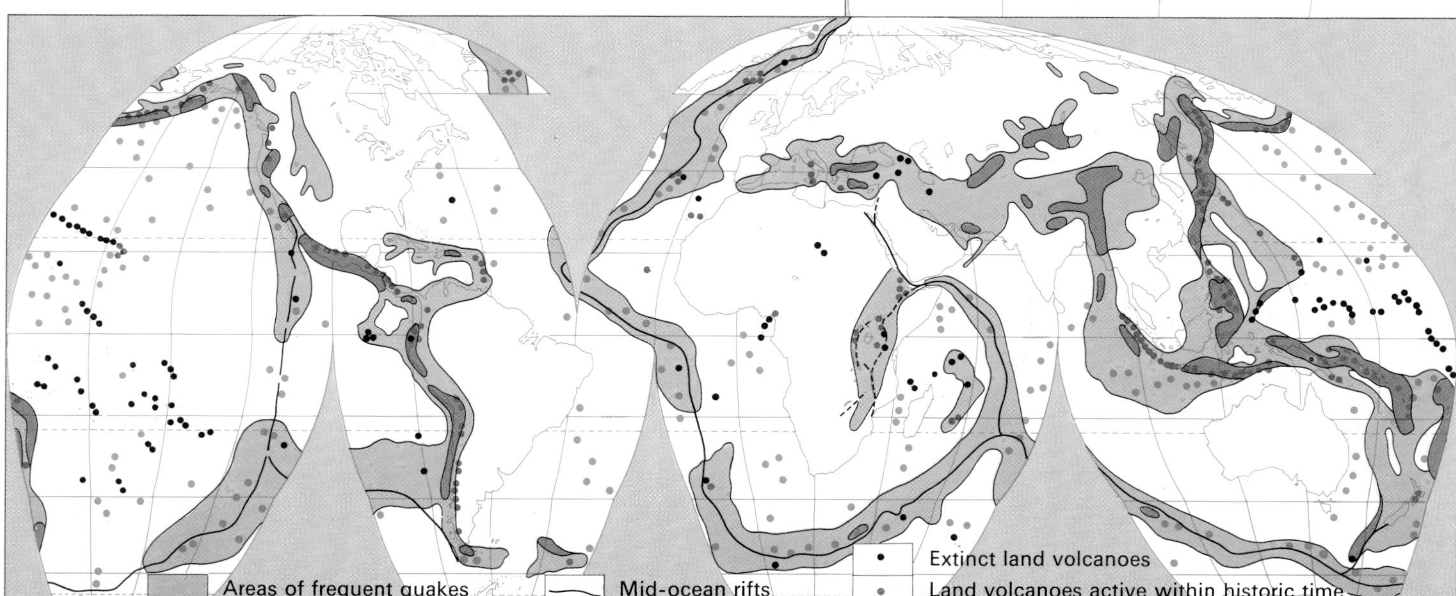

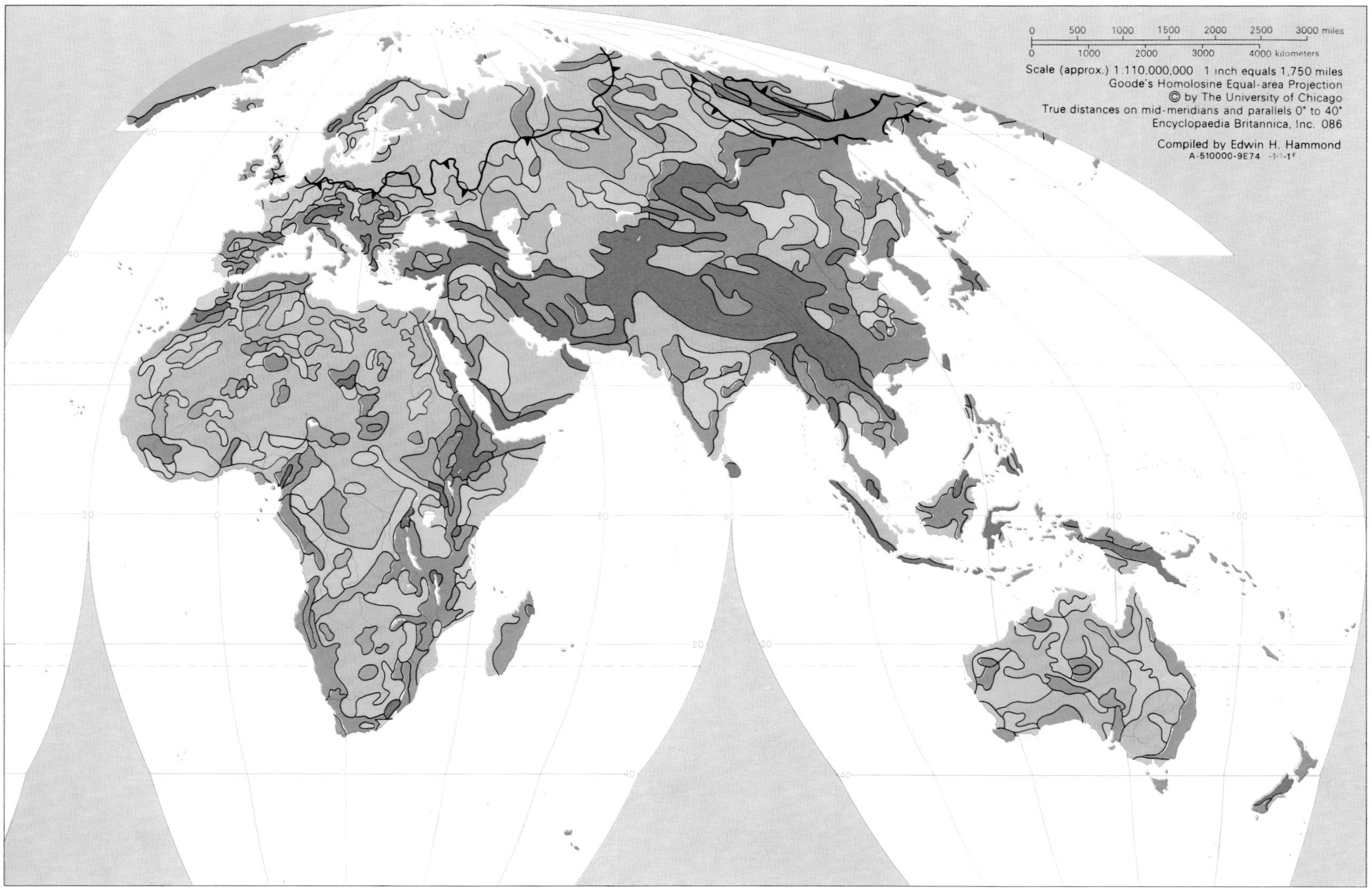

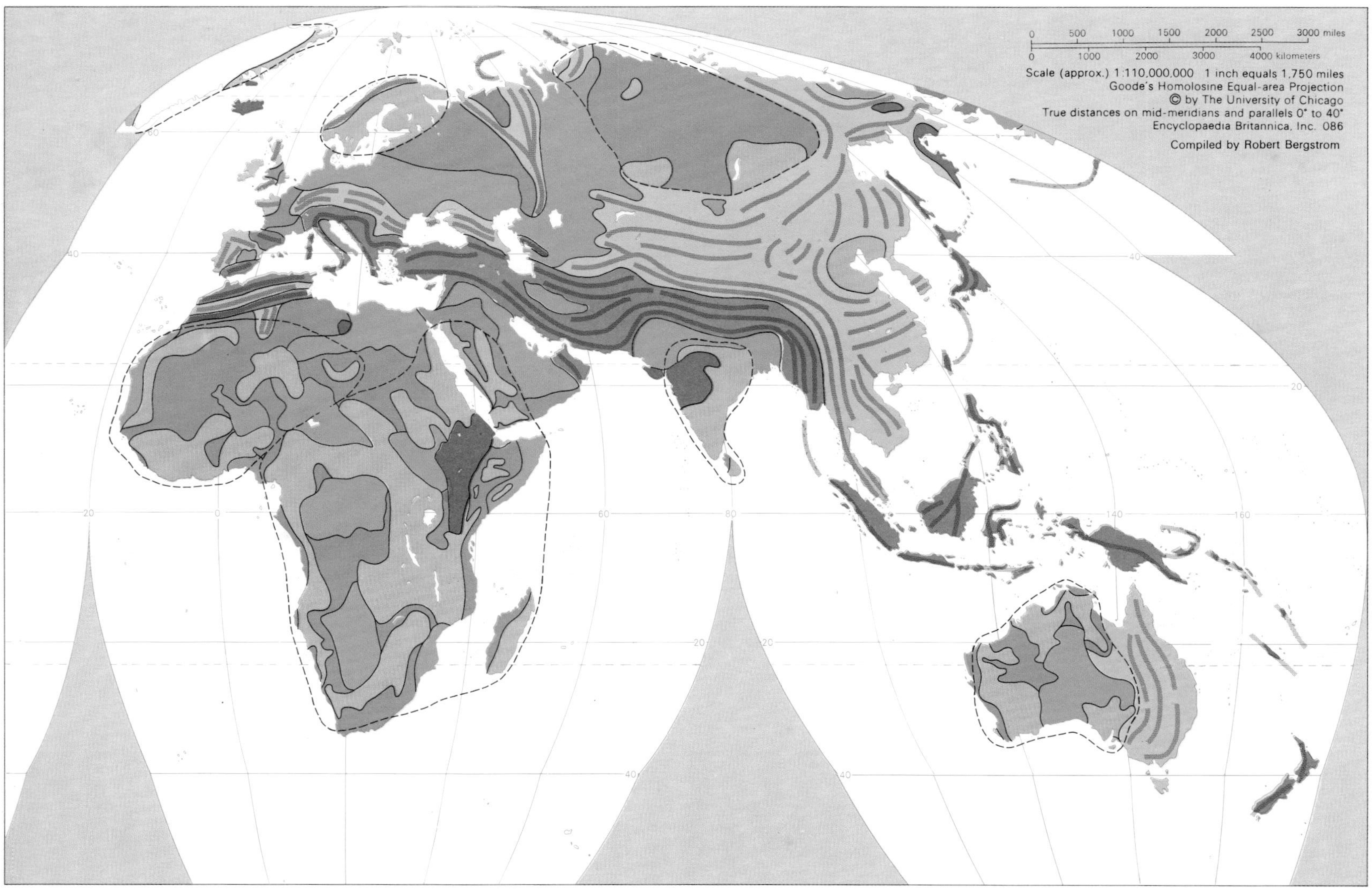

Development of the earth's structure

The earth is in process of constant transformation. Movements in the hot, dense interior of the earth result in folding and fracture of the crust and transfer of molten material to the surface. As a result, large structures such as mountain ranges, volcanoes, lava plateaus, and rift valleys are created. The forces that bring about these structural changes are called *tectonic forces.*

The present continents have developed from stable nuclei, or *shields*, of ancient (Precambrian) rock. Erosive forces such as water, wind, and ice have worn away particles of the rock, depositing them at the edges of the shields, where they have accumulated and ultimately become sedimentary rock. Subsequently, in places, these extensive areas of flat-lying rock have been elevated, folded, or warped, by the action of tectonic forces, to form mountains. The shape of these mountains has been altered by later erosion. Where the forces of erosion have been at work for a long time, the mountains tend to have a low relief and rounded contours, like the Appalachians. Mountains more recently formed are high and rugged, like the Himalayas.

The map above depicts some of the major geologic structures of the earth and identifies them according to the period of their formation. A geologic time chart is included in the legend. The inset map shows the most important areas of earthquakes, rifts, and volcanic activity. Comparison of all the maps will show the close correlation between present-day mountain systems, recent (Cenozoic) mountain-building, and the areas of frequent earthquakes and active volcanoes.

Natural Vegetation

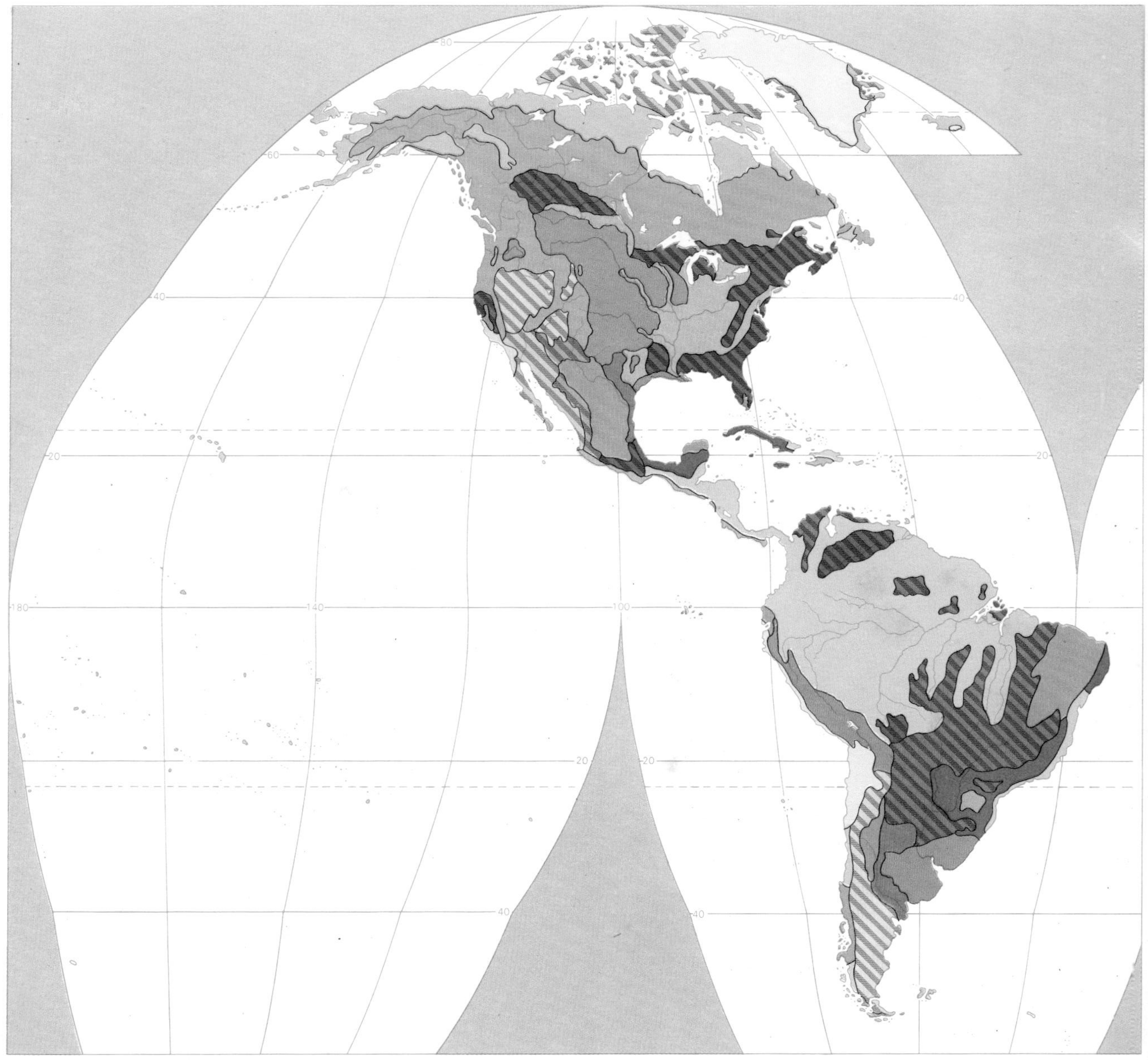

Broad-leaved evergreen vegetation
- Broad-leaved evergreen forest
- Broad-leaved evergreen shrub formation
- Scattered broad-leaved evergreen shrubs
- Scattered broad-leaved evergreen dwarf shrubs

Broad-leaved deciduous vegetation
- Broad-leaved deciduous forest
- Broad-leaved deciduous shrub formation
- Scattered broad-leaved deciduous shrubs
- Scattered broad-leaved deciduous dwarf shrubs

Coniferous vegetation
- Needle-leaved evergreen forest
- Scattered needle-leaved evergreen trees
- Needle-leaved deciduous forest

Mixed vegetation without grass
- Forest of broad-leaved evergreen and deciduous trees
- Forest of broad-leaved and needle-leaved evergreen trees
- Broad-leaved deciduous forests with broad-leaved evergreen shrubs
- Forest of broad-leaved deciduous and needle-leaved evergreen trees

Mixed vegetation with grass
- Grassland with scattered broad-leaved evergreen trees
- Grassland with broad-leaved evergreen shrubs
- Grassland with scattered broad-leaved deciduous trees
- Grassland with broad-leaved deciduous shrubs

Grassland, tundra, barren
- Grassland
- Patches of grass
- Lichens and grasses
- Lichens and mosses
- Barren

Soils

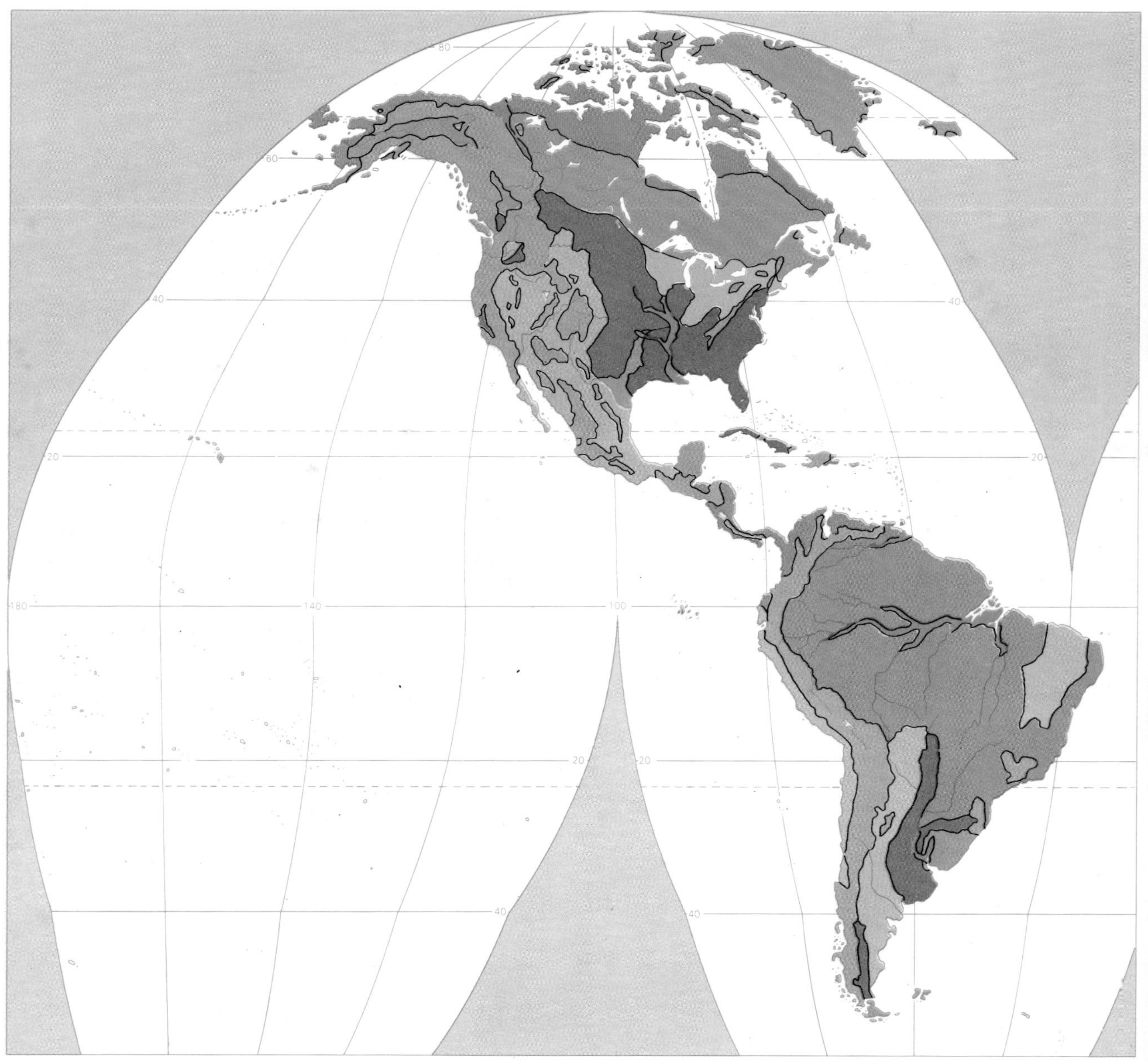

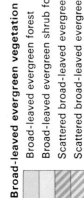

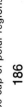

- Tundra soils of frigid climates; commonly with permanently frozen subsoil; supports dwarf shrubs, mosses, and lichens; some used for reindeer pasture
- Podzolic soils of humid, cool climates; covered with predominantly coniferous forest; some farming, mainly subsistence
- Podzolic soils of humid, temperate climates; originally covered with predominantly deciduous forest, much of it removed to accommodate extensive general farming, industry, and cities
- Podzolic soils of humid, warm climates; covered with coniferous or mixed forest; general farming
- Chernozemic soils of subhumid and semiarid, cool to tropical climates; supports mainly grasslands; extensive grain and livestock farming
- Latosolic soils of humid or wet-dry tropical and subtropical climates; supports forest or savanna; shifting cultivation with some plantation agriculture
- Grumusolic soils of humid to semiarid and temperate to tropical climates, with distinct wet and dry seasons; mainly grass-covered; livestock and grain farming
- Desertic soils of arid climates; includes many areas of shallow, stony soils; sparse cover of shrubs and grass, some suitable for grazing; fertile if irrigated; dry farming possible in some areas
- Mountain soils of all climates; shallow, stony; barren, grass-covered, or forested, depending on climate; includes many areas of other soils
- Alluvial soils of all climates; deposited by water in flood plains and deltas of rivers; intensive farming in most temperate and some tropical regions (many smaller areas not shown)
- Ice cap of polar regions

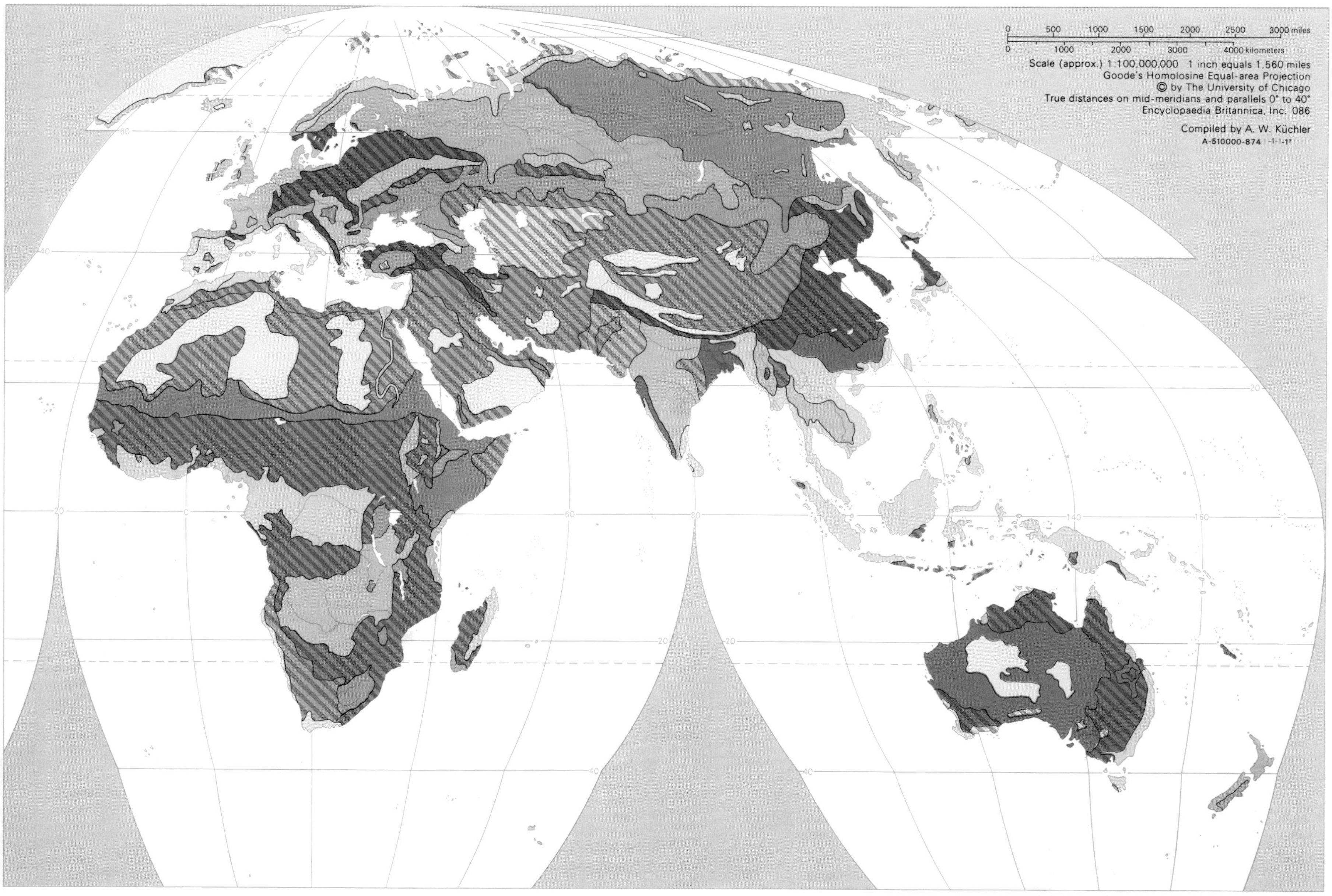
0 500 1000 1500 2000 2500 3000 miles
0 1000 2000 3000 4000 kilometers
Scale (approx.) 1:100,000,000 1 inch equals 1,560 miles
Goode's Homolosine Equal-area Projection
© by The University of Chicago
True distances on mid-meridians and parallels 0° to 40°
Encyclopaedia Britannica, Inc. 086
Compiled by A. W. Küchler
A-510000-874

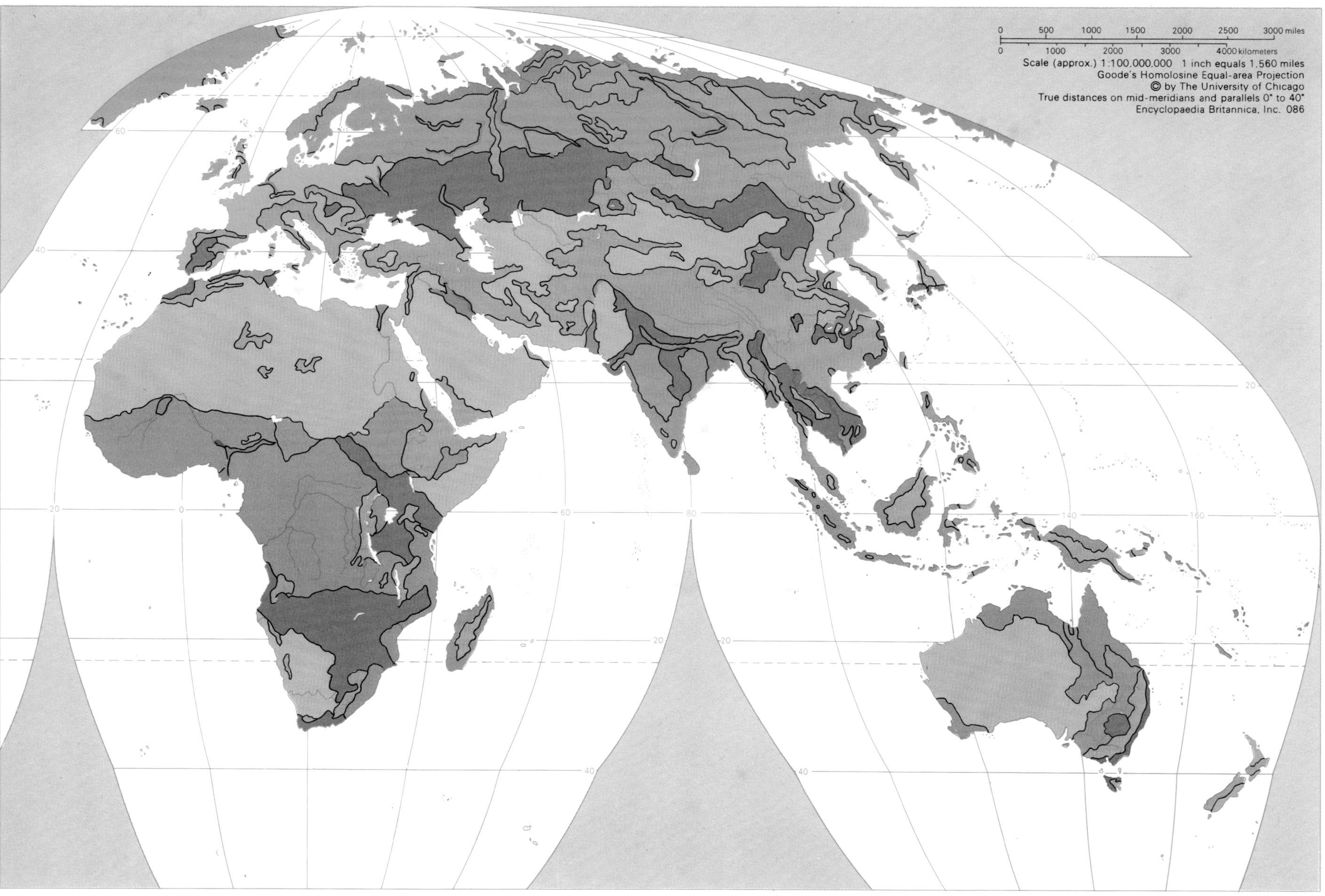
0 500 1000 1500 2000 2500 3000 miles
0 1000 2000 3000 4000 kilometers
Scale (approx.) 1:100,000,000 1 inch equals 1,560 miles
Goode's Homolosine Equal-area Projection
© by The University of Chicago
True distances on mid-meridians and parallels 0° to 40°
Encyclopaedia Britannica, Inc. 086

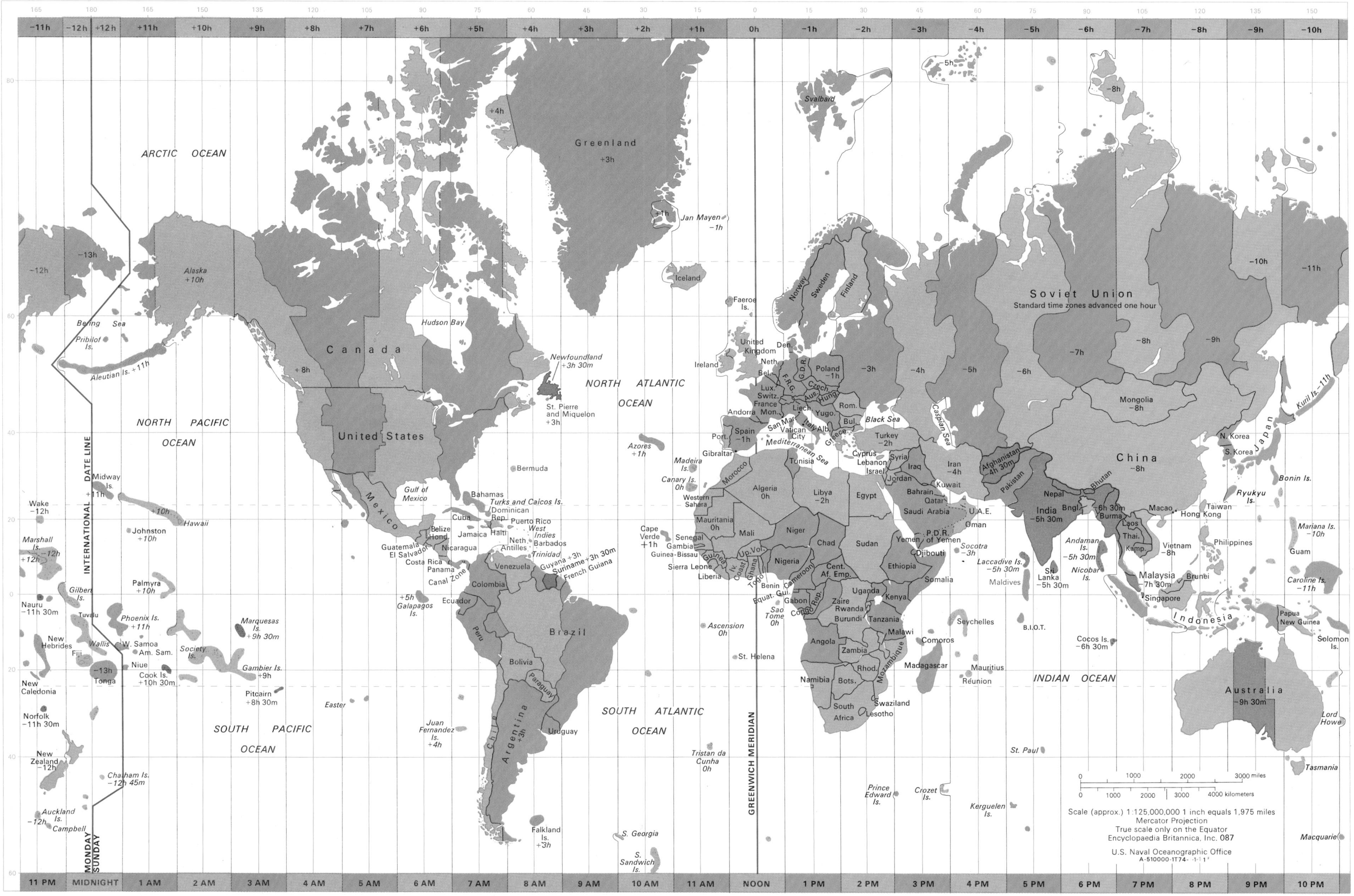

Time Zones

Standard time zone of even-numbered hours from Greenwich time

Standard time zone of odd-numbered hours from Greenwich time

Time varies from the standard time zone by half an hour

Time varies from the standard time zone by other than half an hour

h m hours, minutes

The standard time zone system, fixed by international agreement and by law in each country, is based on a theoretical division of the globe into 24 zones of 15° longitude each. The mid-meridian of each zone fixes the hour for the entire zone. The zero time zone extends 7½° east and 7½° west of the Greenwich meridian, 0° longitude. Since the earth rotates toward the east, time zones to the west of Greenwich are earlier, to the east, later.
Plus and minus hours at the top of the map are added to or subtracted from local time to find Greenwich time. Local standard time can be determined for any area in the world by adding one hour for each time zone counted in an easterly direction from one's own, or by subtracting one hour for each zone counted in a westerly direction. To separate one day from the next, the 180th meridian has been designated as the international date line.
On both sides of the line the time of day is the same, but west of the line it is one day later than it is to the east.
Countries that adhere to the international zone system adopt the zone applicable to their location. Some countries, however, establish time zones based on political boundaries, or adopt the time zone of a neighboring unit. For all or part of the year some countries also advance their time by one hour, thereby utilizing more daylight hours each day.

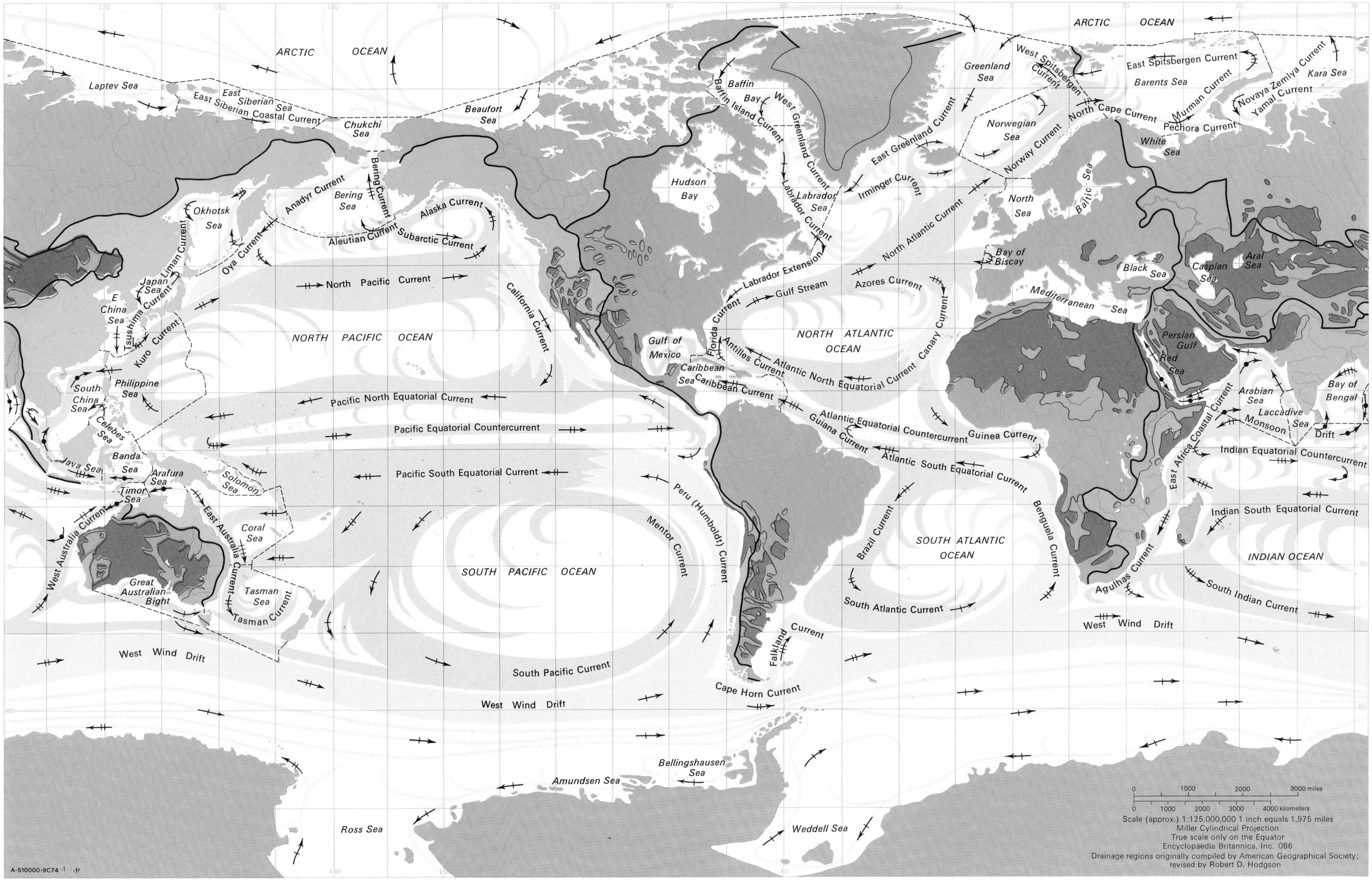

Drainage Regions and Ocean Currents

Currents during Northern Hemisphere winter

- Cold current
- Warm current
- Indicates a current that reverses direction during Northern Hemisphere summer

Speed of current

(1 knot=1 nautical mile[6,076 ft.] per hour)

- Less than 0.5 knots
- 0.5—0.8 knots
- Greater than 0.8 knots
- Limits of seas

Drainage regions

Surface drainage reaching an Ocean

- Outline of oceanic drainage regions
- Atlantic Ocean
- Pacific Ocean
- Indian Ocean
- Arctic Ocean

- Surface drainage not reaching an ocean
- Arid regions
- Ice cap

Atlantic Ocean Floor
Greenland
North America
Europe
Africa
Hudson Bay
Hudson Strait
Great Lakes
Baffin Island
Baffin Bay
Foxe Basin
Labrador Basin
Iceland
Norwegian Sea
Greenland Sea
Barents Sea
Svalbard
North Sea
British Isles
Baltic Sea
Gulf of Bothnia
English Channel
Reykjanes Ridge
Mid-Atlantic Ridge
Midocean Ridge
Gibbs Fracture Zone
Greenland-Iceland Rise
Davis Strait Rise
West European Basin
Biscay Abyssal Plain
Trevelyan Escarpment
Iberian Abyssal Plain
Azores Plateau
Azores-Gibraltar Ridge
Canary Basin
Canary Islands
Madeira
Cape Verde Basin
Cape Verde Islands
Cape Verde Terrace
Sierra Leone Basin
Sierra Leone Rise
Guinea Fracture Zone
Niger Fan
Ceara Abyssal Plain
Amazon Cone
Guiana Basin
Barracuda Fracture Zone
North American Basin
Nares Abyssal Plain
Hatteras Abyssal Plain
Sohm Abyssal Plain
Newfoundland Basin
Newfoundland Ridge
Grand Bank
Flemish Cap
Sable Bank
Georges Bank
Hudson Canyon
New England Seamount Chain
Corner Seamounts
Bermuda Rise
Blake Plateau
Blake Ridge
Great Bahama Canyon
Bahama Bank
Tropic of Cancer
Gulf of Mexico
Mexico Basin
Sigsbee Knolls
Campeche Bank
Yucatan Basin
Cayman Trench
Caribbean Sea
Venezuelan Basin
Colombian Abyssal Plain
Greater Antilles
Lesser Antilles
Puerto Rico Trench
Middle America Trench
Cocos Ridge
Guatemala Basin
Panama Basin
Mediterranean Sea
Mediterranean Ridge
Algerian Basin
Tyrrhenian Abyssal Plain
Adriatic Abyssal Plain
Aegean Sea
Black Sea
Levantine Basin
Arctic Circle

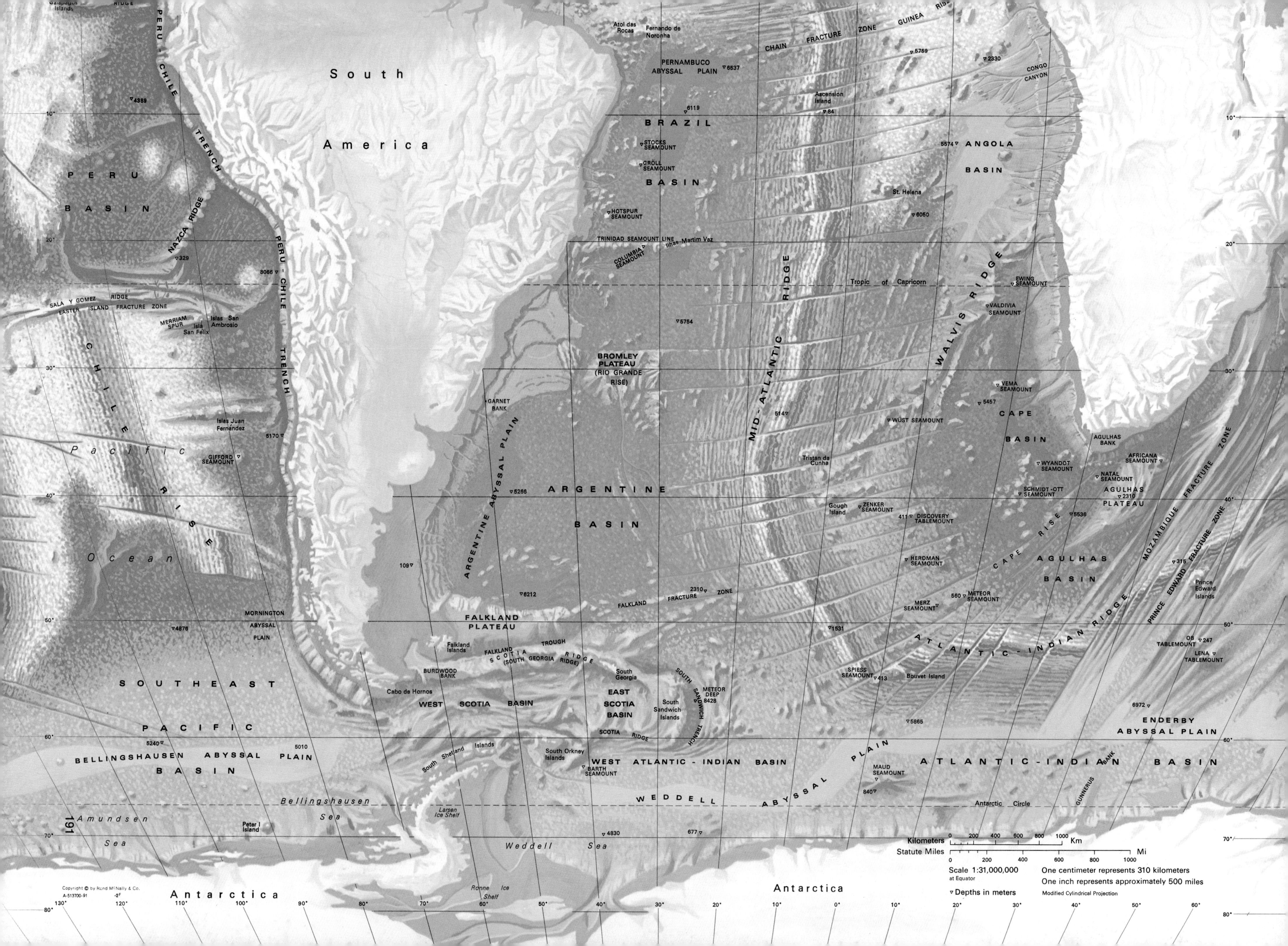
South America
PERU - CHILE TRENCH
PERU BASIN
NAZCA RIDGE
4389
329
8066
SALA Y GOMEZ RIDGE
EASTER ISLAND FRACTURE ZONE
MERRIAM SPUR
Isla San Felix
Islas San Ambrosio
CHILE RISE
Islas Juan Fernández
5170
GIFFORD SEAMOUNT
Pacific Ocean
MORNINGTON ABYSSAL PLAIN
4876
SOUTHEAST PACIFIC BASIN
5240
5010
BELLINGSHAUSEN ABYSSAL PLAIN
BELLINGSHAUSEN BASIN
Bellingshausen Sea
Amundsen Sea
Peter I Island
Atol das Rocas
Fernando de Noronha
PERNAMBUCO ABYSSAL PLAIN
6537
6119
BRAZIL BASIN
STOCKS SEAMOUNT
GRÖLL SEAMOUNT
HOTSPUR SEAMOUNT
TRINIDAD SEAMOUNT LINE
Ilhas Martim Vaz
COLUMBIA SEAMOUNT
5754
BROMLEY PLATEAU (RIO GRANDE RISE)
GARNET BANK
ARGENTINE ABYSSAL PLAIN
5266
ARGENTINE BASIN
109
6212
FALKLAND FRACTURE ZONE
2310
FALKLAND PLATEAU
Falkland Islands
FALKLAND TROUGH
SCOTIA RIDGE (SOUTH GEORGIA RIDGE)
BURDWOOD BANK
Cabo de Hornos
WEST SCOTIA BASIN
South Georgia
EAST SCOTIA BASIN
SOUTH SANDWICH TRENCH
METEOR DEEP 8428
South Sandwich Islands
SCOTIA RIDGE
South Shetland Islands
South Orkney Islands
BARTH SEAMOUNT
WEST ATLANTIC - INDIAN BASIN
WEDDELL ABYSSAL PLAIN
Larsen Ice Shelf
Weddell Sea
4830
677
Ronne Ice Shelf
Antarctica
CHAIN FRACTURE ZONE
GUINEA RISE
5759
2330
CONGO CANYON
Ascension Island
84
5574
ANGOLA BASIN
St. Helena
6050
MID - ATLANTIC RIDGE
WALVIS RIDGE
Tropic of Capricorn
EWING SEAMOUNT
VALDIVIA SEAMOUNT
VEMA SEAMOUNT
5457
CAPE BASIN
514
WÜST SEAMOUNT
Tristan da Cunha
AGULHAS BANK
AFRICANA SEAMOUNT
WYANDOT SEAMOUNT
NATAL SEAMOUNT
SCHMIDT - OTT SEAMOUNT
AGULHAS PLATEAU
2310
Gough Island
ZENKER SEAMOUNT
411
DISCOVERY TABLEMOUNT
5536
CAPE RISE
HERDMAN SEAMOUNT
AGULHAS BASIN
MOZAMBIQUE FRACTURE ZONE
PRINCE EDWARD FRACTURE ZONE
315
Prince Edward Islands
560
METEOR SEAMOUNT
MERZ SEAMOUNT
1531
ATLANTIC - INDIAN RIDGE
OB TABLEMOUNT
247
LENA TABLEMOUNT
SPIESS SEAMOUNT
413
Bouvet Island
5865
6972
ENDERBY ABYSSAL PLAIN
ATLANTIC - INDIAN BASIN
MAUD SEAMOUNT
840
GUNNERUS BANK
Antarctic Circle
Kilometers 0 200 400 600 800 1000 Km
Statute Miles 0 200 400 600 800 1000 Mi
Scale 1:31,000,000 at Equator
One centimeter represents 310 kilometers
One inch represents approximately 500 miles
▽ Depths in meters
Modified Cylindrical Projection
Copyright © by Rand McNally & Co.
A-513700-91
191

Pacific Ocean Floor

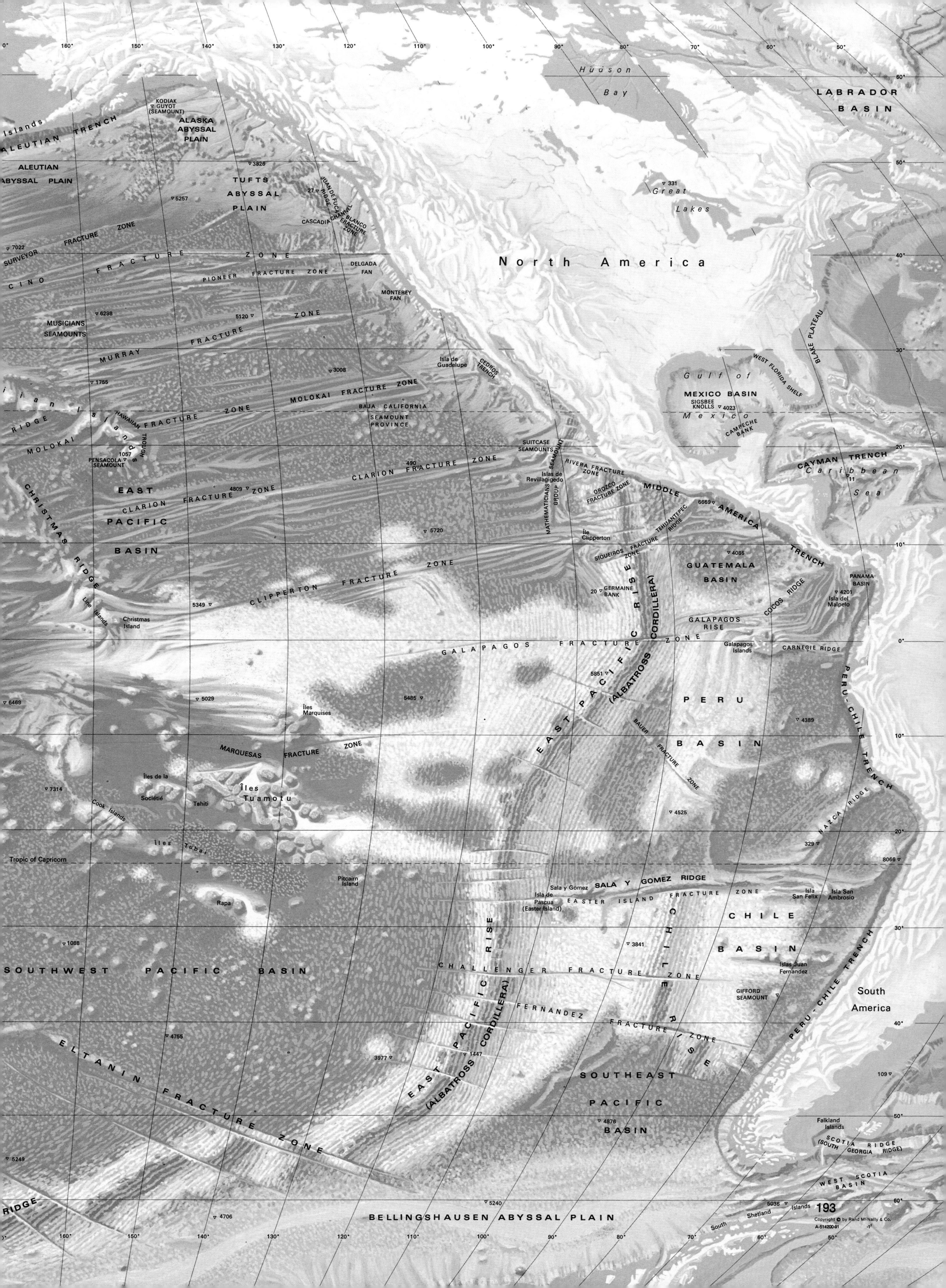
North America
Hudson Bay
LABRADOR BASIN
Great Lakes
KODIAK GUYOT (SEAMOUNT)
ALASKA ABYSSAL PLAIN
ALEUTIAN TRENCH
ALEUTIAN ABYSSAL PLAIN
TUFTS ABYSSAL PLAIN
JUAN DE FUCA RIDGE
CASCADIA CHANNEL
BLANCO FRACTURE ZONE
SURVEYOR FRACTURE ZONE
MENDOCINO FRACTURE ZONE
PIONEER FRACTURE ZONE
DELGADA FAN
MONTEREY FAN
MUSICIANS SEAMOUNTS
MURRAY FRACTURE ZONE
MOLOKAI FRACTURE ZONE
HAWAIIAN FRACTURE ZONE
BAJA CALIFORNIA SEAMOUNT PROVINCE
Isla de Guadelupe
CEDROS TRENCH
Gulf of Mexico
MEXICO BASIN
SIGSBEE KNOLLS
CAMPECHE BANK
WEST FLORIDA SHELF
BLAKE PLATEAU
CAYMAN TRENCH
Caribbean Sea
Hawaiian Islands
HAWAIIAN TROUGH
MOLOKAI RIDGE
PENSACOLA SEAMOUNT
SUITCASE SEAMOUNTS
MATHEMATICIANS SEAMOUNT GROUP
Islas de Revillagigedo
RIVERA FRACTURE ZONE
OROZCO FRACTURE ZONE
MIDDLE AMERICA TRENCH
TEHUANTEPEC RIDGE
CLARION FRACTURE ZONE
EAST PACIFIC BASIN
CHRISTMAS RIDGE
Line Islands
Christmas Island
Île Clipperton
SIQUEIROS FRACTURE ZONE
CLIPPERTON FRACTURE ZONE
GERMAINE BANK
GUATEMALA BASIN
PANAMA BASIN
Isla del Malpelo
COCOS RIDGE
GALAPAGOS RISE
Galapagos Islands
GALAPAGOS FRACTURE ZONE
CARNEGIE RIDGE
EAST PACIFIC RISE (ALBATROSS CORDILLERA)
PERU BASIN
BAUER FRACTURE ZONE
PERU-CHILE TRENCH
NAZCA RIDGE
Îles Marquises
MARQUESAS FRACTURE ZONE
Îles de la Société
Tahiti
Îles Tuamotu
Cook Islands
Îles Tubai
Tropic of Capricorn
Pitcairn Island
Rapa
Sala y Gomez
SALA Y GOMEZ RIDGE
Isla de Pascua (Easter Island)
EASTER ISLAND FRACTURE ZONE
Isla San Felix
Isla San Ambrosio
CHILE BASIN
CHILE RISE
Islas Juan Fernandez
GIFFORD SEAMOUNT
CHALLENGER FRACTURE ZONE
FERNANDEZ FRACTURE ZONE
SOUTHWEST PACIFIC BASIN
South America
ELTANIN FRACTURE ZONE
SOUTHEAST PACIFIC BASIN
Falkland Islands
SCOTIA RIDGE (SOUTH GEORGIA RIDGE)
WEST SCOTIA BASIN
South Shetland Islands
BELLINGSHAUSEN ABYSSAL PLAIN
RIDGE

Indian Ocean Floor

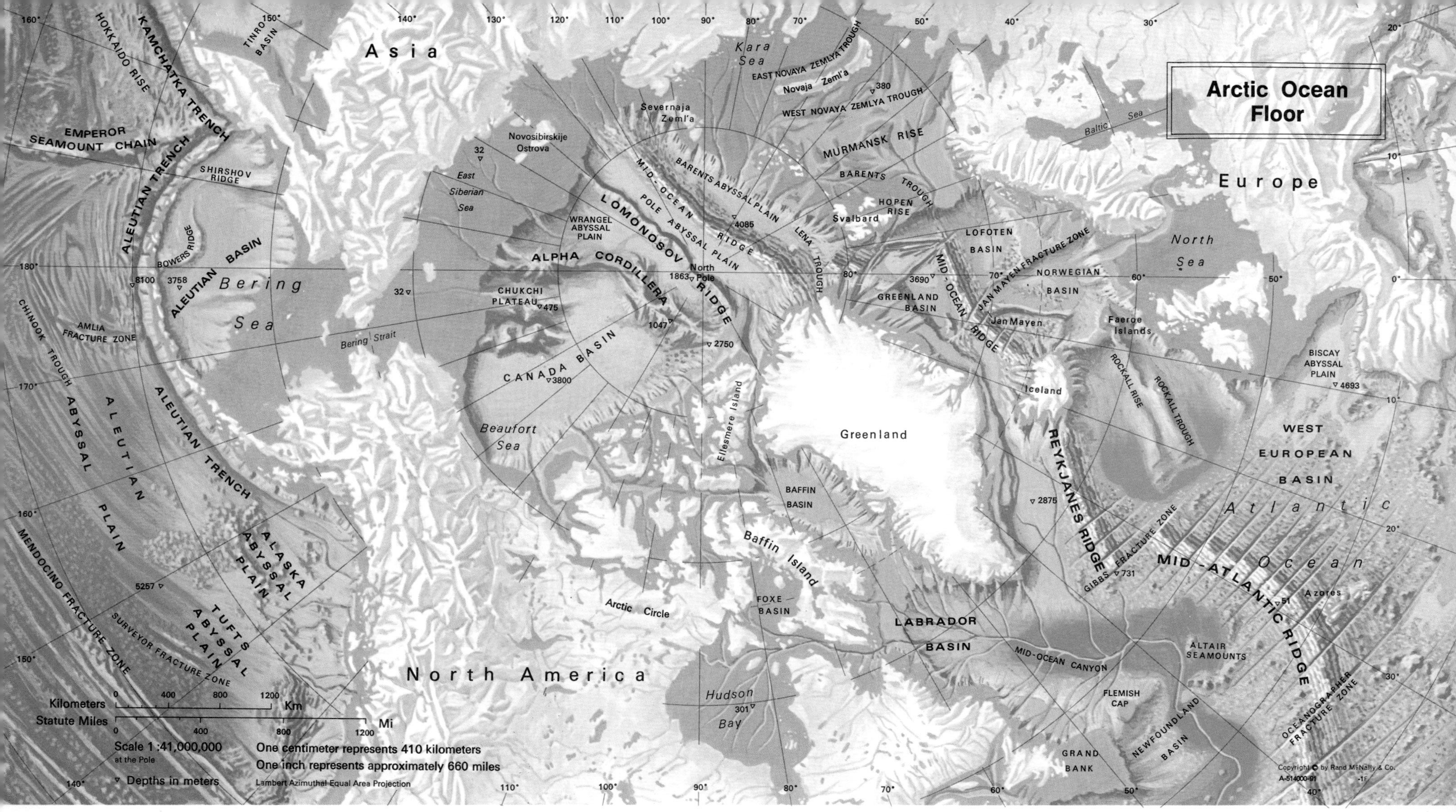
Arctic Ocean Floor
Asia
Europe
North America
Greenland
Kara Sea
Baltic Sea
North Sea
Bering Sea
Beaufort Sea
East Siberian Sea
Hudson Bay
Bering Strait
Arctic Circle
North Pole
KAMCHATKA TRENCH
HOKKAIDO RISE
TINRO BASIN
EMPEROR SEAMOUNT CHAIN
ALEUTIAN TRENCH
SHIRSHOV RIDGE
BOWERS RIDGE
ALEUTIAN BASIN
CHINOOK TROUGH
AMLIA FRACTURE ZONE
ALEUTIAN ABYSSAL PLAIN
ALASKA ABYSSAL PLAIN
TUFTS ABYSSAL PLAIN
MENDOCINO FRACTURE ZONE
SURVEYOR FRACTURE ZONE
Novosibirskije Ostrova
Severnaja Zeml'a
Novaja Zeml'a
EAST NOVAYA ZEMLYA TROUGH
WEST NOVAYA ZEMLYA TROUGH
MURMANSK RISE
BARENTS TROUGH
BARENTS ABYSSAL PLAIN
HOPEN RISE
Svalbard
LENA TROUGH
MID-OCEAN RIDGE
POLE ABYSSAL PLAIN
LOMONOSOV RIDGE
WRANGEL ABYSSAL PLAIN
ALPHA CORDILLERA
CHUKCHI PLATEAU
CANADA BASIN
Ellesmere Island
BAFFIN BASIN
Baffin Island
FOXE BASIN
LOFOTEN BASIN
JAN MAYEN FRACTURE ZONE
Jan Mayen
NORWEGIAN BASIN
GREENLAND BASIN
Faeroe Islands
ROCKALL RISE
ROCKALL TROUGH
Iceland
REYKJANES RIDGE
GIBBS FRACTURE ZONE
BISCAY ABYSSAL PLAIN
WEST EUROPEAN BASIN
Atlantic Ocean
MID-ATLANTIC RIDGE
Azores
ALTAIR SEAMOUNTS
OCEANOGRAPHER FRACTURE ZONE
LABRADOR BASIN
MID-OCEAN CANYON
FLEMISH CAP
NEWFOUNDLAND BASIN
GRAND BANK
Kilometers 0 400 800 1200 Km
Statute Miles 0 400 800 1200 Mi
Scale 1:41,000,000 at the Pole
One centimeter represents 410 kilometers
One inch represents approximately 660 miles
▽ Depths in meters
Lambert Azimuthal Equal Area Projection
Copyright © by Rand McNally & Co.

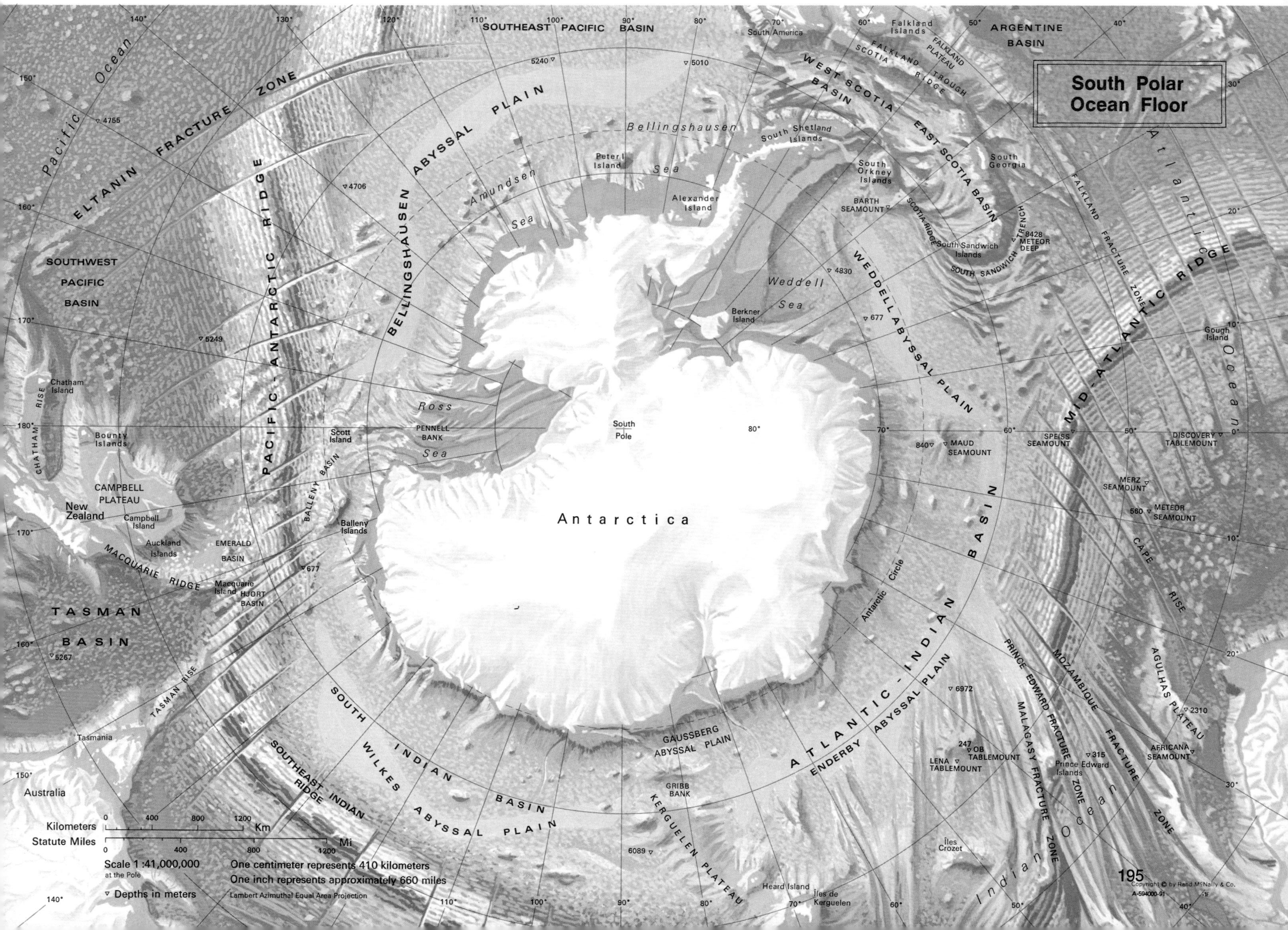
South Polar Ocean Floor
Antarctica
South Pole
Pacific Ocean
Atlantic Ocean
Indian Ocean
Australia
Tasmania
New Zealand
South America
Ross Sea
Amundsen Sea
Bellingshausen Sea
Weddell Sea
Antarctic Circle
SOUTHEAST PACIFIC BASIN
ELTANIN FRACTURE ZONE
BELLINGSHAUSEN ABYSSAL PLAIN
PACIFIC-ANTARCTIC RIDGE
SOUTHWEST PACIFIC BASIN
CHATHAM RISE
Chatham Island
Bounty Islands
CAMPBELL PLATEAU
Campbell Island
Auckland Islands
EMERALD BASIN
MACQUARIE RIDGE
Macquarie Island
HJORT BASIN
TASMAN BASIN
TASMAN RISE
BALLENY BASIN
Balleny Islands
Scott Island
PENNELL BANK
Peter I Island
Alexander Island
Berkner Island
South Shetland Islands
South Orkney Islands
South Georgia
Falkland Islands
FALKLAND PLATEAU
FALKLAND TROUGH
SCOTIA RIDGE
WEST SCOTIA BASIN
EAST SCOTIA BASIN
BARTH SEAMOUNT
South Sandwich Islands
SOUTH SANDWICH TRENCH
METEOR DEEP
ARGENTINE BASIN
FALKLAND FRACTURE ZONE
WEDDELL ABYSSAL PLAIN
MID-ATLANTIC RIDGE
Gough Island
MAUD SEAMOUNT
SPIESS SEAMOUNT
DISCOVERY TABLEMOUNT
MERZ SEAMOUNT
METEOR SEAMOUNT
CAPE RISE
AGULHAS PLATEAU
AFRICANA SEAMOUNT
MOZAMBIQUE FRACTURE ZONE
PRINCE EDWARD FRACTURE ZONE
Prince Edward Islands
MALAGASY FRACTURE ZONE
OB TABLEMOUNT
LENA TABLEMOUNT
Îles Crozet
ATLANTIC-INDIAN BASIN
ENDERBY ABYSSAL PLAIN
GAUSSBERG ABYSSAL PLAIN
GRIBB BANK
KERGUELEN PLATEAU
Heard Island
Îles de Kerguelen
SOUTH INDIAN BASIN
WILKES ABYSSAL PLAIN
SOUTHEAST INDIAN RIDGE
Kilometers 0 400 800 1200 Km
Statute Miles 0 400 800 1200 Mi
Scale 1:41,000,000 at the Pole
One centimeter represents 410 kilometers
One inch represents approximately 660 miles
▽ Depths in meters
Lambert Azimuthal Equal Area Projection
Copyright © by Rand McNally & Co.

World Political Information Table

This table lists all countries and dependencies in the world, U.S. States, Canadian provinces, and other important regions and political subdivisions. Besides specifying the form of government for all political areas, the table classifies them into six groups according to their political status. Units labeled **A** are independent sovereign nations. Units labeled **B** are independent as regards internal affairs, but for purposes of foreign affairs they are under the protection of another country. Areas under military government are also labeled **B.** Units labeled **C** are colonies, overseas territories, dependencies, etc., of other countries. Together the **A, B,** and **C** areas comprise practically the entire inhabited area of the world. The areas labeled **D** are physically separate units, such as groups of islands, which are *not* separate countries, but form part of a nation or dependency. Units labeled **E** are States, provinces, Soviet Republics, or similar major administrative subdivisions of important countries. Units in the table with no letter designation are regions or other areas that do not constitute separate political units by themselves.

Region or Political Division	Area in sq. miles	Estimated Population 1/1/79	Pop. per sq. mi.	Form of Government and Ruling Power	Capital; Largest City (unless same)	Predominant Languages
Afars & Issas, see Djibouti						
Afghanistan†	250,000	21,138,000	85	Republic A	Kābul	Dari, Pushtu
Africa	11,706,727	443,700,000	38		; Al-Qāhirah (Cairo)	
Alabama	51,609	3,766,500	73	State (U.S.) E	Montgomery; Birmingham	
Alaska	586,412	412,400	0.7	State (U.S.) E	Juneau; Anchorage	English, Indian, Eskimo
Albania†	11,100	2,718,000	245	People's Republic A	Tiranë	Albanian
Alberta	255,285	1,889,000	7.4	Province (Canada) E	Edmonton	English
Algeria†	919,595	18,791,000	20	Republic A	Alger (Algiers)	Arabic, French, Berber
American Samoa	76	34,000	447	Unincorporated Territory (U.S.) C	Pago Pago	Polynesian, English
Andaman & Nicobar Is.	3,202	171,000	53	Territory (India) D	Port Blair	Andaman, Nicobar Malay
Andorra	175	19,000	109	Principality A	Andorra	Catalan, Spanish, French
Angola†	481,353	7,448,000	15	People's Republic A	Luanda	Bantu languages, Portuguese
Anguilla	35	6,000	171	Colony (U.K.) C	The Valley; South Hill	English
Antarctica	5,100,000					
Antigua (incl. Barbuda)	171	75,000	439	Associated State (U.K.) B	St. Johns	English
Arabian Peninsula	1,142,050	21,935,000	19		; Al-Kuwayt	Arabic
Argentina†	1,072,162	26,562,000	25	Federal Republic A	Buenos Aires	Spanish
Arizona	113,909	2,411,800	21	State (U.S.) E	Phoenix	
Arkansas	53,104	2,178,300	41	State (U.S.) E	Little Rock	
Arm'anskaja (Armenia) S.S.R.	11,500	2,912,000	253	Soviet Socialist Republic (U.S.S.R.) E	Jerevan	Armenian, Russian
Aruba	69	70,000	1,014	Division of Netherlands Antilles (Neth.) D	; Oranjestad	Dutch, Spanish, English, Papiamento
Ascension I.	34	1,000	29	Dependency of St. Helena (U.K.) D	Georgetown	English
Asia	17,085,000	2,494,000,000	146		; Tōkyō	
Australia†	2,967,909	14,612,000	4.9	Monarchy (Federal) (Comm. of Nations) A	Canberra; Sydney	English
Australian Capital Territory	939	213,000	227	Federal Territory (Australia) E	Canberra	English
Austria†	32,374	7,522,000	232	Federal Republic A	Wien (Vienna)	German
Azerbajdžanskaja (Azerbaidzhan) S.S.R.	33,450	5,850,000	175	Soviet Socialist Republic (U.S.S.R.) E	Baku	Turkic languages, Russian, Armenian
Azores Is.	905	313,000	346	Part of Portugal (3 Districts) D	; Ponta Delgada	Portuguese
Baden-Württemberg	13,803	9,067,000	657	State (Germany, Federal Republic of) E	Stuttgart	German
Bahamas†	5,380	229,000	43	Parliamentary State (Comm. of Nations) A	Nassau	English
Bahrain†	240	273,000	1,138	Emirate A	Al-Manāmah	Arabic
Balearic Is.	1,936	589,000	304	Part of Spain (Baleares Province) D	Palma	Catalan, Spanish
Baltic Republics	67,150	7,502,000	112	Union of Soviet Socialist Republics	; Rīga	Lithuanian, Latvian, Estonian, Russian
Bangladesh†	55,126	83,382,000	1,513	Republic (Comm. of Nations) A	Dacca	Bangla, English
Barbados†	166	263,000	1,584	Parliamentary State (Comm. of Nations) A	Bridgetown	English
Basutoland, see Lesotho						
Bayern (Bavaria)	27,239	10,742,000	394	State (Germany, Federal Republic of) E	München (Munich)	German
Bechuanaland, see Botswana						
Belgium†	11,781	10,012,000	850	Monarchy A	Bruxelles (Brussels) (Brussel)	Dutch, French
Belize	8,867	157,000	18	Colony (U.K.) C	Belmopan; Belize	English, Spanish, Indian languages
Belorusskaja (Byelorussia) S.S.R.†	80,150	9,601,000	120	Soviet Socialist Republic (U.S.S.R.) E	Minsk	Byelorussian, Polish, Russian
Benelux	28,549	24,357,000	853		; Bruxelles (Brussels)	Dutch, French, Luxembourgish
Benin (Dahomey)†	43,484	3,419,000	79	Republic A	Porto-Novo; Cotonou	French, native languages
Berlin, West	185	1,939,000	10,481	State (Germany, Federal Republic of) E	Berlin (West)	German
Bermuda	21	60,000	2,857	Colony (U.K.) C	Hamilton	English
Bhutan†	18,200	1,369,000	75	Monarchy (Indian protection) B	Paro and Thimbu	Tibetan dialects
Bismarck Archipelago	18,965	315,000	17	Part of Papua New Guinea D	; Rabaul	Malay-Polynesian and Papuan languages
Bolivia†	424,164	4,994,000	12	Republic A	Sucre and La Paz; La Paz	Spanish, Quechua, Aymará
Borneo, Indonesian (Kalimantan)	208,286	6,434,000	31	Part of Indonesia D	; Banjarmasin	Indonesian
Botswana (Bechuanaland)†	231,805	730,000	3.1	Republic (Comm. of Nations) A	Gaborone; Francistown	Bechuana, other Bantu languages, English
Brazil†	3,286,487	116,787,000	36	Federal Republic A	Brasília; São Paulo	Portuguese
Bremen	156	706,000	4,526	State (Germany, Federal Republic of) E	Bremen	German
British Antarctic Territory (excl. Antarctic mainland)	2,040	Winter pop. 75	0.04	Dependency (U.K.) C	Administered from Stanley, Falkland Is.	
British Columbia	366,255	2,535,000	6.9	Province (Canada) E	Victoria; Vancouver	English
British Guiana, see Guyana						
British Honduras, see Belize						
British Indian Ocean Territory	18			Dependency (U.K.) C	Administered from London	English
Brunei	2,226	210,000	94	Sultanate (U.K. protection) B	Bandar Seri Begawan	Malay-Polynesian languages, English
Bulgaria†	42,823	8,868,000	207	People's Republic A	Sofija (Sofia)	Bulgarian
Burma†	261,790	32,462,000	124	Federal Republic A	Rangoon	Burmese, English
Burundi (Urundi)†	10,747	4,119,000	383	Republic A	Bujumbura	Bantu and Hamitic languages, French
California	158,693	22,435,100	141	State (U.S.) E	Sacramento; Los Angeles	
Cambodia, see Kampuchea						
Cameroon†	183,569	6,868,000	37	Federal Republic A	Yaoundé; Douala	French, English, native languages
Canada†	3,851,809	23,628,000	6.1	Monarchy (Federal) (Comm. of Nations) A	Ottawa; Montréal	English, French
Canal Zone	553	41,000	74	Under U.S. Jurisdiction C	Balboa Heights; Balboa	English, Spanish
Canary Is.	2,808	1,297,000	462	Part of Spain (2 Provinces) D	; Las Palmas de Gran Canaria	Spanish
Canton & Enderbury	27			U.K.-U.S. Administration C		Malay-Polynesian languages, English
Cape Verde†	1,557	313,000	201	Republic A	Praia; Mindelo	Portuguese
Caroline Is.	463	83,000	179	Part of U.S. Pacific Is. Trust Ter. (4 Districts) D		Malay-Polynesian languages, English
Cayman Is.	100	15,000	150	Colony (U.K.) C	Georgetown	English
Celebes (Sulawesi)	72,987	10,675,000	146	Part of Indonesia D	; Ujung Pandang	Malay-Polynesian languages, Indonesian
Central African Empire†	240,535	1,965,000	8.2	Empire A	Bangui	French, native languages
Central America	202,063	21,040,000	104		; Guatemala	Spanish, Indian languages
Central Asia, Soviet	493,950	24,135,000	49	Union of Soviet Socialist Republics	; Taškent	Uzbek, Russian, Kirghiz, Turkoman, Tadzhik
Ceylon, see Sri Lanka						
Chad†	495,800	4,321,000	8.7	Republic A	Ndjamena	French, native languages
Channel Is. (Guernsey, Jersey, etc.)	75	129,000	1,720		; St. Helier	English, French
Chile†	292,258	10,959,000	37	Republic A	Santiago	Spanish
China (excl. Taiwan)†	3,691,500	868,795,000	235	People's Republic A	Beijing (Peking); Shanghai	Chinese, Mongolian, Turkish, Tungus
China (Nationalist), see Taiwan						
Christmas I. (Indian Ocean)	52	3,500	67	External Territory (Australia) C	; Flying Fish Cove	Chinese, Malay, English
Cocos (Keeling) Is.	5	700	140	External Territory (Australia) C		Malay, English

† Member of the United Nations (1979).

World Political Information Table (continued)

Region or Political Division	Area in sq. miles	Estimated Population 1/1/79	Pop. per sq. mi.	Form of Government and Ruling Power	Capital; Largest City (unless same)	Predominant Languages
Colombia†	439,737	26,200,000	60	Republic....A	Bogotá	Spanish
Colorado	104,247	2,709,700	26	State (U.S.)....E	Denver	
Commonwealth of Nations	10,713,229	1,025,483,000	96		........; London	
Comoros†	694	384,000	553	Republic....A	Moroni	Comoran, French
Congo†	132,000	1,513,000	11	Republic....A	Brazzaville	French, native languages
Congo, The, see Zaire						
Connecticut	5,009	3,135,400	626	State (U.S.)....E	Hartford; Bridgeport	
Cook Is.	93	17,000	183	Self-governing Territory, (New Zealand)....C	Avarua	Malay-Polynesian languages, English
Corsica	3,352	293,000	87	Part of France (2 Departments)....D	........; Bastia	French, Italian
Costa Rica†	19,600	2,150,000	110	Republic....A	San José	Spanish
Cuba†	44,218	9,866,000	223	People's Republic....A	La Habana (Havana)	Spanish
Curaçao	173	175,000	1,012	Division of Netherlands Antilles (Neth.)....D	........; Willemstad	Dutch, Spanish, English, Papiamento
Cyprus†	3,572	642,000	180	Republic (Comm. of Nations)....A	Levkosia (Nicosia)	Greek, Turkish, English
Czechoslovakia†	49,373	15,202,000	308	People's Republic....A	Praha (Prague)	Czech, Slovak
Dahomey, see Benin						
Delaware	2,057	589,100	286	State (U.S.)....E	Dover;Wilmington	
Denmark†	16,629	5,111,000	307	Monarchy....A	København (Copenhagen)	Danish
Denmark and Possessions	857,169	5,203,000	6.1		København (Copenhagen)	Danish, Faeroese, Greenlandic
District of Columbia	67	676,000	10,090	District (U.S.)....E	Washington	
Djibouti†	8,900	140,000	16	Republic....A	Djibouti	Arabic, French
Dominica†	290	81,000	279	Parliamentary State....A	Roseau	English, French
Dominican Republic†	18,816	5,191,000	276	Republic....A	Santo Domingo	Spanish
Ecuador†	109,483	8,053,000	74	Republic....A	Quito; Guayaquil	Spanish, Quechua
Egypt†	386,661	39,812,000	103	Republic‡‡....A	Al-Qāhirah (Cairo)	Arabic
Ellice Is., see Tuvalu						
El Salvador†	8,260	4,416,000	535	Republic....A	San Salvador	Spanish
England (excl. Monmouthshire)	50,332	46,271,000	919	United Kingdom	........; London	English
England & Wales	58,348	49,028,000	840	Administrative division of United Kingdom....E	London	English, Welsh
Equatorial Guinea†	10,830	331,000	31	Republic....A	Malabo	Spanish, native languages
Estonskaja (S.S.R.)	17,400	1,469,000	84	Soviet Socialist Republic (U.S.S.R.)....E	Tallinn	Estonian, Russian
Ethiopia†	471,778	29,597,000	63	Provisional Military Government....A	Addis Abeba	Amharic, Arabic, Hamitic dialects
Eurasia	20,910,000	3,152,620,000	151		........; Tōkyō	
Europe	3,825,000	658,600,000	172		........; London	
Faeroe Is.	540	42,000	78	Self-governing Territory (Denmark)....B	Tórshavn	Danish, Faeroese
Falkland Is. (excl. Deps.)	4,618	2,000	0.4	Colony (U.K.)....C	Stanley	English
Fernando Poo, see Macías Nguema Biyogo						
Fiji†	7,055	626,500	89	Monarchy (Federal) (Comm. of Nations)....A	Suva	English, Fijian, Hindustani
Finland†	130,120	4,756,000	37	Republic....A	Helsinki (Helsingfors)	Finnish, Swedish
Florida	58,560	8,794,100	150	State (U.S.)....E	Tallahassee; Jacksonville	
France†	211,207	53,367,000	253	Republic....A	Paris	French
France and Possessions	229,981	55,146,000	240		Paris	
Franklin	549,253	7,000	0.01	District of Northwest Territories, Canada....E	........; Frobisher Bay	English, Eskimo, Indian
French Guiana	35,100	63,000	1.8	Overseas Department (France)....C	Cayenne	French
French Polynesia	1,550	142,000	92	Overseas Territory (France)....C	Papeete	Malay-Polynesian languages, French
French Somaliland, see Djibouti						
French Southern & Antarctic Ter. (excl. Adélie Coast)	2,918	200	0.07	Overseas Territory (France)....C		French
French West Indies	1,112	755,000	679		........; Fort-de-France	French
Gabon†	103,347	540,000	5.2	Republic....A	Libreville	French, native languages
Galápagos Is. (Colon, Archipélago de)	3,075	4,900	1.6	Province (Ecuador)....D	Puerto Baquerizo Moreno	Spanish
Gambia†	4,361	576,000	132	Republic (Comm. of Nations)....A	Banjul (Bathurst)	English, native languages
Georgia	58,876	5,127,700	87	State (U.S.)....E	Atlanta	
Germany (Entire)	137,727	77,807,000	565		........; Essen	German
German Democratic Republic†	41,768	16,717,000	400	People's Republic....A	Berlin, Ost-(East Berlin)	German
Germany, Federal Republic of (incl. West Berlin)†	95,968	61,090,000	637	Federal Republic....A	Bonn; Essen	German
Ghana†	92,100	10,931,000	119	Republic (Comm. of Nations)....A	Accra	English, native languages
Gibraltar	2	31,000	15,500	Colony (U.K.)....C	Gibraltar	Spanish, English
Gilbert Islands	331	60,000	181	Dependency (U.K.)....C	Tarawa (island);	Malay-Polynesian languages, English
Great Britain & Northern Ireland, see United Kingdom						
Greece†	50,944	9,463,000	186	Republic....A	Athínai (Athens)	Greek
Greenland	840,000	50,000	0.06	Overseas Territory (Denmark)....C	Godthåb	Greenlandic, Danish, Eskimo
Grenada†	133	103,000	774	Parliamentary State (Comm. of Nations)....A	Saint George's	English
Gruzinskaja (Georgia) S.S.R.	26,900	5,089,000	189	Soviet Socialist Republic (U.S.S.R.)....E	Tbilisi	Georgic, Armenian, Russian
Guadeloupe (incl. Dependencies)	687	373,000	543	Overseas Department (France)....C	Basse-Terre; Pointe-à-Pitre	French
Guam	212	114,000	538	Unincorporated Territory (U.S.)....C	Agana	English, Chamorro
Guatemala†	42,042	6,940,000	165	Republic....A	Guatemala	Spanish, Indian languages
Guernsey (incl. Dependencies)	30	54,000	1,800	Bailiwick (U.K.)....C	St. Peter Port	English, French
Guinea†	94,964	4,821,000	51	Republic....A	Conakry	French, native languages
Guinea-Bissau†	13,948	559,000	40	Republic....A	Bissau	Portuguese, native languages
Guyana†	83,000	837,000	10	Republic (Comm. of Nations)....A	Georgetown	English
Haiti†	10,714	4,873,000	455	Republic....A	Port-au-Prince	Creole, French
Hamburg	288	1,688,000	5,861	State (Germany, Federal Republic of)....E	Hamburg	German
Hawaii	6,450	916,500	142	State (U.S.)....E	Honolulu	English, Japanese, Hawaiian
Hessen (Hesse)	8,150	5,506,000	676	State (Germany, Federal Republic of)....E	Wiesbaden; Frankfurt am Main	German
Hispaniola	29,530	10,064,000	341		........; Santo Domingo	French, Spanish
Holland, see Netherlands						
Honduras†	43,277	3,056,000	71	Republic....A	Tegucigalpa	Spanish
Hong Kong	403	4,668,000	11,583	Colony (U.K.)....C	Victoria (Xianggang)	Chinese, English
Hungary†	35,920	10,725,000	299	People's Republic....A	Budapest	Hungarian
Iceland†	39,800	225,000	5.7	Republic....A	Reykjavík	Icelandic
Idaho	83,557	887,500	11	State (U.S.)....E	Boise (Boise City)	
Illinois	56,400	11,321,800	201	State (U.S.)....E	Springfield; Chicago	
India (incl. part of Kashmir)†	1,269,210	648,020,000	511	Republic (Comm. of Nations)....A	New Delhi; Calcutta	Hindi and other Indo-Aryan languages, Dravidian languages, English
Indiana	36,291	5,334,300	147	State (U.S.)....E	Indianapolis	
Indonesia (incl. West Irian)†	741,034	148,261,000	200	Republic....A	Jakarta	Indonesian, Chinese, English
Iowa	56,290	2,890,100	51	State (U.S.)....E	Des Moines	
Iran (Persia)†	636,300	35,400,000	56	Republic....A	Tehrān	Farsi, Turkish dialects, Kurdish
Iraq†	167,925	12,502,000	74	Republic....A	Baghdād	Arabic, Kurdish
Ireland†	27,137	3,239,000	119	Republic....A	Dublin (Baile Átha Cliath)	English, Irish
Isle of Man	227	64,000	282	Possession (U.K.)....C	Douglas	English
Israel†	8,019	3,750,000	468	Republic‡‡....A	Yerushalayim; Tel Aviv-Yafo	Hebrew, Arabic, English
Italy†	116,304	56,905,000	489	Republic....A	Roma (Rome); Milano	Italian
Ivory Coast†	124,504	7,537,000	61	Republic....A	Abidjan	French, native languages

† Member of the United Nations (1979).
‡‡ Areas for Egypt, Israel, Jordan and Syria do not reflect de facto changes which took place during 1967.

World Political Information Table (continued)

Region or Political Division	Area in sq. miles	Estimated Population 1/1/79	Pop. per sq. mi.	Form of Government and Ruling Power	Capital; Largest City (unless same)	Predominant Languages
Jamaica†	4,232	2,127,000	503	Parliamentary State (Comm. of Nations) A	Kingston	English
Japan†	143,751	116,186,000	808	Monarchy A	Tōkyō	Japanese
Java (Jawa) (incl. Madura)	51,033	95,243,000	1,866	Part of Indonesia D	...; Jakarta	Indonesian, Chinese, English
Jersey	45	75,000	1,667	Bailiwick (U.K.) C	St. Helier	English, French
Jordan†	37,738	2,938,000	78	Monarchy‡‡ A	'Ammān	Arabic
Kampuchea†	69,898	6,500,000	93	People's Republic A	Phnum Pénh	Cambodian (Khmer), French
Kansas	82,264	2,365,300	29	State (U.S.) E	Topeka; Wichita	
Kashmir, Jammu &	86,024	7,011,000	82	In dispute (India & Pakistan)	Srīnagar	Kashmiri, Punjabi
Kazachskaja (Kazakh) S.S.R.	1,048,300	14,717,000	14	Soviet Socialist Republic (U.S.S.R.) E	Alma-Ata	Turkic languages, Russian
Keewatin	228,160	4,000	0.02	District of Northwest Territories, Canada E	...; Baker Lake	English, Eskimo, Indian
Kentucky	40,395	3,513,400	87	State (U.S.) E	Frankfort; Louisville	
Kenya†	224,960	15,057,000	67	Republic (Comm. of Nations) A	Nairobi	English, Swahili, native languages
Kerguélen	2,700	90	0.03	Part of French Southern & Antarctic Ter. (Fr.) D		French
Kirgizskaja (Kirghiz) S.S.R.	76,650	3,463,000	45	Soviet Socialist Republic (U.S.S.R.) E	Frunze	Turkic languages, Persian, Russian
Korea (Entire)‡	85,052	54,788,000	644		...; Sŏul (Seoul)	Korean
Korea, North	46,540	17,255,000	371	People's Republic A	P'yŏngyang	Korean
Korea, South	38,025	37,533,000	987	Republic A	Sŏul (Seoul)	Korean
Kuwait†	6,880	1,253,000	182	Sheikdom A	Al-Kuwayt	Arabic
Labrador	112,826	34,000	0.3	Part of Newfoundland Province, Canada D	...; Labrador City	English, Eskimo
Laos†	91,429	3,586,000	39	People's Republic A	Viangchan (Vientiane)	Lao, French
Latin America	7,924,731	349,199,000	44		...; Ciudad de México (Mexico City)	
Latvijskaja (Latvia) S.S.R.	24,600	2,623,000	107	Soviet Socialist Republic (U.S.S.R.) E	Rīga	Latvian, Russian
Lebanon†	4,015	3,221,000	802	Republic A	Bayrūt (Beirut)	Arabic, French, English
Lesotho (Basutoland)†	11,720	1,279,000	109	Monarchy (Comm. of Nations) A	Maseru	Sesotho, English
Liberia†	43,000	1,858,000	43	Republic A	Monrovia	English, native languages
Libya†	679,362	2,769,000	4.1	Republic A	Ṭarābulus (Tripoli)	Arabic
Liechtenstein	62	24,000	387	Principality A	Vaduz	German
Litovskaja (Lithuania) S.S.R.	25,150	3,410,000	136	Soviet Socialist Republic (U.S.S.R.) E	Vilnius	Lithuanian, Polish, Russian
Louisiana	48,523	3,971,700	82	State (U.S.) E	Baton Rouge; New Orleans	
Luxembourg†	998	354,000	355	Grand Duchy A	Luxembourg	Luxembourgish, French, German
Macau	6	287,000	47,833	Overseas Province (Portugal) C	Macau	Chinese, Portuguese
Macías Nguema Biyogo	785	84,000	107	Part of Equatorial Guinea D	Malabo	Spanish, native languages
Mackenzie	527,490	33,000	0.06	District of Northwest Territories, Canada E	...; Yellowknife	English, Eskimo, Indian
Madagascar (Malagasy Republic)†	226,658	8,898,000	39	Republic A	Antananarivo	French, Malagasy
Madeira Is.	308	284,000	922	Part of Portugal (Funchal District) D	Funchal	Portuguese
Maine	33,215	1,105,200	33	State (U.S.) E	Augusta; Portland	
Malawi (Nyasaland)†	45,747	5,971,000	131	Republic (Comm. of Nations) A	Lilongwe; Blantyre	Chichewa, English
Malaya	50,700	11,009,000	217	Part of Malaysia	...; Kuala Lumpur	Malay, Chinese, English
Malaysia†	128,430	13,087,000	102	Constitutional Monarchy (Comm. of Nations) A	Kuala Lumpur	Malay, Chinese, English
Maldives†	115	144,000	1,252	Republic A	Male	Divehi, Arabic
Mali†	478,655	6,218,000	13	Republic A	Bamako	French, Bambara
Malta†	122	365,000	2,992	Republic (Comm. of Nations) A	Valletta	English, Maltese
Manitoba	251,000	1,050,000	4.2	Province (Canada) E	Winnipeg	English
Mariana Is. (excl. Guam)	184	16,000	87	District of U.S. Pacific Is. Trust Ter. D	Saipan (island); ...	Malay-Polynesian languages, English
Maritime Provinces (excl. Newfoundland)	51,963	1,668,000	32	Canada	...; Halifax	English
Marshall Is.	70	27,000	386	District of U.S. Pacific Is. Trust Ter. D	Majuro (island); ...	Malay-Polynesian languages, English
Martinique	425	382,000	899	Overseas Department (France) C	Fort-de-France	French
Maryland	10,577	4,176,100	395	State (U.S.) E	Annapolis; Baltimore	
Massachusetts	8,257	5,801,500	703	State (U.S.) E	Boston	
Mauritania†	397,950	1,487,000	3.7	Republic A	Nouakchott	Arabic, French
Mauritius (incl. Dependencies)†	789	909,000	1,152	Parliamentary State (Comm. of Nations) A	Port Louis	English, French, Creole
Mayotte	144	45,000	313	Overseas Department (France) C	...; Dzaoudzi	French, Malagasy
Mexico†	761,604	67,962,000	89	Federal Republic A	Ciudad de México (Mexico City)	Spanish
Michigan	58,216	9,168,200	157	State (U.S.) E	Lansing; Detroit	
Middle America	1,054,731	117,889,000	112		...; Ciudad de México (Mexico City)	
Midway Is.	2	1,500	750	Possession (U.S.) C		English
Minnesota	84,068	4,036,300	48	State (U.S.) E	St. Paul; Minneapolis	
Mississippi	47,716	2,400,200	50	State (U.S.) E	Jackson	
Missouri	69,686	4,832,600	69	State (U.S.) E	Jefferson City; St. Louis	
Moldavskaja (Moldavia) S.S.R.	13,000	3,935,000	303	Soviet Socialist Republic (U.S.S.R.) E	Kišin'ov (Kishinev)	Moldavian, Russian, Ukrainian
Monaco	0.6	26,000	43,333	Principality A	Monaco	French, Italian
Mongolia†	604,200	1,596,000	2.6	People's Republic A	Ulaanbaatar (Ulan Bator)	Mongolian
Montana	147,138	773,600	5.3	State (U.S.) E	Helena; Billings	
Montserrat	39	14,000	359	Colony (U.K.) C	Plymouth	English
Morocco†	172,415	18,911,000	110	Monarchy A	Rabat; Casablanca (Dar-el-Beida)	Arabic, Berber, French
Mozambique†	302,329	10,018,000	33	People's Republic A	Maputo (Lourenço Marques)	Portuguese, native languages
Namibia (excluding Walvis Bay)	317,827	921,000	2.9	Under South African Administration* C	Windhoek	English, Afrikaans, Native languages, German
Nauru	8	9,000	1,125	Republic (Comm. of Nations) A	Yaren; ...	Nauruan, English
Nebraska	77,227	1,571,300	20	State (U.S.) E	Lincoln; Omaha	
Nepal†	54,362	13,557,000	249	Monarchy A	Kāthmāndu	Nepali, Tibeto-Burman languages
Netherlands†	15,770	13,991,000	887	Monarchy A	Amsterdam and s'-Gravenhage (The Hague); Amsterdam	Dutch
Netherlands and Possessions	16,141	14,256,000	883		Amsterdam and s'-Gravenhage; Amsterdam	
Netherlands Antilles	371	265,000	714	Self-governing Territory (Netherlands) C	Willemstad	Dutch, Spanish, English, Papiamento
Netherlands Guiana, see Surinam						
Nevada	110,540	665,300	6.0	State (U.S.) E	Carson City; Las Vegas	
New Brunswick	28,354	696,000	25	Province (Canada) E	Fredericton; Saint John	English, French
New Caledonia (incl. Deps.)	7,358	143,000	19	Overseas Territory (France) C	Nouméa	Malay-Polynesian languages, French
New England	66,608	12,335,200	185	United States	...; Boston	English
Newfoundland	156,185	573,000	3.7	Province (Canada) E	St. John's	English
Newfoundland (excl. Labrador)	43,359	539,000	12		...; St. John's	English
New Hampshire	9,304	874,100	94	State (U.S.) E	Concord; Manchester	
New Hebrides	5,700	103,000	18	Condominium (France-U.K.) C	Vila	Malay-Polynesian languages, French, English
New Jersey	7,836	7,361,300	939	State (U.S.) E	Trenton; Newark	
New Mexico	121,666	1,239,000	10	State (U.S.) E	Santa Fe; Albuquerque	
New South Wales	309,433	5,152,000	17	State (Australia) E	Sydney	English
New York	49,576	17,897,700	361	State (U.S.) E	Albany; New York	
New Zealand†	103,736	3,280,000	32	Monarchy (Comm. of Nations) A	Wellington; Auckland	English, Maori
Nicaragua†	50,200	2,431,000	48	Republic A	Managua	Spanish
Niedersachsen (Lower Saxony)	18,299	7,185,000	393	State (Germany, Federal Republic of) E	Hannover	German
Niger†	489,200	5,055,000	10	Republic A	Niamey	Hausa, Arabic, French
Nigeria†	356,669	69,425,000	195	Republic (Comm. of Nations) A	Lagos	Hausa, Ibo, Yoruba, English
Niue	100	3,500	35	Island Territory (New Zealand) C	Alofi	Malay-Polynesian languages, English
Nordrhein-Westfalen (North Rhine Westphalia)	13,145	16,980,000	1,292	State (Germany, Federal Republic of) E	Düsseldorf; Essen	German
Norfolk Island	14	2,000	143	External Territory (Australia) C		English

† Member of the United Nations (1979).
‡ Includes 487 sq. miles of demilitarized zone, not included in North or South Korea figures.
‡‡ Areas for Egypt, Israel, Jordan and Syria do not reflect de facto changes which took place during 1967.

* The United Nations declared an end to the mandate of South Africa over Namibia in October 1966. Administration of the territory by South Africa is not recognized by the United Nations.

World Political Information Table (continued)

Region or Political Division	Area in sq. miles	Estimated Population 1/1/79	Pop. per sq. mi.	Form of Government and Ruling Power	Capital; Largest City (unless same)	Predominant Languages
North America	9,420,000	360,900,000	38		........; New York	
North Borneo, see Sabah						
North Carolina	52,586	5,599,900	106	State (U.S.) E	Raleigh; Charlotte	
North Dakota	70,665	661,400	9.4	State (U.S.) E	Bismarck; Fargo	
Northern Ireland	5,463	1,505,000	275	Administrative division of United Kingdom E	Belfast	English
Northern Rhodesia, see Zambia						
Northern Territory	520,280	105,000	0.2	Territory (Australia) E	Darwin	English, Aboriginal languages
North Polar Regions						
Northwest Territories	1,304,903	44,000	0.03	Territory (Canada) E	Yellowknife	English, Eskimo, Indian
Norway†	125,181	4,067,000	32	Monarchy A	Oslo	Norwegian (Riksmål and Landsmål)
Nova Scotia	21,425	851,000	40	Province (Canada) E	Halifax	English
Nyasaland, see Malawi						
Oceania (incl. Australia)	3,295,000	22,700,000	6.9		........; Sydney	
Ohio	41,222	10,711,400	260	State (U.S.) E	Columbus; Cleveland	
Oklahoma	69,919	2,873,100	41	State (U.S.) E	Oklahoma City	
Oman†	82,030	856,000	10	Sultanate A	Masqaţ; Maţraḩ	Arabic
Ontario	412,582	8,493,000	21	Province (Canada) E	Toronto	English
Oregon	96,981	2,449,300	25	State (U.S.) E	Salem; Portland	
Orkney Is.	376	17,000	45	Part of Scotland, U.K. D	Kirkwall	English
Pacific Islands Trust Territory	717	126,000	176	Administered by U.S. C	Saipan (island);	Malay-Polynesian languages, English
Pakistan (incl. part of Kashmir)†	345,753	80,894,000	234	Federal Republic A	Islāmābād; Karāchi	Urdu, English
Panama†	29,209	1,849,000	63	Republic A	Panamá	Spanish
Papua New Guinea†	178,260	3,018,000	17	Parliamentary State (Comm. of Nations) A	Port Moresby	Papuan and Negrito languages, English
Paraguay†	157,048	2,926,000	19	Republic A	Asunción	Spanish, Guaraní
Pennsylvania	45,333	11,835,800	261	State (U.S.) E	Harrisburg; Philadelphia	
Persia, see Iran						
Peru†	496,224	17,282,000	35	Republic A	Lima	Spanish, Quechua
Philippines†	116,000	46,928,000	405	Republic A	Manila	Pilipino, English
Pitcairn (excl. Dependencies)	2	60	30	Dependency (U.K.) C	Adamstown	English
Poland†	120,725	35,205,000	292	People's Republic A	Warszawa (Warsaw); Katowice	Polish
Portugal†	35,553	10,122,000	285	Republic A	Lisboa (Lisbon)	Portuguese
Portugal and Possessions	35,559	10,409,000	293		Lisboa (Lisbon)	
Portuguese Guinea, see Guinea-Bissau						
Prairie Provinces	757,985	3,886,000	5.1	Canada	........; Winnipeg	English
Prince Edward Island	2,184	121,000	55	Province (Canada) E	Charlottetown	English
Puerto Rico	3,435	3,452,000	1,005	Commonwealth (U.S.) C	San Juan	Spanish, English
Qatar†	4,247	103,000	24	Emirate A	Ad-Dawḩah (Doha)	Arabic
Quebec	594,860	6,407,000	11	Province (Canada) E	Québec; Montréal	French, English
Queensland	667,000	2,197,000	3.3	State (Australia) E	Brisbane	English
Reunion	969	513,000	529	Overseas Department (France) C	Saint-Denis	French
Rheinland-Pfalz (Rhineland-Palatinate)	7,657	3,628,000	474	State (Germany, Federal Republic of) E	Mainz	German
Rhode Island	1,214	928,000	764	State (U.S.) E	Providence	
Rhodesia	150,804	7,059,000	47	Self-governing Colony (U.K.)* C	Salisbury	English, native languages
Rio Muni, see Equatorial Guinea						
Rodrigues	42	28,000	667	Part of Mauritius (U.K.) D	........; Port Mathurin	English, French
Romania†	91,699	21,972,000	240	People's Republic A	București (Bucharest)	Romanian, Hungarian
Rossijskaja Sovetskaja Federativnaja Socialističeskaja Respublika	6,592,850	138,223,000	21	Soviet Federated Socialist Republic (U.S.S.R.) E	Moskva (Moscow)	Russian, Finno-Ugric languages, various Turkic, Iranian, and Mongol languages
Rossijskaja S.F.S.R. in Europe	1,527,350	101,418,000	66	Union of Soviet Socialist Republics	........; Moskva (Moscow)	Russian, Finno-Ugric languages
Rwanda†	10,169	4,492,000	442	Republic A	Kigali	Kinyarwanda, French
Saarland (Saar)	992	1,082,000	1,091	State (Germany, Federal Republic of) E	Saarbrücken	German
Sabah (North Borneo)	29,388	865,000	29	Administrative division of Malaysia E	Kota Kinabalu; Sandakan	Malay, Chinese, English
St. Helena (incl. Dependencies)	162	7,000	43	Colony (U.K.) C	Jamestown	English
St. Kitts-Nevis	103	48,000	466	Associated State (U.K.) B	Basseterre	English
St. Lucia	238	114,000	479	Parliamentary State (Comm. of Nations) A	Castries	English
St. Pierre & Miquelon	93	6,000	65	Overseas Territory (France) C	Saint-Pierre	French
St. Vincent	150	119,000	793	Associated State (U.K.) B	Kingstown	English
Samoa (Entire)	1,173	188,000	160		........; Apia	Samoan, English
San Marino	24	21,000	875	Republic A	San Marino	Italian
Sao Tome & Principe†	372	84,000	226	Republic A	São Tomé	Portuguese, native languages
Sarawak	48,342	1,213,000	25	Administrative division of Malaysia E	Kuching	Malay, Chinese, English
Sardinia	9,301	1,582,000	170	Part of Italy D	Cagliari	Italian
Saskatchewan	251,700	947,000	3.8	Province (Canada) E	Regina	English
Saudi Arabia†	830,000	9,942,000	12	Monarchy A	Ar-Riyāḑ (Riyadh)	Arabic
Scandinavia (incl. Finland and Iceland)	509,899	22,505,000	44		........; København (Copenhagen)	Swedish, Danish, Norwegian, Finnish, Icelandic
Schleswig-Holstein	6,046	2,567,000	425	State (Germany, Federal Republic of) E	Kiel	German
Scotland	30,414	5,185,000	170	Administrative division of United Kingdom E	Edinburgh; Glasgow	English, Gaelic
Senegal†	75,750	5,592,000	74	Republic A	Dakar	French, native languages
Seychelles†	156	66,000	423	Republic (Comm. of Nations) A	Victoria	English, Creole
Shetland Is.	550	19,000	35	Part of Scotland, U.K. D	Lerwick	English
Siam, see Thailand						
Sicily	9,926	4,951,000	499	Part of Italy (Sicilia Autonomous Region) D	Palermo	Italian
Sierra Leone†	27,699	3,298,000	119	Republic (Comm. of Nations) A	Freetown	English, native languages
Singapore†	224	2,353,000	10,504	Republic (Comm. of Nations) A	Singapore	Chinese, Malay, English, Tamil
Solomon Is. (Papua New Guinea)	4,100	117,000	29	Part of Papua New Guinea (Bouganville Dist.) D	Sohano; Panguna	Malay-Polynesian languages, English
Solomon Is.†	10,983	219,000	20	Parliamentary State A	Honiara	Malay-Polynesian languages, English
Somalia†	246,201	3,493,000	14	Republic A	Mogadisho	Somali
South Africa (incl. Walvis Bay)†	471,879	27,911,000	59	Federal Republic A	Pretoria, Cape Town; Johannesburg	English, Afrikaans, native languages
South America	6,870,000	231,300,000	34		........; São Paulo	
South Australia	380,070	1,343,000	3.5	State (Australia) E	Adelaide	English
South Carolina	31,055	2,930,300	94	State (U.S.) E	Columbia	
South Dakota	77,047	695,500	9.0	State (U.S.) E	Pierre; Sioux Falls	
Southern Rhodesia, see Rhodesia						
Southern Yemen, see Yemen, People's Democratic Republic of						
South Georgia	1,450	20	0.01	Dependency of Falkland Is. (U.K.) D		English, Norwegian

† Member of the United Nations (1979).
* Rhodesia unilaterally declared its independence from the United Kingdom on November 11, 1965.
‡‡ Areas for Egypt, Israel, Jordan and Syria do not reflect de facto changes which took place during 1967.

World Political Information Table (continued)

Region or Political Division	Area in sq. miles	Estimated Population 1/1/79	Pop. per sq. mi.	Form of Government and Ruling Power	Capital; Largest City (unless same)	Predominant Languages
South Polar Regions						
South West Africa, see Namibia						
Spain†	194,885	37,273,000	191	Monarchy ... A	Madrid	Spanish, Catalan, Galician, Basque
Spain and Possessions	194,897	37,389,000	192		Madrid	
Spanish Possessions in North Africa	12	116,000	9,667	Five Possessions (no central government) (Spain) ... C	........; Ceuta	Spanish, Arabic, Berber
Spitsbergen, see Svalbard						
Sri Lanka (Ceylon)†	25,332	14,147,000	558	Republic (Comm. of Nations) ... A	Colombo	Sinhala, Tamil, English
Sudan†	967,499	17,806,000	18	Republic ... A	Al-Khurṭūm (Khartoum)	Arabic, native languages, English
Sumatra (Sumatera)	182,860	26,035,000	142	Part of Indonesia ... D	........; Medan	Indonesian, English, Chinese
Suriname (Neth. Guiana)†	63,037	468,000	7.4	Republic ... A	Paramaribo	Dutch, Creole
Svalbard (Spitsbergen) and Jan Mayen	24,102	Winter Pop. 3,000	0.1	Dependencies (Norway) ... C	........; Longyearbyen	Norwegian, Russian
Swaziland†	6,705	522,000	78	Monarchy (Comm. of Nations) ... A	Mbabane	English, siSwati
Sweden†	173,732	8,304,000	48	Monarchy ... A	Stockholm	Swedish
Switzerland	15,941	6,284,000	394	Federal Republic ... A	Bern (Berne); Zürich	German, French, Italian
Syria†	71,498	8,216,000	115	Republic‡‡ ... A	Dimashq (Damascus)	Arabic, French
Tadžikskaja (Tadzhik) S.S.R.	55,250	3,568,000	65	Soviet Socialist Republic (U.S.S.R.) ... E	Dušanbe (Dushanbe)	Tadzhik, Turkic languages, Russian
Taiwan (Formosa) (Nationalist China)	13,885	17,118,000	1,233	Republic ... A	T'aipei	Chinese
Tanganyika, see Tanzania						
Tanzania (Tanganyika & Zanzibar)†	364,900	16,925,000	46	Republic (Comm. of Nations) ... A	Dar-es-Salaam	Swahili, English, Arabic
Tasmania	26,383	435,000	16	State (Australia) ... E	Hobart	English
Tennessee	42,244	4,345,700	103	State (U.S.) ... E	Nashville; Memphis	
Texas	267,339	13,133,100	49	State (U.S.) ... E	Austin; Houston	
Thailand (Siam)†	198,500	45,663,000	230	Monarchy ... A	Krung Thep (Bangkok)	Thai, Chinese
Tibet (Xizang Zizhiqu)	471,700	1,303,000	2.8	Autonomous Region (China) ... E	Lasa (Lhasa)	Tibetan, Chinese
Togo†	21,600	2,445,000	113	Republic ... A	Lomé	Native languages, French
Tokelau (Union) Is.	4	1,600	400	Island Territory (New Zealand) ... C	........; Fakaofo	Malay-Polynesian languages, English
Tonga	270	93,000	344	Monarchy (Comm. of Nations) ... A	Nukualofa	Tongan, English
Transcaucasia	71,850	13,851,000	193	Union of Soviet Socialist Republics	........; Baku	
Trinidad & Tobago†	1,980	1,166,000	589	Republic (Comm. of Nations) ... A	Port of Spain	English, Spanish
Tristan da Cunha	40	300	7.5	Dependency of St. Helena (U.K.) ... D	Edinburgh	English
Trucial States, see United Arab Emirates						
Tunisia†	63,170	6,490,000	103	Republic ... A	Tunis	Arabic, French
Turkey†	301,382	44,720,000	148	Republic ... A	Ankara; İstanbul	Turkish, Kurdish, Arabic
Turkey in Europe	9,121	3,859,000	423	Turkey ... E	........; İstanbul	Turkish
Turkmenskaja (Turkmen) S.S.R.	188,450	2,650,000	14	Soviet Socialist Republic (U.S.S.R.) ... E	Ašchabad	Turkic languages, Russian
Turks & Caicos Is.	166	6,000	36	Colony (U.K.) ... C	Grand Turk	English
Tuvalu (Ellice Is.)	9.5	8,000	842	Parliamentary State ... A	Funafuti (island);	Malay-Polynesian languages, English
Uganda†	91,134	12,962,000	142	Republic (Comm. of Nations) ... A	Kampala	English, Swahili
Ukrainskaja (Ukraine) S.S.R.†	233,100	50,368,000	216	Soviet Socialist Republic (U.S.S.R.) ... E	Kijev (Kiev)	Ukrainian, Russian
Union of Soviet Socialist Republics (Soviet Union)†	8,649,500	262,332,000	30	Federal Soviet Republics ... A	Moskva (Moscow)	Russian and other Slavic languages, various Finno-Ugric, Turkic and Mongol languages, Caucasian languages, Persian
Union of Soviet Socialist Republics in Europe	1,920,750	172,824,000	90	Union of Soviet Socialist Republics	........; Moskva (Moscow)	Russian, Ruthenian, various Finno-Ugric and Caucasian languages
United Arab Emirates (Trucial States)†	32,278	247,000	7.7	Self-governing Union ... A	Abū Ẓaby; Dubayy	Arabic
United Kingdom of Great Britain & Northern Ireland†	94,227	55,754,000	592	Monarchy (Comm. of Nations) ... A	London	English, Welsh, Gaelic
United Kingdom & Possessions	288,049	69,019,000	240		London	
United States†	*3,675,545	219,294,000	60	Federal Republic ... A	Washington; New York	English
United States and Possessions	3,680,713	223,171,000	61		Washington; New York	English, Spanish
Upper Volta†	105,800	6,536,000	62	Republic ... A	Ouagadougou	French, native languages
Uruguay†	68,536	2,839,000	41	Republic ... A	Montevideo	Spanish
Utah	84,916	1,307,500	15	State (U.S.) ... E	Salt Lake City	
Uzbekskaja (Uzbek) S.S.R.	173,600	14,454,000	83	Soviet Socialist Republic (U.S.S.R.) ... E	Taškent	Turkic languages, Sart, Russian
Vatican City (Holy See)	0.2	1,000	5,000	Ecclesiastical State ... A	Città del Vaticano (Vatican City)	Italian, Latin
Venezuela†	352,144	13,338,000	38	Federal Republic ... A	Caracas	Spanish
Vermont	9,609	491,000	51	State (U.S.) ... E	Montpelier; Burlington	
Victoria	87,884	3,933,000	45	State (Australia) ... E	Melbourne	English
Vietnam†	128,402	49,882,000	388	People's Republic ... A	Ha-noi; Thanh-pho Ho Chi Minh (Sai-gon)	Vietnamese
Virginia	40,817	5,239,600	128	State (U.S.) ... E	Richmond; Norfolk	
Virgin Is., British	59	10,000	169	Colony (U.K.) ... C	Road Town	English
Virgin Is. of the U.S.	133	109,000	820	Unincorporated Territory (U.S.) ... C	Charlotte Amalie	English
Wake I.	3			Possession (U.S.) ... C		English
Wales (incl. Monmouthshire)	8,016	2,757,000	344	United Kingdom	Cardiff	English, Welsh
Wallis & Futuna	77	9,500	123	Overseas Territory (France) ... C	Mata-Utu	Malay-Polynesian languages, French
Washington	68,192	3,728,700	55	State (U.S.) ... E	Olympia; Seattle	
Western Australia	975,920	1,234,000	1.3	State (Australia) ... E	Perth	English
Western Sahara	102,700	152,000	1.5	Administered by Morocco and Mauritania ... C	El Aaiún	Arabic
Western Samoa†	1,097	154,000	140	Constitutional Monarchy (Comm. of Nations) ... A	Apia	Samoan, English
West Indies	92,041	28,887,000	314		........; La Habana (Havana)	
West Virginia	24,181	1,871,400	77	State (U.S.) ... E	Charleston; Huntington	
White Russia, see Belorusskaja						
Wisconsin	56,154	4,694,500	84	State (U.S.) ... E	Madison; Milwaukee	
World	57,280,000	4,211,000,000	74		........; Tōkyō	
Wyoming	97,914	430,400	4.4	State (U.S.) ... E	Cheyenne	
Yemen†	75,300	7,388,000	98	Republic ... A	Ṣan'ā'	Arabic
Yemen, People's Democratic Republic of,†	111,075	1,873,000	17	People's Republic ... A	Aden	Arabic, English
Yugoslavia†	98,766	21,974,000	222	Socialist Federal Republic ... A	Beograd (Belgrade)	Serbo-Croatian, Slovenian, Macedonian
Yukon	207,076	22,000	0.1	Territory (Canada) ... E	Whitehorse	English, Eskimo, Indian
Zaire (Congo, The)†	905,567	28,042,000	31	Republic ... A	Kinshasa	French, native languages
Zambia (Northern Rhodesia)†	290,586	5,642,000	19	Republic (Comm. of Nations) ... A	Lusaka	English, native languages
Zanzibar	950	488,000	514	Part of Tanzania ... D	Zanzibar	Arabic, English, Swahili

† Member of the United Nations (1979).
‡‡ Areas for Egypt, Israel, Jordan and Syria do not reflect de facto changes which took place during 1967.
* Total area of the United States includes 3,536,855 square miles of land; 78,268 square miles of inland water; and 60,422 square miles of Great Lakes area, not included in any state.

Largest Metropolitan Areas of the World, 1979

This table lists the major metropolitan areas of the world according to their estimated population on January 1, 1979. For convenience in reference, the areas are grouped by major region, and the number of areas in each region and size group is given.

There are 25 areas with more than 5,000,000 population each; these are listed in rank order of estimated population, with the world rank given in parentheses following the name. For example, New York's 1979 rank is second. Below the 5,000,000 level, the metropolitan areas are listed alphabetically within region, not in order of size.

For ease of comparison, each metropolitan area has been defined by Rand McNally & Company according to consistent rules. A metropolitan area includes a central city, neighboring communities linked to it by continuous built-up areas, and more distant communities if the bulk of their population is supported by commuters to the central city. Some metropolitan areas have more than one central city, for example Tōkyō-Yokohama or San Francisco-Oakland-San Jose.

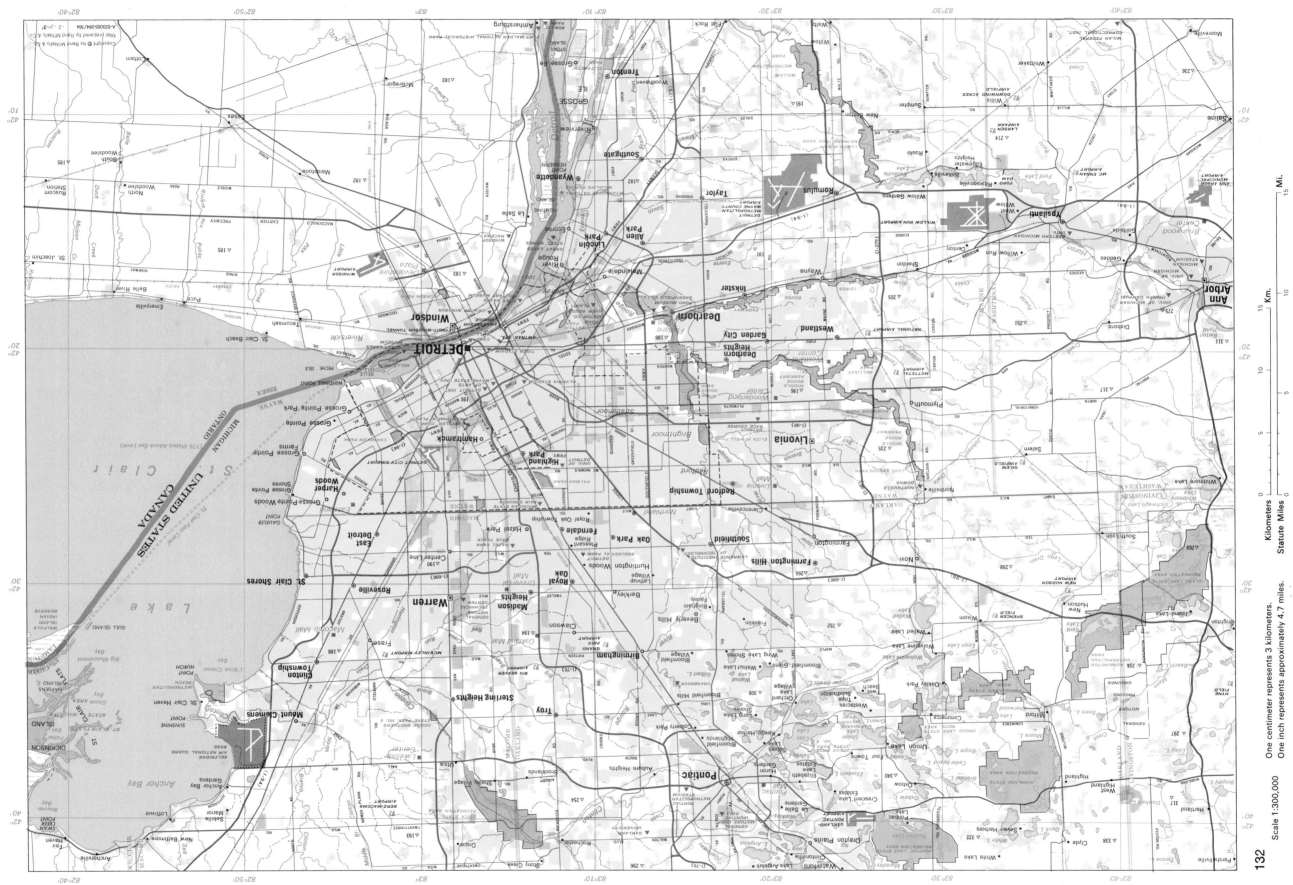

POPULATION CLASSIFICATION	UNITED STATES and CANADA	LATIN AMERICA	EUROPE (excl. U.S.S.R.)	U.S.S.R.	ASIA	AFRICA-OCEANIA
Over 15,000,000 (3)	New York (2)				Tōkyō–Yokohama (1) Ōsaka–Kōbe–Kyōto (3)	
10,000,000–15,000,000 (6)		Ciudad de México (Mexico City) (4) São Paulo (5) Buenos Aires (9)	London (7)	Moskva (Moscow) (6)	Calcutta (8)	
5,000,000–10,000,000 (16)	Los Angeles (12) Chicago (17) Philadelphia (23)	Rio de Janeiro (13)	Paris (11) Essen–Dortmund–Duisburg (The Ruhr) (25)	Leningrad (24)	Sŏul (Seoul) (10) Bombay (14) Shanghai (16) Manila (18) Jakarta (19) Delhi (20) Beijing (Peking) (21) Tehrān (22)	Al-Qāhirah (Cairo) (15)
3,000,000–5,000,000 (28)	Boston Detroit–Windsor San Francisco–Oakland–San Jose Washington	Bogotá Caracas Lima Santiago	Athínai (Athens) Barcelona Berlin İstanbul Madrid Milano (Milan) Roma (Rome)		Baghdād Chongqing (Chungking) Karāchi Krung Thep (Bangkok) Madras Nagoya Shenyang (Mukden) T'aipei (Taipei) Tianjin (Tientsin) Victoria Wuhan	Johannesburg Sydney
2,000,000–3,000,000 (46)	Cleveland Dallas–Fort Worth Houston Miami–Fort Lauderdale Montréal Pittsburgh St. Louis San Diego–Tijuana Toronto	Belo Horizonte Guadalajara La Habana (Havana) Pôrto Alegre Recife	Birmingham Bruxelles (Brussel) (Brussels) București (Bucharest) Budapest Hamburg Katowice–Bytom–Gliwice Lisboa (Lisbon) Manchester Napoli (Naples) Warszawa (Warsaw)	Doneck (Donetsk)–Makejevka Kijev (Kiev)	Ahmādābad Ankara Bangalore Dacca Guangzhou (Canton) Haerbin (Harbin) Hyderābād Lahore Pusan Rangoon Singapore Surabaya Thanh–pho Ho Chi Minh (Saigon) X'ian (Sian)	Alexandria Alger (Algiers) Casablanca Kinshasa Lagos Melbourne
1,500,000–2,000,000 (31)	Atlanta Baltimore Buffalo Minneapolis–St. Paul Seattle–Tacoma	Medellín Monterrey San Juan	Amsterdam Frankfurt am Main Glasgow København (Copenhagen) Köln (Cologne) Leeds–Bradford Liverpool München (Munich) Stuttgart Torino (Turin) Wien (Vienna)	Baku Char'kov (Kharkov) Gor'kij (Gorki) Taškent (Tashkent)	Chengdu (Chengtu) Colombo Dimashq (Damascus) Fukuoka Kānpur Kitakyūshū–Shimonoseki Nanjing (Nanking) Taiyuan	
1,000,000–1,500,000 (83)	Cincinnati Denver El Paso–Ciudad Juárez Hartford Indianapolis Kansas City Milwaukee New Orleans Phoenix Portland Vancouver	Cali Córdoba Fortaleza Guatemala Guayaquil Montevideo Rosario Salvador	Antwerpen (Anvers) (Antwerp) Beograd (Belgrade) Düsseldorf Hannover Lille Łódź Lyon Mannheim Marseille Newcastle–Sunderland Nürnberg Porto Praha (Prague) Rotterdam Sofija (Sofia) Stockholm Valencia	Čel'abinsk (Chelyabinsk) Dnepropetrovsk Jerevan (Yerevan) Kazan' Kujbyšev (Kuybyshev) Minsk Novosibirsk Odessa Omsk Perm Rostov-na-Donu Saratov Sverdlovsk Tbilisi Ufa Volgograd	Anshan Bandung Bayrūt (Beirut) Changchun (Hsinking) Chittagong Fushun Ha-noi Hiroshima–Kure İzmir Jinan (Tsinan) Kaohsiung Kuala Lumpur Kunming Lanzhou (Lanchow) Lucknow Lüda (Dairen) Lyallpur Nāgpur Pune (Poona) P'yŏngyang Qingdao (Tsingtao) Sapporo Shijiazhuang (Shihchiachuang) Taegu Tel Aviv–Yafo Zhengzhou (Chengchow)	Addis Abeba (Addis Ababa) Brisbane Cape Town Durban Tunis
Total by Region (213)	33	24	48	24	70	14

Introduction to the Index

The index includes in a single alphabetical list some 35,000 names appearing on the maps. Each name is followed by a page reference and by the location of the feature on the map. The map location is designated by latitude and longitude coordinates. If a page contains several maps, a lowercase letter identifies the inset map. The page reference for two-page maps is always to the left hand page.

Most map features are indexed to the largest-scale map on which they appear. Countries, mountain ranges, and other extensive features are generally indexed to the map that shows them in their entirety.

The features indexed are of three types: *point, areal,* and *linear.* For *point* features (for example, cities, mountain peaks, dams), latitude and longitude coordinates give the location of the point on the map. For *areal* features (countries, mountain ranges, etc.), the coordinates generally indicate the approximate center of the feature. For *linear* features (rivers, canals, aqueducts), the coordinates locate a terminating point—for example, the mouth of a river, or the point at which a feature reaches the map margin.

NAME FORMS Names in the Index, as on the maps, are generally in the local language and insofar as possible are spelled according to official practice. Diacritical marks are included, except that those used to indicate tone, as in Vietnamese, are usually not shown. Most features that extend beyond the boundaries of one country have no single official name, and these are usually named in English. Many conventional English names and former names are cross referenced to the primary map name. All cross references are indicated by the symbol→. A name that appears in a shortened version on the map due to space limitations is given in full in the Index, with the portion that is omitted on the map enclosed in brackets, for example, Acapulco [de Juárez].

TRANSLITERATION For names in languages not written in the Roman alphabet, the locally official transliteration system has been used where one exists. Thus, names in the Soviet Union and Bulgaria have been transliterated according to the systems adopted by the academies of science of these countries. Similarly, the transliteration for mainland Chinese names follows the Pinyin system, which has been officially adopted in mainland China. For languages with no one locally accepted transliteration system, notably Arabic, transliteration in general follows closely a system adopted by the United States Board on Geographic Names.

ALPHABETIZATION Names are alphabetized in the order of the letters of the English alphabet. Spanish *ll* and *ch*, for example, are not treated as distinct letters. Furthermore, diacritical marks are disregarded in alphabetization—German or Scandinavian *ä* or *ö* are treated as *a* or *o*.

The names of physical features may appear inverted, since they are always alphabetized under the proper, not the generic, part of the name, thus: "Gibraltar, Strait of ɰ". Otherwise every entry, whether consisting of one word or more, is alphabetized as a single continuous entity. "Lakeland," for example, appears after "La Crosse" and before "La Salle." Names beginning with articles (Le Havre, Den Helder, Al-Qāhirah, As-Suways) are not inverted. Names beginning "Mc" are alphabetized as though spelled "Mac," and names beginning "St." and "Sainte" as though spelled "Saint."

In the case of identical names, towns are listed first, then political divisions, then physical features. Entries that are completely identical (including symbols, discussed below) are distinguished by abbreviations of their official country names and are sequenced alphabetically by country name. The many duplicate names in Canada, the United Kingdom, and the United States are further distinguished by abbreviations of the names of their primary subdivisions. (See list of abbreviations on pages 202 and 203).

ABBREVIATION AND CAPITALIZATION Abbreviation and styling have been standardized for all languages. A period is used after every abbreviation even when this may not be the local practice. The abbreviation "St." is used only for "Saint." "Sankt" and other forms of the term are spelled out.

All names are written with an initial capital letter except for a few Dutch names, such as 's-Gravenhage. Capitalization of noninitial words in a name generally follows local practice.

SYMBOL The symbols that appear in the Index graphically represent the broad categories of the features named, for example, ∧ for mountain (Everest, Mount ∧). Superior numbers following some symbols in the Index indicate finer distinctions, for example, ∧[1] for volcano (Fuji-san ∧[1]). A complete list of the symbols and those with superior numbers is given on page 203.

LIST OF ABBREVIATIONS

	LOCAL NAME	ENGLISH
Afg.	Afghānestān	Afghanistan
Afr.	—	Africa
Ala., U.S.	Alabama	Alabama
Alaska, U.S.	Alaska	Alaska
Alg.	Algérie	Algeria
Alta., Can.	Alberta	Alberta
Am. Sam.	American Samoa	American Samoa
And.	Andorra	Andorra
Ang.	Angola	Angola
Anguilla	Anguilla	Anguilla
Ant.	—	Antarctica
Antig.	Antigua	Antigua
Arc. O.	—	Arctic Ocean
Arg.	Argentina	Argentina
Ariz., U.S.	Arizona	Arizona
Ark., U.S.	Arkansas	Arkansas
Ar. Sa.	Al-'Arabīyah as-Sa'ūdīyah	Saudi Arabia
As.	—	Asia
Atl. O.	—	Atlantic Ocean
Austl.	Australia	Australia
Ba.	Bahamas	Bahamas
Bahr.	Al-Baḥrayn	Bahrain
Barb.	Barbados	Barbados
B.A.T.	British Antarctic Territory	British Antarctic Territory
B.C., Can.	British Columbia	British Columbia
Bdi.	Burundi	Burundi
Bel.	Belgique België	Belgium
Belize	Belize	Belize
Benin	Benin	Benin
Ber.	Bermuda	Bermuda
Ber. S.	—	Bering Sea
Bhārat	Bhārat	India
B.I.O.T.	British Indian Ocean Territory	British Indian Ocean Territory
Blg.	Bălgarija	Bulgaria
Bngl.	Bangladesh	Bangladesh
Bol.	Bolivia	Bolivia
Bots.	Botswana	Botswana
Bra.	Brasil	Brazil
B.R.D.	Bundesrepublik Deutschland	Federal Republic of Germany
Bru.	Brunei	Brunei
Br. Vir. Is.	British Virgin Islands	British Virgin Islands
Calif., U.S.	California	California
Cam.	Cameroun	Cameroon
Can.	Canada	Canada
Can./End.	Canton and Enderbury	Canton and Enderbury
Carib. S.	—	Caribbean Sea
Cay. Is.	Cayman Islands	Cayman Islands
Centraf.	Empire centrafricain	Central African Empire
Česko.	Československo	Czechoslovakia
Chile	Chile	Chile
Christ. I.	Christmas Island	Christmas Island
C. Iv.	Côte d'Ivoire	Ivory Coast
C.M.I.K.	Chosŏn Minjujuŭi In'min Konghwaguk	North Korea
Cocos Is.	Cocos (Keeling) Islands	Cocos (Keeling) Islands
Col.	Colombia	Colombia
Colo., U.S.	Colorado	Colorado
Comores	Comores	Comoros
Congo	Congo	Congo
Conn., U.S.	Connecticut	Connecticut
Cook Is.	Cook Islands	Cook Islands
C.R.	Costa Rica	Costa Rica
Cuba	Cuba	Cuba
C.V.	Cabo Verde	Cape Verde
C.Z.	Canal Zone	Canal Zone
Dan.	Danmark	Denmark
D.C., U.S.	District of Columbia	District of Columbia
D.D.R.	Deutsche Demokratische Republik	German Democratic Republic
Del., U.S.	Delaware	Delaware
Den.	Danmark	Denmark
Djibouti	Djibouti	Djibouti
Dom.	Dominica	Dominica
D.Y.	Druk-Yul	Bhutan
Ec.	Ecuador	Ecuador
Eire	Eire	Ireland
Ellás	Ellás	Greece
El Sal.	El Salvador	El Salvador
Eng., U.K.	England	England
Esp.	España	Spain
Eur.	—	Europe
Falk. Is.	Falkland Islands	Falkland Islands (Islas Malvinas)
Fiji	Fiji	Fiji
Fla., U.S.	Florida	Florida
Før.	Føroyar	Faeroe Islands
Fr.	France	France
Ga., U.S.	Georgia	Georgia
Gabon	Gabon	Gabon
Gam.	Gambia	Gambia
Gaza	—	Gaza Strip
Ghana	Ghana	Ghana
Gib.	Gibraltar	Gibraltar
Gilb. Is.	Gilbert Islands	Gilbert Islands
Gren.	Grenada	Grenada
Grn.	Grønland	Greenland
Guad.	Guadeloupe	Guadeloupe
Guam.	Guam	Guam
Guat.	Guatemala	Guatemala
Guer.	Guernsey	Guernsey
Gui.-B.	Guinea-Bissau	Guinea-Bissau
Gui. Ecu.	Guinea Ecuatorial	Equatorial Guinea
Guinée	Guinée	Guinea
Guy.	Guyana	Guyana
Guy. fr.	Guyane française	French Guiana
Haï.	Haïti	Haiti
Haw., U.S.	Hawaii	Hawaii
H.K.	Hong Kong	Hong Kong
Hond.	Honduras	Honduras
H. Vol.	Haute-Volta	Upper Volta
Idaho, U.S.	Idaho	Idaho
I.I.A.	Ittiḥād al-Imārāt al-'Arabīyah	United Arab Emirates
Ill., U.S.	Illinois	Illinois
Ind., U.S.	Indiana	Indiana
Ind. O.	—	Indian Ocean
Indon.	Indonesia	Indonesia
I. of Man	Isle of Man	Isle of Man
Iowa, U.S.	Iowa	Iowa
Īrān	Īrān	Iran
'Irāq	Al-'Irāq	Iraq
Ísland	Ísland	Iceland
It.	Italia	Italy
Jam.	Jamaica	Jamaica
Jersey	Jersey	Jersey
Jugo.	Jugoslavija	Yugoslavia
Kam.	Kampuchea	Cambodia
Kans., U.S.	Kansas	Kansas
Kenya	Kenya	Kenya
Kıpros	Kıpros Kıbrıs	Cyprus
Kuwayt	Al-Kuwayt	Kuwait
Ky., U.S.	Kentucky	Kentucky
La., U.S.	Louisiana	Louisiana
Lao	Lao	Laos
Leso.	Lesotho	Lesotho
Liber.	Liberia	Liberia
Lībiyā	Lībiyā	Libya
Liech.	Liechtenstein	Liechtenstein
Lubnān	Al-Lubnān	Lebanon
Lux.	Luxembourg	Luxembourg
Macau	Macau	Macau
Madag.	Madagasikara	Madagascar
Magreb	Al-Magreb	Morocco
Magy.	Magyarország	Hungary
Maine, U.S.	Maine	Maine
Malawi	Malawi	Malawi
Malay.	Malaysia	Malaysia
Mald.	Maldives	Maldives
Mali	Mali	Mali
Malta	Malta	Malta
Man., Can.	Manitoba	Manitoba
Mart.	Martinique	Martinique
Mass., U.S.	Massachusetts	Massachusetts
Maur.	Mauritanie	Mauritania
Maus.	Mauritius	Mauritius
Md., U.S.	Maryland	Maryland
Medit. S.	—	Mediterranean Sea
Méx.	México	Mexico
Mich., U.S.	Michigan	Michigan
Mid. Is.	Midway Islands	Midway Islands
Minn., U.S.	Minnesota	Minnesota
Miṣr	Miṣr	Egypt
Miss., U.S.	Mississippi	Mississippi
Mo., U.S.	Missouri	Missouri
Moç.	Moçambique	Mozambique
Monaco	Monaco	Monaco
Mong.	Mongol Ard Uls	Mongolia
Mont., U.S.	Montana	Montana
Monts.	Montserrat	Montserrat
Mya.	Myanma	Burma
N.A.	—	North America
Namibia	Namibia	Namibia
Nauru	Nauru	Nauru
N.B., Can.	New Brunswick	New Brunswick
N.C., U.S.	North Carolina	North Carolina
N. Cal.	Nouvelle-Calédonie	New Caledonia
N. Dak., U.S.	North Dakota	North Dakota
Nebr., U.S.	Nebraska	Nebraska
Ned.	Nederland	Netherlands
Ned. Ant.	Nederlandse Antillen	Netherlands Antilles
Nepāl	Nepāl	Nepal
Nev., U.S.	Nevada	Nevada
Newf., Can.	Newfoundland	Newfoundland
N.H., U.S.	New Hampshire	New Hampshire
N. Heb.	New Hebrides Nouvelles-Hébrides	New Hebrides
Nic.	Nicaragua	Nicaragua
Nig.	Nigeria	Nigeria
Niger	Niger	Niger
Nihon	Nihon	Japan
N. Ire., U.K.	Northern Ireland	Northern Ireland
Niue	Niue	Niue
N.J., U.S.	New Jersey	New Jersey
N. Mex., U.S.	New Mexico	New Mexico
Nor.	Norge	Norway
Norf. I.	Norfolk Island	Norfolk Island
N.S., Can.	Nova Scotia	Nova Scotia
N.W. Ter., Can.	Northwest Territories	Northwest Territories
N.Y., U.S.	New York	New York
N.Z.	New Zealand	New Zealand
Oc.	—	Oceania
Ohio, U.S.	Ohio	Ohio
Okla., U.S.	Oklahoma	Oklahoma
Ont., Can.	Ontario	Ontario
Oreg., U.S.	Oregon	Oregon
Öst.	Österreich	Austria
Pa., U.S.	Pennsylvania	Pennsylvania
Pac. O.	—	Pacific Ocean
Pāk.	Pākistān	Pakistan
Pan.	Panamá	Panama
Pap. N. Gui.	Papua New Guinea	Papua New Guinea
Para.	Paraguay	Paraguay
P.E.I., Can.	Prince Edward Island	Prince Edward Island
Perú	Perú	Peru
Pil.	Pilipinas	Philippines
Pit.	Pitcairn	Pitcairn
P.I.T.T.	Pacific Islands Trust Territory	Pacific Islands Trust Territory
Pol.	Polska	Poland
Poly. fr.	Polynésie française	French Polynesia
Port.	Portugal	Portugal
P.R.	Puerto Rico	Puerto Rico
P.S.N.Á.	Plazas de Soberanía en el Norte de África	Spanish North Africa
Qaṭar	Qaṭar	Qatar
Que., Can.	Québec	Quebec
Rep. Dom.	República Dominicana	Dominican Republic
Réu.	Réunion	Reunion
Rh.	Rhodesia	Rhodesia
R.I., U.S.	Rhode Island	Rhode Island
Rom.	România	Romania
Rw.	Rwanda	Rwanda
S.A.	—	South America
S. Afr.	South Africa Suid-Afrika	South Africa
Sah. Occ.	Sahara Occidentale	Western Sahara
Sask., Can.	Saskatchewan	Saskatchewan
S.C., U.S.	South Carolina	South Carolina
S. Ch. S.	—	South China Sea
Schw.	Schweiz; Suisse; Svizzera	Switzerland
Scot., U.K.	Scotland	Scotland
S. Dak., U.S.	South Dakota	South Dakota
Sén.	Sénégal	Senegal
Sey.	Seychelles	Seychelles
Shq.	Shqipëri	Albania
Sing.	Singapore	Singapore
S.L.	Sierra Leone	Sierra Leone
S. Lan.	Sri Lanka	Sri Lanka
S. Mar.	San Marino	San Marino
Sol. Is.	Solomon Islands	Solomon Islands
Som.	Somaliya	Somalia
Sp.	España	Spain
S.S.R.	Sovetskaja Socialističeskaja Respublika	Soviet Socialist Republic
S.S.S.R.	Sojuz Sovetskich Socialističeskich Respublik	Union of Soviet Socialist Republics
St. Hel.	St. Helena	St. Helena
St. K.-N.	St. Kitts-Nevis	St. Kitts-Nevis
St. Luc.	St. Lucia	St. Lucia
S. Tom./P.	São Tomé e Príncipe	Sao Tome and Principe
St. P./M.	St.-Pierre-et-Miquelon	St. Pierre and Miquelon
St. Vin.	St. Vincent	St. Vincent
Sūd.	As-Sūdān	Sudan
Suomi	Suomi	Finland
Sur.	Suriname	Surinam
Sūriy.	As-Sūrīyah	Syria
Sval.	Svalbard og Jan Mayen	Svalbard and Jan Mayen
Sve.	Sverige	Sweden
Swaz.	Swaziland	Swaziland
T.a.a.f.	Terres australes et antarctiques françaises	French Southern and Antarctic Territories
Taehan	Taehan-Min'guk	South Korea
T'aiwan	T'aiwan	Taiwan
Tan.	Tanzania	Tanzania
Tchad	Tchad	Chad
T./C. Is.	Turks and Caicos Islands	Turks and Caicos Islands
Tenn., U.S.	Tennessee	Tennessee
Tex., U.S.	Texas	Texas
Thai.	Prathet Thai	Thailand
Togo	Togo	Togo
Tok. Is.	Tokelau Islands	Tokelau Islands
Tonga	Tonga	Tonga
Trin.	Trinidad and Tobago	Trinidad and Tobago
Tun.	Tunisie	Tunisia
Tür.	Türkiye	Turkey
Tuvalu	Tuvalu	Tuvalu
Ug.	Uganda	Uganda
U.K.	United Kingdom	United Kingdom
'Umān	'Umān	Oman
Ur.	Uruguay	Uruguay
Urd.	Al-Urdunn	Jordan
U.S.	United States	United States

LIST OF ABBREVIATIONS CON'T.

	LOCAL NAME	ENGLISH
U.S.S.R.	Sojuz Sovetskich Socialističeskich Respublik	Union of Soviet Socialist Republics
Utah, U.S.	Utah	Utah
Va., U.S.	Virginia	Virginia
Vat.	Città del Vaticano	Vatican City
Ven.	Venezuela	Venezuela
Viet.	Viet-nam	Vietnam
Vir. Is., U.S.	Virgin Islands	Virgin Islands (U.S.)
Vt., U.S.	Vermont	Vermont
Wake I.	Wake Island	Wake Island
Wales, U.K.	Wales	Wales
Wal./F.	Wallis et Futuna	Wallis and Futuna
Wash., U.S.	Washington	Washington
Wis., U.S.	Wisconsin	Wisconsin
W. Sam.	Western Samoa	Western Samoa
W. Va., U.S.	West Virginia	West Virginia
Wyo., U.S.	Wyoming	Wyoming
Yai.	Yaitopya	Ethiopia
Yaman	Al-Yaman	Yemen
Yam. S.	Al-Yaman ash-Sha'bīyah	People's Democratic Republic of Yemen
Yis.	Yisra'el	Israel
Yukon, Can.	Yukon	Yukon
Zaïre	Zaïre	Zaire
Zam.	Zambia	Zambia
Zhg.	Zhongguo	China

KEY TO SYMBOLS

- ∧ **Mountain**
- ∧[1] Volcano
- ∧[2] Hill
- ∧∧ **Mountains**
- ∧∧[1] Plateau
- ∧∧[2] Hills
-)(**Pass**
- ∨ **Valley, Canyon**
- ≚ **Plain**
- ≚[1] Basin
- ≚[2] Delta
- ≻ **Cape**
- ≻[1] Peninsula
- ≻[2] Spit, Sand Bar
- I **Island**
- I[1] Atoll
- I[2] Rock
- II **Islands**
- II[1] Rocks
- • **Other Topographic Features**
- •[1] Continent
- •[2] Coast, Beach
- •[3] Isthmus
- •[4] Cliff
- •[5] Cave, Caves
- •[6] Crater
- •[7] Depression
- •[8] Dunes
- •[9] Lava Flow
- ≃ **River**
- ≃[1] River Channel
- ≣ **Canal**
- ≣[1] Aqueduct
- ʟ **Waterfall, Rapids**
- ɰ **Strait**
- C **Bay, Gulf**
- C[1] Estuary
- C[2] Fjord
- C[3] Bight
- @ **Lake, Lakes**
- @[1] Reservoir
- ⋮ **Swamp**
- ⌂ **Ice Features, Glacier**
- ⊤ **Other Hydrographic Features**
- ⊤[1] Ocean
- ⊤[2] Sea
- ⊤[3] Anchorage
- ⊤[4] Oasis, Well, Spring
- ✢ **Submarine Features**
- ✢[1] Depression
- ✢[2] Reef, Shoal
- ✢[3] Mountain, Mountains
- ✢[4] Slope, Shelf
- □ **Political Unit**
- □[1] Independent Nation
- □[2] Dependency
- □[3] State, Canton, Republic
- □[4] Province, Region, Oblast
- □[5] Department, District, Prefecture
- □[6] County
- □[7] City, Municipality
- □[8] Miscellaneous
- □[9] Historical
- ʊ **Cultural Institution**
- ʊ[1] Religious Institution
- ʊ[2] Educational Institution
- ʊ[3] Scientific, Industrial Facility
- ⊥ **Historical Site**
- ♠ **Recreational Site**
- ⊠ **Airport**
- ▪ **Military Installation**
- ➛ **Miscellaneous**
- ➛[1] Region
- ➛[2] Desert
- ➛[3] Forest, Moor
- ➛[4] Reserve, Reservation
- ➛[5] Transportation
- ➛[6] Dam
- ➛[7] Mine, Quarry
- ➛[8] Neighborhood
- ➛[9] Shopping Center

Index

Name	Page	Lat° ′	Long° ′
A			
Aachen	72	50.47 N	6.05 E
Aaiun → El Aaiún	106	27.09 N	13.12 W
Aalen	72	48.50 N	10.05 E
Aalst (Alost)	74	50.56 N	4.02 E
Aarau	74	47.23 N	8.03 E
Aare ≃	74	47.37 N	8.13 E
Aarschot	72	50.59 N	4.50 E
Aba, Nig.	114	5.06 N	7.21 E
Aba, Zhg.	88	33.06 N	101.59 E
Abacaxis ≃	60	3.54 S	58.47 W
Ābādān	104	30.20 N	48.16 E
Abaetetuba	56	1.42 S	48.54 W
Abagaqi	88	43.41 N	114.40 E
Abai	62	25.58 S	55.57 W
Abaj	82	49.38 N	72.52 E
Abajo Mountains ∧∧	44	37.50 N	109.25 W
Abajo Peak ∧	44	37.51 N	109.28 W
Abakaliki	114	6.21 N	8.06 E
Abakan	84	53.43 N	91.26 E
Abakan ≃	84	53.43 N	91.30 E
Abancay	56	13.35 S	72.55 W
Abaokoro I	122t	1.30 N	173.01 E
Abashiri	90a	44.01 N	144.17 E
Abasolo	52	20.27 N	101.32 W
Abau	118	10.11 S	148.42 E
Abaya, Lake @	108	6.20 N	37.55 E
Abayita, Lake @	108	7.37 N	38.35 E
Abaza	84	52.39 N	90.06 E
Abbeville, Fr.	74	50.06 N	1.50 E
Abbeville, Ga., U.S.	36	31.59 N	83.18 W
Abbeville, La., U.S.	38	29.58 N	92.08 W
Abbeville, Miss., U.S.	38	34.25 N	89.37 W
Abbeville, S.C., U.S.	36	34.11 N	82.23 W
Abbey Head ≻	70	54.46 N	3.58 W
Abbiategrasso	78	45.24 N	8.54 E
Abbotsford	34	44.57 N	90.19 W
Abbottābād	102	34.09 N	73.13 E
'Abd al-Kūrī I	100	12.12 N	52.15 E
'Abd Allāh, Khawr ɰ	104	29.50 N	48.20 E
Abdulino	82	53.42 N	53.40 E
Abe, Lake @	108	11.06 N	41.50 E
Abéché	108	13.49 N	20.49 E
Abengourou	114	6.44 N	3.29 W
Abeokuta	114	7.10 N	3.26 E
Abercorn → Mbala	110	8.50 S	31.22 E
Aberdare	70	51.43 N	3.27 W
Aberdeen, Scot., U.K.	70	57.10 N	2.04 W
Aberdeen, Idaho, U.S.	46	42.57 N	112.50 W
Aberdeen, Md., U.S.	32	39.30 N	76.10 W
Aberdeen, Miss., U.S.	38	33.49 N	88.33 W
Aberdeen, N.C., U.S.	36	35.08 N	79.26 W
Aberdeen, S. Dak., U.S.	42	45.28 N	98.29 W
Aberdeen, Wash., U.S.	46	46.59 N	123.50 W
Aberdeen Lake @	22	64.27 N	99.00 W
Abernathy	40	33.50 N	101.51 W
Aberystwyth	70	52.25 N	4.05 W
Abhā	100	18.13 N	42.30 E
Abiaca Creek ≃	38	33.20 N	90.15 W
Abidjan	114	5.19 N	4.02 W
Abilene, Kans., U.S.	42	38.55 N	97.13 W
Abilene, Tex., U.S.	40	32.27 N	99.44 W
Abingdon, Ill., U.S.	34	40.48 N	90.24 W
Abingdon, Va., U.S.	36	36.43 N	81.59 W
Abington Reefs ✢[2]	118	18.00 S	149.36 E
Āb-i-Panja (P'andž) ≃	82	37.06 N	68.20 E
Abiquiu	44	36.12 N	106.19 W
Abiquiu Reservoir @[1]	44	36.18 N	106.32 W
Abita Springs	38	30.29 N	90.02 W
Abitau ≃	22	59.53 N	109.03 W
Abitibi, Lake @	34	48.42 N	79.45 W
Abnūb	112	27.16 N	31.09 E
Abohar	102	30.09 N	74.11 E
Abomey	114	7.11 N	1.59 E
Abongabong, Gunung ∧	94	4.15 N	96.48 E
Abong Mbang	106	3.59 N	13.10 E
Abony	72	47.11 N	20.01 E
Aborigen, Pik ∧	84	61.59 N	149.19 E
Abou Deïa	108	11.27 N	19.17 E
Abra Pampa	62	22.43 S	65.42 W
Absaroka Range ∧∧	46	44.45 N	109.50 W
Absarokee	46	45.31 N	109.27 W
Absecon	32	39.26 N	74.30 W
Abū 'Alī I	104	27.20 N	49.33 E
Abū Ḥamad	112	19.32 N	33.19 E
Abū Kamāl	104	34.27 N	40.55 E
Abū Madd, Ra's ≻	104	24.50 N	37.07 E
Abū Mūsā, Jazīreh-ye I	104	25.52 N	55.03 E
Abunã	56	9.42 S	65.23 W
Abuná ≃	56	9.41 S	65.23 W
Abu Road	100	24.29 N	72.47 E
Abū Shajarah, Ra's ≻	112	21.04 N	37.14 E
Abū Ẓaby	104	24.28 N	54.22 E
Acámbaro	52	20.02 N	100.44 W
Acaponeta	52	22.30 N	105.22 W
Acapulco [de Juárez]	52	16.51 N	99.55 W
Acarai Mountains ∧∧	60	1.50 N	57.40 W
Acaraú	56	2.53 S	40.07 W
Acarigua	60	9.33 N	69.12 W
Acatlán [de Osorio]	52	18.12 N	98.03 W
Acay, Nevado de ∧	62	24.21 S	66.12 W
Acayucan	52	17.57 N	94.55 W
Accomac	36	37.43 N	75.40 W
Accoville	36	37.46 N	81.50 W
Accra	114	5.33 N	0.13 W
Acerra	78	40.57 N	14.22 E
Achacachi	56	16.03 S	68.43 W
Achalpur	102	21.16 N	77.31 E
Acheng	88	45.32 N	126.59 E
Achtuba ≃	64	46.42 N	48.00 E
Achtubinsk	82	48.17 N	46.10 E
Achtyrka	82	50.19 N	34.55 E
Ačinsk	84	56.17 N	90.30 E
Acireale	78	37.37 N	15.10 E
Ačisaj	82	43.35 N	68.53 E
Ackerly	40	32.32 N	101.43 W
Ackerman	38	33.19 N	89.10 W
Ackley	34	42.33 N	93.03 W
Acklins Island I	50	22.26 N	73.58 W
Acomita	44	35.03 N	107.35 W
Aconcagua, Cerro ∧	62	32.39 S	70.01 W
Acqui Terme	78	44.41 N	8.28 E
Acre ≃	56	8.45 S	67.22 W
Acton	34	43.37 N	80.02 W
Acton Vale	32	45.39 N	72.34 W
Actopan	52	20.16 N	98.56 W
Acworth	36	34.04 N	84.41 W
Ada, Minn., U.S.	42	47.18 N	96.31 W
Ada, Ohio, U.S.	32	40.46 N	83.49 W
Ada, Okla., U.S.	40	34.46 N	96.41 W
Adair, Iowa, U.S.	42	41.30 N	94.39 W
Adair, Okla., U.S.	38	36.26 N	95.16 W
Adair, Cape ≻	22	71.24 N	71.13 W
Adairsville	36	34.22 N	84.56 W
Adairville	38	36.40 N	86.51 W
Adak	24	51.54 N	176.35 W
Adak Island I	24	51.45 N	176.40 W
Ādam	100	22.24 N	57.32 E
Adam, Mount ∧	58	51.36 S	59.55 W
Adamawa ∧∧	106	7.00 N	12.00 E
Adamello ∧∧	74	46.10 N	10.35 E
Adams, Minn., U.S.	34	43.34 N	92.43 W
Adams, Nebr., U.S.	42	40.28 N	96.31 W
Adams, N. Dak., U.S.	42	48.25 N	98.05 W
Adams, N.Y., U.S.	32	43.49 N	76.01 W
Adams, Tenn., U.S.	38	36.35 N	87.04 W
Adams, Wis., U.S.	34	43.58 N	89.49 W
Adams, Mount ∧	46	46.12 N	121.28 W
Adams Bridge ✢[2]	100	9.04 N	79.37 E
Adams Lake @	26	51.13 N	119.33 W
Adams Peak ∧	100	6.48 N	80.30 E
Adams Rock I[2]	122e	25.04 S	130.05 W
Adamstown	122e	25.04 S	130.05 W
Adamsville	38	35.14 N	88.23 W
Adana	104	37.01 N	35.18 E
Adapazarı	64	40.46 N	30.24 E
Adarama	112	17.05 N	34.54 E
Adavale	118	25.55 S	144.36 E
Adda ≃	78	45.08 N	9.53 E
Ad-Dabbah	112	18.03 N	30.57 E
Ad-Dahnā' ➛[2]	104	24.30 N	48.10 E
Ad-Dāmir	108	17.35 N	33.58 E
Ad-Dammām	104	26.26 N	50.07 E
Ad-Dawādimī	100	24.28 N	44.18 E
Ad-Dawḥah (Doha)	104	25.17 N	51.32 E
Aḍ-Ḍiffah (Libyan Plateau) ∧∧[1]	112	30.30 N	25.30 E
Addis	38	30.21 N	91.16 W
Addis Ababa → Addis Abeba	108	9.00 N	38.50 E
Addis Abeba	108	9.00 N	38.50 E
Addison	34	41.59 N	84.21 W
Ad-Dīwānīyah	104	31.59 N	44.56 E
Ad-Duwaym	112	14.00 N	32.19 E
Adel, Ga., U.S.	36	31.08 N	83.25 W
Adel, Iowa, U.S.	34	41.37 N	94.01 W
Adelaide, Austl.	118	34.55 S	138.35 E
Adelaide, Ba.	54b	25.00 N	77.31 W
Adelaide Peninsula ≻[1]	22	68.09 N	97.45 W
Adèle Island I	118	15.32 S	123.09 E
Aden	100	12.45 N	45.12 E
Aden, Gulf of C	100	12.30 N	48.00 E
Ader ∧∧[1]	114	14.10 N	5.05 E
Adieu, Cape ≻	118	31.59 S	132.09 E
Adige ≃	78	45.10 N	12.20 E
Adigrat	108	14.18 N	39.31 E
Ādilābād	100	19.40 N	78.32 E
Adimi	84	47.20 N	138.56 E
Adin	48	41.12 N	120.57 W
Adirondack Mountains ∧∧	32	44.00 N	74.00 W
Adjuntas	54m	18.10 N	66.43 W
Admiralty Bay C	55h	13.00 N	61.16 W
Admiralty Gulf C	118	14.20 S	125.50 E
Admiralty Inlet C	22	73.00 N	86.00 W
Admiralty Island I, N.W. Ter., Can.	22	69.30 N	101.00 W
Admiralty Island I, Alaska, U.S.	24	57.50 N	134.30 W
Ado-Ekiti	114	7.38 N	5.12 E
Adonara, Pulau I	96	8.20 S	123.10 E
Ādoni	100	15.38 N	77.17 E
Adra	76	36.44 N	3.01 W
Adrano	78	37.40 N	14.50 E
Adrar	106	27.54 N	0.17 W
Adrar ➛[1]	106	20.30 N	13.30 W
Adria	78	45.03 N	12.03 E
Adrian, Ga., U.S.	36	32.32 N	82.35 W
Adrian, Mich., U.S.	34	41.54 N	84.02 W
Adrian, Minn., U.S.	42	43.38 N	95.56 W
Adrian, Mo., U.S.	38	38.24 N	94.21 W
Adrian, Oreg., U.S.	46	43.44 N	117.04 W
Adrian, Tex., U.S.	40	35.16 N	102.40 W
Adrian, W. Va., U.S.	32	38.54 N	80.17 W
Advance	38	37.06 N	89.55 W
Adwa	108	14.10 N	38.55 E
Adyča ≃	84	68.13 N	134.41 E
Aegean Sea ⊤[2]	80	38.30 N	25.00 E
Aeon Point ≻	122o	1.46 N	157.11 W
A'erjinshanmai ∧∧	88	37.30 N	86.30 E
Aershan	88	47.11 N	119.57 E
Afareaitu	122s	17.33 S	149.47 W
Affton	38	38.33 N	90.20 W
Afghanistan □[1]	100	33.00 N	65.00 E
Afikpo	114	5.53 N	7.56 E
Afono Bay C	122u	14.15 S	170.39 W
Afton, Iowa, U.S.	38	41.02 N	94.12 W
Afton, N.Y., U.S.	32	42.14 N	75.32 W
Afton, Okla., U.S.	38	36.42 N	94.58 W
Afton, Wyo., U.S.	44	42.44 N	110.56 W
Agadez	114	16.58 N	7.59 E
Agadir	106	30.26 N	9.36 W
Agadyr'	82	48.17 N	72.53 E
Agalega Islands II	110	10.24 S	56.37 E
Agan ≃	84	61.23 N	74.35 E
Agana	122p	13.28 N	144.45 E
Agapa	84	71.27 N	89.15 E
Agartala	102	23.49 N	91.16 E
Agat	122p	13.24 N	144.39 E
Agat Bay C	122p	13.24 N	144.39 E
Agate	42	39.28 N	103.56 W
Agate Beach	46	44.41 N	124.04 W
Agboville	114	5.56 N	4.13 W
Agege	114	6.37 N	3.20 E
Agen	74	44.12 N	0.37 E
Agency	34	41.00 N	92.18 W
Agency Lake @	46	42.32 N	121.58 W
Aggteleki Barlang •[5]	72	48.30 N	20.32 E
Āghā Jārī	104	30.42 N	49.50 E
Aginskoje	84	55.15 N	94.55 E
Agira	78	37.39 N	14.32 E
Agnew	118	28.01 S	120.30 E
Āgra	102	27.11 N	78.01 E
Agrigento	78	37.18 N	13.35 E
Agrihan I	92	18.46 N	145.40 E
Agrínion	80	38.37 N	21.24 E
Agro Pontino ➛[1]	78	41.25 N	12.55 E
Aguachica	60	8.19 N	73.38 W
Aguada	54m	18.23 N	67.11 W
Aguadas	60	5.37 N	75.27 W
Aguadilla	54m	18.26 N	67.09 W
Aguadulce, Pan.	60	8.15 N	80.33 W
Agua Dulce, Tex., U.S.	40	27.47 N	97.54 W
Agua Fria ≃	44	33.23 N	112.21 W
Aguanus ≃	30	50.13 N	62.05 W
Agua Prieta	52	31.18 N	109.34 W
Aguarico ≃	60	0.59 S	75.11 W
Aguascalientes	52	21.53 N	102.18 W
Agu Bay C	22	70.18 N	86.30 W
Agudos	62	22.28 S	49.00 W
Águeda ≃	76	41.02 N	6.56 W
Aguijan I	92	14.51 N	145.34 E
Aguila	44	33.56 N	113.11 W
Aguilar	42	37.24 N	104.46 W
Águilas	76	37.24 N	1.35 W
Agulhas, Cape ≻	116	34.52 S	20.00 E
Agulhas Negras, Pico das ∧	58	22.23 S	44.38 W
Agusan ≃	98	9.00 N	125.31 E
Agustín Codazzi	60	10.02 N	73.14 W
Ahaggar ∧∧	106	23.00 N	6.30 E
Ahaggar, Tassili du ∧∧[1]	106	21.00 N	6.00 E
Aha Hills ∧∧[2]	116	19.45 S	21.10 E
Ahar	104	38.28 N	47.04 E
Ahklun Mountains ∧∧	24	59.15 N	161.00 W
Ahlen	72	51.46 N	7.53 E
Ahmadābād	102	23.02 N	72.37 E
Ahmadnagar	100	19.05 N	74.45 E
Ahmadpur East	102	29.09 N	71.16 E
Ahmar Mountains ∧∧	108	9.15 N	41.00 E
Ahoskie	36	36.17 N	76.59 W
Ahrensburg	72	53.40 N	10.14 E
Ahtanum Creek ≃	46	46.32 N	120.31 W
Ahuacatlán	52	21.03 N	104.29 W
Ahvāz	104	31.19 N	48.42 E
Ahvenanmaa (Åland) II	68	60.15 N	20.00 E
Aḥwar	100	13.31 N	46.42 E
Aibihu @	88	44.55 N	82.55 E
Aibonito	54m	18.08 N	66.16 W
Aiguá, Arroyo del ≃	62	33.38 S	54.23 W
Aihun	88	50.13 N	127.33 E
Aijal	102	23.44 N	92.43 E
Aiken	36	33.34 N	81.43 W
Ailaoshan ∧∧	94	24.08 N	101.25 E
Ailsa Craig I	70	55.16 N	5.07 W
Aim	84	58.50 N	134.12 E
Aimorés	56	19.30 S	41.04 W
Ainsworth	42	42.33 N	99.52 W
Aïr ∧∧	114	18.00 N	8.30 E
Aire ≃	74	49.19 N	4.49 E
Air Force Island I	22	67.55 N	74.10 W
Aisch ≃	72	49.46 N	11.01 E
Aishihik Lake @	24	61.25 N	137.06 W
Aïssa, Djebel ∧	106	32.51 N	0.30 W
Aitape	92	3.08 S	142.21 E
Aitkin	34	46.32 N	93.43 W
Aiud	80	46.19 N	23.44 E
Aiurua, Passe d' ɰ	122s	17.49 S	149.07 W
Aix-en-Provence	74	43.32 N	5.26 E
Aíyion	80	38.15 N	22.05 E
Aiyon	123b	7.43 N	134.37 E
Aizpute	86	56.43 N	21.38 E
Aizu-wakamatsu	90	37.30 N	139.56 E
Ajaccio	78	41.55 N	8.44 E
Ajaguz	84	47.56 N	80.23 E
Ajan	84	56.27 N	138.10 E
Ajan ≃	84	70.10 N	95.50 E
Ajanta	100	20.30 N	75.48 E
Ajanta Range ∧∧	100	20.30 N	76.00 E
Ajax	34	43.51 N	79.02 W
Ajayan Point ≻	122p	13.15 N	144.43 E
Ajdābiyah	108	30.48 N	20.14 E
Ajjer, Tassili n' ∧∧[1]	106	25.10 N	8.00 E
Ajmer	102	26.27 N	74.38 E
Ajo	44	32.22 N	112.52 W
Ajon, Ostrov I	84	69.50 N	168.40 E
Ajtos	80	42.42 N	27.15 E
Akademii, Zaliv C	84	54.15 N	138.05 E
Akaroa Harbour C	120	43.50 S	172.56 E
'Akasha East	112	21.05 N	30.43 E
Akashi	90	34.38 N	134.59 E
Akeley	34	47.00 N	94.44 W
Akesu	88	41.10 N	80.20 E
Aketi	108	2.44 N	23.46 E
Akharnai	80	38.05 N	23.44 E
Akhisar	80	38.55 N	27.51 E
Akiachak	24	60.55 N	161.27 W
Akimiski Island I	22	53.00 N	81.20 W
Akita	90	39.43 N	140.07 E
Akjoujt	114	19.45 N	14.23 W
Akkerman → Belgorod-Dnestrovskij	82	46.12 N	30.20 E
'Akko (Acre)	104	32.55 N	35.05 E
Akkol', S.S.S.R.	82	45.02 N	75.40 E
Akkol', S.S.S.R.	82	43.25 N	70.47 E
Aklavik	24	68.12 N	135.00 W
'Aklé 'Âduâna ➛[1]	114	18.00 N	5.30 W
Akobo ≃	112	7.48 N	33.03 E
Akola	100	20.42 N	77.00 E
Akordat	108	15.35 N	37.54 E
Akpatok Island I	22	60.25 N	68.00 W
Akranes	66a	64.18 N	22.02 W
Akron, Colo., U.S.	42	40.10 N	103.13 W
Akron, Ind., U.S.	38	41.02 N	86.01 W
Akron, Iowa, U.S.	42	42.49 N	96.33 W
Akron, N.Y., U.S.	32	43.01 N	78.30 W
Akron, Ohio, U.S.	32	41.05 N	81.31 W
Akron, Pa., U.S.	32	40.09 N	76.12 W
Aksaray	100	38.23 N	34.03 E
Aksarka	84	66.36 N	67.46 E
Akşehir	100	38.21 N	31.25 E
Aksuat	84	47.48 N	82.50 E
Aksum	108	14.08 N	38.48 E
Aktogaj	84	46.57 N	79.40 E
Akt'ubinsk	82	50.17 N	57.10 E
Akure	114	7.15 N	5.12 E
Akureyri	66a	65.44 N	18.08 W
Akžar	84	47.35 N	83.42 E
Alabama □[3]	20	32.50 N	87.00 W
Alabama ≃	38	31.08 N	87.57 W
Alabaster	38	33.15 N	86.49 W
Alachua	36	29.47 N	82.30 W
Alagir	82	43.03 N	44.14 E
Alagoa Grande	56	7.03 S	35.38 W
Alagoinhas	56	12.07 S	38.26 W
Alajskij Chrebet ∧∧	82	39.45 N	72.00 E
Alakol', Ozero @	84	46.10 N	81.45 E
Al-'Alamayn	112	30.49 N	28.57 E
Alamagan I	92	17.36 N	145.50 E
Al-'Amārah	104	31.50 N	47.09 E
Alameda, Calif., U.S.	48	37.46 N	122.16 W
Alameda, N. Mex., U.S.	44	35.11 N	106.37 W
Alamein → Al-'Alamayn	112	30.49 N	28.57 E
Alamo, Ga., U.S.	36	32.09 N	82.47 W
Alamo, Nev., U.S.	48	37.22 N	115.10 W
Alamo, Tenn., U.S.	38	35.47 N	89.07 W
Alamo ≃	48	33.14 N	115.39 W
Alamogordo	44	32.54 N	105.57 W
Alamo Heights	40	29.28 N	98.28 W
Alamo Lake @[1]	44	34.20 N	113.30 W
Alamosa	44	37.28 N	105.52 W
Alamosa ≃, Colo., U.S.	44	37.22 N	105.46 W
Alamosa ≃, N. Mex., U.S.	44	33.20 N	107.21 W
Aland Sea ⊤[2]	68	60.00 N	19.30 E
Alanson	34	45.27 N	84.47 W
Alanya	100	36.33 N	32.01 E
Alaotra, Lac @	117b	17.30 S	48.30 E
Alapaha	36	31.23 N	83.13 W
Alapaha ≃	36	30.26 N	83.06 W
Alapajevsk	82	57.52 N	61.42 E
Al-'Aqabah	104	29.31 N	35.00 E
Alarcón, Embalse de @[1]	76	39.36 N	2.10 W
Al-'Arīsh	112	31.08 N	33.48 E
Alashanyouqi	88	40.02 N	103.33 E
Alaska □[3]	24	65.00 N	153.00 W
Alaska, Gulf of C	24	58.00 N	146.00 W
Alaska Peninsula ≻[1]	24	57.00 N	158.00 W
Alaska Range ∧∧	24	62.30 N	150.00 W
Alassio	78	44.00 N	8.10 E
Al-'Aṭrūn	112	18.11 N	26.36 E
Alatyr'	66	54.51 N	46.36 E
Alausí	60	2.12 S	78.50 W
Alazeja ≃	84	70.51 N	153.34 E
Al-'Azīzīyah	108	32.32 N	13.01 E
Alba, It.	78	44.42 N	8.02 E
Alba, Mich., U.S.	34	44.59 N	84.58 W
Alba, Tex., U.S.	40	32.48 N	95.38 W
Albacete	76	38.59 N	1.51 W
Alba-Iulia	80	46.04 N	23.35 E
Albanel, Lac @	22	50.55 N	73.12 W
Albania □[1]	64	41.00 N	20.00 E
Albano Laziale	78	41.44 N	12.39 E
Albany, Austl.	118	35.02 S	117.53 E
Albany, Ga., U.S.	36	31.35 N	84.10 W
Albany, Ill., U.S.	34	41.47 N	90.13 W
Albany, Ind., U.S.	38	40.18 N	85.14 W
Albany, Ky., U.S.	38	36.42 N	85.08 W
Albany, Minn., U.S.	34	45.38 N	94.34 W
Albany, Mo., U.S.	38	40.15 N	94.20 W
Albany, N.Y., U.S.	32	42.39 N	73.45 W
Albany, Ohio, U.S.	32	39.14 N	82.12 W
Albany, Oreg., U.S.	46	44.38 N	123.06 W
Albany, Tex., U.S.	40	32.44 N	99.18 W
Albany, Wis., U.S.	34	42.43 N	89.26 W
Albany ≃	22	52.17 N	81.31 W
Albardón	62	31.26 S	68.32 W
Al-Baṣrah (Basra)	104	30.30 N	47.47 E
Albatross Bay C	118	12.45 S	141.43 E
Al-Bawīṭī	112	28.21 N	28.52 E
Albegna ≃	78	42.30 N	11.11 E
Albemarle	36	35.21 N	80.12 W
Albemarle Sound ɰ	36	36.03 N	76.12 W
Albenga	78	44.03 N	8.13 E
Alberene	36	37.53 N	78.37 W
Alberga Creek ≃	118	27.06 S	135.33 E
Albert	74	50.00 N	2.39 E
Albert, Lake @	110	1.40 N	31.00 E
Alberta	38	32.14 N	87.25 W
Alberta □[4]	22	54.00 N	113.00 W
Albert City	42	42.47 N	94.57 W
Albert Edward Bay C	22	69.32 N	103.00 W
Al'bertin	86	53.05 N	25.23 E
Albertirsa	72	47.15 N	19.38 E
Albert Lea	34	43.39 N	93.22 W
Alberton, P.E.I., Can.	30	46.49 N	64.04 W
Alberton, Mont., U.S.	46	47.00 N	114.29 W
Albertville, Fr.	74	45.41 N	6.23 E
Albertville, Ala., U.S.	38	34.16 N	86.12 W
Albertville → Kalemi, Zaïre	110	5.56 S	29.12 E
Albi	74	43.56 N	2.09 E
Albia	34	41.02 N	92.48 W
Albina	56	5.30 N	54.03 W
Albino	78	45.46 N	9.47 E
Albion, Calif., U.S.	48	39.13 N	123.46 W
Albion, Idaho, U.S.	46	42.25 N	113.35 W
Albion, Ill., U.S.	38	38.23 N	88.04 W
Albion, Ind., U.S.	38	41.24 N	85.25 W
Albion, Mich., U.S.	34	42.15 N	84.45 W
Albion, Nebr., U.S.	42	41.42 N	98.00 W
Albion, N.Y., U.S.	32	43.15 N	78.12 W
Albion, Pa., U.S.	32	41.53 N	80.22 W
Albion, Wash., U.S.	46	46.48 N	117.15 W
Albo, Monte ∧	78	40.29 N	9.33 E
Alborán, Isla de I	76	35.58 N	3.02 W
Alborz, Reshteh-ye Kūhhā-ye ∧∧	104	36.00 N	53.00 E
Ālbū Gharz, Sabkhat @	104	34.45 N	41.15 E
Albuquerque	44	35.05 N	106.40 W
Alburg	32	44.59 N	73.18 W
Albury	118	36.05 S	146.55 E
Alcalá de Guadaira	76	37.20 N	5.50 W
Alcalá de Henares	76	40.29 N	3.22 W
Alcalde	44	36.05 N	106.03 W
Alcamo	78	37.59 N	12.58 E
Alcañiz	76	41.03 N	0.08 W
Alcântara	56	2.24 S	44.24 W
Alcantarilla	76	37.58 N	1.13 W
Alcázar de San Juan	76	39.24 N	3.12 W
Alcester	42	43.01 N	96.38 W
Alcira	76	39.09 N	0.26 W
Alcoa	36	35.48 N	83.59 W
Alcobaça	56	17.30 S	39.13 W
Alcolu	36	33.45 N	80.13 W
Alcorn College	38	31.52 N	91.09 W
Alcovy ≃	36	33.26 N	83.50 W
Alcoy	76	38.42 N	0.28 W
Aldabra Islands I[1]	110	9.25 S	46.22 E
Aldama	52	28.51 N	105.54 W
Aldan ≃	84	63.28 N	129.35 E
Aldanskoje Nagorje ∧∧[1]	84	57.00 N	127.00 E
Alden, Iowa, U.S.	34	42.31 N	93.23 W
Alden, Mich., U.S.	34	44.53 N	85.17 W
Alden, Minn., U.S.	34	43.40 N	93.34 W
Alder Lake @[1]	46	0.00	0.00
Alderney I	70	49.43 N	2.12 W
Aldershot	70	51.15 N	0.47 W
Alderson	36	37.43 N	80.39 W
Aledo	34	41.12 N	90.45 W
Aleg	114	17.03 N	13.55 W
Alegrete	62	29.46 S	55.46 W
Alegros Mountain ∧	44	34.09 N	108.11 W
Alejandro Selkirk, Isla (Isla Más Afuera) I	58	33.45 S	80.46 W
Alejsk	84	52.58 N	82.45 E
Aleknagik	24	59.17 N	158.38 W
Aleksandrija	82	48.40 N	33.07 E
Aleksandro-Nevskij	86	53.28 N	40.13 E
Aleksandrov	86	56.24 N	38.43 E
Aleksandrov Gaj	82	50.09 N	48.34 E
Aleksandrovsk	82	48.35 N	39.12 E
Aleksandrovskoje	84	60.26 N	77.50 E
Aleksandrovsk-Sachalinskij	84	50.54 N	142.10 E
Aleksejevka, S.S.S.R.	82	51.59 N	70.59 E
Aleksejevka, S.S.S.R.	82	50.37 N	38.42 E
Aleksejevsk	84	57.50 N	108.23 E
Aleksin	86	54.31 N	37.05 E
Aleksinac	80	43.32 N	21.43 E
Alemania	62	25.36 S	65.38 W
Alençon	74	48.26 N	0.05 E
Alenquer	56	1.56 S	54.46 W
Alenuihaha Channel ɰ	49a	20.26 N	156.00 W
Alert Bay	26	50.35 N	126.55 W
Alès	74	44.08 N	4.05 E
Alessandria	78	44.54 N	8.37 E
Ålesund	68	62.28 N	6.09 E
Aletai	88	47.52 N	88.07 E
Aleutian Islands II	24	52.00 N	176.00 W
Aleutka	84	45.57 N	150.10 E
Alevina, Mys ≻	84	58.50 N	151.20 E
Alex	40	34.55 N	97.47 W
Alexander	42	47.51 N	103.39 W
Alexander, Cape ≻	123e	6.35 S	156.30 E
Alexander Archipelago II	24	56.30 N	134.00 W
Alexander Bay	116	28.40 S	16.30 E
Alexander City	38	32.56 N	85.57 W
Alexandra	120	45.15 S	169.24 E
Alexandra Falls ʟ	22	60.29 N	116.18 W
Alexandria → Al-Iskandarīyah, Miṣr	112	31.12 N	29.54 E
Alexandria, Rom.	80	43.58 N	25.20 E
Alexandria, Ind., U.S.	38	40.16 N	85.41 W
Alexandria, Ky., U.S.	32	38.58 N	84.23 W
Alexandria, La., U.S.	38	31.18 N	92.27 W
Alexandria, Minn., U.S.	42	45.53 N	95.22 W
Alexandria, Mo., U.S.	38	40.27 N	91.28 W
Alexandria, Nebr., U.S.	42	40.15 N	97.23 W
Alexandria, S. Dak., U.S.	42	43.39 N	97.47 W
Alexandria, Tenn., U.S.	38	36.05 N	86.02 W
Alexandria, Va., U.S.	32	38.48 N	77.03 W
Alexandria Bay	32	44.20 N	75.55 W
Alexandrina, Lake @	118	35.26 S	139.10 E
Alexandroúpolis	80	40.50 N	25.52 E
Alexis	34	41.04 N	90.33 W
Alfaro	60	2.12 S	79.50 W
Al-Fāshir	112	13.38 N	25.21 E
Al-Fayyūm	112	29.19 N	30.50 E
Alfeld	72	51.59 N	9.50 E
Alfenas	62	21.26 S	45.57 W
Alfred, Maine, U.S.	32	43.29 N	70.43 W
Alfred, N.Y., U.S.	32	42.15 N	77.47 W
Alga	82	49.46 N	57.20 E
Algeciras	76	36.08 N	5.30 W
Algemesí	76	39.11 N	0.26 W
Alger (Algiers), Alg.	106	36.47 N	3.03 E
Alger, Ohio, U.S.	32	40.42 N	83.51 W
Algeria □[1]	106	28.00 N	3.00 E
Al-Gharbīyah, Aṣ-Ṣaḥrā' (Western Desert) ➛[2]	108	27.00 N	27.00 E
Al-Ghayḍah	100	16.12 N	52.15 E
Alghero	78	40.34 N	8.19 E
Al-Ghurdaqah	112	27.14 N	33.50 E
Algiers → Alger	106	36.42 N	3.08 E
Algodones	44	35.23 N	106.29 W
Algoma	34	44.36 N	87.27 W
Algona	34	43.04 N	94.14 W
Algonac	34	42.37 N	82.32 W
Algonquin	34	42.10 N	88.18 W
Algood, Tenn., U.S.	36		
	38	36.12 N	85.27 W
Algorta, Esp.	76	43.22 N	3.01 W
Algorta, Ur.	62	32.25 S	57.23 W
Al-Ḥadīthah	104	34.07 N	42.23 E
Al-Ḥajarah ➛[1]	104	30.00 N	44.00 E
Al-Ḥamād ≚	104	32.00 N	39.30 E
Al-Ḥarīq	104	23.37 N	46.31 E
Al-Harūj al-Aswad ∧∧[2]	108	27.00 N	17.10 E
Al-Ḥasakah	104	36.29 N	40.45 E
Alhaurín el Grande	76	36.38 N	4.41 W
Al-Ḥawrah	100	13.49 N	47.37 E
Al-Ḥayy	100	32.10 N	46.03 E
Al-Ḥijāz ➛[1]	104	24.30 N	38.30 E
Al-Ḥillah	104	32.29 N	44.25 E
Al-Hoceima	106	35.15 N	3.55 W
Al Hoceima, Baie d' C	76	35.20 N	3.50 W
Alhucemas, Islas de II	76	35.13 N	3.53 W
Al-Ḥudaydah	100	14.48 N	42.57 E
Al-Hufūf	104	25.22 N	49.34 E
Al-Ḥulwah	100	23.27 N	46.47 E
Aliaksin, Cape ≻	24	55.30 N	160.43 W
Alībāg	100	18.39 N	72.53 E
Alicante	76	38.21 N	0.29 W
Alice	40	27.45 N	98.04 W
Alicedale	116	33.19 S	26.05 E
Alice Springs	118	23.42 S	133.53 E
Aliceville	38	33.08 N	88.09 W
Alīgarh	102	27.54 N	78.05 E
Alima ≃	110	1.36 S	16.36 E
Alingsås	68	57.56 N	12.31 E
Aliquippa	32	40.37 N	80.15 W
Al-'Irq	108	29.02 N	21.33 E
Al-Iskandarīyah (Alexandria)	112	31.12 N	29.54 E
Al-Ismā'īlīyah	112	30.35 N	32.16 E
Aliwal North	116	30.45 S	26.45 E
Al-Jabal al-Akhḍar ∧∧	104	23.15 N	57.20 E
Al-Jaghbūb	112	29.45 N	24.31 E
Al-Jawārah	100	18.55 N	57.17 E
Al-Jawf, Ar. Sa.	104	29.50 N	39.52 E
Al-Jawf, Lībīya	112	24.11 N	23.19 E
Al-Jazīrah ➛[1]	112	14.25 N	33.00 E
Āl-Jilf Al-Kabīr, Hadabat ∧∧[1]	108	23.27 N	26.00 E
Al-Jīzah	112	30.01 N	31.13 E
Al-Julaydah ⊤[4]	104	29.03 N	45.38 E
Al-Junaynah	112	13.27 N	22.27 E
Alkali Creek ≃	46	43.16 N	107.40 W
Alkali Lake @, Nev., U.S.	48	41.42 N	119.50 W
Alkali Lake @, Oreg., U.S.	46	43.10 N	120.02 W
Al-Kāẓimīyah	104	33.22 N	44.20 E
Al-Khābūrah	100	23.59 N	57.08 E
Al-Khalīl	104	31.32 N	35.06 E
Al-Khandaq	112	18.36 N	30.34 E

Symbols in the index entries are identified on page 203.

Symbols in the index entries are identified on page 203.

Symbols in the index entries are identified on page 203.

Symbols in the index entries are identified on page 203.

Symbols in the index entries are identified on page 203.

Symbols in the index entries are identified on page 203.

Symbols in the index entries are identified on page 203.

Symbols in the index entries are identified on page 203.

Symbols in the index entries are identified on page 203.

Symbols in the index entries are identified on page 203.

Symbols in the index entries are identified on page 203.

Symbols in the index entries are identified on page 203.

Symbols in the index entries are identified on page 203.

Symbols in the index entries are identified on page 203.

Symbols in the index entries are identified on page 203.

Symbols in the index entries are identified on page 203.

Symbols in the index entries are identified on page 203.

Symbols in the index entries are identified on page 203.

Symbols in the index entries are identified on page 203.

Symbols in the index entries are identified on page 203.

Symbols in the index entries are identified on page 203.

Symbols in the index entries are identified on page 203.

Symbols in the index entries are identified on page 203.

Symbols in the index entries are identified on page 203.

Symbols in the index entries are identified on page 203.

Symbols in the index entries are identified on page 203.

Symbols in the index entries are identified on page 203.

Symbols in the index entries are identified on page 203.

Symbols in the index entries are identified on page 203.

Symbols in the index entries are identified on page 203.

Symbols in the index entries are identified on page 203.

Symbols in the index entries are identified on page 203.

Symbols in the index entries are identified on page 203.

Symbols in the index entries are identified on page 203.

Symbols in the index entries are identified on page 203.

Symbols in the index entries are identified on page 203.

Symbols in the index entries are identified on page 203.

Name	Page	Lat °′	Long °′
Wind ≃, Wyo., U.S.	46	43.35 N	108.13 W
Windber	32	40.14 N	78.50 W
Winder	36	32.59 N	83.43 W
Windhoek	116	22.34 S	17.06 E
Wind Lake	34	42.50 N	88.09 W
Windom	42	43.52 N	95.07 W
Windom Peak ▲	44	37.37 N	107.35 W
Windorah	118	25.26 S	142.39 E
Window Rock	44	35.41 N	109.03 W
Wind River Peak ▲	46	42.42 N	109.07 W
Windsor, N.S., Can.	30	44.59 N	64.08 W
Windsor, Ont., Can.	34	42.18 N	83.01 W
Windsor, Qué., Can.	32	45.34 N	72.00 W
Windsor, Eng., U.K.	70	51.29 N	0.38 W
Windsor, Calif., U.S.	48	38.33 N	122.49 W
Windsor, Colo., U.S.	44	40.29 N	104.54 W
Windsor, Conn., U.S.	32	41.51 N	72.39 W
Windsor, Ill., U.S.	38	39.26 N	88.36 W
Windsor, Mo., U.S.	38	38.32 N	93.31 W
Windsor, N.C., U.S.	36	36.00 N	76.57 W
Windsor, Vt., U.S.	32	43.29 N	72.23 W
Windsor, Va., U.S.	36	36.48 N	76.45 W
Windsor Forest	36	32.56 N	81.11 W
Windsor Locks	32	41.56 N	72.38 W
Windthorst	40	33.34 N	98.26 W
Windward Islands II	50	13.00 N	61.00 W
Windward Passage ⊔	50	20.00 N	73.50 W
Windy Peak ▲, Colo., U.S.	44	38.21 N	106.16 W
Windy Peak ▲, Wash., U.S.	46	48.56 N	119.58 W
Winfield, Ala., U.S.	38	33.56 N	87.49 W
Winfield, Iowa, U.S.	34	41.07 N	91.26 W
Winfield, Kans., U.S.	42	37.15 N	96.59 W
Winfield, Mo., U.S.	38	39.00 N	90.44 W
Winfield, W. Va., U.S.	32	38.32 N	81.53 W
Wing	42	47.09 N	100.17 W
Wingate	36	34.59 N	80.27 W
Wingham	34	43.53 N	81.19 W
Wingo	38	36.39 N	88.45 W
Winifred	46	47.04 N	109.23 W
Winisk	22	55.15 N	85.12 W
Winisk ≃	22	55.17 N	85.05 W
Winisk Lake ⊜	22	52.55 N	87.22 W
Wink	40	31.45 N	103.09 W
Winkelman	44	32.59 N	110.46 W
Winkler	28	49.11 N	97.56 W
Winneba	114	5.25 N	0.36 W
Winnebago, Ill., U.S.	34	42.16 N	89.15 W
Winnebago, Minn., U.S.	34	43.46 N	94.10 W
Winnebago, Nebr., U.S.	42	42.14 N	96.28 W
Winnebago ≃	34	43.03 N	92.57 W
Winnebago, Lake ⊜	34	44.00 N	88.25 W
Winneconne	34	44.07 N	88.43 W
Winnemucca	48	40.58 N	117.44 W
Winner	42	43.22 N	99.51 W
Winnetka	34	42.07 N	87.44 W
Winnett	46	47.00 N	108.21 W
Winnfield	38	31.55 N	92.38 W
Winnibigoshish, Lake ⊜	34	47.27 N	94.12 W
Winnie	38	29.49 N	94.23 W
Winnipeg	28	49.53 N	97.09 W
Winnipeg ≃	22	50.38 N	96.19 W
Winnipeg, Lake ⊜	28	52.00 N	97.00 W
Winnipegosis, Lake ⊜	28	52.30 N	100.00 W
Winnipesaukee, Lake ⊜	32	43.35 N	71.20 W
Winnsboro, La., U.S.	38	32.10 N	91.43 W
Winnsboro, S.C., U.S.	36	34.22 N	81.05 W
Winnsboro, Tex., U.S.	40	32.58 N	95.17 W
Winnsboro Mills	36	34.22 N	81.06 W
Winona, Kans., U.S.	42	39.04 N	101.15 W
Winona, Mich., U.S.	34	46.52 N	88.55 W
Winona, Minn., U.S.	34	44.03 N	91.39 W
Winona, Miss., U.S.	38	33.29 N	89.44 W
Winona, Mo., U.S.	38	37.06 N	91.19 W
Winona Lake	38	41.14 N	85.49 W
Winooski	32	44.29 N	73.11 W
Winooski ≃	32	44.30 N	73.15 W
Winooski, North Branch ≃	32	44.15 N	72.35 W
Winschoten	72	53.08 N	7.02 E
Winside	42	42.11 N	97.10 W
Winslow, Ariz., U.S.	44	35.01 N	110.42 W
Winslow, Maine, U.S.	32	44.32 N	69.38 W
Winsted, Conn., U.S.	32	41.55 N	73.04 W
Winsted, Minn., U.S.	34	44.58 N	94.03 W
Winston, Fla., U.S.	36	28.02 N	82.01 W
Winston, Oreg., U.S.	46	45.07 N	123.25 W
Winston-Salem	36	36.06 N	80.15 W
Winter	34	45.49 N	91.01 W
Winter Garden	36	28.34 N	81.35 W
Winter Harbor	32	44.24 N	68.05 W
Winterhaven, Calif., U.S.	48	32.44 N	114.38 W
Winter Haven, Fla., U.S.	36	28.01 N	81.44 W
Wintering ≃	42	48.12 N	100.34 W
Winter Island I	22	66.14 N	83.04 W
Winter Park, Fla., U.S.	36	28.36 N	81.20 W
Winter Park, N.C., U.S.	36	34.11 N	77.56 W
Winterport	32	44.38 N	68.51 W
Winters, Calif., U.S.	48	38.31 N	121.58 W
Winters, Tex., U.S.	40	31.57 N	99.58 W
Winterset	34	41.20 N	94.01 W
Winterswijk	72	51.58 N	6.44 E
Winterthur	74	47.30 N	8.43 E
Winterville, Ga., U.S.	36	33.59 N	83.18 W
Winterville, Miss., U.S.	38	33.30 N	91.10 W
Winterville, N.C., U.S.	36	35.32 N	77.24 W
Winthrop, Iowa, U.S.	34	42.28 N	91.44 W
Winthrop, Maine, U.S.	32	44.18 N	69.59 W
Winthrop, Minn., U.S.	34	44.32 N	94.22 W
Winthrop Harbor	34	42.29 N	87.49 W
Winton, Austl.	118	22.23 S	143.02 E
Winton, N.Z.	120	46.09 S	168.20 E
Winton, N.C., U.S.	36	36.24 N	76.56 W
Wipperfürth	72	51.07 N	7.23 E
Wirral ≻[1]	70	53.20 N	3.03 W
Wisbech	70	52.40 N	0.10 E
Wiscasset	32	44.00 N	69.40 W
Wisconsin □[3]	20	44.45 N	89.30 W
Wisconsin ≃	34	43.00 N	91.15 W
Wisconsin, Lake ⊜[1]	34	43.24 N	89.43 W
Wisconsin Dells	34	43.38 N	89.46 W
Wisconsin Dells V	34	43.41 N	89.49 W
Wisconsin Rapids	34	44.23 N	89.49 W
Wisdom	46	45.37 N	113.27 W
Wise	36	36.59 N	82.34 W
Wise ≃	46	45.48 N	112.57 W
Wishek	42	46.16 N	99.33 W
Wisła ≃	72	54.22 N	18.55 E
Wismar, D.D.R.	72	53.53 N	11.28 E
Wismar, Guy.	60	6.00 N	58.18 W
Wisner, La., U.S.	38	31.59 N	91.39 W
Wisner, Nebr., U.S.	42	41.59 N	96.55 W
Wister	38	34.58 N	94.43 W
Witbank	116	25.56 S	29.07 E
Withlacoochee ≃	36	30.24 N	83.10 W
Witney	70	51.48 N	1.29 W
Witt	38	39.15 N	89.21 W
Witten	72	51.26 N	7.20 E
Wittenberg, D.D.R.	72	51.52 N	12.39 E
Wittenberg, Wis., U.S.	34	44.49 N	89.10 W
Wittenberge	72	53.00 N	11.44 E
Wittenoom	118	22.17 S	118.19 E
Wittstock	72	53.10 N	12.29 E
Witwatersrand ✣[1]	116	26.00 S	27.00 E
W. Kerr Scott Reservoir ⊜[1]	36	36.07 N	81.15 W
Włocławek	72	52.39 N	19.02 E
Woburn	32	42.29 N	71.09 W
Wodonga	118	36.07 S	146.54 E
Woking	70	51.20 N	0.34 W
Wolbach	42	41.24 N	98.24 W
Wolcott, Ind., U.S.	38	40.46 N	87.03 W
Wolcott, N.Y., U.S.	32	43.13 N	76.49 W
Wolcottville	38	41.32 N	85.22 W
Woleai I[1]	92	7.21 N	143.52 E
Wolf ≃, U.S.	38	35.09 N	90.04 W
Wolf ≃, Kans., U.S.	42	39.54 N	95.11 W
Wolf ≃, Miss., U.S.	38	30.21 N	89.18 W
Wolf ≃, Wis., U.S.	34	44.11 N	88.48 W
Wolf Creek, Mont., U.S.	46	47.00 N	112.04 W
Wolf Creek, Oreg., U.S.	46	42.42 N	123.24 W
Wolf Creek ≃, U.S.	40	36.35 N	99.30 W
Wolf Creek ≃, Iowa, U.S.	34	42.20 N	92.09 W
Wolf Creek Pass)(	44	37.29 N	106.48 W
Wolfeboro	32	43.35 N	71.12 W
Wolfen	72	51.40 N	12.16 E
Wolfenbüttel	72	52.10 N	10.32 E
Wolfforth	40	33.30 N	102.01 W
Wolf Lake	34	43.14 N	86.10 W
Wolf Point	46	48.05 N	105.39 W
Wolf Rock I[2]	70	49.57 N	5.49 W
Wolfsberg	72	46.51 N	14.51 E
Wolfsburg	72	52.25 N	10.47 E
Wolfville	30	45.05 N	64.22 W
Wolgast	72	54.03 N	13.46 E
Wolin I	72	53.55 N	14.31 E
Wollaston, Cape ≻	22	71.04 N	118.07 W
Wollaston, Islas II	58	55.40 S	67.30 W
Wollaston Lake ⊜	22	58.15 N	103.20 W
Wollaston Peninsula ≻[1]	22	70.00 N	115.00 W
Wollongong	118	34.25 S	150.54 E
Wołomin	72	52.21 N	21.14 E
Wolseley	28	50.25 N	103.19 W
Wolsey	42	44.25 N	98.28 W
Wolverhampton	70	52.36 N	2.08 W
Wolverine	34	45.16 N	84.36 W
Wondai	118	26.19 S	151.52 E
Wonderland	48	40.24 N	121.19 W
Wonewoc	34	43.39 N	90.14 W
Wŏnju	88	37.22 N	127.58 E
Wonotobo Fall ↳	60	4.22 N	57.55 W
Wŏnsan	88	39.09 N	127.25 E
Wonthaggi	118	38.36 S	145.35 E
Wood	42	43.30 N	100.29 W
Wood ≃, Nebr., U.S.	42	41.02 N	98.05 W
Wood ≃, Wyo., U.S.	46	44.07 N	108.58 W
Woodall Mountain ▲[2]	38	34.45 N	88.11 W
Woodbine, Ga., U.S.	36	30.58 N	81.43 W
Woodbine, Iowa, U.S.	42	41.44 N	95.43 W
Woodbine, N.J., U.S.	32	39.14 N	74.49 W
Woodbridge	32	38.39 N	77.15 W
Woodbridge Bay C	54d	15.19 N	61.25 W
Woodburn	46	45.09 N	122.51 W
Woodbury, Conn., U.S.	32	41.33 N	73.13 W
Woodbury, Ga., U.S.	36	32.59 N	84.35 W
Woodbury, N.J., U.S.	32	39.50 N	75.10 W
Woodbury, Tenn., U.S.	38	35.50 N	86.04 W
Woodhull	34	41.11 N	90.20 W
Woodlake, Calif., U.S.	48	36.25 N	119.06 W
Wood Lake, Nebr., U.S.	42	42.38 N	100.14 W
Woodland, Calif., U.S.	48	38.41 N	121.46 W
Woodland, Ga., U.S.	36	32.46 N	84.33 W
Woodland, Maine, U.S.	32	45.09 N	67.24 W
Woodland, N.C., U.S.	36	36.20 N	77.12 W
Woodland Park	44	39.00 N	105.03 W
Woodlark Island I	118	9.05 S	152.50 E
Woodlawn	38	37.04 N	85.04 W
Wood River, Ill., U.S.	38	38.52 N	90.05 W
Wood River, Nebr., U.S.	42	40.49 N	98.36 W
Woodroffe, Mount ▲	118	26.20 S	131.45 E
Woodrow	36	35.08 N	77.05 W
Woodruff, Ariz., U.S.	44	34.47 N	110.03 W
Woodruff, S.C., U.S.	36	34.45 N	82.02 W
Woodruff, Wis., U.S.	34	45.54 N	89.42 W
Woods, Lake ⊜	118	17.50 S	133.30 E
Woods, Lake of the ⊜	22	49.15 N	94.45 W
Woodsboro	40	28.14 N	97.20 W
Woodsfield	32	39.46 N	81.07 W
Woods Hole	32	41.31 N	70.40 W
Woodson	40	33.01 N	99.03 W
Woodstock, N.B., Can.	30	46.09 N	67.34 W
Woodstock, Ont., Can.	34	43.08 N	80.45 W
Woodstock, Ill., U.S.	34	42.19 N	88.27 W
Woodstock, N.Y., U.S.	32	42.02 N	74.07 W
Woodstock, Vt., U.S.	32	43.37 N	72.31 W
Woodstock, Va., U.S.	32	38.53 N	78.31 W
Woodsville	32	44.09 N	72.02 W
Woodville, N.Z.	120	40.20 S	175.52 E
Woodville, Ala., U.S.	38	34.38 N	86.16 W
Woodville, Fla., U.S.	36	30.20 N	84.15 W
Woodville, Ga., U.S.	36	33.40 N	83.06 W
Woodville, Miss., U.S.	38	31.01 N	91.18 W
Woodville, Ohio, U.S.	32	41.27 N	83.22 W
Woodville, Tex., U.S.	38	30.46 N	94.25 W
Woodward, Iowa, U.S.	34	41.51 N	93.55 W
Woodward, Okla., U.S.	40	36.26 N	99.24 W
Woody ≃	28	52.30 N	100.51 W
Woody Island	24	57.47 N	152.22 W
Woolmarket	38	30.31 N	89.02 W
Woomera	118	31.31 S	137.10 E
Woonsocket, R.I., U.S.	32	42.00 N	71.31 W
Woonsocket, S. Dak., U.S.	42	44.03 N	98.16 W
Wooramel	118	25.44 S	114.17 E
Wooramel ≃	118	25.47 S	114.10 E
Wooster	32	40.48 N	81.56 W
Worcester, S. Afr.	116	33.39 S	19.27 E
Worcester, Eng., U.K.	70	52.11 N	2.13 W
Worcester, Mass., U.S.	32	42.16 N	71.48 W
Worden	46	45.58 N	108.10 W
Workington	70	54.39 N	3.35 W
Worksop	70	53.18 N	1.07 W
Worland	46	44.01 N	107.57 W
Worms	72	49.38 N	8.22 E
Wortham	40	31.47 N	96.28 W
Worthing	70	50.48 N	0.23 W
Worthington, Ind., U.S.	38	39.07 N	86.59 W
Worthington, Minn., U.S.	42	43.37 N	95.36 W
Worthington, Ohio, U.S.	32	40.05 N	83.01 W
Worthington Peak ▲	48	37.55 N	115.37 W
Wounded Knee Creek ≃	42	43.26 N	102.32 W
Wowoni, Pulau I	96	4.08 S	123.06 E
Woy Woy	118	33.30 S	151.20 E
Wrangell	24	56.28 N	132.23 W
Wrangell, Mount ▲	24	62.00 N	144.06 W
Wrangell Island I	24	56.15 N	132.10 W
Wrangell Mountains ⛰	24	62.00 N	143.00 W
Wrath, Cape ≻	70	58.37 N	5.01 W
Wray	42	40.05 N	102.13 W
Wreck Reef ✣[2]	118	22.13 S	155.17 E
Wrecks, Bay of C	122o	1.52 N	157.17 W
Wrens	36	33.12 N	82.23 W
Wrexham	70	53.03 N	3.00 W
Wright, Mount ▲	46	47.58 N	112.49 W
Wright City, Mo., U.S.	38	38.50 N	91.01 W
Wright City, Okla., U.S.	40	34.03 N	95.01 W
Wrightstown	34	44.19 N	88.09 W
Wrightsville	36	32.44 N	82.43 W
Wrightsville Beach	36	34.12 N	77.49 W
Wrightwood	48	34.21 N	117.38 W
Wrigley	24	63.16 N	123.37 W
Wrocław (Breslau)	72	51.06 N	17.00 E
Września	72	52.20 N	17.34 E
Wuchin → Changzhou	88	31.47 N	119.57 E
Wuchuan	94	21.25 N	110.40 E
Wudangshan ⛰	88	32.30 N	110.50 E
Wudu	88	33.21 N	105.00 E
Wuershunhe ≃	88	49.00 N	117.41 E
Wugang	88	26.40 N	110.31 E
Wugongshan ⛰	88	27.21 N	113.50 E
Wuhan	88	30.36 N	114.17 E
Wuhsing → Huzhou	88	30.52 N	120.06 E
Wuhu	88	31.21 N	118.22 E
Wulanhaote	88	46.05 N	122.05 E
Wuliangshan ⛰	94	24.30 N	100.45 E
Wulumuqi (Urumchi)	88	43.48 N	87.35 E
Wulunguhe ≃	88	46.59 N	87.27 E
Wunnummin Lake ⊜	22	52.55 N	89.10 W
Wunstorf	72	52.25 N	9.26 E
Wuppertal	72	51.16 N	7.11 E
Würzburg	72	49.48 N	9.56 E
Wurzen	72	51.22 N	12.44 E
Wushan	88	31.05 N	109.48 E
Wushenqi	88	38.58 N	109.01 E
Wusu	88	44.27 N	84.37 E
Wusulijiang (Ussuri) ≃	84	48.27 N	135.04 E
Wutai	88	38.44 N	113.17 E
Wutaishan ▲	88	39.04 N	113.35 E
Wutongqiao	88	29.26 N	103.51 E
Wuvulu Island I	92	1.45 S	142.50 E
Wuxi	88	31.35 N	120.18 E
Wuyishan ⛰	88	27.52 N	117.40 E
Wuyuan	88	41.06 N	108.29 E
Wuzhishan ▲	94	18.57 N	109.43 E
Wuzhong	88	37.57 N	106.10 E
Wuzhou (Wuchow)	94	23.30 N	111.27 E
Wyaconda	38	40.24 N	91.55 W
Wyaconda ≃	38	40.04 N	91.30 W
Wyalusing	32	41.40 N	76.16 W
Wyandotte	34	42.12 N	83.10 W
Wyandra	118	27.15 S	145.59 E
Wyatt	38	36.55 N	89.13 W
Wyeville	34	44.01 N	90.23 W
Wykoff	34	43.42 N	92.16 W
Wylie	40	33.01 N	96.32 W
Wylie, Lake ⊜[1]	36	35.07 N	81.02 W
Wymore	42	40.07 N	96.40 W
Wyndham	118	15.28 S	128.06 E
Wyndmere	42	46.16 N	97.08 W
Wynne	38	35.14 N	90.47 W
Wynnewood	40	34.39 N	97.10 W
Wynniatt Bay C	22	72.55 N	110.30 W
Wynona	40	36.33 N	96.20 W
Wynot	42	42.45 N	97.10 W
Wynyard	28	51.47 N	104.10 W
Wyocena	34	43.30 N	89.19 W
Wyodak	42	44.18 N	105.24 W
Wyoming, Ill., U.S.	34	41.04 N	89.47 W
Wyoming, Iowa, U.S.	34	42.04 N	91.00 W
Wyoming, Mich., U.S.	34	42.54 N	85.42 W
Wyoming □[3]	20	43.00 N	107.30 W
Wyoming Range ⛰	44	42.00 N	111.00 W
Wyong	118	33.17 S	151.25 E
Wyszków	72	52.36 N	21.28 E
Wytheville	36	36.57 N	81.05 W
Wytopitlock	32	45.38 N	68.05 W
X			
Xam Nua	94	20.25 N	104.02 E
Xánthi	80	41.08 N	24.53 E
Xapuri	56	10.39 S	68.31 W
Xenia, Ill., U.S.	38	38.38 N	88.38 W
Xenia, Ohio, U.S.	32	39.41 N	83.56 W
Xiaguan	88	33.37 N	111.46 E
Xiahe	88	35.06 N	102.40 E
Xiamen (Amoy)	88	24.28 N	118.07 E
Xi'an (Sian)	88	34.15 N	108.52 E
Xiangfan	88	32.03 N	112.01 E
Xiangjiang ≃	88	29.00 N	112.56 E
Xiangkhoang	94	19.20 N	103.22 E
Xiangride	88	36.02 N	98.08 E
Xiangtan	88	27.51 N	112.54 E
Xianyang	88	34.23 N	108.40 E
Xianyou	88	25.23 N	118.40 E
Xiaogan	88	30.55 N	113.54 E
Xiaoxing'anling-shanmai ⛰	88	48.45 N	127.00 E
Xiapu	88	26.52 N	120.01 E
Xichang	88	27.58 N	102.13 E
Xihe ≃	88	41.44 N	121.30 E
Xijiang ≃	94	23.10 N	111.50 E
Xilinhaote	88	43.58 N	116.04 E
Xinavane	116	25.02 S	32.47 E
Xincheng	88	39.15 N	115.59 E
Xingan	88	25.37 N	110.31 E
Xinghe	88	40.48 N	113.58 E
Xinghua	88	32.57 N	119.50 E
Xingkathu (Ozero Chanka) ⊜	84	45.00 N	132.24 E
Xingtai	88	37.04 N	114.29 E
Xingu ≃	56	1.30 S	51.53 W
Xingyi	94	25.06 N	104.58 E
Xinhailian	88	34.39 N	119.16 E
Xinhua	88	27.37 N	111.02 E
Xining	88	36.38 N	101.55 E
Xinjiang	88	35.40 N	111.11 E
Xinxiang	88	35.20 N	113.51 E
Xinyang	88	32.19 N	114.01 E
Xique-Xique	56	10.50 S	42.44 W
Xuancheng	88	30.58 N	118.45 E
Xuanhua	88	40.37 N	115.03 E
Xuchang	88	34.03 N	113.49 E
Xuefengshan ⛰	88	27.44 N	111.00 E
Xuwen	94	20.21 N	110.11 E
Xuyong	88	28.10 N	105.24 E
Xuzhou	88	34.16 N	117.11 E
Y			
Yaan	88	30.03 N	103.02 E
Yablonovy Range → Jablonovyj Chrebet ⛰	84	53.30 N	115.00 E
Yabucoa	54m	18.03 N	65.53 W
Yaco (Iaco) ≃	56	9.03 S	68.34 W
Yacuiba	62	22.02 S	63.45 W
Yacyretá, Isla I	62	27.25 S	56.30 W
Yadkinville	36	36.08 N	80.39 W
Yadong	88	27.29 N	88.55 E
Yafran	108	32.04 N	12.31 E
Yagoua	106	10.20 N	15.14 E
Yaguarón (Jaguarão) ≃	62	32.39 S	53.12 W
Yahara ≃	34	42.48 N	89.07 W
Yaheladazeshan ▲	102	35.12 N	95.20 E
Yahualica	52	21.08 N	102.51 W
Yainax Butte ▲	46	42.20 N	121.16 W
Yaizu	90	34.52 N	138.20 E
Yakima	46	46.36 N	120.31 W
Yakima ≃	46	46.15 N	119.02 W
Yakobi Island I	24	58.00 N	136.30 W
Yakoma	108	4.05 N	22.27 E
Yaku-shima I	91b	30.20 N	130.30 E
Yakutat	24	59.33 N	139.44 W
Yakutat Bay C	24	59.45 N	140.45 W
Yakutsk → Jakutsk	84	62.13 N	129.49 E
Yale, Mich., U.S.	34	43.08 N	82.48 W
Yale, Okla., U.S.	40	36.07 N	96.42 W
Yale, Mount ▲	44	38.51 N	106.18 W
Yalgoo	118	28.20 S	116.41 E
Yalinga	108	6.31 N	23.15 E
Yalobusha ≃	38	33.33 N	90.10 W
Yalongjiang ≃	88	30.01 N	101.07 E
Yalujiang (Amnok-kang) ≃	88	39.55 N	124.22 E
Yamagata	90	38.15 N	140.15 E
Yamaguchi	90	34.10 N	131.29 E
Yambio	108	4.34 N	28.23 E
Y'Ami Island I	92	21.07 N	121.57 E
Yamma Yamma, Lake ⊜	118	26.20 S	141.25 E
Yampa	44	40.09 N	106.55 W
Yampa ≃	44	40.32 N	108.59 W
Yampa Plateau ⛰[1]	44	40.25 N	109.00 W
Yampi Sound	118	15.15 S	123.30 E
Yamsay Mountain ▲	46	42.56 N	121.22 W
Yamuna ≃	102	25.25 N	81.50 E
Yanam	100	16.40 N	82.10 E
Yan'an	88	36.41 N	109.19 E
Yanbu'	104	24.05 N	38.03 E
Yanceyville	36	36.24 N	79.20 W
Yanchang	88	36.35 N	110.15 E
Yancheng	88	33.24 N	120.09 E
Yanchi	88	37.52 N	107.22 E
Yandina	123e	9.07 S	159.13 E
Yangasa Levu I	123g	18.57 S	178.26 W
Yangjiang	88	21.51 N	111.56 E
Yangor	122b	0.31 S	166.54 E
Yangquan	88	37.52 N	113.36 E
Yangtze → Changjiang ≃	88	31.48 N	121.10 E
Yangzhou	88	32.24 N	119.26 E
Yangzhuoyonghu ⊜	102	28.58 N	90.44 E
Yanji	88	42.57 N	129.32 E
Yankeetown	36	29.02 N	82.43 W
Yankton	42	42.53 N	97.23 W
Yanqi	88	42.00 N	86.15 E
Yantai (Chefoo)	88	37.33 N	121.20 E
Yanzhou	88	35.33 N	116.50 E
Yaoundé	106	3.52 N	11.31 E
Yap	122q	9.31 N	138.08 E
Yap I	122q	9.31 N	138.06 E
Yaqui ≃	52	27.37 N	110.39 W
Yaraka	118	24.53 S	144.04 E
Yarí ≃	60	0.23 S	72.16 W
Yarīm	100	14.29 N	44.21 E
Yaritagua	60	10.05 N	69.08 W
Yarmouth, N.S., Can.	30	43.50 N	66.07 W
Yarmouth, Maine, U.S.	32	43.48 N	70.12 W
Yarumal	60	6.58 N	75.24 W
Yasawa Group II	123g	17.00 S	177.23 E
Yass	118	34.50 S	148.55 E
Yata ≃	56	10.29 S	65.26 W
Yaté	123f	22.09 S	166.57 E
Yatesboro	32	40.48 N	79.20 W
Yates Center	42	37.53 N	95.44 W
Yates City	34	40.47 N	90.01 W
Yathkyed Lake ⊜	22	62.41 N	98.00 W
Yatsushiro	90	32.30 N	130.36 E
Yatta Plateau ⛰[1]	110	2.00 S	38.00 E
Yauco	54m	18.02 N	66.51 W
Yavarí (Javari) ≃	56	4.21 S	70.02 W
Yaví, Cerro ▲	60	5.32 N	65.59 W
Yaxian	94	18.20 N	109.30 E
Yazd	104	31.53 N	54.25 E
Yazoo ≃	38	32.22 N	91.00 W
Yazoo City	38	32.51 N	90.28 W
Ybbs ≃	72	48.10 N	15.06 E
Ye	94	15.15 N	97.51 E
Yecheng	102	37.54 N	77.25 E
Yecla	76	38.37 N	1.07 W
Yeerqianghe (Yarkand) ≃	102	40.28 N	80.52 E
Yei ≃	112	6.15 N	30.13 E
Yélimané	114	15.08 N	10.34 W
Yellow ≃, U.S.	38	30.33 N	87.00 W
Yellow ≃, Ind., U.S.	38	41.16 N	86.50 W
Yellow ≃, Iowa, U.S.	34	43.05 N	91.11 W
Yellow ≃, Wis., U.S.	34	46.01 N	92.22 W
Yellow → Huanghe ≃, Zhg.	88	37.32 N	118.19 E
Yellow Creek ≃, U.S.	38	33.34 N	88.20 W
Yellow Creek ≃, Tenn., U.S.	38	36.26 N	87.34 W
Yellowhead Pass)(	26	52.53 N	118.28 W
Yellowknife	22	62.27 N	114.21 W
Yellowknife ≃	22	62.31 N	114.19 W
Yellow Medicine ≃	42	44.44 N	95.25 W
Yellow Sea ⊤[2]	88	36.00 N	123.00 E
Yellowstone ≃	20	47.58 N	103.59 W
Yellowstone, Clarks Fork ≃	46	45.39 N	108.43 W
Yellowstone Falls ↳	46	44.43 N	110.30 W
Yellowstone Lake ⊜	46	44.25 N	110.22 W
Yellowstone National Park	46	44.58 N	110.42 W
Yellville	38	36.14 N	92.41 W
Yemassee	36	32.41 N	80.51 W
Yemen □[1]	100	15.00 N	44.00 E
Yemen, People's Democratic Republic of □[1]	100	15.00 N	48.00 E
Yenangyaung	94	20.28 N	94.52 E
Yen-bai	94	21.42 N	104.52 E
Yendi	114	9.26 N	0.01 W
Yeo Lake ⊜	118	28.04 S	124.23 E
Yeovil	70	50.57 N	2.39 W
Yeppoon	118	23.08 S	150.45 E
Yerington	48	38.59 N	119.10 W
Yermo	48	34.54 N	116.50 W
Yerupajá, Nevado ▲	56	10.16 S	76.54 W
Yerushalayim (Jerusalem)	104	31.46 N	35.14 E
Yesa, Embalse de ⊜[1]	76	42.36 N	1.09 W
Yeso	40	34.26 N	104.37 W
Ye-u	92	22.46 N	95.26 E
Yeu, Île d' I	74	46.42 N	2.20 W
Yi ≃	62	33.07 S	57.08 W
Yian	88	47.55 N	125.20 E
Yiannitsá	80	40.48 N	22.25 E
Yibin	88	28.47 N	104.38 E
Yichang	88	30.42 N	111.11 E
Yichun, Zhg.	88	27.50 N	114.23 E
Yichun, Zhg.	88	47.42 N	128.55 E
Yilan	88	46.19 N	129.34 E
Yiliang	94	24.58 N	103.07 E
Yinchuan	88	38.30 N	106.18 E
Yinghe ≃	88	32.30 N	116.32 E
Yingjisha	88	38.57 N	76.03 E
Yingkou	88	40.40 N	122.14 E
Yingtan	88	28.14 N	117.00 E
Yining (Kuldja)	88	43.55 N	81.14 E
Yirga Alem	108	6.52 N	38.22 E
Yishan	94	24.40 N	108.35 E
Yishui	88	35.50 N	118.41 E
Yitulihe	88	50.38 N	121.57 E
Yiyang	88	28.36 N	112.20 E
Ylig Bay C	122p	13.24 N	144.46 E
Ynykčanskij	84	60.15 N	137.43 E
Yoakum	40	29.17 N	97.09 W
Yockanookany ≃	38	32.40 N	89.40 W
Yocona ≃	38	34.11 N	90.11 W
Yogyakarta	96	7.48 S	110.22 E
Yokkaichi	90	34.58 N	136.37 E
Yokohama	90	35.27 N	139.39 E
Yokosuka	90	35.18 N	139.40 E
Yola	106	9.12 N	12.29 E
Yom ≃	94	15.52 N	100.16 E
Yona	122p	13.25 N	144.47 E
Yonago	90	35.26 N	133.20 E
Yoncalla	46	43.36 N	123.17 W
Yonezawa	90	37.55 N	140.07 E
Yongan	88	25.58 N	117.22 E
Yongdeng	88	36.48 N	103.14 E
Yongding	88	24.46 N	116.43 E
Yongdinghe ≃	88	39.39 N	116.13 E
Yongdingzhen	88	26.08 N	101.40 E
Yongfeng	88	27.19 N	115.24 E
Yongshan	88	28.15 N	103.24 E
Yonkers	32	41.00 N	73.52 W
York, Austl.	118	31.53 S	116.46 E
York, Eng., U.K.	70	53.58 N	1.05 W
York, Ala., U.S.	38	32.29 N	88.18 W
York, Nebr., U.S.	42	40.52 N	97.36 W
York, N. Dak., U.S.	42	48.19 N	99.34 W
York, Pa., U.S.	32	39.58 N	76.44 W
York, S.C., U.S.	36	35.00 N	81.14 W
York ≃	36	37.15 N	76.23 W
York, Cape ≻	118	10.42 S	142.31 E
Yorke Peninsula ≻[1]	118	35.00 S	137.30 E
York Factory	28	57.00 N	92.18 W
York Sound ⊔	118	14.50 S	125.05 E
Yorkton	28	51.13 N	102.28 W
Yorktown, Tex., U.S.	40	28.59 N	97.30 W
Yorktown, Va., U.S.	36	37.14 N	76.30 W
Yorkville, Ill., U.S.	34	41.38 N	88.27 W
Yorkville, N.Y., U.S.	32	43.07 N	75.16 W
Yoron-jima I	91b	27.02 N	128.26 E
Yosemite National Park	48	37.45 N	119.35 W
Yŏsu	88	34.46 N	127.44 E
Youjiang ≃	94	22.50 N	108.06 E
Young, Austl.	118	34.19 S	148.18 E
Young, Ariz., U.S.	44	34.06 N	110.57 W
Youngs Rock I[2]	122e	25.03 S	130.07 W
Youngstown, Fla., U.S.	36	30.22 N	85.27 W
Youngstown, N.Y., U.S.	32	43.15 N	79.03 W
Youngstown, Ohio, U.S.	32	41.06 N	80.39 W
Youngsville, La., U.S.	38	30.06 N	92.00 W
Youngsville, N.C., U.S.	36	36.01 N	78.29 W
Youngsville, Pa., U.S.	32	41.51 N	79.19 W
Yountville	48	38.24 N	122.22 W
Youssoufia	106	32.16 N	8.33 W
Youyang	88	28.58 N	108.41 E
Ypané ≃	62	23.29 S	57.19 W
Ypsilanti	34	42.15 N	83.36 W
Yreka	46	41.44 N	122.38 W
Ystad	68	55.25 N	13.49 E
Ystwyth ≃	70	52.24 N	4.05 W
Yuanling	88	28.20 N	110.16 E
Yuanmou	94	25.38 N	101.54 E
Yuba City	48	39.08 N	121.37 W
Yūbari	90a	43.04 N	141.59 E
Yucaipa	48	34.02 N	117.02 W
Yucatán □[3]	52	20.50 N	89.00 W
Yucatan Channel ⊔	50	21.45 N	85.45 W
Yucatan Peninsula ≻[1]	52	19.30 N	89.00 W
Yucca	44	34.52 N	114.09 W
Yucca Lake ⊜	48	36.59 N	116.01 W
Yucca Valley	48	34.07 N	116.35 W
Yuci	88	37.45 N	112.41 E
Yueyang	88	29.23 N	113.06 E
Yugoslavia □[1]	64	44.00 N	19.00 E
Yujiang ≃	94	23.24 N	110.05 E
Yukon	40	35.30 N	97.45 W
Yukon □[8]	22	64.00 N	135.00 W
Yukon ≃	24	62.33 N	163.59 W
Yulin, Zhg.	88	38.20 N	109.29 E
Yulin, Zhg.	94	22.36 N	110.07 E
Yuma, Ariz., U.S.	44	32.43 N	114.37 W
Yuma, Colo., U.S.	42	40.08 N	102.43 W
Yumbo	60	3.35 N	76.28 W
Yumen	88	39.56 N	97.51 E
Yuncheng	88	35.00 N	110.59 E
Yunhe (Grand Canal) ⊼	88	32.12 N	119.31 E
Yunxian	88	32.49 N	110.49 E
Yupanyang C	88	30.30 N	121.46 E
Yurimaguas	56	5.54 S	76.05 W
Yuriria	52	20.12 N	101.09 W
Yushu	88	33.28 N	96.18 E
Yutian	102	36.51 N	81.40 E
Yuty	62	26.32 S	56.18 W
Yuxian	88	34.10 N	113.28 E
Yverdon	74	46.47 N	6.39 E
Z			
Zaandam	72	52.26 N	4.49 E
Zabajkal'sk	84	49.38 N	117.19 E
Zabarjad, Jazīrat I	112	23.37 N	36.12 E
Zabīd	100	14.10 N	43.17 E
Žabinka	86	52.12 N	24.01 E
Ząbkowice Śląskie	72	50.36 N	16.53 E
Zābol	104	31.02 N	61.30 E
Zabrze	72	50.18 N	18.46 E
Zacapa	52	14.58 N	89.32 W
Zacapu	52	19.50 N	101.43 W
Zacatecas	52	22.47 N	102.35 W
Zacatlán	52	19.56 N	97.58 W
Zachary	38	30.39 N	91.09 W
Zacoalco de Torres	52	20.14 N	103.35 W
Zadar	78	44.07 N	15.14 E
Zadetkyi Kyun I	94	9.58 N	98.13 E
Zadonsk	86	52.23 N	38.57 E
Zafra	76	38.25 N	6.25 W
Żagań	72	51.37 N	15.19 E
Žagarė	86	56.21 N	23.15 E
Zagorsk	86	56.18 N	38.08 E
Zagreb	78	45.48 N	15.58 E
Zāgros, Kūhhā-ye ⛰	104	33.40 N	47.00 E
Zagros Mountains → Zāgros, Kūhhā-ye ⛰	104	33.40 N	47.00 E
Zāhedān	104	29.30 N	60.52 E
Zaḩlah	104	33.51 N	35.53 E
Zaire □[1]	110	4.00 S	25.00 E
Zaječar	80	43.54 N	22.17 E
Zajsan	84	47.28 N	84.55 E
Zajsan, Ozero ⊜	84	48.00 N	84.00 E
Zakamensk	84	50.23 N	103.17 E
Zákinthos I	80	37.52 N	20.44 E
Zakopane	72	49.19 N	19.57 E
Zalaegerszeg	72	46.51 N	16.51 E
Zalău	80	47.11 N	23.03 E
Zalegošč'	86	52.56 N	36.53 E
Žaltyr	82	51.40 N	69.50 E
Zama	38	32.53 N	89.23 W
Zambezi (Zambeze) ≃	110	18.55 S	36.04 E
Zambia □[1]	110	15.00 S	30.00 E
Zamboanga	96	6.54 N	122.04 E
Zambrów	72	53.00 N	22.15 E
Zamfara ≃	114	12.05 N	4.02 E
Zamora	76	41.30 N	5.45 W
Zamora de Hidalgo	52	19.59 N	102.16 W
Zamość	72	50.44 N	23.15 E
Zanaga	110	2.51 S	13.50 E
Zandvoort	72	52.22 N	4.32 E
Zanesville	32	39.56 N	82.01 W
Zanjān	104	36.40 N	48.29 E
Zanjón ≃	62	31.16 S	67.41 W
Žannetty, Ostrov I	84	76.43 N	158.00 E
Zanthus	118	31.02 S	123.34 E
Zanzibar	110	6.10 S	39.11 E
Zanzibar Island I	110	6.10 S	39.20 E
Zaouia el Kahla	106	28.09 N	6.43 E
Zaoz'ornyj	84	55.58 N	94.42 E
Zap	42	47.17 N	101.55 W
Zapadnaja Dvina (Daugava) ≃	86	57.04 N	24.03 E
Zapadno-Sibirskaja Nizmennost' ⊻	84	60.00 N	75.00 E
Zapala	62	38.54 S	70.04 W
Zapata	40	26.52 N	99.19 W
Zapata, Ciénaga de ⩸	54p	22.25 N	81.20 W
Zapatosa, Ciénaga de ⊜	60	9.05 N	73.50 W
Zapl'usje	86	58.26 N	29.43 E
Zapol'arnyj	66	69.26 N	30.48 E
Zapolje	86	58.23 N	29.41 E
Zaporožje	64	47.50 N	35.10 E
Zapotlanejo	52	20.38 N	103.04 W
Zaprudn'a	86	56.34 N	37.26 E
Zaragoza, Esp.	76	41.38 N	0.53 W
Zaragoza, Méx.	52	28.29 N	100.55 W
Zarajsk	86	54.46 N	38.53 E
Zarand, Munţii ⛰	80	46.10 N	22.15 E
Zaranj	104	31.06 N	61.53 E
Zárate	62	34.06 S	59.02 W
Zaraza	60	9.21 N	65.19 W
Zard Kūh ▲	104	32.22 N	50.04 E
Zarembo Island I	24	56.20 N	132.50 W
Zarghūn Shahr	102	32.51 N	68.25 E
Zaria	114	11.07 N	7.44 E
Žarma	84	48.48 N	80.50 E
Zaruma	60	3.41 S	79.37 W
Żary (Sorau)	72	51.38 N	15.09 E
Zarzal	60	4.24 N	76.04 W
Zāskār Mountains ⛰	102	33.00 N	78.00 E
Žatec	72	50.18 N	13.32 E
Zavalla	38	31.09 N	94.26 W
Zavitinsk	84	50.07 N	129.27 E
Zavolžsk	86	57.30 N	42.10 E
Zawiercie	72	50.30 N	19.25 E
Zāwiyat al-Bayḍā'	108	32.46 N	21.43 E
Zaza ≃	54p	21.37 N	79.32 W
Ždanov	64	47.06 N	37.33 E
Zduńska Wola	72	51.36 N	18.57 E
Zearing	34	42.10 N	93.18 W
Zebulon, Ga., U.S.	36	33.06 N	84.21 W
Zebulon, N.C., U.S.	36	35.49 N	78.19 W
Zedang	88	29.16 N	91.46 E
Zeehan	118	41.53 S	145.20 E
Zeeland, Mich., U.S.	34	42.49 N	86.01 W
Zeeland, N. Dak., U.S.	42	45.58 N	99.50 W
Zeerust	116	25.33 S	26.06 E
Zehdenick	72	52.59 N	13.20 E
Zeigler	38	37.54 N	89.03 W
Zeil, Mount ▲	118	23.24 S	132.23 E
Zeila	108	11.21 N	43.30 E
Zeist	72	52.05 N	5.15 E
Zeitz	72	51.03 N	12.08 E
Zeja	84	53.45 N	127.15 E
Zeja ≃	84	50.13 N	127.35 E
Zele	72	51.04 N	4.02 E
Zelee, Cape ≻	123e	9.45 S	161.34 E
Zelenogorsk	86	60.12 N	29.42 E
Zelenogradsk	86	54.58 N	20.29 E
Železnodorožnyj	86	54.22 N	21.19 E
Železnogorsk	86	52.22 N	35.23 E
Železnogorsk-Ilimskij	84	56.37 N	104.08 E
Zelienople	32	40.48 N	80.08 W
Zella-Mehlis	72	50.39 N	10.39 E
Zel'onodol'sk	66	55.51 N	48.33 E
Želudok	86	53.36 N	24.59 E
Zel'va	86	53.08 N	24.48 E
Zemetčino	86	53.30 N	42.38 E
Zenica	80	44.12 N	17.55 E
Zephyr	40	31.41 N	98.48 W
Zephyrhills	36	28.14 N	82.11 W
Zeravšan ≃	82	39.22 N	63.45 E
Zerbst	72	51.58 N	12.04 E
Žerdevka	86	51.51 N	41.28 E
Zereh, Gowd-e ⊜	104	29.45 N	61.50 E
Zernograd	82	46.50 N	40.19 E
Zeulenroda	72	50.39 N	11.58 E
Zevenaar	72	51.56 N	6.05 E
Zgierz	72	51.52 N	19.25 E
Zhalinghu ⊜	88	34.53 N	97.58 E
Zhalinhu ⊜	102	31.10 N	88.15 E
Zhalutegi	88	44.37 N	120.58 E
Zhangguangcailing ⛰	88	45.25 N	129.20 E
Zhangjiakou (Kalgan)	88	40.50 N	114.53 E
Zhangping	88	25.19 N	117.25 E
Zhangye	88	38.57 N	100.37 E
Zhangzhou	88	24.33 N	117.39 E
Zhanjiang	94	21.16 N	110.28 E
Zhanyi	88	25.38 N	103.43 E
Zhaoan	88	23.44 N	116.11 E
Zhaoqing	88	23.03 N	112.27 E
Zhaotong	88	27.19 N	103.48 E
Zhaxigang	88	32.32 N	79.41 E
Zhengding	88	38.10 N	114.34 E
Zhengzhou	88	34.48 N	113.39 E
Zhenjiang	88	32.13 N	119.26 E
Zhenping	88	33.08 N	112.19 E
Zhenyuan	88	26.53 N	108.19 E
Zhide	88	30.04 N	116.58 E
Zhob ≃	102	32.04 N	69.50 E
Zhongba	88	29.54 N	83.40 E
Zhongdian	88	27.50 N	99.40 E
Zhongning	88	37.27 N	105.38 E
Zhongshan	88	22.31 N	113.22 E
Zhongxiang	88	31.11 N	112.33 E
Zhoucun	88	36.47 N	117.48 E
Zhoushan	88	30.02 N	122.06 E
Zhoushanqundao II	88	30.00 N	122.00 E
Zhuangaerpendi ⊻[1]	88	45.00 N	88.00 E
Zhujiangkou C	88	23.36 N	113.44 E
Zhungeerqi	88	39.49 N	111.10 E
Zhuoxian	88	39.30 N	115.58 E
Zhushan	88	32.10 N	110.19 E
Zhuzhou	88	27.50 N	113.09 E
Žiar nad Hronom	72	48.36 N	18.52 E
Zibo	88	36.47 N	118.01 E
Zielona Góra (Grünberg)	72	51.56 N	15.31 E
Ziftā	112	30.43 N	31.15 E
Žigalovo	84	54.48 N	105.08 E
Zigana Dağları ⛰	100	40.37 N	39.30 E
Žigansk	84	66.45 N	123.20 E
Zigong	88	29.24 N	104.47 E
Ziguinchor	114	12.35 N	16.16 W
Žigulevsk	66	53.25 N	49.27 E
Zihuatanejo	52	17.38 N	101.33 W
Žilina	72	49.14 N	18.46 E
Zillah, Lībīya	108	28.33 N	17.35 E
Zillah, Wash., U.S.	46	46.24 N	120.16 W
Zillertaler Alpen ⛰	72	47.00 N	11.55 E
Žil'ovo	86	54.59 N	38.02 E
Zilwaukee	34	43.28 N	83.55 W
Zima	84	53.55 N	102.04 E
Zimnicea	80	43.39 N	25.21 E
Zinder	114	13.48 N	8.59 E
Zion	34	42.27 N	87.50 W
Zionsville	38	39.57 N	86.16 W
Zipaquirá	60	5.02 N	74.00 W
Zishui ≃	88	28.45 N	112.25 E
Žitomir	64	50.16 N	28.40 E
Zittau	72	50.54 N	14.47 E
Ziway, Lake ⊜	108	8.00 N	38.50 E
Ziyun	88	25.43 N	106.05 E
Zizhong	88	29.48 N	104.50 E
Zlatoust	82	55.10 N	59.40 E
Zlītan	108	32.28 N	14.34 E
Žlobin	86	52.54 N	30.03 E
Złotoryja	72	51.08 N	15.55 E
Złotów	72	53.22 N	17.02 E
Zmeinogorsk	84	51.10 N	82.13 E
Znamenka	82	48.43 N	32.40 E
Znamenskoje	84	57.08 N	73.55 E
Znojmo	72	48.52 N	16.02 E
Žochova, Ostrov I	84	76.04 N	152.40 E
Žodino	86	54.06 N	28.21 E
Zolfo Springs	36	27.30 N	81.48 W
Zolotkovo	86	55.32 N	41.06 E
Žoltyje Vody	82	48.21 N	33.31 E
Žolymbet	82	51.45 N	71.44 E
Zomba	110	15.23 S	35.18 E
Zonguldak	64	41.27 N	31.49 E
Zouar	108	20.27 N	16.32 E
Zrenjanin	80	45.23 N	20.24 E
Zubcov	86	56.10 N	34.34 E
Zubova Pol'ana	86	54.04 N	42.51 E
Zudañez	56	19.06 S	64.44 W
Zug	74	47.10 N	8.31 E
Zugdidi	82	42.30 N	41.53 E
Zugspitze ▲	72	47.25 N	10.59 E
Zuiderzee → IJsselmeer ⊤[2]	72	52.45 N	5.25 E
Zujevka	66	58.25 N	51.10 E
Žukovskij	86	55.35 N	38.08 E
Zulia ≃	60	9.04 N	72.18 W
Zumbo	110	15.36 S	30.25 E
Zumbro ≃	34	44.18 N	91.56 W
Zumbrota	34	44.17 N	92.40 W
Zuni	44	35.04 N	108.51 W
Zuni ≃	44	34.39 N	109.40 W
Zuni Mountains ⛰	44	35.10 N	108.15 W
Zunyi	88	27.39 N	106.57 E
Zuqar, Jazīrat I	100	14.00 N	42.45 E
Zürich	74	47.23 N	8.32 E
Zürichsee ⊜	74	47.13 N	8.45 E
Zutphen	72	52.08 N	6.12 E
Zuwārah	108	32.56 N	12.06 E
Zvolen	72	48.35 N	19.08 E
Zweibrücken	72	49.15 N	7.21 E
Zwickau	72	50.44 N	12.29 E
Zwischenahn	72	53.11 N	8.00 E
Zwolle, Ned.	72	52.30 N	6.05 E
Zwolle, La., U.S.	38	31.38 N	93.38 W
Zyr'anka	84	65.45 N	150.51 E
Zyr'anovsk	84	49.43 N	84.20 E
Żyrardów	72	52.04 N	20.25 E
Żywiec	72	49.41 N	19.12 E

Symbols in the index entries are identified on page 203.